DIGITAL
MOSAIC

DIGITAL MOSAIC

Media, Power, and Identity in Canada

DAVID TARAS

 UNIVERSITY OF TORONTO PRESS

Higher Education Division

www.utppublishing.com

LIBRARY AND ARCHIVES CANADA CATALOGUING IN PUBLICATION

Taras, David, 1950–, author
    Digital mosaic : media, power, and identity in Canada / David Taras.

Includes bibliographical references and index.
Issued in print and electronic formats.

ISBN 978-1-4426-0887-0 (bound).—ISBN 978-1-4426-0886-3 (pbk.).—
ISBN 978-1-4426-0888-7 (pdf).—ISBN 978-1-4426-0889-4 (epub).

    1. Mass media—Social aspects—Canada.   2. Mass media—Political aspects—
Canada.   I. Title.

HN110.M3T37 2015   302.230971   C2014-903882-8
                                                  C2014-903883-6

We welcome comments and suggestions regarding any aspect of our publications—please feel free to contact us at news@utphighereducation.com or visit our Internet site at www.utppublishing.com.

North America
5201 Dufferin Street
North York, Ontario, Canada, M3H 5T8

2250 Military Road
Tonawanda, New York, USA, 14150

ORDERS PHONE: 1-800-565-9523
ORDERS FAX: 1-800-221-9985
ORDERS E-MAIL: utpbooks@utpress.utoronto.ca

UK, Ireland, and continental Europe
NBN International
Estover Road, Plymouth, PL6 7PY, UK
ORDERS PHONE: 44 (0) 1752 202301
ORDERS FAX: 44 (0) 1752 202333
ORDERS E-MAIL: enquiries@nbninternational.com

The University of Toronto Press acknowledges the financial support for its publishing activities of the Government of Canada through the Canada Book Fund.

Printed in the United States of America.

CONTENTS

ACKNOWLEDGEMENTS

Writing *Digital Mosaic* has taken me on an extraordinary journey. It has been a road that I have travelled happily, even though it has been full of detours, accidents, and a lot of stop-and-go driving. The irony is that the velocity of change that I describe in the book became the main problem in writing it. There was always a new platform, a new development, a new study that had to be absorbed, interpreted, and explained. I was always trying to catch up to the next storm brewing just over the horizon. This means that the book remains a work in progress. It is my attempt to assemble as many pieces of the puzzle as I can, hold each one up to the light, and see how and if they fit together. All of the errors are of course mine.

I am grateful to Michael Harrison of the University of Toronto Press for his great patience, confidence, and professionalism. I can't thank Michael enough for believing in this project and for his wisdom and guidance. Richard Davis, Thierry Giasson, Sean Holman, Alex Marland, Margy MacMillan, Florian Sauvageau, and Christopher Waddell provided invaluable advice and saved me from making fundamental errors. They have my deepest gratitude. Peter Zuurbier was a keen editor and an exceptional researcher. I am thankful to have had him in my corner.

There are also those who, over the years, provided inspiration, insights, guidance, and a helping hand, although they may not realize the role that they played in my career or my thinking. Elly Alboim, Keith Brownsey, Duane Bratt, Lorry Felske, Fred Fletcher, Roger Gibbins, Ken Goldstein, Georgina Grosenick, Marsha Hanen and Robert Weyant, Clifford Lincoln, Karim-Aly Kassam, Michael Keren, Ruth Klinkhammer, David Marshall, Patrick McCurdy, Michael McMordie, Ian Morrison, David Nayman, Marc Raboy, Beverly and Anthony Rasporich, Chasten Remillard, David Schneiderman, Tamara and Robert Seiler, Tamara Small, Shannon Sampert, Rebecca Sullivan and Bart Beaty, Richard Sutherland, Wisdom Tettey, Harold Troper, Allan Tupper, and Aritha Van Herk are just some of the people that have made a difference.

I owe a special thanks to Dean Marc Chikinda of the Faculty of Communication Studies at Mount Royal University for his faith and vision. My colleagues and students at MRU have taught me more about the future of the media than they will ever know.

Caralee Hubbell provided an expert eye in shaping the layout of the manuscript and finding mistakes. I am grateful to Martin Boyne for his excellent copyediting.

Within my family orbit, our five men—Matthew T., Joel, Asher, David, and Matthew M.—contributed to the book by letting me into their digital worlds and sharing their reactions and experiences with me. My wife, Joan, dealt with my writing obsession with good cheer and great understanding. I am grateful to her for making my life better and more meaningful in so many ways.

one
The New Architecture
of Media Power

Like many people, I look forward to reading hard-copy newspapers with my morning coffee, I love bookstores, and I remember black-and-white television sets and telephones that did not play music and video games, take photos, allow me to watch TV shows, or do my banking. As a young boy I couldn't wait for the newspaper to arrive in the morning so that I could find out the hockey scores from the night before. TSN, Rogers Sportsnet, ESPN, league and team websites, sports blogs, and smart phone apps with instant updates and highlight packages didn't exist. Aside from newspapers, my lens on the world was the handful of TV stations that I watched. Popular shows would attract as much as 20 per cent of the audience, and with so few choices almost everyone was exposed to the same experiences: the same news, comedy, dramas, sports events, and celebrities. Television was the great—and one can argue the only real—meeting place of Canadian society. During those halcyon days of the mass media, newspapers and television networks, and to a lesser extent radio stations, had overwhelming and what seemed like unshakeable power and authority.

There was also little sense when I was growing up that readers or audiences were anything but receivers of information. The closest that anyone in my family came to being part of the media production process was my great-grandmother, who sold newspapers from a kiosk at the corner of Peel and St. Catherine in Montreal. Information flowed in a one-way torrent from the top down, and aside from letters to the editor and callers to radio hotline shows, there was little room for what my friend and colleague Michael Keren has called "the citizen's voice."[1]

Much later in life, I served, together with Marc Raboy from McGill University, as one of two expert advisors to the House of Commons Standing Committee on Canadian Heritage during a two-year examination of Canada's broadcasting policy (2001–03). After pouring over mountains of documents, hearing testimony from scores of witnesses, travelling to corporate head offices and broadcasting studios across Canada, and studying the experiences of other countries, the Committee, led by the distinguished parliamentarian Clifford Lincoln, concluded that much of the broadcasting system needed substantial overhaul and rethinking.[2] The old assumptions could no longer be sustained. But the Lincoln Report never envisioned the massive shock that was about to stun and transform Canada's media industries. While the Committee could see changes looming on the horizon, the speed and devastating force of the approaching media storm was never anticipated. We were entering a post-broadcasting era in which every medium would merge with every other medium, every screen would become every other screen, and web-based media giants such as Google, Apple, Amazon, and Facebook would become not only main platforms for news, culture, and business but also gateways and meeting places for all other media. The world that we knew was drifting away even as we were working on the report.

Canadians now occupy a media world that is vastly different from the one that I grew up in. In addition to the traditional media of newspapers, network TV, and radio stations, Canadians have access to an endless sea of web-based media: powerful search engines that scour the vast reaches of the Internet finding information on any and every topic; social media sites such as Facebook, Twitter, Pinterest, and LinkedIn, which have become the new meeting places of society as well as connecting links to other media; a daily onslaught of millions of videos; news aggregators that cull newspapers, blogs, and magazines from around the world for the latest and most poignant opinion pieces; and smart phones and tablets that are a platform for millions of applications of every imaginable function and taste.

The tectonic plates of the media world have shifted so suddenly and powerfully that much of the old landscape is now unrecognizable. Or, to put it differently, what was once unimaginable has now become routine, even ordinary. A simple click of the mouse can take us to cameras on probes that are exploring the surface of Mars or careening through the endless reaches of the solar system and beyond. Big data can now predict flu outbreaks or the timing of future house sales by tracking Google searches, and during the 2012 American presidential election the Obama campaign was able to track and "score" the political preferences of every single voter. We can contact long-lost friends, bear witness to faraway events, create online protests, shop online at virtually any store in the world, and interact with journalists, politicians, and celebrities. More frighteningly, our whereabouts, purchases, and preferences and the aspects of our private lives are routinely tracked by others.

The title of this book, *Digital Mosaic*, is a takeoff from the idea that Canada exists as a series of regional, ethnic, and linguistic fragments, which, while never quite blending together, manage to coexist and create a vibrant, even brilliant, tapestry. The concept owes much to the work of sociologist John Porter, who saw Canada as a vertical mosaic in which power was distributed unequally.[3] Today, the fragments of loyalty and connection are being altered. Digital media are weakening and disrupting the traditional media of newspapers and conventional over-the-air TV networks that produce the news and journalism that are critical to a healthy democracy and act as the central stages on which Canadian political and cultural life takes place. While web-based and social media have created new and exciting ways of communicating, the effects on democracy are as yet unclear. Online communication can move with great velocity, but it can also be sporadic and evaporate quickly. A new mosaic is forming, one that cross-cuts and is very much unlike the old one.

A description that I use throughout the book is *media shock*. I'm aware that this description is hardly original. Even a brief Google search will find many instances in which the word *shock* is used to describe the impact of the current media revolution. One Canadian scholar, Herve Fischer, used the term "digital shock" in a book on the effects of the computer revolution.[4] Futurist Alvin Toffler employed the term "future shock" in his 1970s bestseller on how information overload could overwhelm our lives.[5] And Douglas Rushkoff coined the phrase "present shock" in a 2013 book on how technologies have created a world of ever-present and inescapable demands.[6] But the term is a convenient handle for capturing the magnitude and jolt-like force of media change. I am also aware that the current media environment has so many moving parts, and is moving with such speed, that trying to capture its essence is difficult and often elusive. Studying media change often resembles trying to solve a Rubik's Cube. Just as you think all of the pieces fit together, one or two pieces fall out of place or an entirely new piece appears. Nonetheless, for the purposes of this analysis, media shock has at least ten characteristics:

1) The rapidity and suddenness of media change.
2) The degree to which web-based media have permeated virtually every aspect of daily life.
3) The ability of individuals to alter the top-down flow of information and create their own highly customized media worlds. We can now produce, alter, re-schedule, store, and comment on media experiences and products based on our own preferences and circumstances. Media choices are increasingly fragmented, customized, and personalized.
4) There is now a greater concentration of media ownership than has existed in decades. Just a handful of companies control online search, music production, the key video-watching platforms, and social media. Rarely has so much power existed in so few hands.
5) Every medium is merging with every other medium, and every screen is converging with every other screen. Or, to put it differently, every medium is in the process of becoming every other medium.

3

For instance, in their digital form, newspapers now broadcast news stories, contain photo galleries, host blogs, connect with social media sites, allow for citizen interactions, aggregate data, and have become a storefront to sell products, among other activities.

6) The traditional media, such as newspapers and conventional TV networks, are losing audiences and advertising to the point where there are questions about their continued survival. While they continue to be the main producers of news and journalism, their ability to carry out these vital functions is in grave jeopardy. At the same time, new genres of "citizen journalism" have emerged that both disrupt and are being co-opted by traditional news organizations.

7) Television continues to dominate public and cultural life, but in radically new ways. Serialized productions from cable and online broadcasters such as HBO, AMC, Showtime, Amazon Prime, YouTube, and Netflix are remaking the television landscape and changing the ways in which people watch TV. We now find ourselves in an era of Big TV, where the mass audience, once thought close to extinction, has re-emerged.

8) The connectivity and globalization of communication have meant that events and people in distant places can be easily accessed. Skype, Twitter, Google Maps, and YouTube, among other portals, can create "a presence in absence," where we can in a sense be in places without being there.

9) Social media such as Twitter, Facebook, LinkedIn, and Google+ have created a new dynamic that has transformed the ways in which we conduct business, enjoy culture, socialize, and mobilize politically. While we have entered a new world of exchange, much of this territory remains unexplored in terms of the effects that it is having on our lives and institutions.

10) Governments, political parties, and corporations now have the ability to gather vast amounts of information about people's tastes, habits, purchases, leisure activities, and political and religious views. Much of commerce and politics is now governed by Big Data, but at the same time there are concerns about the emergence of a surveillance society where privacy is threatened.

This book deals with media shock as a whole, rather than focusing separately on each of these strands. Instead of dealing with individual bolts of lightning, I treat media shock as a giant storm that contains many elements. Some of these elements, such as the concentration of media ownership, the challenges faced by the traditional media, and the downward shift of media production to groups and individuals, are discussed at great length, while others receive less attention.

This changing media landscape has altered many other landscapes. The old ways of teaching and learning, socializing and interacting with others, conducting business, experiencing culture, and fighting political battles are all undergoing dramatic changes. While *Digital Mosaic* will touch on most of these areas, the main focus will be on the changes being brought to the Canadian media system, to the news industry, and to Canadian cultural and public life. A central concern, the thread that weaves its way throughout the book, is the issue of citizen engagement and the degree to which media shock is both energizing and deflating democratic life.

A main problem for Canada is that so much of its political and cultural life has been dependent on newspapers and broadcasting. While the main transmission lines of Canadian public life still run through institutions such as the CBC/Radio-Canada, CTV, *Maclean's*, the *Globe and Mail*, *TVA*, *La Presse*, and *Postmedia* newspapers, to name some of the leading media brands, they are all under attack from web-based media and are scrambling to reinvent themselves. While much of the traditional media remains intact, and some of the major institutions may endure and even prosper, quite a number are likely to fall by the wayside. Moreover, the whole architecture of Canadian media policy that has been erected over decades could come crashing down. Policies governing foreign ownership, TV licences, Canadian content regulations, public broadcasting, and simultaneous substitution (where American programs and advertising are blocked by Canadian cable operators so that Canadian TV networks and advertisers can have unchallenged access to audiences) may not be sustainable amid the endless tidal wave of apps and video streaming, and the presence of powerful new gatekeepers such as Google, Facebook, and Twitter. While Canadian TV broadcasters are required to spend a certain amount of money each year on Canadian productions, "over the top" broadcasters such as Netflix, Crackle, Amazon, and YouTube have no such worries—they don't have to contribute at all.

The book will focus most of all on the future of the news industry. Democracy cannot thrive without quality journalism. The news media scan the horizon on behalf of ordinary citizens; they warn of dangers, celebrate achievements, and provide both a record of daily events and—most critically—a sense of place. Most of all, great journalism provides context, analysis, and perspective. Ideally the news media are also a check on the power of the powerful, ensuring that political, religious, and corporate leaders have to answer for their actions. People need to know the basic facts about the world in which they live in order to be able to make good choices for themselves and for their society. This can't happen if people "don't know what they don't know."[7]

Failures by the news media have enormous consequences for society. If we never learn about scandals or approaching economic or political storms, then we can't adjust. We can't make our lives better. The fact that the news media for years failed to notice the culture of corruption that had engulfed the construction industry in Quebec, report vigorously about climate change, and have for the most part lost interest in covering hospital waiting times or reporting on the widening gulf between rich and poor in Canada has had enormous repercussions for society. The media's failure to signal the financial crisis that began with the fall of Lehman Brothers in 2008 did extraordinary harm.[8] The resulting devastation damaged, and continues to damage, much of the global economy and brought great suffering to millions of people.

The effects of media shock on the news industry in Canada have been particularly devastating. It's not only that digital competitors have taken away audiences and advertising; it's that the very nature of news consumption has changed. The vast majority of Canadians now expect news to be instant, constant, interactive, and free. As one of Canada's leading media experts, Florian Sauvageau, has noted, younger people in particular are now used to news "snacks" rather than "meals."[9] They devour news in headlines and short bursts, in scrawls and in 140 characters. But most crucially they are used to getting news for free. A 2011 study found that over 80 per cent of Canadians would abandon their favourite news sources and find others if they had to pay for news.[10] A similar American survey conducted by the Pew Research Center in 2011 found that a large majority of tablet users are reluctant to pay for news "even if that was the only way to get news from their favorite sources."[11] Most startling perhaps is that more and more people are becoming "news-less"; they seem uninterested in the news and are willing to live without it.

A second concern is that as audiences are being splintered and ghettoized by the cable explosion and web-based media, the capacity of the Canadian traditional media to assemble a mass audience is fading quickly. Many people now live in self-enclosed media bubbles, which they rarely leave. They have their own Facebook communities, visit a few favourite websites or YouTube channels, and are increasingly drawn to a small number of popular TV programs. Ironically, the great concern is that amid a vast cornucopia of media abundance, more and more people are increasingly disengaged from public life. People under 30 in particular have lower levels of voting, joining civic organizations, and donating to causes and know a lot less about history and public affairs than people did at the same stage of their lives in previous generations.[12] The concern is that we are producing a "drop-out culture," or what I will call "peek-a-boo" citizens, who are actively involved in some ways but disappear from sight on so many other occasions.

Of course, web-based media are producing new meeting places, new public squares, and new connections. But these new phenomena are different—and it's not apparent that they will be nation-building institutions in the same way that newspapers and television networks were and to some degree still are. Social media allow those who are already active to become even more active, but they have little effect on those who are disconnected from public affairs. For instance, data from the 2011 federal election suggest that while social media were marvellous tools for furthering and deepening the engagement of those who were already engaged, the majority of Canadians did not use social media to learn about the election and very few used it to follow the news.[13]

The question is how and even whether Canadians will be able to communicate with each other amid the shock of media change. I will argue that the Canadian system is facing multiple crises, all of which are hitting at the same time: a crisis in the traditional media, a crisis in public broadcasting, a crisis in news and journalism, and a crisis in citizen engagement. These overlapping crises bring both exciting opportunities for re-imagining and reform as well as grave dangers to the health and vitality of our democratic system.

Understanding Media Shock

One of the most extraordinary characteristics of media shock is the very newness of the new media world. There have been few instances in history where change has come so quickly and dramatically and with such explosive energy. In the space of the last 10 to 15 years an entire architecture of human communication has been created that didn't exist before. Google, arguably the most powerful media organization of the first two decades of the twenty-first century and the spinal cord of the new media system, was founded only in 1998. Wikipedia was launched in 2001, Facebook in 2004, YouTube in 2005, and Tumblr blogs in 2007. The first, and by our current standards primitive, version of the Blackberry did not appear until 1999. Blogging did not catch fire in the popular imagination until 2001, and Twitter did not come on stream until 2006. Facebook Connect, arguably one of the most important developments in the entire media landscape because it linked Facebook to websites, was activated as recently as 2008. Apple famously launched the iPad in 2010; it was soon followed by over 100 other tablets developed by a myriad of competitors. Cloud computing began to be packaged as a popular media product only in 2011. During that same year Microsoft released Kinect, a device attached to its Xbox gaming console that allows players to direct the action through gestures.

A Rip van Winkle waking up from a 20-year-long sleep today would find that most of the assumptions on which his media world had been based would have disappeared. The pace of development has now become so frenetic that products are literally obsolete the moment they hit the market. Even as new products are released, the next versions are in production. Look at a smart phone from, let's say, five years ago, and it looks like it belongs in a museum. New laptops now lose their value at a rate of $100 a month—within months of a new purchase their value has been eaten up. If we accept the conventional wisdom that human knowledge doubles every five years—although evidence based on numbers of publications and patents would suggest that the real rate is far less—then we cannot escape what one pundit has described as the "acceleration of the acceleration."[14] Take a long siesta, stop paying attention even for a couple of years, and entire fields will have changed.

It's only the acceleration of change in technology but also its scale and pervasiveness that are breathtaking. The advance of web-based media is massive, enveloping, and unstoppable. At the time of writing there were an estimated 500 million websites, and almost the same number of active blogs, and well over a billion people were on Facebook. Facebook alone accounts for a trillion page views a month—with over half of its users checking it once a day.[15] Almost four billion videos are watched on YouTube every day, with 60 hours of video posted every minute.[16] The number of videos on YouTube doubled from 2010 to 2012. Remarkably, videos now make up some 40 per cent of all Internet traffic.[17] This figure is likely to rise to 60 per cent by the end of the decade, if not sooner. Images are becoming the new language of the Internet, far outstripping words as a means of communication. And then there's Google. The massive conglomerate now records four billion searches a day. A single search requires 700 to 1,000 computers located in huge data farms scattered across the US.[18] The number of applications now available on smart phones and tablets has mushroomed to well over a million and is climbing by the day.

According to one estimate, if one were to add together all of the programs broadcast on network TV in Canada and the US over the last 60 years, it would equal the amount of content uploaded on YouTube in only a 2- or 3-week period.[19] Or, to put it differently, over 60 years of TV history is now merely a drop in the YouTube bucket. In a short period of time, YouTube has become the largest and best-organized video archive in history. It has become, in effect, the memory bank for much of the world's culture.

Interestingly, because of the need to connect people and communities across vast distances, Canada has always been at the forefront of adopting new media technologies. The first telephone call, in 1876, took place in Canada, as did some of the first radio broadcasts, in 1901 and 1902. Canada was the first country to use satellites for domestic television and was a pioneer in cable technology, having one of the highest rates of cable use in the world. Perhaps not surprisingly a Canadian company, Research in Motion, now known simply as Blackberry, was at the forefront of smart-phone development, although its influence has been waning for quite some time.

The appetite of Canadians for online and digital communication is staggering. According to comScore, Canadians spent more time online in 2013 than citizens of any other country except the United States.[20] We spend an average of 41 hours per month in cyberspace, with the average Canadian clicking through more than 120 page views per day.[21] Moreover, in 2012 Canadians were the largest per-capita users of social media in the world. Close to 90 per cent of Canadians who were online had joined Facebook, while close to 20 per cent were on Twitter. There is some evidence that Facebook usage may be slipping, however, simply because we may have reached a saturation point and the novelty may have worn off for many users. But the most astonishing statistic comes in the area of watching videos. In 2013, Canada ranked second in video consumption worldwide, lagging behind only the UK. The average Canadian watched close to 300 videos a month, roughly 10 per day. In addition, over two-thirds of Canadians have a smart phone, over 40 per cent of Canadians read blogs, close to 4 million Canadians subscribe to Netflix, and over 40 per cent of anglophones own a tablet.

Most telling, perhaps, is that revenue from online advertising in Canada rose from $364 million in 2004 to close to $3.5 billion in 2012 and is now greater than the amount that advertisers spend on newspapers and radio.[22] US Internet advertising amounted to $40 billion in 2012, a figure that was expected to double by 2016.[23] The most popular online ads can register hundreds of millions of visits.

A third characteristic of media shock, and perhaps the most dramatic change, is that the flow of information and entertainment is no longer just top down, from producers to consumers. "Digital natives," a description first coined by Marc Prensky,[24] refers to those who came of age with web-based media and are immersed in the culture that these media have created—they are not just inert receivers of information but active producers. They tweet, blog, make their own videos, post photographs, swap and redact products from the traditional media, form communities, and create viral tidal waves that can reach millions of people. While most of what is discussed, posted, and circulated online is still the product of the traditional media and is about news stories, celebrities, TV shows, sports events, and music that is produced and owned by the major media conglomerates, a zone of creative independence exists on a scale that was unimaginable just a decade ago. There is now such a cornucopia of choices that people are able to map out their own individualized media eco-systems, creating in effect their own "Me-media." We can now live in the media equivalent of gated communities, visiting the media sites that reflect our own views and interests while avoiding information and images that make us feel uncomfortable. The creation of online ghettos based on selective exposure means that many citizens are increasingly isolated from the views of others.

Markus Prior, the author of an influential book entitled *Post Broadcast Democracy*, has argued that the existence of so many choices, particularly in entertainment, has had a corrosive effect on public awareness and civic engagement.[25] This is because in many if not most cases, people construct their own Me-media worlds around entertainment, and this often means that they have little exposure to news. Pushing the news away has created a downward spiral; the less exposure to news, the less interest people have in public affairs, and the less likely they are to vote.

One irony of the new situation is that the same technological revolution that has allowed citizens to have greater choice and autonomy than ever before has also led to greater corporate concentration, the fourth characteristic of media shock. A large part of this book is devoted to describing the tension between the power of audiences to shape their own media worlds, the hyper–fragmentation that this has created, and the overwhelming, often crushing, power of corporate centralization and control. The two phenomena exist side by side in a kind of teeter-totter relationship, with each pushing and galvanizing the other. But the stark reality is that much of the web is now accessible only through pay-walls, subscriptions, and micro-payments. Despite the hope expressed by many at the beginning of the Internet age "that information wants to be free," the web is being monetized so that more and more of what is available on the web now has to be paid for.

One of the keys to both of these contradictory impulses is "search." Ken Goldstein believes that "search" is one of the most important words and functions of the twenty-first century.[26] Information that once took days or weeks to retrieve, if it could be accessed at all, is now available in split seconds using powerful search engines such as Google, Yahoo, or Bing. Search has shifted power in two ways. It has decentralized power by giving users the ability to create their own private media spaces based on their individual tastes and beliefs. But at the same time search has shifted power upwards by allowing just a handful of corporations to exercise extraordinary control over the choices available to those audiences. At the apex of the new hierarchy of media power are platforms such as Google, Facebook, Microsoft,

Wikipedia, and Apple (as well as their Chinese counterparts Alibaba, Baidu, and Tencent), which act as meeting places and gateways and more accurately tollbooths through which users have to pass to access other media. These conglomerates organize the web and act as its guidance system—they are webs within the web.

By any conceivable standard, Google is a colossus. At the time of writing, Google controlled close to 70 per cent of web searches worldwide, including 70 per cent in the US, 80 per cent in Canada, 90 per cent in Japan, and 85 per cent of the European market.[27] It also has 90 per cent of the mobile search market. Google attracts a staggering 30 billion searches a week, leaving Yahoo and Microsoft's Bing to share the leftovers. Like it or not, a single corporation now functions as the air traffic control system for much of the world's information. As author Ken Auletta bluntly puts it, Google has become "the front door to the world for many people."[28]

But Google's claim to being among the world's most powerful media conglomerates rests on at least two other foundations. First, it competes along the entire length of the digital and technological frontier: it owns YouTube, whose domination of the online video world seems unassailable; its Android smart phone software leads the global smart-phone race; Google Chrome is now the world's most used web browser; Google+ competes against Facebook; Google Fiber is a broadband Internet network that is in the early stages of adoption; Gmail is the world's largest free email service; the video functions on Google+ allow it to compete against Skype and Facetime; and Google TV is a leader in making the Internet available on home TV screens. In addition, Google has developed a myriad of other products including Google Earth, Google Maps, Google Street View, Google Scholar, and Google Books, each of which controls a sizable share of lucrative beach-front property on the Internet.

Most critically media companies have expanded their horizons, becoming producers of products rather than just transmitters of information. The so-called Internet of things has the capacity to transform much of the industrial landscape, as artificial intelligence and robotics produce a new generation of products.[29] Take for instance the Google car. Loaded with advanced sensors and a GPS navigation system, the car is programmed to drive safely through traffic without a driver. Google has already tested these vehicles in rush-hour traffic on California freeways, and the car has been approved for driving in Utah. While it's wonderful to imagine yourself watching a movie or playing video games on a smart phone while in the back seat as the car drives itself, the loss of control would probably unnerve most people. Former US Vice President Al Gore believes that the Google car and others like it are about to transform the auto industry and take hundreds of thousands of jobs away from people who now make a living as truck and taxi drivers. With its acquisition of Boston Dynamics, along with a phalanx of other robot design and production companies, Google has moved to the very front of the robotics industry. The merging of data, computers, and robotics will likely make Google a major industrial player for at least the next generation.

In 2014, Google bought a leading drone manufacturer, Titan Aerospace, hoping to use drone technology to reduce the cost of Internet access. Perhaps someday it will have its own air force.

The second foundation of Google's power is that through its ownership of programs such as Adwords, Adsense, and Double Click, it controls roughly 40 per cent of advertising revenue on the web.[30] By matching searching with advertising, Google has been able to turn its main product, search, into a money machine. Its master stroke was to set up a system of mechanized online auctions for web ad space that allows people and businesses to bypass ad agencies and bid on their own. As sites now have to be visually attractive in order to compete for advertisers, Google is credited with triggering a design revolution that has transformed the web.

The real key to Google's success has been the mesmerizing sophistication of its algorithms. Google Analytics allows advertisers to measure daily and hourly ad traffic and the number of clicks per sale. With such a finely tuned scorecard at their disposal, the old adage that advertisers knew that at least half of their advertising was successful, they just didn't know which half, is no longer true.

The same types of precise measurements are evident in virtually every aspect of online activity. Philip Napoli of Fordham University believes that there is now a new science of "audience information systems" based on the fact that every time "audiences interact with media [they] leave some sort of measurable data trail that can be aggregated, analyzed and in some cases monetized."[31] In short, every time we go online we create a data footprint that can be aggregated, studied, and sold as a product. I will discuss the digital footprints that we leave, both later in this introductory chapter as well as in Chapter Four.

While Google's domination of "search" has given it immense power, by 2009 Facebook had displaced Google as the home page for most users. This means that by simply turning on their computer, users are invited into the Facebook world and enjoy access to millions of other blogs and websites. By 2011, Facebook attracted over a trillion page views a month, was home to over 100 billion friendship combinations, and regularly attracted over 750 million photographs on a single day.[32] Like Google, Facebook is a "fast-churning data machine" that aggregates, "datafies," and sells its data to third parties and, of course, uses the information itself to attract advertising.[33] In addition, it acts as a tollbooth through which those who want to connect to other media have to pass.

The survival of large numbers of newspapers, magazines, music labels, and broadcasters may depend on the revenue that they can generate from applications that are hosted on platforms such as Facebook, Apple, and Google. But unlike domestic phone companies, cable and satellite providers, or broadcasters that are regulated by the Canadian Radio-Television and Telecommunications Commission (CRTC) and must abide by its rules with regard to such matters as TV licences, funding Canadian content, and the rates that they can charge customers, the new digital giants lie largely outside of Canadian control. Apple, Facebook, and Microsoft are now much more important to Canadians and to the culture in which we live than is the CRTC. Adding to the dilemma is the fact that much of TV viewing now comes from websites such as Netflix, YouTube, Hulu, Amazon, and Crackle, which exist in a netherworld beyond our regulatory grasp. Where the Canadian state was once able to call the shots when it came to what Canadians watched and listened to, those days are long gone. Richard Schultz of McGill University has described Ottawa's role in cultural policy as having gone from "master, to partner to bit player." Unfortunately "spectator" may be a better description.[34]

One of the factors that has led to increased corporate concentration is that major content companies such as Disney, Comcast, News Corporation/21st Century Fox, and Time Warner in the US, and BCE, Rogers, Quebecor, and Shaw in Canada, seek to control every part of the media spinal cord, from TV stations to cable channels to smart phones and tablets. The barriers to entry for would-be competitors have arguably never been higher or more imposing, and few companies can compete with these giants before being bought out, undercut or out-muscled in some way.

Columbia University Professor Tim Wu has coined the term the "master switch" to describe what he sees as the natural evolution of media empires.[35] According to Wu, "History shows a typical progression of information technologies: from somebody's hobby to somebody's industry; from jury-rigged contraption to slick production marvel: from a freely accessible channel to one strictly controlled by a single corporation or cartel—from open to closed system. It is a progression so common as to seem inevitable."[36] Wu believes that a super-consortium consisting of Hollywood content, AT&T lines, and Apple devices dominates the information supply chain. While Wu's thesis may be overblown, cynics might argue that the media world now resembles a scene from the movie *The Godfather Part II* where Hyman Roth (Lee Strasberg) and Michael Corleone (Al Pacino) cut a cake with the map of

Cuba on it, symbolically dividing up the country among themselves.[37] At the very least it's difficult for small upstarts to get a piece of the action.

Another important factor in the new concentration of media power is the winner-take-all nature of the web. The Internet is dominated by relatively few giant killer whales—eBay, Google, Facebook, Amazon, Wikipedia, Groupon, Netflix, Craigslist, PayPal, Redddit, and YouTube, among others—that exist alongside many hundreds of millions of minnows. The top ten websites now account for roughly 75 per cent of page views, with 35 per cent of visits going to just four sites. Robert McChesney bemoans the lack of a middle class among news websites, noting that audiences have gravitated to just a few news powerhouses while a whole layer of mid-level news organizations "are being wiped out."[38] Even in the highly rarified world of political blogs, there are a handful of A-list blogs that have influential readerships and are part of the wider political conversation, and tens of thousands of castoff blogs with tiny readerships.[39]

The existence of giant conglomerates with unprecedented power has reopened the question of corporate concentration and whether media giants have too much power. The fear is that these slow-moving behemoths suppress innovation and competition, charge exorbitant rates, set the parameters of political debate, and dominate the cultural and entertainment landscape while allowing few other voices to be heard. While corporate concentration can produce great dangers, there are offsetting arguments with respect to Canada's situation. Some argue that Canada needs "national champions" in order to compete against global media giants and create at least some Canadian cultural landmarks. Only super-sized conglomerates such as Bell Media, Quebecor, or Rogers, it is argued, have the size and scale needed to swim among the global whales—and even these companies may not be big enough.

A fifth characteristic of media shock is that every screen is merging with every other screen, every medium is merging with every other medium, and they are all converging on the Internet. This means that many of the old boundaries, many of the old distinctions, are disintegrating as traditional media are being reassembled and reshaped. Holland Wilde, an award-winning television set designer and popular blogger, predicts that fundamentally "all screens are the same. It's all TV. Size, kind, and style are of little importance. Our reality is shifting away from the real world and INTO the screen; Period."[40]

This type of convergence is happening both with content and hardware. On the content side, sites such as The Daily Beast, Reddit, The Huffington Post, Slate, Buzzfeed, and Politico are at once magazines, blogs, broadcast centres, aggregators, photo galleries, archives, social media sites, and stores.

These hybrid media have considerable financial backing, are attached to more established media companies, and already claim important audience and advertising niches. This has left the newspaper industry in particular in crisis. While newspapers have been creeping step by step into hybrid form, they have come late to the party. They are attempting to occupy much of the same ground that the established hybrids already occupy. As we will discuss in Chapter Six, the question is whether the advantage that they have in local news will allow them to survive. British scholar Andrew Chadwick has described the hybrid and polycentric nature of almost all news reporting. His argument is that hybrid media have created a hybrid newsroom and that the media logic that dominated traditional media is melding with news forms of newsgathering and news-making.[41]

Convergence is taking place even more emphatically on the hardware side. Take smart phones. Versatile, compact, portable, and interactive, they are the exact opposite of traditional stand-alone media. The integration of the phone with the computer has made smart phones into "the electronic equivalent of the Swiss Army knife."[42] Mobile devices provide text messaging, GPS systems, and Internet TV, and through a storehouse of applications users can access an avalanche of films, TV programs, video games, live sports events, comic books, shopping, and archives. Even the creation of ring tones has become an art form—and a profitable business. More importantly, smart phones have become the central organizer of daily life for many, if not most, Canadians. They have become our constant companions: indispensable, ubiquitous, addictive, and always on. The social and psychological implications of the smart-phone culture will be discussed at some length throughout the book.

One of the most interesting developments on the convergence frontier is "wearable computing." Companies such as Apple, Samsung, and Google are integrating watches and glasses with everyday fashions. Smart watches, for instance, are fitted with health-related monitors and apps so that users are able to read their health charts while they read news headlines, watch a video, and of course tell the time. A further striking example of how new technology has already changed the cultural landscape is that David Hockney, one of the most important artists of the twenty-first century, now uses the iPad Brushes application to create works of art. In fact, his iPhone and iPad creations are so remarkable that they have been shown at major galleries.[43]

While the video game console tends to get little attention from scholars, in some ways it's been just as revolutionary as the smart phone. Owners of the latest game consoles can connect to the Internet and Facebook, send text messages, download movies, TV programs, and old video games, and some games even allow players to order pizza so that they don't have to get up from the games that they are playing. Users can attend concerts, re-create historical events, run fictional households, and play with or against people from across the globe. They can enter a fantasy world over which they will have more control than they will have over almost anything that they will experience in the real world: this no doubt is the key to the great pleasure that these games provide.

The time and resources that now go into the development of a major video game exceeds or at least parallels the time and resources needed to produce a major Hollywood movie. Top games can take four or five years to develop, employ more than 1,000 people, and cost more than $100 million (US) to produce. The games themselves have become multimedia extravaganzas with movie-like introductions, startling graphics, sophisticated scripts, life-like characters, in-game advertising (billboards for Coke or Pepsi, sports figures wearing Nike equipment, etc.), and places where gamers, in the guise of their online characters, can meet each other. The integration of gaming with social media on sites such as Steam allows for a continuous conversation as well as never ending deal making, exchanges, and purchases. Perhaps the best example of the power that video games possess occurred when Electronic Arts developed the Madden NFL video game in 1985. NFL coaching legend John Madden wanted the video game to resemble a TV broadcast. Over 25 years later, Fox Sports CEO David Hill returned the compliment by using the video game as a model for Fox's TV telecasts.[44]

A sixth characteristic of media shock is the impact that these changes are having on the survival of traditional media. Newspapers are seen as the most prominent victim of web-based media's assault on traditional media. And there can be little doubt that the newspaper industry is in the process of being blown apart as advertisers increasingly go online and young readers disappear. As an article in the *Economist* explained in 2009,

> A newspaper is a package of content—politics, share prices, weather and so forth—which exists to attract eyeballs to advertisements. Unfortunately for newspapers, the Internet is better at delivering some of that than paper is. It is easier to search through job and property listings on the web, so classified advertising ... is migrating to the Internet. Some content, too, works better on the Internet— news and share prices can be more frequently updated, weather can be more geographically specific so readers are migrating too. The package is thus being picked apart.[45]

There is little question that the Canadian newspaper industry has been in a nosedive from which it has been unable to level off. Circulation in Canada declined from over 100 per cent of households in 1950 (when many Canadians read more than one daily newspaper) to about 27 per cent today. Circulation figures in the US and in the UK are only a little higher than in Canada. Circulation in the US plummeted from 123 per cent in 1950 to roughly 30 per cent of households in 2012. Average circulation in the UK fell from approximately 150 per cent of households in 1950 to just about 33 per cent in 2012.[46]

Once-thriving papers have seen their circulations plummet. Between 1995 and 2010, the *Toronto Star* lost close to 44 per cent of its circulation, the *Winnipeg Free Press* lost over 12 per cent, the *Ottawa Citizen* over 26 per cent, *La Presse* 14 per cent, and the *Toronto Sun* over 42 per cent.[47] By any reasonable estimate, newspapers have lost at least half of their value since 2000. Ad revenue has been in free fall, stock prices have been battered, and investors are few and far between. Another problem, apart from the great disassembling of the newspaper industry described above, is that young people are no longer newspaper readers. Florian Sauvageau likes to tell the story of how after arriving at Laval University one morning he happened to see a young man in one of the cafeterias reading *Le Devoir*, Quebec's most respected newspaper. Professor Sauvageau quickly went back to his department to tell his colleagues about his remarkable sighting, a sighting he treated with the same awe as seeing other endangered species such as a whooping crane or a blue whale.

But even amid the carnage created by media shock, some of the old battleships are unlikely to sink any time soon. This is partly because there are still people (like me) who enjoy the sensation of holding a newspaper in their hands and believe that reading a hard-copy newspaper with their morning coffee is one of life's great pleasures. Newspapers are also the main producers of news—arguably the one medium without which the other media could not operate. Although media expert Clay Shirky warns that newspaper lovers "risk sounding like a fuddy-duddy gentleman preaching the virtues of ascots and walking sticks,"[48] and Barbara Ehrenreich told graduating students at California-Berkeley that newspaper reporters now "feel a certain kinship with blacksmiths and elevator operators," I will argue later in the book that there are forces that are likely to keep newspapers afloat at least for a time. As the old saying goes, "it's not over till it's over."[49]

Conventional over-the-air broadcasters such as Global, CTV, and TVA are under similar pressures. Although personal video recorders, large flat high-definition screens, surround sound, and a kaleidoscope of cable and satellite channels and web broadcasting sites have made TV viewing more spectacular than ever, the audience for conventional over-the-air network television has steadily dropped. In Canada the audience share enjoyed by private conventional broadcasters dropped from 45.3 per cent in 1993 to 33.3 per cent in

2001 to just 22 per cent in 2008–09.[50] Between 2008 and 2012, revenues for Canadian private broadcasters dropped by 1.2 per cent on the English language side and 2.8 per cent on the French side, a sizable downturn if one factors in taxes and inflation.[51]

Ironically, the very technology that is making television such a visual paradise for viewers is making it a nightmare for conventional broadcasters. A main factor is the emergence of a new form of TV—high quality, expansive, serialized programs that have altered the direction of the TV business. As discussed above, this is the seventh characteristic of media shock. Where the TV business was until recently attracting smaller and smaller niche audiences, it has again become a mass medium and a central meeting place. Programs such as *Mad Men*, *Game of Thrones*, *Homeland*, *House of Cards*, *Breaking Bad*, *The Walking Dead*, and *True Detectives* have adult themes, deal with anti-heroes, feature cinema-like production techniques, and are designed for binge viewing. These new hyper-serials are, according to some experts, the way in which "our brains *want* to watch TV"—not in short ad-filled slivers of 22 minutes per week but in long bursts of 3 and 4 hours at a time. As pundit Alan Sepinwall has described the massive impact being made by this latest version of Big TV, "The revolution was televised."[52]

To the chagrin of the conventional over-the-air networks, however, these shows are produced mainly by specialty cable channels such as HBO, AMC, and Showtime or by online broadcasters such as Netflix, YouTube, Amazon Prime, and Hulu Plus, among a host of others. Netflix alone now supplies over 30 per cent of all down-stream traffic in North America during prime time hours, an astonishing percentage.[53] But networks also face an avalanche of other online competition. YouTube, peer-to-peer sharing, illegal sites such as Pirate Bay and Kickass Torrents, as well as archives created by virtually every broadcaster and studio have eaten into the territory once comfortably occupied by traditional broadcasters.

While Canada's over-the-air broadcasters are owned by highly diversified media conglomerates—BCE (CTV), Shaw (Global), Quebecor (TVA), and Rogers (City)—their positions are increasingly precarious. While broadcasters are trying to extend their reach through video archives, mobile phones, tablets, and Internet broadcasting, trying in effect to own every link in the media spinal cord, keeping their audiences may be difficult simply because of the onslaught of competition from every imaginable direction. Quebec broadcasters, principally TVA and Radio-Canada, remain an exception because of the protective barriers of the French language and the tug of popular programs rooted in Quebec culture.

CBC television seems to be in the greatest danger. Largely denied the opportunity to expand along the cable frontier, facing private competitors that are vertically integrated and have multiple media platforms, having shredded much of their local programming because of budget cuts, and being unable to plan effectively because the public broadcaster never quite knows what its budget will be from year to year, the CBC is fighting to keep its head above water. This is less true of Radio-Canada television, which enjoys a privileged position in Quebec.

Although as a group they continue to be profitable, the long-term prospects for radio stations don't seem to be much brighter. Music downloading continues to be epidemic, Internet radio has migrated into cars, threatening the age-old relationship between listeners and local stations, and applications such as Pandora, Songza, and Spotify allow users to construct their own highly personalized listening experience. Most worrying for the radio industry is not only the slow erosion of audience numbers but the increasing absence of younger listeners.[54] The point has been reached where the audience for commercial talk radio in particular (with the exception of sports) is verging on geriatric. If the trend continues, most hotline listeners will be people who wear hearing aids and read in large print. Interestingly, amid these changes, and perhaps because of them, CBC/SRC radio has retained its audience. In 2012 it still commanded 13.4 per cent of daily English-language listeners (combining audiences for Radio One and Radio Two).[55] Its distinctive voice, home-grown character, and in-depth discussions are becoming more difficult to find elsewhere.

The traditional mass media are likely to co-exist for quite some time in a kind of limbo dance with web-based media: not quite prospering but not quite disappearing. Big media brands may prosper purely because they carry a certain authority and are multi-headed monsters with many assets. So perhaps will local or niche media that have a monopoly over certain kinds of information: the small-town newspaper, magazines directed at different groups or industries, specialized cable or Internet channels, for example. The problem perhaps is with media organizations that are in the middle of the pack in terms of size and have no special cause, identity or mission. They are likely to face extinction or reappear in new forms. This is not a small issue for a country such as Canada that has depended on the traditional media to carry the heavy load of national identity. The burning question then becomes this: if not the traditional media, then what or who will do this heavy lifting?

An eighth characteristic of media shock is the degree to which we have become globally connected. As Joshua Meyrowitz once put it, television "now escorts children across the globe even before they have permission to cross the street." In his classic work, *No Sense of Place*, Meyrowitz argued that the great achievement of electronic media was that it created a "shared arena" by taking viewers to "back regions" of society from which they had previously been excluded.[56] In fact, television now revels in trespassing onto private spaces—making the private public. For the first time in history, poor people can enter the homes of the rich, Jews and Muslims can see how Christmas is celebrated or how a Pope is chosen, women can enter once-forbidden bastions of male power such as board rooms and locker rooms, and viewers can accompany the police on patrol, entering where they would normally be afraid to go. Cable TV has become an endless travelogue into once-hidden worlds, including those of ghost hunters, convicts, gamblers, tattoo artists, swamp people, ice pilots, pickers, the obese, hospital emergency-room personnel, gypsies, and believers in alien invasions.

The ability to peer into other people's lives is also true internationally. Thomas Friedman, the three-time Pulitzer Prize–winning columnist for the *New York Times*, has described the role that the news media played in spawning the uprisings that exploded across the Middle East in 2011.[57] Presumably the same analysis could be applied to the events that shook Turkey, Brazil, and Egypt in 2013. While the Middle East uprisings of 2011 were caused by shocking levels of unemployment, sky-rocketing food prices, authoritarian regimes that ruled by torture and fear, and a pervasive sense of hopelessness, web-based media acted as a catalyst in two ways. YouTube, Twitter, Facebook, *Al Jazeera*, and Google Earth (which allowed people to see the luxurious homes of government officials) all played a part in both setting and spreading the fire of revolt by allowing dissidents to learn about and connect with each other. In fact, Manuel Castells has argued in his study of social movements that opposition forces have been able to create their own online societies— with their own news networks, rituals, symbols, and sense of belonging.[58] Friedman also believes that the ability of ordinary people to breach the walls erected by their national media had an extraordinary impact. Young Arabs saw that other societies were creating democratic institutions and achieving higher standards of living while theirs were stagnating. The same held true for the uprising in Brazil in 2013, where people demanded that the country's leadership provide the same types of public institutions and standards that Europeans and North Americans enjoyed.

The instant nature of global communication is most evident, perhaps, in the behaviour of stock markets. Where stock markets were once rooted in national or regional economies, today there is in effect a global market-place with traders—mostly computer algorithms—able to react instantly to the latest news from Tokyo, London or Shanghai. Trillions of dollars a day ping back and forth across the world in a never-ending game of financial pinball.

The ninth element in media shock is the transformation created by social media. Social media such as Facebook, Twitter, Pinterest, and Google+ have created opportunities for political involvement and interaction that were unimaginable even a short time ago. Users can be informed quickly about events, demonstrations, meet-ups, and forums. They can sign online petitions, donate to causes, help create viral fire storms, follow tweets from political leaders and journalists, and join discussions on any topic at any time of the day or night. In short, they have the capacity to "produce" politics either by themselves or in confluence with large campaigns. As was demonstrated during Barack Obama's run for the presidency in 2008 and his re-election campaign in 2012, social media have a breathtaking capacity to mobilize large number of voters. The Obama campaign used social media to organize tens of thousands of meetings, raise hundreds of millions of dollars, and run an extraordinary get-out-the-vote effort. But the Obama campaigns in 2008 and 2012 remain a singular political achievement; most other online campaigns have fallen far short in terms of results. As will be discussed in much greater length in Chapter Four, political leaders also have to be continually on guard, as missiles in the form of embarrassing videos or overheard conversations can disrupt their campaigns and in some cases do incalculable damage.

Some observers, however, aren't so sure that a new political world is rising. A study conducted by the Pew Internet Project of Internet use during the 2010 US mid-term elections found that while Internet use was widespread for accessing news, learning about candidates or fact checking, only a small minority used the Internet to become personally involved in the campaign.[59] Online activists also tended to be wealthier and better educated. Although this more privileged group was using social and web-based media intensively, most citizens remained disengaged from politics and didn't bother to vote.

The same is true in Canada. As mentioned earlier, a survey taken during the 2011 Canadian federal election found that while social media allowed the small number of Canadians who were already involved in politics to become more involved, it did not create a wider circle of involvement.[60] Yaroslav Baran, who was instrumental in the Conservative Party's communications operations during the 2004, 2006, and 2008 federal elections, is critical of what he sees as the media's infatuation with Twitter during the 2011 campaign. Baran describes the euphoria that was created around Twitter: "But it was perhaps the Twitter political bubble that in fact convinced itself—inside the same bubble—that this medium would be the revolutionizing feature that it failed to be." He also recounts how he received a tweet during the third week of the campaign from a Liberal supporter bragging that "We are KICKING your ass in social media." As Baran notes sarcastically, "Perhaps they did kick our ass in social media … but how did that turn out for you?"[61]

In a study of "public connectedness" conducted in the UK, Nick Couldry, Sonia Livingstone, and Tim Markham were able to substantiate the theory of the "virtuous circle" first elaborated by Harvard professor Pippa Norris— those who were already politically engaged use media to become even more engaged.[62] But they also found the opposite was true: a "vicious circle" of non-involvement also existed. Those who were not involved were "less interested, less engaged and more inattentive." Internet use did not alter this basic equation.

Aside from the charge that political activism on social media is the preserve of a privileged or activist minority, some scholars believe that it has a "narcotizing" effect; it gives users the illusion of involvement without its substance. Sometimes referred to as "slacktivism" or "clicktivism," the notion is that Internet activism is cheap and convenient and is often a substitute for real activity or commitment. While some users may feel the warm glow of engagement because they have signed an online petition, watched a video, re-tweeted an article, or discussed crime, climate change or an election with Facebook friends, the reality is that unless people join organizations, attend meet-ups, donate money, volunteer time, and vote, they are just spectators watching from the sidelines rather than true participants.

Indeed, in a scathing critique of what he sees as the passivity of the Facebook culture, popular author Malcolm Gladwell believes that "Facebook activism succeeds not by motivating people to make real sacrifice but by motivating them to do the things that people do when they are not motivated enough to make real sacrifices."[63] He argues that social networks lack the hierarchy and clear lines of authority needed to make decisions or operate strategically. Simply put, users don't have the collective will to take a campaign to the next level. A similar argument is made by Zizi Papacharissi of the University of Illinois at Chicago. She believes that it is a mistake to see social media as part of the public sphere. As she puts it, "the nexus of collaborative social networks—blogs, tweets, video-blogs, YouTube videos, videos, diggs, and other forms of citizen media—amalgamates around the self and the territory of the self—that is the private sphere, which serves as the starting point and the core of all such activity."[64] Hence the public sphere is being brought into private spaces, rather than the reverse. While this doesn't diminish the power and importance of social media, we should not be under any illusions that the public sphere is about to be reinvigorated.

The reality may fall somewhere between these two opposing positions. The simple truth is that we are not sure about the influence that social media will have in the long run. In Canada, social media seems to have had little effect in galvanizing action during elections. On other occasions, however, such as during the Quebec student strike of 2012 and the Idle No More movement in 2013, they became vital instruments for communicating within the movements and mobilizing demonstrations.

The last characteristic of media change that we will cover is the issue of privacy. We are now under surveillance to a degree that would have shocked George Orwell; to paraphrase Winston Churchill, "never before have so few known so much about so many." Gatekeepers such as Google, Facebook, and Apple track the sites that users visit, getting to know where they shop, the products that they like, the music that they listen to, the TV programs they watch, where they travel, the organizations they join, and who their friends are. Companies aggregate information and create user profiles that they use in advertising or sell to third parties. Tracking companies such as Twitalyzer, PeerIndex, and Klout analyze information from social media sites in order to determine and "score" the influence that various users have within their network.[65]

The Internet has become a forest of tracking devices. An investigation in 2011 by the *Wall Street Journal* into the operations of the 50 most popular websites, including the main news sites, found that they contained an average of 64 tracking devices.[66] Remarkably there were 12 sites that had over 100 tracking tools. The only major site that did not have tracking devices was Wikipedia. The *WSJ* concluded that "a defining feature of the Internet" was people's willingness to give up their most private information in exchange for the information that the Internet could give them.[67] In other words, people enter a devil's bargain where they have to give up a great deal of private information in exchange for the advantages that Facebook and Apple can give them.

While Big Data can help produce much better public policies—by using Google searches to predict when and where flu outbreaks are likely to occur, which TV shows are likely to be hits, the likely locations of crimes and even the rate of inflation—they are also used by companies to target consumers with ads based on sensitive personal characteristics such as their medical and romantic histories, religious beliefs, race or sexual orientation. Most members of the public, however, remain sublimely unaware of the degree to which they are under continuous surveillance. They are unaware that their smart phones are in effect spying on them—revealing their whereabouts, mapping their digital profiles, and directing their purchases. Even more brazen is the ability of e-readers to record readers' thoughts. Every time, for instance, someone highlights a passage in a book or magazine that they are reading, a record of that passage is being stored and can be available to strangers. The same is true for personal fitness bracelets and other wearables. The data that they store about your location, health and even sleep patterns is being collected and can be sold to third parties.

Particularly disturbing is the degree to which political parties track the voting intentions and political associations of virtually every citizen. In 2012, barackobama.com had 75 tracking devices that allowed the Obama campaign to place a "score" on the political beliefs of every American of voting age.[68] While Canadian parties are not nearly as sophisticated as their American counterparts, they are building inventories of information about ordinary citizens that could easily lead to abuses. Why should political parties be able to peer into the private lives of citizens? Why should they know which party or candidate you support and whether you can be counted as a friend or as a critic?

On another level, thanks to National Security Agency whistleblower Edward Snowden, we now know that American government agencies conduct warrant-less examinations of phone conversations, emails, and text messages of millions of Americans every day. In effect, Google and Facebook, among other corporations, have allowed the US government to have access to their information through a backdoor that is always open. The daily drag-net also captures the private activities and information of millions of people around the world, including Canadians. For its part, Canada has aided the US in spying on foreign leaders, among them the leaders of the G8, and has also spied on leaders of countries such as Brazil. The current logic of international diplomacy is that everyone is spying on everyone else all the time.

While people may believe that their information is safe, legal scholars warn that constitutional protections are razor thin. The federal government has the ability to "go deep" on individual users, although police require a warrant to search through a person's computer or smart phone. But this is only the tip of the iceberg: there are "investigation" sites such as Spokeo, which, for a small cost, will provide subscribers with information on anyone that they choose. These sites scour the Internet using deep web crawlers for any available information on their targets, including their financial informa-tion, associations they belong to, professional history, and photos of their homes, workplaces, and friends. Much as in international diplomacy, new technologies allow everyone to spy on everyone else all the time.

Particularly distressing in this regard was the case of the education stu-dent who was denied a teaching degree after a picture of her attending a Halloween party as a "drunken pirate" was posted on a social media site.[69] While this is a particularly grievous example of someone being unable to outrace her past, she is just one casualty among thousands of others who didn't realize that their Facebook histories were open to scrutiny by corpora-tions and other institutions and that pictures, opinions, and friendships from years before could come back to bite them. The reality is that a majority of recruiters and human-resources personnel scour social media sites to find out about prospective employees.[70] Providing access to these sites is often a condition of being interviewed. Not surprisingly, some people never make it to the interview despite having all of the paper qualifications needed for the job. The problem is that the worst thing that you ever did can become the first thing that people learn about you, and you have little chance to erase that history and in many cases even know that it exists.

Nor is personal information safe from hackers, including hacking by governments. In 2011, for instance, computers in the federal Finance Department and Treasury Board were attacked and apparently overwhelmed by a cyber-attack originating in China. No one knows how much personal and corporate information was pillaged. Attacks against government agencies, major corporations, and major websites are routine and sometimes devastating. While data-scrubbing technologies have become more sophisticated, allowing people to set time limits after which their postings disappear, tagged photos that have been widely distributed are difficult to find and erase. Moreover, paying for a "social media audit" can be very expensive—well beyond what most people can afford. Law professor Jeffrey Rosen has described the dilemma that we are all in,

> We've known for years that the Web allows for unprecedented
> voyeurism, exhibitionism and inadvertent indiscretion, but we
> are only beginning to understand the costs of an age in which so
> much of what we say, and of what others say about us, goes into
> our permanent—and public—digital files. The fact that the Internet
> never seems to forget is threatening, at an almost existential level, our
> ability to control our identities, to preserve the option of reinventing
> ourselves and starting anew: to overcome our checkered pasts.[71]

★★★

Examined individually, any one of the developments that constitute media shock has had a major impact on our culture and public life. Taken together they represent a profound revolution—arguably the deepest and most fundamental change in communication since the invention of the printing press, the telegraph, or the telephone. It would be a mistake to see web-based media as merely a sideshow, as representing just a new bag of tricks that have to be learned if we want to run a business or communicate with friends. In reality, media shock has produced a reordering of power relationships, the breaking of old institutions, and the building of new frontiers of creativity and invention. It goes to the core of how societies work and how we connect with each other. Yet surprisingly little has been written about how these new realities of power are colliding with and changing identity and public life in Canada. It is to this task that we now turn.

Media Change and Canadian Public Spaces

Much has been written about the notion of the "public sphere," a term popularized by the much-venerated German scholar Jürgen Habermas. To Habermas, the public sphere is that narrow and precious space where the real work of a society gets done—those places where people can meet freely to learn about and discuss issues and ideas and where a consensus about future actions takes shape.[72] The existence of a public sphere cannot, however, be taken for granted. Governments, interest groups, and corporations have the capacity to close off or co-opt public spaces, to narrow and skew debate. The problem of how to keep public spaces open for genuine debate and interaction has consumed much of the thinking of media scholars. Even at their very best, public spheres are chaotic, disorganized, unequal, and always in flux.

The public spheres provided by the mass media are as critical to how a society is organized and governed as formal institutions such as legislatures, courts, schools, and political parties. In fact, as David Altheide and Robert Snow, as well as Richard Ericson and his colleagues, have shown, the media set the stage and condition how these other actors play their roles.[73] The American scholar Jay Rosen has argued that the primary mission of the news media is "to make politics 'go well' so that it produces a discussion in which the polity learns more about itself, its current problems, its real divisions, its place in time, its prospects for the future."[74] But just as easily and surely, poor media and poor journalism can make political and economic life go poorly. When media don't work, when people don't have the basic information that they need to live healthy lives or to make good decisions, then the damage to society can be immense.

Dean Starkman of the *Columbia Journalism Review* argues that the health of democracies is inextricably linked to the strength and vitality of what he calls "accountability journalism." Accountability journalism ensures that the powerful are held responsible for their actions. Hence the watchdog has to be alert, independent, and willing to bite. To Starkman, accountability journalism is "the great agenda-setter, public trust builder and value creator. It explains complex problems to a mass audience and holds the powerful to account."[75] His great worry is that "the very architecture of the Internet militates against such work."[76]

Media change may have greater consequences for Canadians than it does for those in other countries because other societies are not as dependent on the media to be a vital connecting link. Countries with "hard" identities such as Japan, Sweden, South Korea, Italy, Turkey, or Spain are bound by a common ethnic heritage, are confined within narrow geographies, have strong religious traditions and deep histories, and have a rich terrain of shared symbols and heroes. Even their architecture reminds them of who they are. The very bones of Canadian identity are different. With vast distances and a harsh climate, sharp linguistic and cultural divisions, the overpowering influence of American mass media and popular entertainment, along with the fact that Canada has since World War II taken in more immigrants per capita than any other country in history, Canadian culture and identity can't be taken for granted in the same way.

Because of these challenges, the Canadian media system has largely been a construct of the federal government. Whether it was the establishment of and support for public broadcasting, the creation of rules and incentives for Canadian content, a tax system that penalized advertising in non-Canadian publications, rules that limited foreign ownership and allowed for the emergence of "national champions," a system of simultaneous substitution that blocks American TV signals—and more specifically American advertising—from reaching Canadian viewers when Canadian broadcasters are airing the same shows at the same times as the American networks, or the generous infusions of government advertising dollars, the fingerprints of government intervention are everywhere. While media owners often complain about the obligations that Ottawa imposes on them, they rarely complain when they get lucrative franchises or licences. In fact, one could argue that the creation of a national media system has been one of the country's great nation-building exercises, rivalled in scale and significance only by John A. Macdonald's National Policy, the creation of Medicare and other social programs in the 1950s and 1960s, and the rights revolution brought about by the Charter of Rights and Freedoms that began in the 1980s.

American scholars such as Douglas Cater, Timothy Cook, and Noam Chomsky have gone as far as to argue that the news media have become a branch of government, that government and media are part of the same organism, part of the same co-production system.[77] Governments need media to perform certain functions without which they wouldn't be able to operate. This is the inverse of what American founders such as Thomas Jefferson had originally intended, namely that journalism would be a check on the power of government—a check against tyranny. In reality, the news media's relationship with government is a complex amalgam of conflict and symbiosis, alliance and opposition.

One of the consequences of media shock is that the Canadian government is losing the capacity to maintain the media system. Search engines, social media, websites, applications, media archives, personal video recorders, and YouTube, to name just a few of the new digital realities, not only undermine conventional media but are to some degree beyond the reach of governments and regulators. The once unmovable building blocks of media policy are being swept away by the pace and force of media change.

So what's at stake? The significance of the traditional mass media was that they were, and to some degree still are, the central meeting places of the culture. This is especially the case for television. In anthropologist Benedict Anderson's famous description, viewers are drawn into "imagined communities" because they come to identify with and are moved by events, issues, and people that are otherwise far from their personal experiences.[78] As British scholar Robert Hartley has put it, "representative political space is literally made of pictures—they constitute the public domain."[79] To Roger Silverstone "the media presents a version of the world that in the absence of direct experience effectively constitutes *the* world."[80] To the eminent Swedish scholar Peter Dahlgren, media are "the dominant symbolic environment of a society."[81]

In the period from the 1950s to the early 1970s, when Canadians could receive only five or six TV channels, half of them American, virtually the entire population was exposed to the same news programs, comedy, and variety shows and shared the same cultural experience. Programs such as *The Wayne and Shuster Hour, Juliette, La famille Plouffe, The Friendly Giant, Front Page Challenge, Don Messer's Jubilee, Les belles histoires des pays d'en haut, This Hour Has Seven Days*, and *Pointe de Mire* reached huge audiences. While they are now only fading shadows in our collective memory, these shows set standards of taste and sensibility, particularly in comedy, that were far different from those in the US. These shows created a star system in Canada and allowed political leaders, celebrities, athletes, or artists to be seen, heard, liked or disliked, and viewed at close range. In a symbolic sense we all occupied the same living room.

TV moments are still the signposts of collective memory and identity. For years, Canadians were moved by graphic scenes from the war in Afghanistan and especially the moving ramp ceremonies for fallen Canadian soldiers. The battle for the Stanley Cup, the drama of election nights, Olympic coverage, the sombre reflections of Remembrance Day ceremonies from Parliament Hill—all of these still provide a sense of belonging. In fact, sports television offers a poignant example of the power of the traditional media. It is important to remember that for more than half a century, *Hockey Night in Canada* has been more than just a TV program. It is a spectacle that has transcended divisions based on region and language and provided the country with a common experience.

Perhaps the pinnacle event of recent Canadian collective memory was the Vancouver Olympics of 2010. A broadcast consortium led by CTV produced so much coverage—4,800 hours in all—that the Olympics became both inescapable and all-enveloping. Some 15.5 million Canadians watched the opening ceremonies, and TVs in an astounding 80 per cent of Canadian households were tuned to the Canada–US gold-medal men's hockey game. A pride in hosting the games, the country's gold-medal haul (which was the largest of any country in the history of the Winter Games), stories of personal triumph by Canadian athletes, and an avalanche of patriotic advertising by Canadian corporations produced a collective experience and a patriotic euphoria rarely seen in Canadian history. Given the disruptive power of media shock, one wonders whether the Vancouver Olympics will be the last great mass-media event in Canadian history, the last time that Canadians share a single mythical media moment together. Audiences for the Sochi Olympics, including the hockey final against Sweden, fell short of Vancouver's numbers, although they were still substantial. The deeper question is whether societies need such spectacles, need these moments of collective memory and belonging, to stay together.

Although the Canadian mass media can still summon large audiences, competition for viewers has never been as intense. The battle for audiences is being fought on two fronts. On the one hand, large global conglomerates such as Google, Apple, and Disney are assuming greater control of the media landscape, a control that threatens and diminishes the role that governments can play in promoting a national media system. On the other hand, web-based media are eroding audiences and advertising at an astonishing rate. The stark reality is that Me-media isn't necessarily Canadian media. In fact, in most cases it isn't.

While Habermas's "floor plan" envisions "vast numbers of sprawling communicative spaces of immense variety," he did not envision the slow erosion of the conventional media, the cable explosion, Big Data, peer-to-peer communication, YouTube, or the rise of social media, nor did he anticipate the impact that these developments could have on the public sphere and the workings of democracy.[82] In short, he did not envision what the media would eventually become.

Looking Ahead

The purpose of *Digital Mosaic* is to view the problems of Canadian identity and democracy through the prism of media change. The book will examine the new shape of media power and the impact that these changes are having on the Canadian media system, and particularly on the future of journalism and the news media in Canada. A main theme in the book is that the country is experiencing a number of overlapping crises simultaneously. There is a crisis of citizen engagement and participation, as Canadians in general—and younger people in particular—are less involved in or even do not follow public affairs. There is a journalistic crisis, as established media institutions become weaker and less able to shoulder the responsibilities of in-depth reporting. The future of news and the question of who will pay for it are very much in the air. And there is a crisis in Canada's media policy, too, with global media conglomerates such as Google, Apple, and Facebook having usurped much of the power that the government and the CRTC once had to "administer" the media lives of Canadians. Issues such as the future of public broadcasting, our ability to produce Canadian drama and cultural programming, as well as disturbing questions about protecting personal privacy now haunt our media and communications policies.

At the same time, some of our political institutions are in need of drastic reform. For better or worse, our political institutions are artifacts of nineteenth-century political understandings and deal-making. The Senate, Question Period in the House of Commons, the messy hodge-podge of federal and provincial jurisdictions, and the way in which elections are fought are just some of the areas that need to be re-thought and re-imagined. Along with these systemic issues are some important policy matters that often suffer as a result of the nature of our institutions; the lack of funding for our burgeoning cities and the state of Aboriginal relations are just two of these pressing concerns.

Digital Mosaic is divided into nine chapters including a conclusion. The second chapter, following this introduction, discusses the complex nature of Canadian citizenship. Much as we dress for winter, Canadians often wear many layers of identity that we take on and off when circumstances change. Canadian political nationality has been shaped by a culture of accommodation and an adherence to legal rights that are at once remarkably strong and deeply fragile. Given our patchwork sense of nationality, one can argue that Canada is more vulnerable to the pounding and corrosive effects of media shock than are other countries.

A second part of the chapter is devoted to the disengagement crisis: the fact that so many Canadians, and digital natives in particular, appear to have become peek-a-boo citizens engaged in some ways but largely disappearing from view when it comes to joining civic organizations, knowing the basic facts of public life, following the news, volunteering, or voting in elections. A last section discusses some of the factors that have contributed to the "disengagement culture" and touches briefly on the role that the media may have played in suppressing citizen involvement—a theme that will be discussed in much greater depth in Chapter Six.

Chapter Three deals with what can be described as "the iron laws of corporate concentration." The focus is mostly on corporate convergence and the strategies employed by giant technology and entertainment conglomerates to dominate the media landscape. Despite the emergence of Me-media and the vast smorgasbord of choices available to users, a handful of communication giants remain the key producers of culture. A small cohort of giant conglomerates such as Disney, Google, News Corporation, Comcast, and Time Warner in the US, and companies such as BCE, Shaw, Rogers, and Quebecor in Canada, have the ability to impose cultural and political agendas and control media consumption. This is because most of what is discussed in cyberspace—news, celebrities, sports, TV programs, music, and so on—are overwhelmingly the products of the established media. In addition, powerful conglomerates have created checkpoints and tollbooths so that more and more of web-based media is accessible only to those who can pay for subscriptions. The implications of corporate control for journalism and media content are discussed in detail.

The flip-side of corporate concentration has been the ability of people to create their own micro-media environments. Chapters Four and Five describe the politics of Me-media and people's ability to construct their own media universes out of the connective tissue of websites, cable channels, blogs, videos, and social media including Facebook and Twitter. Chapter Four begins by describing current research and theories about the impact that web-based media have had on political involvement and behaviour. Battle lines have formed over whether web-based and social media empower and enhance citizenship or whether they create merely an illusion of activity.

The chapter also focuses in particular on the cable explosion and blogging. While the cable revolution is largely ignored by scholars, the chapter will argue that cable has been at the forefront of change in a number of critical ways; it has created a "shock culture" that has legitimized and glamorized behaviours that were once considered marginal, such as gambling, getting a tattoo, going to pawn shops, searching for extra-terrestrials, and ghost hunting, and it has redefined news to emphasize crime and ideological politics. At the same time, cable has allowed broadcasters to offload programming about Canadian politics and history, as well as shows that feature Aboriginal Canadians, from conventional to cable channels. The effect, I will argue, has been to signal to the audience that these topics are unimportant. The chapter also takes readers on a tour of the Canadian blogosphere, arguing that it is much like the Internet as a whole: there is a distinct blogging hierarchy with a few influential players and a vast sea of those who are writing for themselves and their friends.

The fifth chapter continues the discussion of Me-media, concentrating on YouTube, Facebook, and Twitter. These are vast subjects, so the discussion focuses for the most part on how they are used in the political arena. The overriding theme is surveillance: the extent to which both political figures as well as ordinary citizens are under continual scrutiny. Digital technologies have taken us well beyond anything ever imagined by George Orwell in his dark novel *Nineteen Eighty-Four*. Both for good and ill, we are always observing others or being observed ourselves.

The sixth and seventh chapters deal with the challenges being faced by the traditional media. Chapter Six will discuss the future of newspapers, conventional TV, and radio. While rumours of their deaths may be greatly exaggerated, the wounds that they have suffered at the hands of web-based media are life-threatening. The business models that made the newspaper and network TV businesses prosperous for decades are under serious attack. While traditional media are likely to persist in their current forms for quite some time, some of the great lions of the Canadian media are likely to vanish. Others will take on different shapes as they merge with and incorporate other media. A key problem to be discussed is that Canadian democracy is still very much attached to and dependent on the informa-tion roadbeds of newspaper and broadcasting. The traditional media have been among Canada's great "nation-building" institutions. As the traditional media weaken, it's not clear what institutions will take their place.

Chapter Seven will focus on the future of public broadcasting. In a pre-vious book I wrote that, due to political pressures, public broadcasting had been "chilled to the bone."[82] The CBC was afraid to be too controversial, to take strong positions, and most of all to offend those in power. It was also experiencing drastic budget cuts and had starved local and regional programming to save programming at the centre. Currently, it's not so much chilled to the bone as surrounded on all sides. This is especially the case with respect to the English language TV network. It faces intense competition from broadcasters such as CTV and Global that are now part of vast media conglomerates and are spread across multimedia plat-forms. It has to withstand the tidal waves of Big TV coming from online broadcasters such as Netflix and YouTube, as well as cable giants such as HBO. Its budgets have been eviscerated and local programming has been diminished. CBC television, at least in English Canada, is becoming "min-iaturized." Its footprint grows smaller and smaller, never quite disappearing but no longer making a difference. At the same time, and more positively, CBC radio has a loyal if older audience and Radio-Canada continues to produce exciting drama and current-events programs that draw large audiences in Quebec.

This chapter will describe the goals of public broadcasting and the chances for building it anew. The argument is that public broadcasting is integral to having a media policy at all and to having a journalistic culture that is not only driven by commercial values.

Chapter Eight shifts direction by dealing with the relationship between journalists and politicians and the ways in which each of the two estates is in the process of disengaging from the other. The chapter tests a hypothesis first spelled out by political consultant Elly Alboim, a former parliamentary bureau chief for CBC TV news. Alboim claims that the news media are on the verge of total dysfunction. They can no longer have the budgets needed to report on public affairs and, worse still, they have lost interest in and no longer have a stake in Canada's democratic institutions.

The chapter reviews the main routines and assumptions of news reporting, concluding that in subtle and not-so-subtle ways the news media are disengaging from politics. There are fewer political reporters, both crime reporting and celebrity news have come to dominate news agendas, journalists do less investigative work, and journalistic repertories such as trying to achieve "balance" and the obsession with the "horse race" have all too often become excuses for not having to drill below the surface and provide real facts. As Alex Jones argues, the news media are "less able to stay with a story rather than simply visit it."[83] At the same time, a main strategy of political leaders and parties is to bypass journalists so that they can avoid the media filter. Much of politics is now devoted to controlling the message and avoiding media scrutiny.

The end result of this process of mutual disengagement is that Canadians are less knowledgeable about, and less interested in, public affairs. While the disengagement crisis has, as discussed in Chapter Two, a number of causes and explanations, journalists and politicians are at least partly to blame. Ironically, the principal victim of peek-a-boo citizens is the news media themselves. Without avid readers and viewers, they have little future.

The last chapter poses a series of questions. Among other questions, the chapter will ask about the future of news, the nature of citizen disengagement, the prospects for re-inventing public broadcasting, whether privacy can be protected, whether politics can be reformed, and about the policies needed to ensure that Canadians can communicate with each other in an age when each of us is able to construct our own personal media eco-systems and in doing so exclude Canadian media entirely. In short, the last chapter asks about whether we can build new and vital public spaces in the age of media shock. The reality is that while we may gain powerful new instruments of communication and there are many new and splendid possibilities, there is also much to lose.

Notes

1 Michael Keren, *The Citizen's Voice: Twentieth Century Politics and Literature* (Calgary: University of Calgary Press, 2003).

2 Standing Committee on Canadian Heritage, *Our Cultural Sovereignty: The Second Century of Canadian Broadcasting* (Ottawa: House of Commons Canada, 2003).

3 John Porter, *The Vertical Mosaic: An Analysis of Social Class and Power in Canada* (Toronto: University of Toronto Press, 1965).

4 Herve Fischer, *Digital Shock: Confronting the New Reality* (Montreal: McGill-Queen's University Press, 2006).

5 Alvin Toffler, *Future Shock* (New York: Bantam, 1970).

6 Douglas Rushkoff, *Present Shock: When Everything Happens Now* (New York: Penguin, 2013).

7 Elly Alboim, "On the Verge of Total Dysfunction: Government, Media and Communications," in *How Canadians Communicate IV: Media and Politics*, ed. David Taras and Christopher Waddell (Edmonton: Athabasca University Press, 2012), 52.

8 Anya Schiffrin, ed., *Bad News: How America's Business Press Missed the Story of the Century* (New York: New Press, 2011).

9 Florian Sauvageau, "The Uncertain Future of the News," in *How Canadians Communicate IV: Media and Politics*, ed. David Taras and Christopher Waddell (Edmonton: Athabasca University Press, 2012), 32–33.

10 Canadian Media Research Consortium, "Canadian Consumers Unwilling to Pay for News Online," March 29, 2011, http://www.cmrcccrm.ca/documents/CMRC_Paywall_Release.pdf.

11 Barbara Ortutay, "Pew Study Finds Tablet Users Don't Want to Pay for News," *Associated Press*, October 25, 2011.

12 For deeper insights see Howard Gardner and Katie Davis, *The App Generation: How Today's Youth Navigate Identity, Intimacy and Imagination in the Digital World* (New Haven, CT: Yale University Press, 2013).

13 See David Taras and Christopher Waddell, "The 2011 Federal Election and the Transformation of Canadian Media and Politics," in *How Canadians Communicate IV: Media and Politics*, ed. David Taras and Christopher Waddell (Edmonton: Athabasca University Press, 2012), 95–102.

14 For further reading on this estimate see Thomas Fuller, "Does Human Knowledge Double Every 5 Years?," last modified May 28, 2007, http://newsfan.typepad.co.uk/does_human_knowledge_doub/2007/05/index.html.

15 Robert W. McChesney, *Digital Disconnect: How Capitalism Is Turning the Internet against Democracy* (New York: New Press, 2013), 149.

16 Eric Schmidt and Jared Cohen, *The New Digital Age* (New York: Knopf, 2013), 181.

17 McChesney, *Digital Disconnect*, 129.

18 Ibid., 136.

19 Ibid., 1.

20 Omar El Akkad, "Silver Surfers Boost Canada's Web Usage," *Globe and Mail*, March 9, 2011: A3.

21 Statistics drawn from *Canada Digital Future in Focus 2013* (Reston, VA: comScore, March 2013), http://www.comscore.com/Insights/Presentations_and_Whitepapers/2013/2013_Canada_Digital_Future_in_Focus.

22 Interactive Advertising Bureau of Canada, *2011 Actual + 2012 Estimates Canadian Online Advertising Revenue Survey*, http://iabcanada.com/files/Canadian_Online _Advertising_Revenue_Survey_English.pdf, 6.

23 McChesney, *Digital Disconnect*, 148.

24 Marc Prensky, "Digital Natives, Digital Immigrants Part 1," *On the Horizon* 9, no. 5 (October 2001): 1–6; Marc Prensky, "Digital Natives, Digital Immigrants Part 2: Do They Really Think Differently?," *On the Horizon* 9, no. 6 (October 2001).

25 Markus Prior, *Post-Broadcast Democracy* (Cambridge: Cambridge University Press, 2007).

26 Kenneth J. Goldstein (presentation), University of Calgary, January 2007.

27 See "Google Grows Too Successful for Washington," *Real Clear Markets*, June 28, 2011, http://www.realclearmarkets.com/articles/2011/06/28/google_grows_too _succesful_for_washington_99101.html.

28 Ken Auletta, *Googled: The End of the World as We Know it* (New York: The Penguin Press, 2009), 283.

29 Erik Brynjolfsson and Andrew McAfee, *The Second Machine Age: Work, Progress and Prosperity in a Time of Brilliant Technologies* (New York: Norton, 2014).

30 "Google Grows Too Successful."

31 Philip Napoli, *Audience Evolution: New Technologies and the Transformation of Media Audiences* (New York: Columbia University Press, 2011), 10.

32 McChesney, *Digital Disconnect*, 147; Viktor Mayer-Schonberger and Kenneth Cukier, *Big Data: A Revolution That Will Transform How We Live, Work, and Think* (New York: Houghton Mifflin Harcourt, 2013), 92.

33 McChesney, *Digital Disconnect*, 149.

34 Richard Schultz, "From Master to Partner to Bit Player: The Diminishing Capacity of Government Policy," in *How Canadians Communicate*, ed. David Taras, Frits Pan- nekoek and Maria Bakardjieva (Calgary: University of Calgary Press, 2003), 27–49.

35 Timothy Wu, *The Master Switch: The Rise and Fall of Information Empires* (New York: Alfred A. Knopf, 2010).

36 Wu, *The Master Switch*, 6.

37 See http://Vimeo.com/24935, 369 (accessed November 13, 2014).

38 McChesney, *Digital Disconnect*, 210.

39 Matthew Hindman, *The Myth of Digital Democracy* (Princeton, NJ: Princeton Univer- sity Press, 2009).

40 Correspondence with Holland Wilde, November 2009.

41 Andrew Chadwick, *The Hybrid Media System: Power and Politics* (New York: Oxford University Press, 2014).

42 Henry Jenkins, *Convergence Culture: Where Old and New Media Collide* (New York: New York University Press, 2006), 5.

43 Richard Benefield, et al., *David Hockney: A Bigger Exhibition* (New York: Prestel Publishing, 2013).

44 Bryan Curtis, "Summa Cum Madden," *New York Times Magazine*, September 13, 2008: 31–32.

45 *Economist*, "The Rebirth of News," May 16, 2009 http://www.economist.com/ node/13649304.

46 Communic@tions Management Inc., "Sixty Years of Daily Newspaper Circulation Trends: Canada, United States, United Kingdom," discussion paper, May 6, 2011, http://media-cmi.com/downloads/Sixty_Years_Daily_Newspaper_Circulation _Trends_050611.pdf; also Communic@tions Management Inc., "Daily Newspaper

Circulation Trends 2000–2013: Canada, United States, United Kingdom," discussion paper, October 28, 2013, http://www.media-cmi.com/downloads/CMI_Discussion_Paper_Circulation_Trends_102813.pdf.

47 Christopher Dornan, "Newspapers and Magazines: Of Crows and Finches," in *Cultural Industries.ca: Making Sense of Canadian Media in the Digital Age*, ed. Ira Wagman and Peter Urquhart (Toronto: James Lorimer, 2012), 54.

48 Quoted in Howard Kurtz, "The Death of Print?," *Washington Post*, May 11, 2009, http://www.washingtonpost.com/wp-dyn/content/article/2009/05/11/AR2009 051100782.html.

49 Quoted in Robert W. McChesney and John Nichols, *The Death and Life of American Journalism: The Media Revolution That Will Begin the World Again* (Philadelphia: Nation Books, 2010), 57.

50 See Standing Committee on Canadian Heritage, *Our Cultural Sovereignty*, 87–93; CRTC (Canadian Radio-television and Telecommunications Commission), *Communications Monitoring Report*, 2010 (Ottawa: Government of Canada, July 2010), 55, Table 4.3.4: "Viewing Share of Canadian and Non-Canadian Services by Language and Type of Service—All Canada, Excluding Quebec Franco Market 2005/2006—2008/2009 Television Seasons," http://www.crtc.gc.ca/eng/publications/reports/policymonitoring/2010/cmr2010.pdf.

51 CRTC, *Communications Monitoring Report*, 2013 (Ottawa: Government of Canada, September 2013), 90, Table 4.3.12: "Advertising and Other Revenues by English- and French-Language Market for Private Conventional Television Stations." http://www.crtc.gc.ca/eng/publications/reports/policymonitoring/2013/cmr2013.pdf.

52 Alan Sepinwall, *The Revolution Was Televised: The Cops, Crooks, Slingers and Slayers Who Changed TV Drama Forever* (New York: Simon & Schuster, 2012).

53 Ken Auletta, "Outside the Box: Netflix and the Future of Television" *New Yorker*, February 3, 2014, 54.

54 CRTC, *Communications Monitoring Report*, 2010 (Ottawa: Government of Canada, July 2010), 34, Table 4.2.4: "Average Weekly Hours Tuned Per Capita by Age Group," http://www.crtc.gc.ca/eng/publications/reports/policymonitoring/2010/cmr2010.pdf.

55 CRTC, *Communications Monitoring Report*, 2013 (Ottawa: Government of Canada, September 2013), 60, Figure 4.2.2: "Radio Tuning by Station Type in an Average Week in Daily Markets," http://www.crtc.gc.ca/eng/publications/reports/policymonitoring/2013/cmr2013.pdf.

56 Joshua Meyrowitz, *No Sense of Place: The Impact of Electronic Media on Social Behavior* (New York: Oxford University Press, 1985).

57 Thomas L. Friedman, "This Is Just the Start," *New York Times*, April, 6, 2011, http://www.nytimes.com/2011/03/02/opinion/02friedman.html?_r=0.

58 Manuel Castells, *Networks of Outrage and Hope: Social Movements in the Internet Age* (Cambridge: Polity Press, 2012).

59 Aaron Smith, "The Internet and Campaign 2010," *Pew Internet & American Life Project*, March 17, 2011, http://www.pewinternet.org/files/old-media//Files/Reports/2011/Internet%20and%20Campaign%202010.pdf.

60 Taras and Waddell, "The 2011 Canadian Federal Election."

61 Yaroslav Baran, "Social Media in Campaign 2011: A Noncanonical Take on the Twitter Effect," *Policy Options* 32, no. 6 (June/July 2011): 85.

62 Nick Couldry, Sonia Livingstone, and Tim Markham, *Media Consumption and Public Engagement* (London: Palgrave Macmillan, 2010); Pippa Norris, *Democratic Deficit: Critical Citizens Revisited* (Cambridge: Cambridge University Press, 2011).

63 Malcolm Gladwell, "Small Change: Why the Revolution Will Not Be Tweeted," *New Yorker*, October 4, 2010, http://www.newyorker.com/reporting/2010/10/04/101004fa_fact_gladwell?currentPage=all.

64 Zizi Papacharissi, *A Private Sphere: Democracy in a Digital Age* (Cambridge: Polity Press, 2010), 157.

65 Sue Halpern, "Mind Control & the Internet," *New York Review of Books* LVIII, no. 11 (June 23, 2011): 33–35, http://www.nybooks.com/issues/2011/jun/23/; Stephanie Rosenbloom, "Got Twitter? You've Been Scored," *New York Times*, June 25, 2011, http://www.nytimes.com/2011/06/26/sunday-review/26rosenbloom.html.

66 Julia Angwin and Tom McGinty, "Sites Feed Personal Details to New Tracking Industry," *Wall Street Journal*, July 30, 2010, http://online.wsj.com/articles/SB10001424052748703977004575393173432219064.

67 Angwin and McGinty, "Sites Feed Personal Details to New Tracking Industry."

68 Colin Bennett, "What Political Parties Know about You," *Policy Options* 34, no. 2 (February 2013): 51–53.

69 Jeffrey Rosen, "The Web Means the End of Forgetting," *New York Times*, July 21, 2010, http://www.nytimes.com/2010/07/25/magazine/25privacy-t2.html?pagewanted=all.

70 Cited in Elias Aboujaoude, *Virtually You: The Dangerous Powers of the E-Personality* (New York: Norton, 2011), 242.

71 Rosen, "The Web Means the End of Forgetting."

72 Jürgen Habermas, *The Structural Transformation of the Public Sphere* (Cambridge, MA: Massachusetts Institute of Technology, 1989).

73 David Altheide and Robert Snow, *Media Logic* (Beverly Hills, CA: Sage, 1979); Richard Ericson, Patricia Baranek, and Janet Chan, *Negotiating Control: A Study of News Sources* (Toronto: University of Toronto Press, 1989).

74 Jay Rosen, "Politics, Vision and the Press," in *The New News v. The Old News* (New York: Twentieth Century Fund, 1992), 10.

75 Dean Starkman, *The Watchdog That Didn't Bark: The Financial Crisis and the Disappearance of Investigative Journalism* (New York: Columbia University Press, 2014), 9.

76 Starkman, *The Watchdog*, 306.

77 Douglas Cator, *The Fourth Branch of Government* (Boston: Houghton Mifflin, 1959); Timothy Cook, *Governing with the News: The News Media as a Political Institution* (Chicago: University of Chicago Press, 1998); Noam Chomsky, *Manufacturing Consent: The Political Economy of the Mass Media* (New York: Pantheon, 1988).

78 Benedict Anderson, *Imagined Communities: Reflections on the Origin and Spread of Nationalism* (London: Verso, 1983).

79 Robert Hartley, *The Politics of Pictures: The Creation of the Public in the Age of Popular Media* (London: Routledge, 1992), 35.

80 Quoted in Papacharissi, *A Private Sphere*, 94.

81 Peter Dahlgren, *Media and Political Engagement: Citizens, Communication and Democracy* (Cambridge: Cambridge University Press, 2009), 34.

82 Ibid., 72.

83 David Taras, *Power & Betrayal in the Canadian Media* (Toronto: University of Toronto Press, 2001).

84 Alex Jones, *Losing the News: The Future of the News that Feeds Democracy* (New York: Oxford University Press, 2009), 5.

Two
Identity and Citizenship in Canada.ca

In their classic work *The Civic Culture*, published in 1963, Gabriel Almond and Sidney Verba analyzed democratic values in five countries: the US, Mexico, Italy, Germany, and the UK.[1] They applied the equivalent of a political stress test, measuring the strength and quality of democracy in each country based on survey results that reflected people's knowledge about and awareness of their political institutions and their willingness to accept differences, achieve consensus, and embrace change. The underlying premise was that democracy could thrive only if there was a healthy civic culture in which there was a trust and respect for institutions, a willingness to exchange ideas, and engaged citizens. Over 50 years later, Mexico and Italy, the two countries that scored the lowest in democratic values, have plunged into deeper waters. Despite recent progress, Mexico is still engulfed in a catastrophic drug war that has claimed over 40,000 lives, corruption is rampant, and adherence to and respect for laws and authority is mixed at best. Italy is mired in debt, has a profound unemployment crisis, and, under former President Silvio Berlusconi at least, there was little in the way of either an independent press or an independent judiciary. This has changed at least to some degree with Berlusconi's ouster from power and from the Italian Senate. Arguably, though, in both Mexico and Italy democratic institutions, and more importantly the culture needed to sustain them, have never fully blossomed.

A main argument in the book is that democratic institutions and cultures have to be continually maintained, reformed, and fought for or they can fall into disrepair—ultimately undermining and damaging both the lives of citizens and any hopes for social and economic progress. The reality is that all societies can fail if democratic institutions aren't attended to. As I will point out in the next section, Canada has also had its share of roadblocks, upheavals, and near-death experiences.

One of the great lessons from the global financial meltdown that began symbolically at least with the fall of Lehman Brothers in 2008 is that even supposedly stable and prosperous societies are vulnerable to paralysis and even collapse unless their political and media institutions work well. Part of the reason for the financial crisis was the failure of US regulators, aided by an inattentive media, to effectively monitor the banking, brokerage, and insurance industries, and the exotic and dangerous practices that had penetrated the business culture. But the dysfunctional nature of the American political system was also to blame. The requirement for super majorities in the Congress, the use of filibusters at every pretext, the rise of negative advertising as the main instrument of elections, runaway campaign spending, the rise of third party super PACs (political action committees) that allow powerful individuals and interests to intervene in elections, and a media culture that thrives on negative news and legitimizes extreme positions—all have made it difficult for the US to deal with its problems. The erosion of civic culture and growing economic inequalities have humbled and damaged one of the world's great democracies.

The findings of *The Civic Culture* have been buttressed by more than a generation of studies, including findings from the World Values Surveys.[2] The bottom line in all of these studies is that active and informed citizens help ensure a healthy political system. The reality, however, is that by any tangible measure—voting, volunteering, joining, giving money to causes or attending public events—there has been a sharp downturn in civic participation in almost all Western democracies. Scholars routinely lament "the loss of social capital," increasing "democratic deficits," "public disconnection," and the degree to which "citizens are adrift."[3] Harvard scholar Robert Putnam in particular has linked the decline of social capital to higher crime rates, poorer health, greater social inequality, and the development of a me-first society.

John W. Holmes, the distinguished Canadian diplomat and scholar of the postwar era, argued that while people don't always have to know the facts or understand the technical details of issues or policies, what matters is that they knew enough to be "rational' about the limits of power and the compromises that need to be made for a political system to survive. In other words, citizens have to have a realistic sense of "the possible" so that they won't be swayed by momentary impulses, simplistic solutions, or the overheated promises of popular politicians.[4]

The media are a crucial part of the equation in any analysis of civic culture. The media system is the linchpin between citizens and governments and also the stage on which public and cultural life takes place. The Canadian media system has always been more than just a transmission line; it has been a major instrument of both nation and citizen-building and the main conveyor of symbols and identity.

One prominent scholar, John Zaller, believes that at the very least we should be producing "monitorial" citizens: people who, while unaware of the details of civic life, are still aware enough to know if dangerous storm clouds are gathering over the horizon, if institutions are working well or if political leaders are doing their jobs effectively.[5] To Zaller, the crucial role of the news media is to sound the "alarm" bell when things go wrong. But if the media system is broken or is too weak to respond, society's other institutions will fail because societal realities will be hidden from view, debates won't take place, alternative solutions won't be aired, and problems will be allowed to fester and worsen. An attentive public is crucial not only to the functioning of democracy but also to the survival of the news media itself. Without an engaged audience, news organizations can't survive and serious journalism can't be sustained. The two are locked in a symbiotic relationship where the failure of one leads to the failure of the other. The disconnectedness of young people in particular could be the great silent killer for much of the news media.

This chapter will begin by examining the special characteristics of the Canadian mosaic. Canada's loosely defined sense of identity, along with global-ization and vast increases in immigration and the country's remarkable ability to encourage multiple identities and loyalties are at once great strengths but also great vulnerabilities. The irony is that the very qualities that have made Canada one of the world's great success stories have also made it among the most vulnerable to the effects of media shock. Arguably countries that have "hard" identities—a single language or religion, a confined space, a long his-tory and less diversity, such as Italy, Japan, Sweden or Brazil—may be better able to withstand the disruption created by media shock than Canada can.

A second section will focus on whether the values associated with "civic culture" are thriving in Canada. The evidence is disheartening. By almost any measure, citizen involvement is tilting downwards. Digital natives have largely become peek-a-boo citizens, at once technologically savvy, progressive, con-nected, and global and at the same time increasingly rootless, distrustful, dis-connected, and arguably unhappy. Political scientist Henry Milner captured these contradictory impulses when he described the Internet generation as being both "Green and Apolitical."[6] Milner is worried about what he terms "political dropouts"—people "so inattentive to the political world around them that they lack the minimal knowledge needed to distinguish and thus choose among parties and candidates."[7] As is the case with other advanced countries, Canada has produced a dropout culture.

This second section tries to pinpoint some of the reasons for the disen-gagement crisis. While there is no one smoking gun, no one great overarching cause, there are, however, a number of contributing factors. Some of the more obvious villains, such as the widespread failure to teach Canadian history in the schools, the collapse of civic organizations, increased secular-ization, and the failures of the political system to inspire trust, are described in some detail.

A last section of the chapter discusses some of the more recent economic and societal changes that have led to the creation of peek-a-boo citizens. These are tough economic times for young Canadians in particular. While many get good jobs, a great number are trapped in low-paying, dead-end jobs from which there are few chances for escape. One of the great ironies of media shock is that new technologies are eating up jobs at an alarming rate, due in part to global competition, but also because old industries are being digitized. As a consequence, Canada, like the US, is becoming a more unequal society, a development that is exceedingly harmful not only for the poor but for everyone else as well. All of these factors have had an impact on citizen involvement and levels of participation in civic life.

The Unlikely Country

Any discussion of the strength of civic culture in Canada has to begin with the fact that Canada is one of the great places in the world to live. As *Globe and Mail* columnist John Ibbitson claimed in his book *The Polite Revolution*, "Sometime, not too long ago, while no one was watching, Canada became the world's most successful country."[8] A survey conducted in 27 countries by the British Broadcasting Corporation in 2007 found that Canada was the most highly regarded country in the world.[9] A 2010 survey of people living in the world's 24 leading economies found that many people would move to Canada if they could.[10] For many people across the globe, Canada was their preferred place to be, the place of dreams. A study published by the OECD in 2011 determined that next to Australia, Canada had the best quality of life among 34 major industrialized countries.[11] The study was based on a mix of indicators including education, life expectancy, and environmental quality. In an Angus Reid/*Maclean's* survey conducted in 2011, 90 per cent of Canadians rated their country as "the best place for them to raise a family," and an overwhelming majority believed that Canada ranked far ahead of the United States and the United Kingdom in offering them a bright economic future.[12] The 2013 World Happiness Report ranked Canada the sixth happiest country in the world.

The country's many blessings are beyond dispute: our freedoms of expression under the Charter of Rights and Freedoms; a multicultural diversity that rivals anywhere else on the planet; the country's breathtaking beauty; our enviable standard of living based on high educational standards, an ability to master technology, and bountiful resources; as well as the political peace that we have achieved through habits of compromise and conciliation—all these factors have created one of the world's most successful political projects.

While there is much room for self-congratulation (perhaps a very un-Canadian thing to do), there is another side of the coin. Canadians know that much of the country's success is built on fragile foundations that can't be taken for granted. There are antiquarian political institutions that are drastically in need of reform, a political culture that all too often rewards inaction, increasing economic inequalities, and glaring injustices. Moreover, establishing common meeting places has never been an easy task in a country where populations are scattered and separated by vast distances, where there have been painful linguistic and regional divides, and where American power and influence pervade almost every aspect of economic and cultural life.

To outsiders, Canada is an unlikely country. First, the distances are forbidding. Cape Spear on the eastern fringe of Newfoundland is closer to Ireland than it is to Winnipeg. It is separated from Vancouver Island on the west coast by no less than five and half time zones. Both Britain and Ireland could fit easily inside Saskatchewan, and all of Western Europe could fit into the Canadian North with plenty of room to spare. But also, as Northrop Frye, one of Canada's most venerated scholars and thinkers, pointed out, "Every part of Canada is shut off by its geography, British Columbia from the prairies by the Rockies, the prairies from the Canadas by the immense hinterland of northern Ontario, Quebec from the Maritimes by the upthrust of Maine, the Maritimes from Newfoundland by the sea.... Everywhere in Canada we find solitudes: every part of Canada has strong separatist feelings because every part of it is in fact a separation."[13]

To some degree Canada can be seen as an archipelago of "city-states" stretching for thousands of kilometres along the US border. Most of the Canadian population is now concentrated in relatively few hubs; Halifax, Quebec City, Montreal, Ottawa-Gatineau, Toronto, Winnipeg, the Calgary–Edmonton corridor, and Vancouver. But beyond these city-states there still looms a stark, majestic, and imposing vastness. In the words of Louis Hemon, author of the classic novel *Maria Chapdelaine*, it is a wilderness that still closes around us "with a savage grip that must be loosened little by little, year by year."[14] In much of early and even later Canadian literature, the land beyond the settlements and the cities inspired something akin to sheer terror. The natives told of mythic figures such as the Wendigo, who had "Eyes of Blood and a Heart of Ice." Poet Archibald Lampman wrote about "winds that touch like steel" and of "a world of winter and death."[15] A.J. Pratt's poems are filled with torture, sudden death, and an unforgiving natural world. Even recent novels such as Joseph Boyden's powerful and troubling *Three Day Road* and *The Orenda* recount a history in which brutal cold, consuming fires, and desperate isolation meant bare survival, if survival at all. And while painters such as Tom Thomson, the Group of Seven, and Emily Carr did much to soften these terrorizing images, evoking a view of the Canadian landscape as tranquil, pristine, accessible, and possessing intoxicating spiritual power, it's also true, as art critic John O'Brien reminds us, that Canadians remained obsessed with the wilderness to an extent not seen in most other cultures.[16]

Some observers credit Canada's harsh geography with imposing unity rather than division. Economist Harold Innis, and his friend and colleague historian Donald Creighton, believed that Canada was the product of its natural geography.[17] More precisely, the river systems created an east–west corridor for what would become a burgeoning trade in staple products such as furs, cod, wheat, and minerals. Developing his own variation on Innis's "staples theory," Creighton's "Laurentian thesis" argued that the Canadian state was the product of what he called "the commercial empire of the St. Lawrence." In his view, exploration and settlement were driven by a commercial imperative that brought elites and capital together in a single cause or, in Creighton's famous description, "an obsession."

Aside from the formidable challenges of distances and geography, a second major factor in the shaping of Canadian identity is that Canada shares a border with the world's greatest economic and cultural power—the United States. In Pierre Trudeau's famous analogy, Canadians are in bed with an elephant, and even if it is a friendly elephant its slightest move is a cause for worry. To the Dutch scholar Rob Kroes, US influence rests on the fact that it embodies, or at least for much of its history represented, what he termed the "great modernist project of trans-nationalism."[18] By this he means that American identity is based on a way of life and on the acceptance of shared civic ideals, rather than on an ethnic or religious identity. This made American values transcendent and exportable. Dominique Moisi of France's Institute of International Affairs expresses the attraction of the American dream this way:

> In contrast with Europe, America has traditionally been characterized by hope. Its very history ... is based on an almost messianic hope, a belief in America as a land of redemption, liberation and new beginnings. It is this hopeful optimism that has enabled this modest, plain-living, idealistic early American Republic to grow to imperial status in less than two centuries. That same spirit of hope has remained the basis of America's soft power and its enormous attractiveness to people around the world as well.... Where twentieth century Europe was built on the idea of transcending history, its special strength and weakness being its ability to evoke or to conjure up its past, America is all about the future.[19]

While there have been times when anti-Americanism has swept across much of Europe, the Middle East, and Latin America, in what the French philosopher Bernard-Henri Levy has described as an "anti-American phantasmagoria," there can be little doubt that for much of the twentieth century, American political ideals were a great example, a beacon, for many around the world.[20]

For Canadians, the American cultural presence is everywhere and inescapable. By one count, over 95 per cent of movies, 84 per cent of the retail sales of sound recordings, 85 per cent of the prime-time drama that Canadians watch on English language TV, and almost 85 per cent of magazine sales at newsstands are American.[21] The figures for games, online TV, comics, blogs, videos, for example, are if anything even higher.

While Canadians have created islands of expression through our own media production and by resisting, rejecting or appropriating American cultural products, these islands exist in a very large ocean. For many Canadians the US is the place where culture is created: from "California dreaming" to Lady Gaga, from *American Idol* to *Glee*, from Disneyland to the NFL. As Canadian TV producer David Barlow once described the magnitude of the problem, "An interesting phenomenon occurs when a country looks to a foreign culture for its popular entertainment over a long period of time. If a society consistently chooses the dramatic fantasies of another culture, they come to believe that their own reality is not a valid place on which to build their dreams. Their reality isn't good enough for dreaming."[22]

But one can also argue that the overwhelming presence of American culture has created a "pushback" effect: the more that Canadians are exposed to American culture, the greater their resistance to it. In fact, pollster Michael Adams found that despite the overpowering influence of the United States, the two countries have moved further apart in terms of their core values, to the point where they have become "fire and ice."[23] With its greater disparities between rich and poor, its rejection of universal health insurance, its veneration of the military, the vaunted place that it gives to religion, and the greater prevalence of both guns and violence, the US remains remarkably different. Northrop Frye once observed that when travelling in the United States Canadians can easily be lulled into believing that they are in a society not much different from their own—until something happens that jolts them into the realization that they really are in a foreign country and that the rules are different.[24]

McGill communications scholar Richard Schultz believes that the "we are what we watch" thesis is nothing more than ritualistic fear mongering by Canadian cultural nationalists and powerful media interests.[25] To Schultz, the threat of Americanization is a phantom conjured up by those who have an interest in promoting Canadian cultural protectionism. He believes that Canadian culture is strong enough to stand on its own and doesn't need to be coddled as if it were an endangered species. Christopher Dornan of Carleton University also believes that Canadian media corporations cynically play the nationalist card in order to keep protectionist measures and support for Canadian programming in place. The great irony, according to Dornan, is that having convinced politicians and regulators to protect them as much as possible from US network competition, these very same broadcasters then flood the airwaves with American programming.[26] Canadian broadcasters argue that without the revenue generated by Hollywood shows, they would have little money to spend on Canadian programming. In other words, they can only "Canadianize" by first "Americanizing."

Others do not dismiss the problems of Americanization so easily. John Meisel, a retired Queen's University professor and former chair of the CRTC, has suggested that "inside every Canadian, there is in fact an American"—the degree of Americanness varying from person to person depending on their values, education, and exposure to popular culture."[27] In a first attempt to explain his position, Meisel argued that Canadian culture tends to appeal to an elite group, while the mass of Canadians prefer American culture. This has produced a self-fulfilling prophecy. Having become addicted to American mass culture, most Canadians are reluctant to support Canadian cultural institutions such as the CBC or the Canada Council (which supports Canadian artists and musicians) because they don't see these institutions as playing an important role in their lives. As a consequence of this chronic underfunding, Canadian culture is less able to compete and as a result is less attractive to mass audiences. In a later article, Meisel modified his position, arguing that support for Canadian culture stretched more widely and penetrated more deeply than he had previously suggested.[28] But Meisel's overall conclusion was essentially the same: while Canadian writers, artists, and musicians are making their mark internationally, Canadian culture remains the minority culture in Canada. The dominant culture is American.

The scholar who is perhaps the most pessimistic about Canada's future is Michael Bliss.[29] Bliss believes that for most Canadians history is a forgotten land. Canadians have few attachments to their past and consider Canadian history to be either painfully boring or mindlessly irrelevant. Bliss blames Canadian historians for "sundering" the historical profession by focusing on narrow tributaries, sub-specialties within sub-specialties, rather than on broader and more compelling national questions.[30] But he also believes that the country has little to hold it together, because the foundations on which it has been built have been largely swept away. The values, symbols, and allegiances of what once was British Canada, the vision of Canada as a northern country with a special sense of pioneering and destiny, the striving for social justice that fuelled the creation of Canada's social programs, and finally the goal of creating a bilingual and bicultural country have been eroded, rejected or forgotten.

Writing in 2006, Bliss saw Canada as a place of broken dreams and a broken identity: "From a more traditional perspective Canada's evolution may appear to be moving increasingly toward decline into global irrelevance and incoherence.... In the histories of the contemporary world outside of Canada, this country does almost nothing worth noticing. I am not as optimistic about Canada's future in 2006 as my mother and I were in 1951."[31] In contrast to the "fire and ice" hypothesis, Bliss believes that there may be fewer major differences between Canada and the United States, between "'us' and 'them'" than was the case a generation ago, to the point where it may now be only "'us' and 'us.'"[32] He believes that the differences that do exist may now be so small that Canada is in danger of becoming no more than "an outlying northern suburb of the United States."[33] In fact, we "are less different from Americans in their fundamental values and orientations than Maritimers were from Canadians in 1867."[34]

Those sympathetic to Bliss's Americanization argument will not be surprised by the results of a 2008 survey of Canadians and Americans conducted by the Strategic Council for the *Globe and Mail* and CTV.[35] The survey found that 50 per cent of Canadians viewed Canadians and Americans as being either "essentially" or "mainly" the same. But these numbers paled beside the American results; an astonishing 70 per cent of Americans believed that the two countries are now either essentially or mainly the same. It is hard to think of another instance in which the citizens of one country see so few differences with the citizens of another.

While Bliss raises troubling questions, and his emotional blast, his sense of bereavement, needs to be respected, he is far too ready, in my view, to dismiss the country's great achievements. For instance, he considers the Canadian Charter of Rights and Freedoms, a document that has both produced and reflected a profound rights revolution and is characterized by a very distinctive approach to legal reasoning and judgments, as being just another example of rampant Americanization, an imitation of the US Bill of Rights. He also seems unimpressed by the fact that Canada has taken in proportionally more immigrants from more places than virtually any country in the world and has done so with extraordinary success. Since World War II, Canada has welcomed at least three times the number of immigrants per capita as has the United States, the great self-proclaimed nation of immigrants. While German Chancellor Angela Merkel and British Prime Minister David Cameron can talk openly about the failure of the multicultural experiments in their countries, this is not the case in Canada. The country's capacity to integrate immigrants has been astonishing. By 2031, for example, almost 65 per cent of Toronto's population will be made up of visible minorities, including an estimated 2.1 million people with East Asian origins. At its current rate of growth, Vancouver will soon become the "first Asian city outside of Asia," with the largest community being Chinese.[36] The new Canada may be jumbled and complex and floating in multiple identities, but it is also vital, open, and, by the standards of the rest of the world, a model of tolerance. In short, a wonderful and complex mosaic.

Nor is it clear that Canadians have abandoned the quest for social justice and equality. Although most studies place Canada in the middle among advanced democratic countries on most measures of equality, support for Medicare is still rock solid and few politicians seem willing to risk their political necks by advocating increased privatization.[37] A public university system, pension plans, employment insurance, and equalization programs that support poorer provinces are still mainstays of the Canadian social bargain even if these programs are fraying at the edges.

But Bliss is not alone in criticizing the fragile nature of Canadian identity. In Noah Richler's grand tour of the Canadian literary landscape, *This is My Country, What's Yours?*, he devotes an entire chapter to writers who believe that they are living in the "nowhere in particular" of uninteresting subdivisions and soulless shopping malls.[38] Author Yann Martel has described the country as a "multicultural hotel," a place where you can live comfortably without having to put down roots. For writer George Jonas the country is a "railway station," a transit stop on the way to other, more fulfilling identities.[39] Whatever the analogy, there is now, according to a whole host of observers, an extraordinary lightness to being Canadian.

A great third problem facing Canadians, aside from our vast distances and harsh climate and the onslaught of American economic and cultural power, is the political divisions that have limited and distorted Canadian political life. Canada's federal system is the most decentralized in the world, with much of the spending power and policy responsibility housed at the provincial level. The *British North America Act* of 1867 left a tangled web of divided jurisdictions that has made policy-making in areas such as natural resources, health care, labour, and the environment complex and often futile. Getting anything accomplished usually involves endless wrangling and deal-making, awkward compromises and patchwork agreements, with one or more of the provinces usually opting out. Quebec has its own pension plan, every province has its own sometimes very different environmental standards and practices, and Canadians are forced to pay higher costs for drugs because, instead of combining forces to negotiate more effectively with pharmaceutical companies, each province negotiates separately. Attempts to create a national body to measure health-care outcomes, develop a national energy strategy or establish a national securities regulator run up against political and constitutional barriers that make progress next to impossible.

Of course, strands of cooperation do exist. As mentioned above, "have not" provinces receive equalization payments from the federal government, while "have" provinces, especially Alberta, contribute far more to federal government coffers than they ever get back. But the prevailing ethic in federal–provincial relations was perhaps best described by Pierre Trudeau as "you scratch my back, or I'll scratch your face."

University of Toronto political scientist Nelson Wiseman believes that Canada is the very opposite of the vacant "nowhereland" that some authors describe. In his excellent book *In Search of Canadian Political Culture*, Wiseman contends that far from there being too little political consciousness, the problem is that there is far too much.[40] Quebec, Newfoundland, Aboriginal Canada, and Alberta, for instance, have deeply rooted identities and searing memories of grievances and injustice. Each has its own symbolic culture and sees the country though its own storylines. This has made it difficult for a common symbolic culture to emerge.

It hasn't taken much to set fire to the dry kindling of linguistic and regional grievances. A particularly painful example was the Meech Lake and Charlottetown constitutional battles of the late 1980s and early 1990s. During these attempts to rewrite the Constitution, provinces and interest groups forcefully pushed their demands. Once having taken hard-line positions, adhering to these positions became matters of honour from which they could not retreat. As a result, the negotiating process became overloaded with too many conflicting demands and agendas, eventually collapsing under its own weight. The process was so destructive that for over a generation, politicians have treated with horror the prospect of opening up the Constitution—the political equivalent of an outbreak of bubonic plague.

One of the consequences of Canada's constitutional stalemate is that the demarcation lines and power relationships established in 1867, when Canada was a much different country, remain in place regardless of how dysfunctional and even counterproductive they have become. The Senate continues to exist as a kind of zombie institution, neither fully alive nor fully dead, with appointed senators able on occasion to block legislation from the elected House of Commons. Even large cities, some of which have become almost like city-states, are still creatures of the provinces to which they have to go cap in hand for funding. Calgary Mayor Naheed Nenshi has expressed his frustration thus: "I'm the mayor of a city that has more people in it than five provinces, yet, I have the exact same legislative authority as any village of 30 or 40 people. And that has to change."[41]

The 1995 Quebec referendum on sovereignty, which was the direct outcome of the painful and divisive constitutional battles of the late 1980s and early 1990s—and which the federalist side won by only a hair's breadth, 50.6 per cent to 49.4 per cent—demonstrated just how close to the edge of survival the country can come when political passions are ignited. Of course, passions need leaders who can embody and express them. During the referendum campaign, sovereigntist leader Lucien Bouchard touched raw nerve endings of identity and emotion in a way that no federal politician came close to matching. In fact, it was the lack of response by federalist leaders, their inability to make a strong case for Canada, that was most startling. Under Bouchard's harsh attacks, his politics of humiliation, and his staccato-like delivery, attachments to Canada for some at least seemed to dissolve almost overnight. Had the sovereigntists been able to squeeze out just a few more votes, Quebec's then-premier Jacques Parizeau has admitted that he would have moved quickly towards Quebec's independence, although the moves may have been stymied by splits within the independence movement.[42] Canada has spent years recovering from what was the equivalent of a national nervous breakdown.

Younger Québécois who did not experience the Quiet Revolution or the language wars of the 1970s, hear René Lévesque's fiery speeches or live through the wrenching emotional turmoil of the two great referendums on sovereignty held in 1980 and 1995 now live in a far different political reality than was the case during the white-hot days of Quebec nationalism. According to a CROP survey taken in 2011, 71 per cent of Québécois believed that the sovereignty debate is "outdated," with only 25 per cent wanting to separate from Canada. More telling perhaps is that 76 per cent felt "very or somewhat proud" of being Canadian. Just 5 per cent, a small fringe, were not proud to be Canadian.[43] Still, surveys vary, and support for some form of sovereignty or a much looser confederation is never far below the surface. Even so, the Bloc Québécois, a sovereigntist party, was all but decimated during the 2011 federal election by the federalist New Democratic Party. Seen as passé, the party fell before the appeal of NDP leader Jack Layton and the "Orange crush." Similarly, Parti Québécois premier Pauline Marois lost the 2014 provincial election largely because Quebec voters did not want the pain and disruption that would come with another referendum and wanted to remain in Canada.

Arguably the animosity and distrust produced by generations of conflict with English-speaking Canada have given way to what can be described as "Canadianization through globalization." The emergence of Montreal as a global city, both economically and in terms of immigration, has had the effect of deepening its connections to Canada. According to historian Jocelyn Letourneau, a technocratic elite has emerged in Quebec that is highly educated, mobile, and postmodern, and while it is sympathetic to Quebec nationalism it is also open to other experiences and identities.[44] Urban and cosmopolitan, the people of "Montreality," as Letourneau describes them, would be just as comfortable in Paris, New York or Vancouver.

In Letourneau's view, however, this more cosmopolitan Quebec based in Montreal contrasts with a "Quebecitude" that is largely rural, far more insular, less self-confident, and dependent for its livelihood on traditional and declining industries. According to Letourneau, these two Quebecs live uncomfortably together while having less and less in common. Although the differences between Montreal and the rest of the province may be overdrawn, there can be little doubt that Quebec, like the rest of Canada, finds itself swimming in a sea of changing identities.

Despite the failure of the sovereigntist movement to achieve official independence, one can argue that Quebec has in fact achieved a form of symbolic independence within Canada. The *BNA Act* allows Quebec to exercise what amounts to cultural sovereignty. The province controls language and education, manages the selection process in choosing new immigrants, and is governed by a civil legal code that is different from the legal system used in other provinces. It has the power to opt out of federal programs, has its own pension plan, and benefits massively from federal transfers and equalization payments. Arguably by remaining in Canada it also has more clout on the international stage than it would as a small independent country. It may be that the two societies are now like an old quarrelsome couple that has agreed to go on living together despite the fact that strong differences remain. As Jeffrey Simpson has observed, "The rest of Canada, for the most part, does not seem to menace or interest Quebeckers; rather it barely exists."[45] But political columnist Chantal Hébert has warned that "time is not so much healing the untended Quebec-Canada fracture as turning it into a permanent vulnerability."[46] Further rifts and sudden volte-faces are not out of the question.

While political animosities may have cooled, two solitudes still exist in the realm of the Canadian media. The country has two media systems: one that functions in English, and one that functions in French. Without the public broadcaster, the CBC/Radio-Canada, which has reporters from the two language groups stationed across the country, there would almost be no journalists from English Canada in Quebec, and vice versa. While many of the same news stories splash across both media systems, there are news stories that have consumed Quebec society that receive little coverage in the rest of Canada and hot stories in other parts of Canada that are of little interest in Quebec.[47] It has been argued, only half-jokingly, that the Quebec press reports Ottawa in much the same way that the Americans cover the

Olympics—it follows the home team, while largely ignoring the other athletes. Another critical difference is that home-grown TV productions attract large audiences in Quebec, while the top shows watched by English language viewers are almost always American. The same can be said for almost all other cultural products.

Another unsettled reality of Canadian life is the condition of Aboriginal Canadians. The relationship between the federal government and First Nations is a veritable hodgepodge. Some First Nations live under treaties; some like the Tsilhqot'in in British Columbia have never relinquished their sovereignty and must consent to any developments that take place on their land; Aboriginals are the largest population groups in Nunavut and the Northwest Territories, where they can control at least some of the levers of power; and the Métis have only recently had their status as a First Nation confirmed by the Supreme Court of Canada. Only half of Canada's native population is made up of "status" Indians who are located on reserves and receive benefits and funding from the federal government. Almost all Aboriginal leaders agree, however, that the Indian Act under which status Indians live is a remnant of the past that is ineffectual and insulting. Meanwhile the Aboriginal population in cities, particularly on the prairies, is both young and growing, suffers from high rates of poverty and homelessness, and is deeply marginalized.

The relationship between First Nations peoples and the majority of Canadians is complex and multilayered. On one hand, some observers argue that Aboriginals are "inconvenient" and invisible. This is how writer Thomas King has expressed his frustration and anger:

> ... most of the history of Indians in North America has been
> forgotten, and what we are left with is a series of historical artifacts,
> and more importantly, a series of entertainments.... Native history is
> an imaginative cobbling together of fears and loathings, romances and
> reverences, facts and fantasies into a cycle of creative performances,
> in Technicolor and 3-D, with accompanying soft drinks, candy and
> popcorn.
>
> In the end, who really needs the whole of native history when we
> can watch the movie.[48]

In some ways, the Aboriginal presence seems to be everywhere. Aboriginal symbols are on display at airports, in government buildings and embassies, in museums and galleries, and in the work of some of the country's most prominent artists. This is especially the case in British Columbia, where Haida art and the work of master sculptor Bill Reid have become part of the collective imagination. Similar prominence has been given to Inuit sculptors and images that have long been part of the country's symbolic landscape.

There is also, as Troy Patenaude has pointed out, an increasing fascination with contemporary Aboriginal art by non-Aboriginals.[49] According to Patenaude, the attachment to Aboriginal art is often emotional and spiritual and a way for other Canadians "to imagine themselves in another manner."[50] It has also allowed Aboriginal artists to stretch the boundaries of Aboriginal culture by creating "storywork" that is a meeting place and form of sharing with other Canadians. The great irony is that Aboriginal symbols are being appropriated as part of national identity at the same time as so many Aboriginal Canadians feel increasingly invisible and powerless. In fact, the more central these symbols become to Canadian identity, the more marginalized Aboriginals seem to be in Canadian life.

A leading policy expert, Gilles Paquet, has argued that as a consequence of our divisions, a "sociality of consensus" has emerged that keeps potentially divisive debates from taking place.[51] Unable to absorb contentious political battles for very long, Canadians have become expert at studiously avoiding or muffling disagreement. This is in sharp contrast to what Paquet has seen in countries such as Australia, where hard-fought political brawls seem to have been encouraged.

One of the keys to keeping political peace is that politicians have been able to redirect to the Supreme Court of Canada controversial issues such as abortion, Aboriginal rights, the rules governing Quebec's right to secede from Canada, the legality of private health insurance, the extent of police powers, and the limits on freedom of expression. Arguably the ability of the courts to act as a "safety-valve" has spared the country political battles that would have otherwise caused considerable damage.

On some occasions accommodation has meant swallowing hard, ignoring, and moving on. When the former Premier of Newfoundland and Labrador, Danny Williams, ordered the removal of Canadian flags from provincial government buildings in 2004 because he was angry that the federal government had reneged on promises it had made about transfer payments, federal politicians seemed to dive for cover. It is difficult to imagine the governor of an American state ordering the removal of the US flag without encountering a hailstorm of anger and experiencing an abrupt end to her or his political career. In Canada, the very opposite occurred. Williams was lionized as a Newfoundland patriot and a tough negotiator (which proved to be the case when the Martin government eventually agreed to Williams's terms).

As a further example, when in 2006 the House of Commons passed a resolution declaring that the Quebecois formed a nation within a united Canada, the resolution produced a "ho-hum—so what's the big deal?" response that would have been inconceivable had a similar situation occurred in other countries. One can only imagine the reaction if Mississippi or Scotland or Catalonia had tried to have itself recognized as a "nation" in the US, the UK, or Spain. Although the declaration of Quebec as a nation may well be a ticking time bomb that explodes unexpectedly at a future date, for now it seems to have had little meaning or impact. Mercifully, perhaps, other "nations," including Acadians, the Métis, Inuit, First Nations, and Newfoundlanders, did not press for similar resolutions.

Canada is also one of the few countries where historical amnesia, the convenient act of forgetting, seems to be a virtue. While much is made of the fact that Canadians tend to find their history boring and as a consequence know little about it, the problem might be far deeper. As Quebec author Gil Courtemanche points out, it may be that we don't really like our history.[52] Much of Canada's past consists of what Noah Richler describes as "myths of disappointment"—broken dreams, tragic injustices, heroes defying and succumbing to the odds, great plans dashed. Richler has described the endless litany of disappointments that make up so much of the telling of Canadian history:

> The story of residential schools, Canadian's participation in the First World War, the internment of Japanese Canadians, Diefenbaker's cancellation of the Avro Arrow jet-fighter project, the Acadians, the alleged failure of Canadian historians to adequately report the history of black slavery in Canada, the cancellation of the fabled CBC news program, *This Hour Has Seven Days*, in 1966, the disastrous National Energy Policy of then–prime minister Pierre Trudeau in 1980 and even the 2004–5 NHL strike all fit into a common mould in which good Canadians are let down by institutions they serve and that should protect them.[53]

In *Survival*, her classic review of the Canadian literary landscape, Margaret Atwood puts it even more bluntly: "... stick a pin in Canadian literature at random, and nine times out of ten you'll hit a victim."[54] She went on to observe that "all Canadian revolutions are failed revolutions, and our writer, searching for Hero material, will find himself almost inevitably writing a drama in which an individual defending the rights of a small group finds himself up against faceless authority."[55] Although *Survival* was published over 40 years ago when Canada was a very different country, one can argue that the victim motif has not entirely disappeared.

Historian Jocelyn Letourneau has arrived at a similar conclusion about Quebec's history. Letourneau contends that in the hands of Quebec intellectuals history became a chronicle of endless despair and defeat. As Letourneau has described these themes, for the Québécois "the past is a breeding ground of painful, depressing memories rather than a pretext for positive remembering.... Stuck in an inconsolable sadness resulting from a supposed situation as 'failed rebels,' they are unable, or barely able, to escape from the imaginary of a victim and the mentality of a person owed a debt."[56] For these reasons, both Letourneau and Courtemanche believe that carrying the weight of the past can be deeply destructive. Glorifying history is only useful if it produces conditions that lead to a better future and not to dead ends and out-dated dreams. As Courtemanche expresses it, "The loyalty to Canada is not a loyalty to history.... It's a loyalty to equality, and some kind of a midsummer night's dream. Quietness. Peace and good neighbourliness. Not much arguing. No conflicts—or just small conflicts that can be resolved by shaking hands. It's a loyalty to values, but values don't make great novels."[57] The lesson is that if one wants to maintain a peaceful midsummer night's dream, then forgetting can go a long way.

In his eloquent submission to the Supreme Court of Canada when it was adjudicating the rules that would govern Quebec's secession from Canada, John Whyte argued that "the threads of a thousand acts of accommodation are the fabric of a nation...."[58] Perhaps he's right.

As a consequence of this need to continually compromise and look the other way, some would argue that the country suffers from an emotional incompleteness. John Meisel has noted that while he has come to "greatly appreciate Canada's 'namby-pamby approach to la patrie,'" he believes that "the absence of a boastful nationalism also exacts a price."[59] But the reason he adores Canada is that "when judging people, it is important to consider not only what they *do* but also that to which they *aspire*. One of Canadians' most attractive and enduring features is that their self-image and national ideal so closely correspond to the benign, appealing, kind, tolerant, slightly milquetoastian model...."[60]

Other observers argue that the very open-endedness of Canadian identity, its softness, is in fact its greatest strength. Philosopher Charles Taylor has argued that Canada has achieved what he calls "deep diversity"—an approach that allows citizens the freedom to choose how and in what ways they wish to be Canadian.[61] To Taylor, there is no "one size fits all" Canadian identity, no single blueprint for what it means to be Canadian. A Québécois living in Rivière-du-Loup may choose to identify differently than an Asian immigrant living in Burnaby or an Aboriginal living on a First Nations reserve. They each view the country through a different set of lenses and with a different heart. And yet this complex and contradictory formula, which at first glance shouldn't work, might just contain the right ingredients for survival in the twenty-first century.

Harold Innis wrote about "the lack of unity which has preserved Canadian unity,"[62] and *Globe and Mail* columnist John Ibbitson claims that "we owe our success as a country to our failure as a nation."[63] Having failed to create a strong overarching national identity, we have instead created spaces that allow for multiple loyalties and choices. In fact, one can argue that diversity itself has become the country's defining characteristic, the signature of its existence. While there are, of course, drawbacks to Canada's puzzling identity, Ibbitson sees Canada as one of the great political experiments of the twenty-first century and a model for other countries to follow:

> In reality, it is a marvelous way to run a country. In fact, it's probably the way every country should be run. In that sense, Canada is a model for the world, a place that, to a greater degree than most others, has set aside ethnic conflicts based on national identity, in favour of a loosey-goosey multiculturalism based on individual opportunity and inter-group respect. Call it a post-national state. Some of us think that it's quite wonderful.[64]

Because Ibbitson's vision of Canada presents such a different model from those of conventional nation-states, I will leave the last word in this section to him.

The Public Participation Scorecard

Coincident with the arrival of media shock, and perhaps because of it, is another extraordinary phenomenon: the degree to which Canadians have become disconnected from public affairs and are melting away as citizens. By any reasonable measure, civic disengagement has increased dramatically. This is especially the case among digital natives. According to most yardsticks—voting, joining, donating money, knowing about public affairs or following the news—digital natives are largely missing in action. Scholars now routinely refer to "information deficits," a "dropout culture," "passive citizenship," "public disconnectedness," and "political de-skilling," and some worry that young people lack even minimal knowledge about the world in which they live. To use Walter Lippmann's famous description, so many of today's citizens seem like deaf spectators looking on from the back rows as the orchestra plays.[65] The analogy is a bit brutal, but there are genuine concerns that will be addressed later about the ability of digital natives to read, think, and listen deeply amid the quick hits of activity demanded by media shock.

The great irony is that while digital natives are on the one hand more pluralistic, global, and technologically savvy than previous generations and appear to be interested in and even passionate about issues such as climate change, human rights, and social inequality, they disappear suddenly from the political landscape when conventional political campaigns need to be organized or votes counted. They have increasingly become peek-a-boo citizens: connected in some ways and disconnected in others. Even if one believes that Canada is experimenting with a new, softer form of political nationality, the lack of knowledge that Canadians seem to have about their own country is shocking. If anything, one would think that the country's obvious successes would elicit some measure of pride in its history and achievements or at the very least that there would be some common understanding of how the country functions. This is not the case.

While the problem of missing citizens or missing information is especially acute among young Canadians, a majority of Canadians would fail a basic citizenship test.[66] A survey conducted in 2007 by Ipsos Reid and the former Dominion Institute found that only one in five Canadians could name the political parties in the House of Commons or were aware of the Charter of Rights and Freedoms, the document that sanctifies and embodies the country's basic values. Similarly, only slight majorities could identify prominent Canadian political leaders or tell interviewers when major historical events such as Confederation or the invasion of Normandy took place. According to a survey conducted in 2009 by the Dominion Institute, fewer than 50 per cent of Canadians knew that the wily and inscrutable John A. Macdonald was Canada's first prime minister (1867–73, 1878–91), and just 56 per cent of those who were in the 18–35 age group could identify Pierre Trudeau, arguably Canada's most charismatic and controversial prime minister (1968–79, 1980–84) from a photograph.[67] The names of major Canadian artists, scientists, and writers were unrecognizable to the vast majority of those surveyed. In a study comparing Canadians to people in Finland, Henry Milner found that while 67 per cent of Finns could name that country's finance minister, only 33 per cent of respondents in the Canadian sample could name even a single federal cabinet minister. He also found that only 57 per cent of respondents could name Canada's second largest political party—which when the survey was taken was the Liberal Party.[68]

Not surprisingly, perhaps, Canadians appear to know a lot more about American history than they do about their own.[69] America's history seems far more compelling. The American Revolution, the country's fateful and bloody civil war, its venerated heroes and its global power seem far more spectacular than the equivalents in Canadian history: the fight for responsible government, the monumental sacrifices that Canada made in World Wars I and II, the fashioning of a universal health insurance system, the country's pioneering role in establishing UN peacekeeping, or the creation of a unique Charter of Rights and Freedoms that is respected across the world. These achievements seem to have little of the same glow, the same magnificence.

Arguably the lack of knowledge about Canadian public life is approaching a kind of danger point—dipping below the level needed to sustain a healthy democracy. According to election studies carried out in the early 2000s by Elisabeth Gidengil and her colleagues, a majority of Canadians cannot differentiate between left- and right-wing political parties or locate specific parties on the political spectrum. Most of those surveyed had either a "shaky grasp" or "no grasp" at all of the basic ideological terrain.[70] While political pundits frequently talk about political parties appealing to voters who are on the "right" or the "left," it would appear that large segments of the public would not know what these pundits are talking about. It's as if they are talking in a foreign language.

According to Elly Alboim, the commonly held perception among communication professionals is that roughly 70 per cent of Canadians are disconnected from public affairs, except for momentary flashes of interest when there is a riveting issue or event. As Alboim has put it, "Reaching them is extraordinarily difficult. Informing them directly, let alone educating them, is even more so. Most of these people have chosen to disconnect because they have decided that most public affairs is of no practical relevance to them."[71] In short, if we are to believe Alboim, many Canadians have disappeared as citizens—they no longer constitute a "public."

Political disconnectedness can have a devastating effect on democracy. Without a vigilant public, leaders and institutions become complacent, false assumptions are more easily accepted, and problems are allowed to linger and become more intractable. Moreover, when voters either don't or cannot follow the issues, gut feelings, prejudices, and the likeability of political leaders become more important. It's also the case that uninformed citizens can be more easily manipulated by shrewd advertising. As Swedish scholar Peter Dahlgren has warned, "Without a minimal level of involvement from its citizens, democracy loses its legitimacy and may cease to function in a genuine way."[72] We become in effect a democracy without citizens.

One of the most glaring indicators of a disappearing public is the declining audience for news. As will be discussed at some length in Chapter Five, one of the reasons for the slow death spiral of newspapers and TV news shows is that a sizable percentage of digital natives are no longer interested in the news. As Florian Sauvageau points out, even when they do consume news they prefer having "snacks" rather than meals; they are used to headlines, tweets, short snippets of information, and a rapid turnover of stories.[73] Although longer stories can be downloaded, Twitter, Buzzfeed, Reddit, Facebook, and Yahoo supply copious amounts of jolt-like news, with many users never going beyond the headlines or the short snippets that are presented. Not surprisingly, audiences for TV news broadcasts, newspapers, and radio talk shows—long-form news—are verging on geriatric. On TV news shows in the US, where pharmaceutical advertising is permitted, ads for laxatives, wheelchairs, high blood pressure medications, and sexual aids such as Viagra are primary sources of revenue. TV news basically runs side-by-side with what is in effect an on-air pharmacy.

Indeed, the participation crisis among young people is a phenomenon that is occurring across the Western world.[74] For instance, while considerable mythology has developed about the involvement of young people in Barack Obama's 2008 race for the presidency, voter turnout (61.6 per cent) was barely above previous lows and only about half of those under 30 bothered to vote—hardly inspiring numbers considering that the US had been hit by the deepest economic recession since the Great Depression, was fighting two wars, and had in Barack Obama an electrifying speaker and the first African American to run for president on a major party ticket. The 2012 presidential election wasn't much different. Although the economic stakes were more critical than ever and well over $2 billion was spent on TV ads and voter contact during the 2012 presidential race, voter turnout plummeted by 9 per cent from the previous election.[75] Some 119 million registered voters stayed home, and turnout among those under 30 dropped by 3 per cent from 2008. Turnout in the 2014 US mid-term elections plummeted to just 36 per cent, the lowest in 72 years. Just 13 per cent of those under 30—a little over 1 in 10—bothered to vote.[76] In European parliamentary elections, the downturn in voting has been slower, but turnout still dropped by 10 per cent from 1960 to 2009.[77]

Peter Dahlgren has argued that those who use conventional markers such as voting, volunteering or political knowledge as the test for measuring civic engagement are missing the point. This is because the boundaries of what we think of as "political" now have to be stretched to include popular culture. He argues that popular culture and politics feed off each other and are inextricably linked.[78] TV shows, comics, jokes, popular novels, video games, art, sports, and films allow people to occupy symbolic spaces, express or be exposed to different views on social, political, and moral issues, and challenge or legitimize authority. According to Dahlgren, popular culture also "invites us to fantasize about the ideals and hopes we have for society, as well as to process things that we fear."[79] The assumption is that once an idea or an aspect of societal change is accepted within pop culture, it's only a matter of time before it becomes accepted in society. His argument is that while digital natives may have retreated from conventional politics, they "vote" daily as consumers and creators of popular culture.

Although Dahlgren's argument is compelling, it ignores some hard truths. First, much of politics takes place in arenas or situations where popular culture cannot have an immediate or tangible influence because what is required is direct political action and persuasion. Problems such as dangerously long waiting lists for medical tests and operations, the lack of investment in public transit, the problems of homelessness, or the deplorable shortage of adequate housing and safe drinking water on many First Nations reserves are rarely addressed by popular culture. Moreover, in real life, ground-level politics often involves messy and uncomfortable compromises, taking slow steps toward a more distant goal, and the need to choose the least undesirable among a number of undesirable options. None of that translates easily into music, TV shows or video games. In the end, policy changes have to be ratified by Parliament, provincial legislatures, and courts. This means that elections and voting are still gateways to change, gateways that can't be easily avoided.

We also have to address the argument that surveys that measure political knowledge and involvement often ask the wrong questions. Knowledge about political parties or about which political leaders are championing which issues may not tell us very much about what people actually know and how they process information. Asking questions about how people spend their leisure time, their aspirations in the housing market, whether they shop for food at local markets, the sports teams that they follow, how they rate their family doctors (if they have one), or whether the local music scene is vibrant and popular may provide a more grassroots sense of what people know and find meaningful.

However, even if we acknowledge that our sense of what constitutes pertinent knowledge needs to be broadened, voting is still a key litmus test of a country's political health because it not only determines the shape of governments and policy decisions but also has great symbolic value. Voting is an expression, perhaps the ultimate expression, of participation and equality.

And if voting is the scorecard, we are clearly faltering. Turnout in federal elections has declined steadily, from slightly over 75 per cent of eligible voters in 1988 to just 58.8 per cent in the 2008 election, the lowest in the history of Confederation. In 2011, turnout inched back up to 61.4 per cent. If the present trend continues, the number of non-voters in Canada may soon exceed the number of voters. Moreover, all that a federal political party needs to do to win a majority government is to get roughly 40 per cent of the votes. In 2011, Stephen Harper's Conservatives formed a majority government with the support of just 24.3 per cent of eligible voters, a relatively small minority of Canadians. Not surprisingly, then, the strategies of the major political parties are now geared almost entirely toward mobilizing their base—those voters who have voted for the party in the past and are considered loyalists—as well as winning over clutches of swing voters (seniors, environmentalists, multi-cultural communities, etc.) by targeting them with specific messages and appeals. One can argue that as long as a governing party can maintain the loyalty of its own troops and appeal to certain identifiable groups of swing voters, the majority of Canadians can be ignored both during elections and in the governing of the country.

Voter turnouts in provincial elections are also on a downward slide. The elections in 2011 in Ontario (49.2 per cent), in 2008 in Alberta (41.4 per cent), and in 2013 in Nova Scotia (58.9 per cent) all produced record or near-record low voter turnouts. Turnout in the 2008 Quebec election (56.5 per cent) was the lowest since 1927. Turnout in British Columbia elections seems to have levelled off at just 51 per cent in 2009 and 52 per cent in 2013. Turnout in the 2012 Alberta election, the most hotly contested in generations, was 57 percent, while a little less than 56 per cent of voters trudged to the polls in the 2011 Manitoba election and only 61 per cent voted in the 2011 Newfoundland election. However, turnout in the 2014 Quebec election was 71 per cent, a slight decrease from the 2012 election but still high because of the re-emergence of sovereignty as an issue.

According to survey results, the sharp decline in voter turnout is due almost entirely to an increase in non-participation by younger Canadians.[80] Here the evidence is disturbing. A survey of first-time voters conducted by Elections Canada found that only 38.7 per cent had voted in the 2004 federal election, a percentage lower than first-time voters in the UK, the US, France, and nearly all other industrialized countries.[81] Based on a survey conducted in 2007–08, Paul Howe estimated that at least a third of those under 30 paid virtually no attention to electoral politics. To revisit Lippmann's analogy, they remained deaf as the orchestra played. He also found that drop-outs were not just confined to the poor and poorly educated; non-voters cut across the entire socio-economic spectrum.[82] In a 2011 study for Elections Canada, André Blais and Peter Loewen pooled results from all of the federal elections from 1997 to 2008, finding that turnout averaged 37 per cent for those aged 18–24 and 47 per cent for those aged 25–30.[83] Marc Mayrand, the Chief Electoral Officer of Canada, reported that only 38.8 per cent of those aged 18–24 and 45.1 per cent of those aged 25–34 voted in 2011.[84] The good news is that voting increases significantly with age; the bad news is that it still remains relatively low. In addition, and not surprisingly, William Cross and Lisa Young found that young people have all but vanished from political party memberships. According to a sample taken in 2000, the average age of party members was 59 and almost half were senior citizens. Only 1 in 20 was under 30.[85]

When political parties and the pool of likely voters become disproportionately older, a distorting effect is created. Arguably political parties now give less priority to policies that might appeal to younger voters—such as providing more affordable education, encouraging the creation of entry-level jobs, helping with first-time mortgages, subsidizing daycare, or developing more aggressive environmental policies—than they do to policies that are attractive to older voters. Inevitably parties load the election dice in favour of attracting those who are most likely to vote, meaning older Canadians. Yet Henry Milner is particularly mystified by the absence of younger voters from the climate change debate:

> The absence of a generation-based politically sophisticated environmental movement is an acute symptom of a wider political phenomenon: the generation reaching maturity is seemingly not prepared to take its full part in the political process. Climate change dramatically brings to light the results of continued low levels of informed political participation by the generation most affected by it, and the fact that even on this most global issue, there is no avoiding politics.[86]

The heart of the problem may be a breakdown of trust. Trust in politicians of all stripes has fallen dramatically. Surveys routinely rank politicians at the very bottom or close to the very bottom of all professions in terms of public esteem. Luckily, surveys don't measure politicians against car thieves, leaders of crackpot religious cults or members of biker gangs—because we might be unpleasantly surprised by the results. In fact, a poll taken during the 2008 election by Ipsos Reid found that a majority of those surveyed saw both the Conservatives and the Liberals as "stale," "phoney," "unfeeling," and "risky."[87] A survey taken during the 2011 federal election showed that voters viewed the election with varying degrees of mistrust, cynicism, and suspicion. Almost two-thirds told interviewers that none of the parties had satisfactory positions on the issues and that the political system had descended into crisis.[88] The results of an Ipsos Reid online poll conducted in 2012 were even more brutal. Ninety-five per cent of those surveyed believed that politicians in Ottawa had either little or nothing in common with average Canadians. Eighty-four per cent thought that the political elite in Ottawa wasn't "tuned" into what was really important to people.[89]

For evidence one need look no further than Question Period in the House of Commons. Aside from elections, Question Period is the part of the political process that's most visible to Canadians. It is also the part of politics that has become the most dysfunctional. Political leaders and journalists both cling to Question Period because it's a guaranteed media moment for politicians and an easy story for journalists. As a result it has become little more than a kind of theatre performance with a predicable repertoire of spitball attacks, outrageous charges, cute one-liners, and grandstanding. In the words of Conservative MP Michael Chong, who has been at the forefront of those who would like to reform Question Period by encouraging more substantive questions and responses, "Far too often, it descends into a testosterone-laden, anger-filled screaming match, characterized by aggressive body language and by those who can yell the loudest and hurl the biggest insults."[90] In fact, Question Period has become a parallel universe where a politician's political skills are judged by how well they "perform" in the House rather than by their ideas or policy solutions. While important issues are raised, questions are almost never answered. In fact, genuine exchanges of any kind rarely take place.

Canadians have not been impressed. A survey taken in September 2010 by Pollara for Canada's Public Policy Forum found that two-thirds of Canadians think that Question Period needs to be reformed and that most Canadians "think less of our political system" from the little that they may see of the daily knife-fight on TV.[91] Admittedly, keeping governments on their toes, allowing opposition parties to raise issues that might otherwise be buried or forgotten, and the give and take, the political jousting, that takes place are all important functions in a democracy—but it ceases to be important if people have stopped watching or come to see the political process as little more than an opportunity for partisan attacks and one-upmanship.

Moreover, becoming a politician is hardly on the bucket list of most Canadians. While politics has never been the most attractive profession, it seems to have become even less attractive than it once was. The rigid nature of party discipline that leaves little room for individual expression or initiative, the media spotlight and its potential to pry into and turn personal lives upside down, the tedium, exhaustion and disruptions to family life produced by endless travel (particularly for western and northern MPs who have to travel longer distances to get to Ottawa), and the sheer nastiness and hyper-adversarial nature of the parliamentary politics—all of these are enough to discourage even the heartiest true believer from considering a political career. As a consequence the talent pool has narrowed.

Although the Canadian political stage has been occupied by its share of magnetic and compelling figures—one need only mention Wilfrid Laurier, John Diefenbaker, René Lévesque, Joey Smallwood, Peter Lougheed, Tommy Douglas, David Lewis, Pierre Trudeau, and Jack Layton among many others—one wonders if we are in the midst of a miniaturization of Canadian political life, with the current cast of characters, minus a few exceptions of course, made up of greyer, more mundane figures than was the case in the past. Their personal stories seem quite unremarkable, there are few whose oratory can hold audiences transfixed, and there seems to be little magic. One of the country's most astute political observers, Jeffrey Simpson of the *Globe and Mail*, contends that, "Apart from Pierre Trudeau, who could also be profane on occasion and pedantic when reading a text, it's hard to think of any Canadian leader in the past three decades who could craft a phrase, conjoin them into a speech, lift them from a page, draw tears or galvanize action by the power and clarity of their voice."[92]

Interestingly, Paul Howe found that trust is not the issue for younger Canadians. In fact, his data showed that "satisfaction with government is not of critical importance to the disengagement of young Canadians" and that "young Canadians are, if anything, more confident in government."[93] Howe's survey was taken before the economic downturn that began in 2008 and the job disappointments that have been so painful for young people in particular. It also may be that digital natives do not see a link between their lives and government policies.

Just as the disappearing and distrustful voter remain a major challenge for Canadian democracy, so too do the missing volunteer and the absent donor. Service organizations are a case in point. Over the last 30 to 40 years, membership in service clubs has nose-dived, and these once-powerful organizations are beginning to look like empty shells. The significance of this cannot be underestimated. Harvard professor Theda Skocpol believes that mass-member service organizations such as the Elks, the Shriners, the Grange, the Knights of Columbus, Scouts and Guides, B'nai Brith, and veterans' and women's groups once played a critical role as incubators of democracy.[94] They broke down class barriers, absorbed new immigrants, taught democratic principles and procedures including elections, constitutions, and rules of order, and mobilized support for vital community projects—taking care of the poor, building hospitals, and so on. Skocpol argues that as these organizations began to wither in the 1970s and 1980s, largely becoming "check-book" organizations, the fabric of democracy and community life was weakened.

There can be little doubt that service organizations are in sharp decline and that quite a number are on the verge of extinction. The fate of the Shriners and the Scouts seems typical. While trying to pinpoint the Canadian membership of an organization such as the Shriners is difficult because it is a North America–wide organization, international membership in the Shriners has shrunk from close to 1 million in 1980 to approximately 350,000 today.[95] Given the extraordinary work that the Shriners have done in building hospitals for handicapped children, among their other charitable endeavours, their slow evaporation has meant that there are far fewer helping hands in the community.

Scouts Canada is another example of an organization that appears to be in serious decline. This is especially the case after investigations by the CBC revealed a raft of child-abuse cases and cover-ups about the existence of suspected pedophiles by the organization in 2011. But the die was cast many years before these revelations. Membership in Scouts Canada dropped by 15 per cent from 1990 to 1995, fell by another 15 per cent between 1995 and 2000, and plummeted by another 40 per cent between 2000 and 2005. In overall terms there has been a 75-per-cent drop in membership from its heyday in 1965.[96] While some people may see scouting, with its uniforms, rituals, and pledges, as arcane and out of step with the twenty-first century, the Scouts' emphasis on developing life skills, giving children opportunities for outdoor experiences that they might not otherwise have, and volunteering produced considerable benefits for the community.

Participation in organized sports, once the fulcrum of community involvement, is also in sharp decline. According to Richard Gruneau, one of the country's leading experts on sports and society, the percentage of Canadians who report being involved in sports at least once a week declined from 45 per cent in 1992 to just 28 per cent in 2005. Rates of participation dropped even among 11- to 14-year-olds.[97] Among the reasons for this drop are the rising costs of equipment, especially for hockey, the withdrawal of public subsidies for leagues and community centres so that people now have to "pay to play," and a sports system that segregates star athletes at an early age, thus ignoring and sidelining recreational athletes. Gruneau's fear is that working-class males are being shut out of sports—at least as prospective athletes.

Religious organizations have had to deal with similar forces of gravity. It is critical to remember that until well after World War II churches played a vital role in hospitals, universities, school systems, and welfare agencies. Those days have long since vanished, and religious organizations have largely retreated from the social and educational spheres. While this is not true of all religions, and one can argue that spirituality as opposed to attendance in organized religious institutions is thriving and even burgeoning, the organizational power of most religious groups is but a shadow of what it once was. Reginald Bibby, who has tracked religious identification and practices over several decades, believes that the trend lines are clear: there is less affiliation combined with greater belief.[98] But the extent of the erosion in church memberships—perhaps collapse is a better description—is still startling, and there can be little doubt that the country has undergone a vast secularization; almost half of adult Canadians have either no religious affiliation or don't regularly attend churches, temples, synagogues, or mosques.[99]

The Catholic Church has probably suffered the sharpest decline. The situation in Quebec in particular is almost a textbook case of a once-venerated institution being unable to survive social change. One survey taken in Quebec found that regular attendance had slipped from close to 90 per cent in the 1950s, perhaps the highest rate of church attendance in the world at that time, to just 6 per cent in 2008—the lowest attendance rate in any Western society. Moreover, only a small percentage of those who attend are under 50.[100] The United Church of Canada has experienced a similar fate. With nearly 60 per cent of its members disappearing since 1965, its ranks have been thinned to the point where one commentator has gone as far as to predict that church membership will evaporate entirely by 2022.[101] While the prediction may be overstated, the age of the average church member is in the mid-60s.[102] And the losses suffered by the Anglican Church are no less devastating: its membership plummeted by 53 per cent between 1961 and 2001. Between 1991 and 2001 alone, fully 20 per cent of the church's congregants disappeared. At its current rate of decline, the Church will all but disappear by mid-century.[103]

At the same time it is important to point out that there are religious communities, especially the Christian evangelical and Mormon churches, where memberships are rising, and there is a corresponding increase in social networks and civic involvement. But these communities remain islands in an increasingly secular sea.

Canadians also give less generously than they used to. In 2010, Statistics Canada reported that the number of taxpayers making a charitable donation had hit a 30-year low, falling from one-third of Canadians to less than a quarter. Compounding the problem was that those who gave to charities also gave less.[104] Giving undoubtedly suffered as a result of the great recession, but the long-term trend is worrying.

While there have been extraordinary instances of "flash" giving made possible by the Internet, such as the responses to the tsunamis that devastated southeast Asia in 2004 and Japan in 2011, and the earthquake that levelled Haiti in 2010, there are many examples like the horrific famine that ravaged Somalia in 2012 and beyond where Canadians have not responded in a meaningful way. Some observers worry about the sporadic and unpredictable nature of "giving explosions" on the Internet. People will be moved by headlines or a YouTube video, and a campaign of mass giving will be quickly organized. The danger is that fundraising for mainstream causes, whether for medical research, to help the homeless, or for local good works, may suffer as attention is diverted to the latest Internet campaigns.

While other indices of involvement have fallen, volunteering has gone in the opposite direction. The proportion of Canadians aged 15 and over who volunteer rose from 45 per cent in 2004 to 47 per cent in 2010. Most critically, 58 per cent of those between 15 and 24, the digital generation, volunteered in 2010, compared to 55 per cent in 2004.[105] This was the highest rate of volunteering of any age group. While it's easy to downplay these figures—because over 20 per cent of all volunteering is related to sports, many schools make volunteering mandatory, and jobseekers often volunteer in order to build their résumés and connections—the level of involvement is still impressive. Still, only a small cohort—10 per cent of volunteers—accounts for over half of all volunteer hours.

The question perhaps is whether we are looking for political or community involvement in the wrong places. Some observers argue that a great deal of civic connectedness now takes place online. There can be no question that some online campaigns have been immensely successful, have created or at least accelerated social movements, and have involved deep levels of participation. But there are also questions about whether online communication suppresses rather than galvanizes political and social activity, giving people the illusion of involvement without asking for much in terms of energy and commitment. This paradox will be discussed briefly in the next section of this chapter and in much greater detail in Chapter Four. A more pressing question, however, is why so many people appear to be so disconnected from their communities and from public affairs at the same time that they are "connected" by web-based and social media. The last section in this chapter briefly discusses some of the other factors that may have helped create a culture of peek-a-boo citizens.

Turbulent Times: The Effects of Economic and Media Change

For the first time in decades, politics in Canada is taking place on the streets. The Vancouver riots of 2011, the Quebec student strike of 2012, and the Idle No More demonstrations of 2013 seem to be part of a wider global phenomenon of grassroots protest that has spread from Cairo to Wall Street, from Iceland to Brazil. While on the surface, at least, there may be little similarity between a hockey riot, a strike by Quebec students over increased tuition fees, and a movement for change among Aboriginals, the underlying conditions that spawned these outbursts may not be that dissimilar: growing alienation, feelings that dreams were becoming unattainable, and a loss of respect for governments and authority. In each case the raw nerve endings of rage and disconnectedness were suddenly and nakedly exposed. What they also had in common was the role that social media played in organizing and publicizing events, and in the case of the Vancouver riots, in both triggering them and bringing them to an end. While in each case some of the rioters and protesters were thrill seekers who enjoyed their brief moments of power, and while it was only a minority of people who were involved in these events, it would be a mistake to dismiss them as temporary blips on the screen rather than indications of far deeper divides.

Some commentators believe that the increasing disconnectedness described in the previous section is in part the result of the alienation that has become endemic in our high-demand, high-speed, "always-on" society.[106] The changing nature of the family, high divorce rates, the tensions, long hours, and impermanence of work and careers, the relentless drive for material pleasures, as well as the impact of media shock have created what Iris Young has called the "vertigo" of modern life.[107] Many people find themselves in a state of permanent dislocation, their feet never quite touching solid ground: Canadians now move residences on average once every four years, can expect to have many different jobs and even careers in their lifetimes, and have a myriad of partners and, in all too many instances, spouses. The sense of being in constant motion is even greater among digital natives; in the US one-third of those in their 20s move to a new residence every year, will already have had an average of seven jobs, and two-thirds will live with a romantic partner that they won't end up marrying.[108] The vast majority also have no idea who their neighbours are and probably wouldn't recognize them if they saw them on the street or were sitting next to them on the bus or at the local coffee emporium.[109] Why bother to learn their names if you will be moving away almost as soon as you have arrived?

In his book *The Corrosion of Character*, Richard Sennett argues that almost all of the institutions that once brought stability and shaped people's characters, such as close-knit communities, strong religious beliefs, close families, and deep commitments to and pride in one's work, are all on the verge of disappearing.[110] To make his point, Sennett compared the lives of a postwar father, an Italian immigrant who worked at menial jobs, with that of his son, a successful business executive. The father seemed to have a much fuller life and was in a sense far richer than his son, who was financially better off. Deeply attached to his community and to his church, the father dedicated his life to achieving long-term family goals and was grateful for the slow and hard-fought gains that he made. His far more affluent son, however, lived in a maelstrom of instability: going from company to company, moving from city to city, juggling schedules and relationships—all of which eroded or depleted his "character," that is, took away from the person that he wanted to be.

Similarly, Christopher Lasch has described the life of the new executive class that moves from place to place, and often from country to country, never quite settling down or belonging anywhere.[111] Privileged and rootless, they have little at stake in the quality of local schools or the state of health care because they are constantly on the move, constantly on their way to somewhere else. Blue-collar workers experience much of the same disruption, but without the attendant lifestyles. Harry Hiller in his excellent book on migration to Alberta, *Second Promised Land*, characterizes such workers as "a reserve army of labour" that is continually being pushed from place to place in Canada and indeed globally.[112] Not surprisingly they experience shifting identities and the loss of a sense of belonging to any one place.

The economic situation created by the financial meltdown that began in 2008 has only added to the sense of dislocation that so many people are experiencing. This is especially the case with the vast armada of young men who are increasingly, in the words of the *Globe and Mail*'s Margaret Wente, "unskilled, unmarried and unwanted."[113] Young men do not attend college or university in nearly the same numbers as women do, traditional male-oriented jobs in manufacturing and construction are disappearing, and without education or job prospects many have "no path to manhood." Not attending college is particularly destructive. According to data made available by Statistics Canada in 2009, employment prospects increase with education. Those with graduate degrees do better on the job market than those with undergraduate degrees, who in turn have lower rates of unemployment than those who attend only high school. At the time of the survey, people with a master's degree earned an average of $21,000 more than those with only a high-school education, while those who had a bachelor's degree earned an average of $17,000 more.[114] As Jeffrey Simpson has observed, "The income gap between those with university credentials and those without starts slowly in the first years after graduation, but after a decade, the gap is wide and stays there."[115]

In *The Unheavenly Chorus*, an award-winning book on economic inequality and political engagement in the US, Kay Schlozman, Sidney Verba, and Henry Brady stress that economic inequalities have been a factor in explaining low levels of community involvement for generations.[116] But the situation has become worse over time. The greatest loss has been in educational opportunities and the accompanying sense of efficacy that motivates people to believe that they can make a difference in their lives and in the lives of those around them. The basic and inexorable reality is that the well-off have the resources needed to donate, volunteer, join groups, and become knowledgeable about public affairs. The end result is that as the voices of those who are better off have become louder, the less well-off have become increasingly voiceless. Research conducted by James Galbraith has confirmed that increasing inequality is a factor in voter turnout. The wider the gap between rich and poor, the less likely poor people are to vote.[117] While Canadians have not experienced the same levels of inequality that have so deeply scarred American life, on most indicators of equality Canada is only in the middle of the pack among advanced democracies.[118] The frightening part is that inequality grew faster in Canada in the last 20 years than in all but one other OECD country.[119]

Economist Jeffrey Sachs argues that in addition to economic and societal stresses, we are increasingly behaving in ways that "undermine our very balance as individuals."[120] Among these behaviours are excessive TV watching and consumer addictions such as binge eating and drinking, shopping, gambling, and borrowing that signal a "loss of self-control."[121] Sachs's main concern is with evidence that suggests that TV viewing, and by inference general media use, is inversely correlated with high levels of social trust; the more TV we watch, the less involved we are in civic and public life.[122] Using Canadian data, political scientist Brenda O'Neill also found lower levels of civic engagement among heavy TV viewers.[123]

Canadians watch TV in such high doses that it's hard to find people who are not part of the TV culture. As discussed at greater length in Chapter Six, many if not most Canadians spend what amounts to at least a full day out of every week watching TV, or the equivalent of 50 days a year. Many people watch TV while eating (displacing conversation with family members at mealtimes) and have TVs in their bedrooms. The effects of TV on interactions and relationships within families are so profound that even beginning to describe them is difficult. Although families and friends sometimes come together to watch their favourite shows or major events such as the Super Bowl or the Oscars, TV watching is usually a signal to others that one wishes to be left alone. In most cases it's downtime, a form of "I'm in my own space" time. Perhaps the best indication that a person will watch TV at night is if they are feeling blue, have had a hard day at work, or are overcome with worries or problems. Losing ourselves in the white noise and blur of TV allows us to escape to another world.[124] We also know that heavy TV viewers tend to be less happy and that there is a strong correlation between heavy TV viewing and obesity.[125]

Robert Putnam, a Harvard political science professor, created a great deal of controversy when he first proposed his "bowling alone" thesis.[126] Putnam demonstrated that the downward slide in civic engagement, what he refers to as "social capital" (the extent to which a person and the society at large are enriched by a high level of civic involvement and connectedness), coincided with the emergence of television as the primary means of mass communication. Putnam blames TV for "privatizing our leisure time"; people who watch TV are not spending time with family or friends, attending plays or concerts, going to community events or down to city hall. They are also not exercising or doing charity work. TV endlessly displaces other activities to the point where other activities become real only if they take place on TV.

The crucial point for Putman, and for theorists such as Markus Prior, is that people tend to turn to TV, and by extension the Internet, not for news or information or to learn more about the world, but for entertainment. With so much entertainment available at every turn, news can be easily bypassed and ignored. As Putman puts it, "Nothing—not low education, not full-time work, not long commutes in urban agglomerations, not poverty or financial distress—is more broadly associated with civic disengagement and social disconnection than is dependence on television for entertainment."[127] Put simply, entertainment is the silent killer of civic engagement.

To make matters worse, Joshua Meyrowitz and other scholars argue that television has psychological effects that may limit active involvement in civic affairs.[128] TV's intimacy, its riveting pictures, and its ability to place us in the middle of the action, whether it be natural disasters, election campaigns, crime scenes or war zones, give us the feeling that we are "there" and have somehow come to "know" the people that we are watching. Early pioneers of communications studies such as Paul Lazarsfeld and Robert Merton used the term "narcotizing dysfunction" to describe how some people become convinced that watching or listening to an event is the same as participating in it.[129] Roderick Hart has stretched the argument even further, arguing that TV has made viewers into "remote control citizens" who somehow "feel engaged without the effort of actually being engaged."[130] These feelings of make-believe empowerment are encouraged by a popular culture that has made audience voting, whether on shows such as *American Idol* or *Dancing with the Stars* or for products, people or TV shows that we "like" into an everyday occurrence.

A critical question is whether new web-based and social media have a similar narcotizing effect. As will be discussed at greater length in Chapter Four, some observers such as Malcolm Gladwell believe that watching a video, signing an online petition, joining a Facebook site that is devoted to a cause or tweeting a link to a friend can often give people a false sense of political participation, the illusion of activity without its substance.[131] As we shall also see in Chapter Four, optimists such as Clay Shirky take the opposite view. Shirky contends that the web has created a "cognitive surplus" of sharing and problem solving. Whether through Ted Talks, eBay, Wikipedia, aggregators, apps, blogs, file sharing, or collaborative problem-solving sites such as Innocentive or Kaggle, both our knowledge and our ability to help each other have expanded.[132]

At the very least, the conclusion of the early research is that web-based media, including social media sites such as Facebook and Twitter, allow people who are already engaged in politics to become even more engaged, and those who are already well connected to become even more connected. They allow "super-citizens" to have access to vast reservoirs of information, enter discussions, interact with others, and mobilize campaigns for their causes with a speed, immediacy, and effectiveness that were unimaginable even a short time ago. This resembles the "virtuous circle" thesis first identified by Harvard political scientist Pippa Norris. In her research about TV viewing, Norris found that those who were already knowledgeable about public affairs watched more news and current affairs programs on TV. This deepened their knowledge about public affairs—which led them to consume even more news.[133]

But web-based media have little effect on those who have already dropped out, who never follow politics, and who are disconnected from public affairs. They cannot ignite political interest when there is little or none to begin with. Surveys conducted by Samara in 2012 found that the vast majority of Canadians, over 70 per cent, have never used social media to discuss or read about politics.[134] Even when politics is discussed, conversations tend to be infrequent and unfocused.

The problem for Canada is that while web-based media are unlikely to replace traditional media as the main transmission lines of national identity any time soon, the traditional media have been so devastated by media shock that they are unlikely to survive in their current form and may be unable to continue their nation-building role. But as we have seen in this chapter, what's at stake is the very idea of citizenship, of being connected to each other and to our communities. The next four chapters will deal directly with the effects of media shock and the ways in which media change has both enhanced and endangered Canadian democracy.

Notes

1 Gabriel Almond and Sidney Verba, *The Civic Culture: Political Attitudes and Democracy in Five Nations* (Princeton, NJ: Princeton University Press, 1963).
2 See David Easton, *A Systems Analysis of Political Life* (New York: Wiley, 1965); Norris, *Democratic Deficit*.
3 See Couldry, Livingstone, and Markham, *Media Consumption*; Dahlgren, *Media and Political Engagement*; Henry Milner, *The Internet Generation: Engaged Citizens or Political Dropouts* (Boston: Tufts University Press, 2010); Paul Howe, *Citizens Adrift: The Democratic Disengagement of Young Canadians* (Vancouver: UBC Press, 2010); Norris, *Democratic Deficit*; and Robert Putnam, *Bowling Alone: The Collapse and Revival of American Community* (New York: Simon & Schuster, 2000), among other works.

4 Denis Stairs, "The Pedagogics of John W. Holmes," in *An Acceptance of Paradox: Essays on Canadian Diplomacy in Honour of John W. Holmes*, ed. Kim Richard Nossal (Toronto: Canadian Institute of International Affairs, 1982), 11–12.

5 John Zaller, "A New Standard of News Quality: Burglar Alarms for the Monitorial Citizen," *Political Communication* 22, no. 2 (2003): 109–30.

6 Milner, *The Internet Generation*, 4.

7 Milner, *The Internet Generation*, 24.

8 John Ibbitson, *The Polite Revolution: Perfecting the Canadian Dream* (Toronto: McClelland & Stewart, 2005), 1.

9 BBC World Service, "Israel and Iran Share Most Negative Rating in Global Poll," March 6, 2007.

10 Joe Friesen, "The World Would Love to Be Canadian," *Globe and Mail*, June 22, 2010: A14.

11 Derek Abma and Peter O'Neil, "Canadians Trail Only Aussies in Quality of Life: Study," *Canada.com* May 26, 2011, http://www.canada.com/business/Canadians+trail+only+Aussies+quality+life+Study/4830801/story.html.

12 "Canadians Happy with Daily Lives, While Americans and Britons Ponder Moves," *Angus Reid Public Opinion*, December, 28, 2011, http://www.angusreidglobal.com/wp-content/uploads/2011/12/2011.12.28_Greatest.pdf.

13 Northrop Frye, "Sharing the Continent," in *Divisions on a Ground: Essays on Canadian Culture* (Toronto: House of Anansi Press, 1982), 58.

14 Louis Hemon, *Maria Chapdelaine*, trans. W.H. Blake (Toronto: Macmillan, 1973), 121.

15 Quoted in Ross King, *Defiant Spirits: The Modernist Revolution of the Group of Seven* (Vancouver: Douglas & McIntyre; Kleinburg: McMichael Canadian Art Collection, 2010), 42.

16 John O'Brian, "Wild Art History," in *Beyond Wilderness: The Group of Seven, Canadian Identity, and Contemporary Art*, ed. John O'Brian and Peter White (Montreal: McGill-Queen's University Press, 2007), 21.

17 Harold Innis, *The Fur Trade in Canada* (Toronto: University of Toronto Press, 1956); Donald Creighton, *The Commercial Empire of the St. Lawrence* (Toronto: University of Toronto Press, 1937).

18 Rob Kroes, *Them & Us: Questions of Citizenship in a Globalized World* (Chicago: University of Illinois Press, 2000), 6.

19 Dominique Moisi, *Geopolitics of Emotion* (New York: Doubleday, 2009), 113.

20 Bernard-Henri Levy, *American Vertigo: Traveling America in the Footsteps of Tocqueville*, trans. Charlotte Mandell (New York: Random House, 2006), 9.

21 Cited in Schultz, "From Master to Partner," 30.

22 Quoted in CRTC and Telefilm, *Dramatic Choices: A Report on Canadian English-language Drama* (Ottawa: Government of Canada, May 2003), 10, prepared by Trina McQueen.

23 Michael Adams, *Fire and Ice: The United States, Canada, and the Myth of Converging Values* (Toronto: Penguin, 2003).

24 Frye, "Sharing the Continent," 57.

25 Richard Schultz, "Canadian Communications and the Spectre of Globalization: Just Another Word …," in *How Canadians Communicate II: Media, Globalization, and Identity*, ed. David Taras, Maria Bakardjiva, and Frits Pannekoek (Calgary: University of Calgary Press, 2007), 25.

26 Christopher Dornan, "Other People's Money: The Debate over Foreign Ownership in the Media," in *How Canadians Communicate II: Media, Globalization and Identity*, ed.

David Taras, Maria Bakardjiva, and Frits Pannekoek (Calgary: University of Calgary Press, 2007), 47–64.

27 John Meisel, "Escaping Extinction: Cultural Defence of an Undefended Border," in *Southern Exposure: Canadian Perspectives on the United States*, ed. David Flaherty and William McKercher (Toronto: McGraw-Hill Ryerson, 1986), 152.

28 John Meisel, "Extinction Revisited: Culture and Class in Canada," in *Seeing Ourselves: Media Power and Policy in Canada*, ed. Helen Holmes and David Taras (Toronto: Harcourt Brace & Company, 1996), 249–56.

29 Michael Bliss, "The Identity Trilogy: The Multicultural North American Hotel," *National Post*, January 15, 2003: A16; also Michael Bliss, "Has Canada Failed?," *Literary Review of Canada* (March 2006): 3–5.

30 Michael Bliss, "Privatizing the Mind: The Sundering of Canadian History, the Sundering of Canada," *Journal of Canadian Studies* 26, no. 4 (Winter 1991–92): 5–17.

31 Bliss, "Has Canada Failed?," 5.

32 Bliss, "The Multicultural North American Hotel."

33 Bliss, "Has Canada Failed?," 4.

34 Bliss, "The Multicultural North American Hotel."

35 Gloria Galloway, "Canadians Share American Anxiety," *Globe and Mail*, June 28, 2008: A4.

36 Eric Malenfant, Andre Lebel, and Laurent Martel, *Projections of the Diversity of the Canadian Population 2006 to 2031* (Ottawa: Statistics Canada), March 2010, http://www.statcan.gc.ca/pub/91-551-x/91-551-x2010001-eng.pdf.

37 See Richard Wilkinson and Kate Pickett, *The Spirit Level: Why Equality is Better for Everyone* (London: Penguin, 2010).

38 Noah Richler, *This is My Country, What's Yours?: A Literary Atlas of Canada* (Toronto: McClelland & Stewart, 2006), chapter one.

39 Quoted in Michael Adams, *Unlikely Utopia: The Surprising Triumph of Canadian Pluralism* (Toronto: Viking Canada, 2007), 34.

40 Nelson Wiseman, *In Search of Canadian Political Culture* (Vancouver: UBC Press, 2007).

41 Siri Agrell, "Nenshi Spreads a Gospel of Revenue Sharing," *Globe and Mail*, September 22, 2011: A6.

42 Alan Cairns, "The Quebec Secession Reference: The Constitutional Obligation to Negotiate," *Constitutional Forum*, Fall 1998, 26; Rhéal Séguin and Graham Fraser, "Parizeau Book Stuns Separatists. Bouchard, Duceppe Deny Any Knowledge of Plan to Declare Independence Unilaterally," *Globe and Mail*, May 8, 1997.

43 Quoted in Jeffrey Simpson, "Quebeckers Want Power, Not Independence," *Globe and Mail*, October 15, 2011: F9.

44 Jocelyn Letourneau, *Le Québec, Les Québécois: un parle historique* [*Quebec, Quebecers: a historical journey*] (Montreal: Editions Fides/Quebec: Musée de la Civilisation [Museum of Civilization], 2004).

45 Jeffrey Simpson, "To Quebec, Canada Barely Exists," *Globe and Mail*, August 31, 2012: A11.

46 Chantal Hébert, "Quebecers Have Become More Detached than Ever," *Toronto Star*, January, 19, 2011, http://www.thestar.com/opinion/columnists/2011/01/19/hbert_quebecers_have_become_more_detached_than_ever.html.

47 Florian Sauvageau, David Schneiderman, and David Taras, *The Last Word: Media Coverage of the Supreme Court of Canada* (Vancouver: UBC Press, 2006).

48 Thomas King, *The Inconvenient Indian* (Toronto: Doubleday Canada, 2012), 20.

49 Troy Patenaude, "Contemporary Canadian Aboriginal Art: Storyworking in the Public Sphere," in *How Canadians Communicate IV: Media and Politics*, ed. David Taras and Christopher Waddell (Edmonton: Athabasca University Press, 2012), 317–48.

50 Patenaude is quoting John Ralston Saul. Patenaude, "Contemporary Canadian Aboriginal Art," 318.

51 Gilles Paquet, *Deep Cultural Diversity: A Governance Challenge* (Ottawa: University of Ottawa Press, 2008), 117.

52 Quoted in Richler, *This is My Country*, 302.

53 Richler, *This is My Country*, 285.

54 Margaret Atwood, *Survival: A Thematic Guide to Canadian Literature* (Toronto: House of Anansi, 2012), 39.

55 Ibid., 170.

56 Letourneau, *Le Québec, Les Québécois*, 15.

57 Richler, *This is My Country*, 302.

58 In their judgment on Quebec secession the justices borrowed this phrase from constitutional expert, John Whyte. See *Reference re Certain Questions Relating to the Secession of Quebec from Canada*, [1998] 2 S.C.R 217, https://scc-csc.lexum.com/scc-csc/scc-csc/en/1643/1/document.do.

59 John Meisel, "Canada: J'accuse/J'adore: Extracts from a Memoir," in *Uneasy Partners: Multiculturalism and Rights in Canada*, ed. Janice Stein, David Robertson Cameron, John Ibbitson, Will Kymlicka, John Meisel, Haroon Siddiqui, and Michael Valpy. (Waterloo: Wilfrid Laurier University Press, 2007), 100.

60 Ibid, 101.

61 Charles Taylor, *Reconciling the Solitudes: Essays on Canadian Federalism and Nationalism* (Montreal: McGill-Queen's University Press, 1993).

62 Quoted in John Ralston Saul, *A Fair Country: Telling Truths About Canada* (Toronto: Penguin, 2008), 144.

63 John Ibbitson, "Let Sleeping Dogs Lie," in *Uneasy Partners: Multiculturalism and Rights in Canada*, ed. Janice Stein, David Robertson Cameron, John Ibbitson, et al. (Waterloo: Wilfrid Laurier University Press, 2007), 55.

64 Ibbitson, "Let Sleeping Dogs Lie," 58.

65 Walter Lippmann, *Public Opinion* (New York: Macmillan, 1922).

66 Ipsos Reid/Dominion Institute, *National Citizenship Exam: 10 Year Benchmark Study*, June 29, 2007, https://www.historicacanada.ca/sites/default/files/PDF/polls/dominion_institute_press_release_mock_exam_en.pdf.

67 The Dominion Institute, *The Dominion Institute's New Canadian Icons Survey Reveals Some Not-So-Familiar Faces*, June 29, http://www.newswire.ca/en/story/467277/the-dominion-institute-s-canadian-icons-survey-reveals-some-not-so-familiar-faces; see also The Dominion Institute (now known as The Historica-Dominion Institute)/ Magna/Arthur Kroeger College of Public Affairs commissioned from Innovative Research Group, *Canadian Views on Prime Ministers*, February 3, 2006, https://www.historicacanada.ca/sites/default/files/PDF/polls/2006_canadian_pm_en.pdf; *Globe and Mail*, "Canadian Authors Celebrated Abroad, Misspelled at Home," Op-ed, December 31, 2008: A12.

68 Milner, *The Internet Generation*, 100.

69 Ipsos Reid, *O Canada: Our Home and Naïve Land*, July 1, 2008, https://www.historicacanada.ca/sites/default/files/PDF/polls/canadaday.survey.dominioninstitute.1july08_en.pdf.

70 Elisabeth Gidengil, *Citizens* (Vancouver: UBC Press, 2004), 67.

71 Alboim, "On the Verge of Total Dysfunction," 45–53.

72 Dahlgren, *Media and Political Engagement*, 1.

73 Sauvageau, "The Uncertain Future of the News," 32–33.

74 Jeffrey Sachs, *The Price of Civilization* (New York: Random House, 2011), 148–49.

75 Andrew McCarthy, "The Voters Who Stayed Home," *National Review Online*, November 10, 2012, http://m.nationalreview.com/articles/333135/voters-who-stayed-home-andrew-c-mccarthy.

76 Jennifer De Pinto, "The Young Voter Turnout in 2014," CBS Interactive, November 13, 2014. www.cbsnews.com/news/the-young-voter-turnout-in-2014/.

77 Norris, *Democratic Deficit*, 221.

78 Dahlgren, *Media and Political Engagement*, 137.

79 Ibid., 140.

80 Elisabeth Gidengil, "Turned Off or Tuned Out? Youth Participation in Politics," *Electoral Insight* 5, no. 2 (July 2003): 2–3.

81 Elections Canada, *Estimate of Voter Turnout by Age Group at the 38th Federal Election* (Gatineau, QC: Elections Canada, June 28, 2004).

82 Howe, *Citizens Adrift*, 21–23.

83 André Blais and Peter Loewen, "Youth Electoral Engagement in Canada," working paper (Gatineau, QC: Elections Canada, January 2011).

84 Marc Mayrand, "Declining Voter Turnout: Can We Reverse the Trend?," *Hill Times Online*, February 6, 2012, https://www.hilltimes.com/opinion-piece/2012/02/06/declining-voter-turnout-can-we-reverse-the-trend/29511.

85 Quoted in Milner, *The Internet Generation*, 127–28.

86 Ibid., 5–6.

87 *Calgary Herald*, "Voters See Liberals as Stale, Dishonest: Poll," September 29, 2008: 5; see also Kathleen Harris, "Canadians Losing Their Trust in Politicians," *Canoe.ca*, December 3, 2007, http://cnews.canoe.ca/CNEWS/Canada/2007/12/03/4704388-sun.html.

88 Susan Delacourt, "Voters Filled with Dashed Hopes, Angus Reid-Star Poll Suggests," *Toronto Star*, April 25, 2011, http://www.thestar.com/news/canada/2011/04/25/voters_filled_with_dashed_hopes_angus_reidstar_poll_suggests.html.

89 Jason Fekete, "Canadians Just Don't Trust Politicians, Poll Says," *Calgary Herald*, July 3, 2012: A4.

90 Michael Chong, "The Increasing Disconnect between Canadians and their Parliament," *Policy Options* 33, no. 8 (September 2012): 27.

91 Pollara, "Question Period Not Working for Most Canadians," The PPF–Pollara National Dialogue Poll (Ottawa: Canada's Public Policy Forum, September 15, 2010), http://www.ppforum.ca/sites/default/files/PPF-Pollara%20FINAL%20ENG.pdf.

92 Jeffrey Simpson, "Imagine Our Politicians' Words Stirring Us," *Globe and Mail*, September 1, 2008: A11.

93 Howe, *Citizens Adrift*, 41.

94 Theda Skocpol, *Diminishing Democracy: From Membership to Management in American Civic Life* (Norman, OK: University of Oklahoma Press, 2003).

95 Robert Remington, "Endangered Species: Service Clubs Struggle to Attract New Members," *Calgary Herald*, January 18, 2009: A1, A6.

96 "Scouts Canada, On the Brink? Is This Century Old Institution on the Verge of Bankruptcy?," *SCOUT eh!*, http://scouteh.ca/; Dakshawa Bascaramurty, "It's Not Your Leave It to Beaver Scouts Anymore," *Globe and Mail*, August 9, 2010, http://www.theglobeandmail.com/news/national/its-not-your-leave-it-to-beaver-scouts-any-more/article1376409/?page=all.

97 Richard Gruneau, "Goodbye Gordie Howe: Sport Participation and Class Inequality in the 'Pay for Play' Society," in *How Canadians Communicate V: Sports*, ed. David Taras and Christopher Waddell (Edmonton: Athabasca University Press, forthcoming).

98 See Reginald Bibby, *Beyond the Gods & Back* (Lethbridge, AB: Project Canada Books, 2011).

99 Warren Clark and Grant Schellenberg, "Who's Religious?," *Canadian Social Trends*, no. 81 (Summer 2006): 2–9.

100 Konrad Yakabuski, "Neither Practicing nor Believing, but Catholic Even So," *Globe and Mail*, August 15, 2009: A17.

101 Margaret Wente, "The Collapse of the Liberal Church," *Globe and Mail*, July 28, 2012: F9; David Ewart, "United Church of Canada Trends: How We Got Here," January 16, 2006, http://www.davidewart.ca/UCCan-Trends-How-Did-We-Get-Here.pdf.

102 Wente, "The Collapse of the Liberal Church."

103 Daniel Blake, "Statistics Suggest Anglican Church of Canada in Huge Decline," *Christian Today*, February 13, 2006, http://www.christiantoday.com/; Michael Valpy, "Anglican Church Facing the Threat of Extinction," *Globe and Mail*, February, 9, 2010, http://www.theglobeandmail.com/news/british-columbia/anglican-church-facing-the-threat-of-extinction/article4352186/.

104 Paul Waldie, "Charities See Alarming Trends as Donors Become Older, Fewer," *Globe and Mail*, December 3, 2010: A1, A22.

105 Mireille Vezina and Susan Crompton, "Volunteering in Canada," *Canadian Social Trends*, no. 93 (Summer 2012), http://www.statcan.gc.ca/pub/11-008-x/2012001/article/11638-eng.pdf.

106 The phrase in taken from Brian X. Chen, *Always On: How the iPhone Unlocked the Anything-Anytime-Anywhere Future—and Locked Us In* (Cambridge, MA: Da Capo Press, 2011).

107 Quoted in Dahlgren, *Media and Political Engagement*, 28.

108 Robin Henig, "What Is It about 20-Somethings?," *New York Times*, August 22, 2010, http://www.nytimes.com/2010/08/22/magazine/22Adulthood-t.html?pagewanted=all.

109 Bill McKibben, *The Age of Missing Information* (New York; Random House, 1992), 170.

110 Richard Sennett, *The Corrosion of Character* (New York: Norton, 1998).

111 Christopher Lasch, *The Revolt of the Elites* (New York: Norton, 1995).

112 Harry Hiller, *Second Promised Land: Migration to Alberta and the Transformation of Canadian Society* (Montreal: McGill-Queen's University Press, 2009), 125.

113 Margaret Wente, "Unskilled, Unmarried, Unwanted…," *Globe and Mail*, August 16, 2011: A13.

114 Jeffrey Simpson, "A University Degree's Value Is Incontestable," *Globe and Mail*, July 20, 2012: A11.

115 Ibid.

116 Kay Lehman Schlozman, Sidney Verba, and Henry E. Brady, *The Unheavenly Chorus: Unequal Political Voice and the Broken Promise of American Democracy* (Princeton, NJ: Princeton University Press, 2012).

117 Cited in McChesney, *Digital Disconnect*, 60–61.

118 Wilkinson and Pickett, *The Spirit Level*.

119 Barrie McKenna, "Mind the Gap," *Globe and Mail*, November 9, 2013: F6.

120 Sachs, *The Price of Civilization*, 144.

121 Ibid.

122 Ibid., 140.

123 Brenda O'Neill, "The Media's Role in Shaping Canadian Civic and Political Engagement," *The Canadian Political Science Review* 3, no. 2 (June 2009): 105–27.

124 John Robinson and Steven Martin, "What Do Happy People Do?," *Social Indicators Research* 89 (December 2008): 565–71.

125 Sachs, *The Price of Civilization*, 141.

126 Putnam, *Bowling Alone*.

127 Putnam, *Bowling Alone*, 231.

128 Meyrowitz, *No Sense of Place*.

129 Paul Lazarsfeld and Robert Merton, "Mass Communication, Popular Taste and Organized Social Action," in *The Process and Effects of Mass Communication*, ed. Wilbur Schramm and Donald F. Roberts (Chicago: University of Illinois Press, 1971), 554–78.

130 Roderick Hart, "Easy Citizenship: Television's Curious Legacy," *Annals of the American Academy of Political Science* 546 (July 1996): 114.

131 Gladwell, "Small Change."

132 Clay Shirky, *Here Comes Everybody: The Power of Organization without Organizations* (New York: Penguin, 2008).

133 Pippa Norris, *A Virtuous Circle: Political Communication in Postindustrial Societies* (New York: Cambridge University Press, 2000).

134 Christopher Waddell, "Engaging the Public through Social Media" (draft).

Three
The Ownership Juggernaut

Scholars such as Harold Innis, Ithiel de Sola Pool, Joshua Meyrowitz, and James Curran famously argued that the way in which the media are organized and structured determines the nature of political and economic power. The media are the central organizing platform of politics. Some media forms produce more centralized control, while others decentralize power by dispersing production and information more widely. The classic example is the printing press, which broke the monopoly of a small and cloistered religious elite that controlled the production of written manuscripts, and hence the distribution of knowledge, by allowing information and ideas to flow to a wider public. The printing press helped create a burgeoning mercantile economy and made democracy possible. In contrast, the telegraph had a centralizing rhythm. As James Carey has explained, "The telegraph ... reworked the nature of the written language.... The wire services demanded language stripped of the local, the regional and the colloquial.... The origins of objectivity then lie in the necessity of stretching language in space over the long lines of the Western Union."[1] The centralization of news and popular culture, and as a result the creation of national audiences and advertising, washed away local tastes and even accents.

Television is the centralizing medium par excellence. During its first golden age from the 1950s to the 1980s, broadcasting required large production facilities, sizable staffs, and a massive distribution network. Most critically, TV was able to assemble mass audiences. As a result, TV became the stage on which political and cultural life took place, and it in turn reshaped much of the style and content of both politics and culture. In terms of politics, leaders had to be able to make it on TV; they had to have that certain magic that would allow them to reach through the screen and touch audiences. Those who were not telegenic enough or appeared awkward in some way would almost inevitably fail. TV also reshaped the nature of elections, political parties, and journalism. Messages had to be telescoped into short sound bites and images and actions choreographed for the cameras. TV ads became the main weapon of political persuasion, and political leaders had to fit the frames demanded by television. Moreover, as leaders got more TV time they became the image and embodiment of their parties. Their power became magnified, while that of other political actors was diminished.[2]

Marshall McLuhan was perhaps the most ardent believer in what can be called media determinism. He argued that each new medium introduces its own modes of consciousness and has the capacity to alter people's nervous systems and sensory balance. The result is that these "extensions of the senses" determine how life is organized. McLuhan summarized the idea in the famous phrase "the medium is the message." A rival school of thought, known as "social constructionism," contends that society plays a determining role in accepting, adapting to, or rejecting new technologies. Technologies are moulded by their users, and prevailing values and cultures condition how media will be used.[3] To take just one example, in a book about Internet use in election politics in 12 countries, the editors (of which I was one) concluded that democratic traditions, election financing rules, the nature of party organizations, and ideology and religion shaped Internet campaigning and that its impact varied widely from country to country.[4] Other theories, such as "social shaping" and "domestication," strike a balance between the power of a new medium to alter social behaviour and the capacity of individuals to bend it to their will and "embed media within daily life."[5]

There can be no doubt, however, that we are now in the midst of a dramatic reordering of the media landscape, equal in its effects to any of the previous media revolutions. But it is not yet clear in which direction the democratic pendulum will swing. Media shock is characterized by both extraordinary centralization and massive decentralization. While corporate ownership and influence have never been greater, just as great is the power of individuals to create their own highly customized media universes and indeed to produce, edit, reschedule, redirect, and react to media messages. On one side of the tug of war, giant corporations are trying to turn the web into a commercial space, and have largely succeeded in doing so. They have created new platforms and gateways through which users access other media content. Information may "want to be free," but increasingly we are forced to pay, whether in the form of subscriptions or micro-payments or by trading our personal information in exchange for access. In addition, as we will soon see, content is controlled mostly by giant corporate behemoths.

Those who see the web as an open space that allows for easy access, unfettered interactions, free and instant information, and the opportunity for individuals to produce and distribute their own media products are increasingly disheartened. At the centre of the struggle is the notion of "net neutrality": the idea that powerful platforms and service providers should not prevent other players from operating online or place limits on the access that citizens enjoy. We are now in the midst of a protracted war for control of the web, with each side making major incursions against the other. For now, the forces of increasing commercialization appear to be winning.

This chapter will examine the factors that have contributed to an increase in corporate concentration and power. No serious observer of media shock can ignore the trend toward increased centralization, concentration, and uniformity and the effect that this is having on political power.

The Powers That Be

As discussed in Chapter One, many, if not most, roads now lead through platforms created by Google, Facebook, Apple, Microsoft, Alibaba, Amazon, and a few other large companies. By dominating access to search, applications, websites, and mainstream media, they have become the meeting place for all other media—and hence for people using those media. John Naughton summarizes the degree to which a handful of tech giants now constitute a public square:

> Facebook is now a public space in which political and other
> potentially controversial views are expressed. Amazon is well on its
> way to becoming a dominant publisher. Google has the power to
> render any website effectively invisible. Given that freedom of speech
> is crucial for democracy, these giant companies are now effectively
> part of our political system. But the power they wield is, as Stanley
> Baldwin famously observed of the British popular press in the 1920s,
> "the harlot's prerogative"—power without responsibility.[6]

Also as discussed in Chapter One, in some ways at least Google has become the signature company in terms of media power. This is because "search" is still the essential key to most media interactions and Google controls that function. With over four billion searches every day, Google acts as the guidance system that allows people to find the information that they need quickly. This gives the company a storehouse of data about how people spend their money, what they are interested in, and how they live their lives. To put it bluntly, Google now knows as much about people's private lives as the church did in medieval times, and perhaps more.

Another point to consider is that Google's dominance over advertising on the Internet has, according to one commentator, "basically turned the web into a giant Google billboard." The effect of Google's auctions and algorithms has been monumental. One of its most important auctions is run by its AdSense arm, which connects advertisers with hundreds of millions of websites and blogs. In any transaction, Google keeps roughly 20 per cent of ad revenue, with the rest going to websites. These ads provide a lifeline that keeps hundreds of millions of sites afloat. Google's auction systems also helped trigger a design revolution by forcing websites and blogs to be visually interesting, well laid out, and compelling.

Moreover, as noted in Chapter One, Google competes across the entire length and breadth of communications media. Its array of products and inventions is simply dazzling. Among its many products, the Android mobile platform dominates the smart-phone market and hosted over 1.3 million applications in 2014. Author Ken Auletta quotes one prominent CEO of a media company as stating, "What terrifies media companies ... is Google's ability and appetite to reach into other businesses, from mobile phones to computer operating systems to video and advertising and even banking. 'Name a business that they're not going to disrupt.'"[7] Another of Auletta's sources described the situation somewhat more graphically: "Google stalks a market ... then strikes quickly and in a cold-blooded way.... Googzilla is voracious, and it will consume companies presently unaware they are the equivalent of a free-range chicken burrito...."[8]

While Google has strong competitors in virtually every sector in which it competes, its main rivals are Facebook, Apple, Amazon, and Microsoft, simply because they are also gateways to all other media. In fact, Facebook has surpassed Google as the home page for most users. Facebook has made a number of innovations that have given the social network immense power. The first is the Social Graph, brought on-stream in 2008, which allows users to see what their friends are buying, visiting, reading, or listening to. This led to Graph Search in 2013, which effectively put Facebook in the search business as a rival to Google.

Apple is another colossus. Founded by the late Steve Jobs, arguably one of the most brilliant and innovative minds of the digital era, the company has become synonymous with innovation. Jobs's biographer, Walter Isaacson, credits him with overturning and revolutionizing at least six industries: personal computers, animated movies, music, phones, tablets, and digital publishing.[9] Apple's popular products include the Mac, the iPod, iTunes, the iPhone, the iPad, iTV, and the iCloud. While Apple's technology has been transformative in many ways, including the ways in which our private and work lives are organized, its influence also comes from the fact that it hosts other media through the applications that it makes available to its customers. By 2014, the Apple Store contained over 1.2 million applications. The success and perhaps even the survival of newspapers, TV networks, film studios, game makers, and music entrepreneurs may depend on the popularity of their applications and on their ability to realize profits after Apple has taken its usual 30-per-cent cut. Apple has to some degree become the platform of platforms, and for many users it is the largest public square.

When it comes to content, as opposed to infrastructure, a small clutch of corporations control most of the world's media: Disney, Time Warner, News Corporation/21st Century Fox, Comcast, Sony, Viacom, as well as the European giant Bertlesmann. Each of these enormous corporations is anchored by a major film and/or TV studio and has a finger in almost every imaginable media pie. These corporate empires extend both vertically to include almost all aspects of production and distribution, and horizontally across almost every conceivable media platform. Timothy Wu describes them as a "gang of octopuses."[10]

Although they are often bitter competitors, media giants sometimes forge strategic alliances, operate joint ventures, and have worked together to dictate the rules of the road. For instance, content companies have agreed in the past to choose one technology over another, such as when they all agreed to adopt the DVD and then Blu-Ray. They have formed partnerships to control video licensing and film distribution and lobby governments, and their executives often sit on each other's boards of directors. In fact, strategic cooperation is woven into the very fabric of how the media industry operates. US TV networks, for instance, never bid against each other when a successful series comes up for renewal, the sports schedule is carefully parsed so that major sports events never conflict with each other, and movie openings are coordinated so that films aimed at the same demographic groups don't open on the same weekend.[11]

Partnerships and alliances come in all shapes and sizes: CBS has an agreement with YouTube to promote its TV shows; Microsoft was an early investor in Facebook and collaborates with it on a whole series of fronts; Facebook also has deals with the *Washington Post*, now owned by Amazon, as well as with Netflix; Disney has an agreement with iTunes; and the TV subscription service Hulu is jointly run by NBC, Fox, and Disney. In addition, cable giants Comcast, Cox, and Time Warner have joined forces to create a national WiFi network to stream programming to smart phones, tablets, and laptops. And of course, big-budget films almost always have more than one studio behind them.

Perhaps the best example of cooperation and competition in Canada is the relationship between Rogers and Bell Media. Together they own a 75-per-cent stake in Maple Leaf Sports and Entertainment (MLSE), which owns the Toronto Maple Leafs and Toronto Marlies hockey teams, the Toronto Raptors basketball team, the Toronto FC soccer team, and the Air Canada Centre, among other ventures. Simply put, MLSE is the largest piece in the Canadian sports jigsaw puzzle. At the same time, Rogers signed an exclusive $5.2-billion deal with the National Hockey League to broadcast hockey for 12 years beginning in 2014. Although Bell Media has regional agreements to broadcast a smattering of Maple Leafs, Ottawa Senators, Winnipeg Jets, and Montreal Canadiens games until 2021, it has been largely cut out of the action. Rogers did, however, sign an agreement for French-language broadcasting rights with Quebecor, another competitor.

Another Canadian example of cooperation and competition is a joint video streaming platform called Shomi, which Rogers and Shaw launched in 2014. The goal is not so much to derail Netflix or HBO Go, which would be unlikely even in the best of circumstances, but to gain a foothold in what is seen as a burgeoning market for on-demand.

Media scholar Robert McChesney believes that large media corporations are now so tightly woven together that they operate as "classic oligopolies."[12] So instead of seeing media corporations as resembling different flavours of ice cream, it is more accurate to see them as a kind of multi-flavoured swirl, with various flavours blending into and mixing with each other. US cable and radio titan John Malone has described the rules of combat this way: "Virtually everyone who is not on your team or in your company will be both a friend and a competitor. We're partners with Time Warner on a whole bunch of stuff. Yet we are also competitors.... If you have cross-investments it increases the likelihood that your purposes are aligned."[13]

According to Ben Bagdikian, who has tracked media-ownership patterns in the US for over 30 years, the number of companies with substantial media holdings shrank from almost 50 in 1983 to just 5 (by his count) in the first decade of the twenty-first century.[14] Today, two groups, Sony Music Entertainment and Universal/EMI, account for close to 70 per cent of global music sales.[15] Just 6 media giants account for over 90 per cent of world film revenues. Of the 30 most viewed cable channels in the US, 23 are owned or partially owned by the leading media behemoths. A single company, Comcast, controls 40 per cent of the cable market.

The concentration of power in web-based media is even greater. A single company, Google, controls almost 80 per cent of "search." Just two providers, Google and Apple, run the operating system software for 90 per cent of smart phones. An extraordinary 70 per cent of music downloads take place on iTunes, and almost three-quarters of all online videos are watched on YouTube.[16] In the first half of 2012, a single company—Google again—amassed more money from advertising than all US magazines and newspapers combined.[17] One company, Amazon, controls close to 20 per cent of the entire US e-commerce market.[18]

The Canadian media landscape is dominated by four large conglomerates—Bell Media, Quebecor, Rogers, and Shaw—as well as a public broadcaster, the CBC/Radio-Canada. Industry dynamics are somewhat different than they are in the US. The CBC remains the largest journalistic organization in the country, while its American equivalent, PBS, is a sideshow at best, with little capacity to set the public or political agenda. The Canadian sandbox is also a lot smaller. The revenues (adjusted for exchange rate) generated by all of Canada's media corporations combined amount to less than that generated by any one of the large American media conglomerates.[19]

What has happened in the media industry both supports and contradicts the theory of "creative destruction," first proposed by economist Joseph Schumpeter.[20] The essence of capitalism, in Schumpeter's view, is the "creative destruction" that sweeps away companies that haven't kept up with the pace of change. Capitalism is always in forward motion, replenishing itself by ceaselessly and mercilessly destroying the old and replacing it with the new. React too slowly, fall one or two steps behind the curve, and you may never recover. Remember Netscape? It rose quickly, dominated for a time (controlling 80 per cent of the browser market), and then came crashing down like a meteor. Nortel, once the pride of the Canadian high-tech sector, is now just a whisper from the past.

Some would argue that the Canadian media industry is a case study in creative destruction. Companies such as CanWest Global, Hollinger newspapers, Astral, CHUM, and Western International Communication (WIC), all of which were major players in the 1990s and early 2000s, no longer exist today. The financial collapse of CanWest Global, founded by the irrepressible Izzy Asper, and the shredding of Hollinger—as well as the jailing in the US of its principal proprietor and driving force, Conrad Black, the larger-than-life conservative intellectual—have almost a Shakespearean quality. To some degree both Asper and Black were victims of their own hubris and made investments in newspapers just as the industry had fallen into a tailspin.

Those who believe in Schumpeter's theory will also point to the new corporate skyline created by media shock. Corporate giants such as Google, Alibaba, Apple, Facebook, eBay, Groupon, and Amazon accumulated immense power in a short period of time by breaking old moulds, founding new industries, and creating new products. While profoundly disruptive to the old media economy, they succeeded in part because they invented or refined products that hadn't existed before: smart phones, search engines, online auctions, new forms of animation, website advertising, and video sharing, to name a few. Rather than fighting over old terrain, they created new markets and new frontiers. Arguably, if these companies had had to compete against entrenched competitors who dominated their sectors, or if they had needed to wait years for regulatory permission to implement their new ideas, they might never have gotten off the ground.

However, Timothy Wu believes that Schumpeter's version of history fails the acid test because it doesn't take into account the fact that some of today's media giants have become "too big to fail" and that legislators and regulators have the capacity to rig the system to protect favoured companies.[21] To put it differently, somewhere along the way, creative destruction seems to have turned into "creative protectionism." Indeed, the major conglomerates employ a number of strategies to ensure their success. One is to maintain barriers to entry that are too high for their competitors to scale. The first and main barrier to entry is financial. Founding a TV network, building a theme park, financing a cable franchise or creating a mobile-phone company that can compete successfully against these giants would require a massive investment. A start-up would have to marry a brave new idea or product with major financial backing. Even if it received funding, it would then face other formidable barriers.

One strategy used by conglomerates is to squash would-be competitors through predatory pricing. Corporations with deep pockets can drive prices down to the point where rival companies can't compete. After having bled their competitors white, they then hike prices back up. This was one of Rupert Murdoch's favourite tactics. Again and again he would bludgeon his rivals by lowering newspaper prices to the point where they found it difficult to survive. Amazon has gone as far as to institutionalize the practice through its Price-Check app. Users who access the app on their iPhones can check on the prices at local stores for the products that they are looking for. They are then directed to Amazon's products, which are invariably available at a lower price. Amazon's strategy is to use its economies of scale to undercut all would-be competitors, all the time.

In addition, new companies must sometimes run through a gauntlet of legal roadblocks that are intended to impede their progress. Wu gives the example of how in the US, Bell purposely flouted government regulations in order to force its competitors to take it to court. The goal was to trap its rivals into years of expensive litigation while Bell lobbied Congress into overturning the laws that had forced the litigation in the first place. In the end, Bell was able to stall and then outlast the competition.[22]

Corporate behemoths can also block competitors by disrupting their distribution chains.[23] In many areas, key distributors depend on major conglomerates for the lion's share of their business. Consequently they are usually reluctant, to put it mildly, to jeopardize these relationships by doing business with rivals. The Canadian film industry is a prime example of the key role played by distributors. While it costs relatively little to make films, marketing them is expensive and gaining access to major theatre chains, or TV channels is difficult and often impossible, since the pipeline is controlled by distributors who depend for their survival on major studios. Having learned these lessons the hard way, Canadian film producers rely on film festivals, educational institutions, second-tier cable broadcasters, and small repertory theatres for exposure—with predictable results. The same holds true for the music industry. Being sold in Wal-Mart or being on a DJ's playlist or being available on Amazon can make a big difference to an artist's or a company's sales. But again it's hard to get a foothold when so much of the mountaintop is already dominated by the major media conglomerates and their sherpas.

Perhaps the ultimate defensive strategy used by major players is to buy out small competitors as soon as they appear to be gaining traction or if they seem to be posing a threat. In fact, the objective of many start-ups is to be bought out by a major conglomerate so that investors can make a quick windfall without incurring the expenses and sacrifices needed to take their companies to the next level.

The highest barriers to entry, however, are often regulatory. As Jonathan Knee and his colleagues explain,

> Whenever the government establishes business regulations ostensibly to protect consumers or the public at large, it often serves to reinforce or even establish a competitive advantage to the existing market leaders. Such regulations, whether environmental, safety-related, procedural, or otherwise, typically impose an incrementally larger fixed financial burden on anyone wishing to operate a business. To the extent that scale economies are driven by the existence of fixed costs, these consumer protections also provide additional competitive protection to the industry incumbent with the greatest customer base across which to spread these burdens.[24]

Regulations can tilt the playing field in one direction rather than another, creating a rigged game. New specialty channels are a prime example of how regulators can determine success or failure. The Canadian Radio-television and Telecommunications Commission (CRTC) has the power to decide if new specialty channels are in the "must carry" category on basic cable. In the end there's a big difference between being channel 23 or 53 or 233—and of course not being carried by some cable providers at all. Similarly, Canadian telecommunications companies Bell Canada Enterprises, Rogers Communication, and Telus have fought for years to ensure that the spectrum remained closed to large American competitors. Winning the battle with the CRTC has ensured years of unbridled profits and the ability to charge high rates to customers.

Small wonder, then, that American media conglomerates spend millions annually on lobbying Congress and donate large amounts to the election campaigns of their political allies. In 2010, Rupert Murdoch's News Corporation spent over $5 million on lobbying and gave over $2 million to right-wing political interest groups that supported Republican candidates.[25]

Comcast applied even more grease to the wheels than News Corporation, employing close to 80 former politicians as lobbyists in 2010.[26] To put this in perspective, Comcast has roughly one lobbyist for every seven members of Congress. Google employs even more. It has approximately 100 lobbyists and gave money to close to 150 business groups, advocacy groups, and think tanks in 2014.[27] These lobbying efforts have allowed Silicon Valley giants to get away with practices that are clearly not in the public interest. Companies like Google and Apple are notorious tax-dodgers, maintaining piles of money in offshore accounts. They create relatively few jobs compared to many other industries; in 2012 Google had 50,000 employees, Facebook employed less than 5,000 people, and Twitter less than 1,000.[28] They also traffic in personal information in ways that violate any common-sense understanding of privacy.

In Canada, CRTC policies have played a critical role in the success of Canadian media conglomerates. For many years a guiding assumption seemed to be that Canada needed "national champions" with the financial firepower needed to offset American cultural influence. To do so, the CRTC has generally approved mergers and acquisitions in a bureaucratic blink of an eye, and until recently there were no limits on cross-media ownership. Companies could own newspapers, TV and radio stations, as well as cable franchises in the same market. Even now, cross-media ownership polices are threadbare and have been all but invalidated by media change. More importantly, Ottawa limits competition by allocating local TV and radio licences to a select group of broadcasters. When local over-the-air TV or radio licences come up for renewal they are usually approved with little fanfare, even though operators may have failed to live up to their promises, although the conditions of licence may be adjusted. Rival bids are never considered. Most crucially, cable providers have been allowed to increase their monthly charges for "basic" cable by roughly four times the rate of inflation since 2002, with barely a whimper from the CRTC.[29]

In addition, Canadian media companies are shielded against foreign ownership. No foreign company can own more than 46.7 per cent of any Canadian broadcaster. Canadian media companies are also protected by provisions of the tax code that discourage Canadian companies from advertising in American publications and broadcasting outlets, and by a system of simultaneous substitution (the blocking of American signals, and hence advertising, in favour of Canadian ones) that is worth over $300 million to the Canadian broadcasting system each year.[30] Canadian media companies benefit indirectly from a phalanx of tax breaks and subsidies for independent producers that encourage Canadian programming and, most crucially, the hiring of Canadians.

The downside of creative protectionism is that Canadian consumers pay more for various services, including smart-phone charges, than do users in many other countries, cable fees are high, and Canadian broadcasters shamelessly "rebroadcast" American programming while producing few top-flight Canadian shows. Critics argue that what has been produced is a culture of complacency that encourages copy-cat programming and little innovation or creativity.

While large corporations have the means to reinforce and reproduce their own power, they are still vulnerable to the forces of creative destruction. While some of these corporate behemoths are "too big to fail," at least for now, the question is whether today's giants will survive the high waves created by media shock—or be drowned by them.

The Power of the Powerful

Perhaps nothing has changed the landscape of media power as much as changes in technology. Every medium, whether newspapers, TV, or magazines, is now a multimedia platform, or, to use Derrick de Kerckove's graphic description, every medium has had to change its "skin."[31] Where each medium once had its own distribution technology—copper wire for telephones, the printing press for books and newspapers, electromagnetic waves for broadcasting, the LP vinyl record for music, and so on—digital technology now provides a single common language that allows the conversion of signals into codes that can be translated and used across media. As Henry Jenkins explains, "new media technologies enabled the same content to flow through many different channels and assume many different forms at the point of reception."[32] Digitalization also allows for almost speed-of-light delivery, higher-quality images, and much larger storage and transmission capacity. Where there was once media scarcity because transmission and distribution were so expensive, digitalization has helped create a vast cornucopia of media abundance.

Until the 1980s, a small clutch of companies tended to dominate a single industry, whether it be television, telephones, music, or book publishing. These companies seldom spread their wings beyond the confines of their own sectors. Newspaper companies remained newspaper companies. Music labels produced music. TV networks were only TV networks. However, these tight enclaves of single-sector dominance began to collapse by the early 1990s. And while technology was the key driver of change, other factors were at work as well. One factor was that, with the explosion of cable, satellite TV, and the Internet, traditional media companies had to stretch their boundaries in order to catch up with where their audiences were going. Simply put, as their audiences began to migrate to other media, media companies followed the parade. They sought to reassemble their audiences by owning key properties in as many media platforms as possible. This was largely a defensive reaction, an attempt to hold on to what they had. Ken Goldstein's conclusion is that audience fragmentation forced media consolidation rather than the other way around.[33]

Another factor in this cross-media expansion was the insatiable appetites of media moguls such as the legendary Steven Ross, Sumner Redstone, David Geffen, Michael Eisner, Steve Jobs, Sergey Brin and Larry Page, and Rupert Murdoch, among others. In Timothy Wu's clever description, "the mogul made the medium."[34] These were men whose vision and ambition, not to mention their monumental egos and ruthless competitiveness, could not be contained within the old boundaries. In Canada, outsized figures such as Conrad Black, Paul Desmarais, Ted Rogers, Pierre Peladeau, Andre Chagnon, and Izzy Asper carved out vast media territories. Compulsive, brilliant, some would say diabolical, and possessing the nerves of riverboat gamblers—with debt loads to match—they left an indelible mark on Canadian media and journalism. Even the fall from grace of titans such as Black was as epic and breathtaking as their rise.

Another factor in the rise of these mega-conglomerates was the scrapping of the so-called Fin/Syn rules (financial interest and syndication rules) in the US in 1994. This is yet another example of how regulators can change the game. Before the rule change, American TV networks were largely prevented from airing programs supplied by their own studios so that they were forced to buy the bulk of their programs from independent producers. After 1994, the networks were given the green light to produce virtually all of their own shows. What this meant was that studios and networks could become part of the same production unit. Owning a major studio soon became essential if a media company wanted to control costs and develop a predictable supply chain of programs and production. Studios became the cornerstone, the fulcrum, for developing a fully integrated media empire. While independent producers haven't disappeared, their share of the TV production pie is much smaller—roughly one in five productions.

In order to appreciate the size and influence of media conglomerates we will briefly examine the corporate wing spans of Disney, one of the world's largest media conglomerates; of Comcast, the largest cable and Internet provider in the US; and of Rupert Murdoch's media empire, which is arguably the most politically powerful of any of the world's media fiefdoms. We will also look at two powerful Canadian media giants, Bell Media and Quebecor. While references will be made to the strategies and holdings of other companies, they won't be examined in the same detail. I will start with the US corporations because their products and strategies have conditioned much of what has taken place in the Canadian media.

Disney

We will begin by looking at Disney, a media empire that has had an extraordinary influence on global entertainment and culture. The company generated over $45 billion in revenues in 2013, roughly the same amount as the bitumen-soaked government of Alberta took in during that same year.[35] While Disney is famous for its theme parks and its cast of mischievous cartoon characters, these properties are only the tip of a much larger iceberg. The company operates cruise ships, resorts, and residential communities, and sells over 40 per cent of the licensed merchandise bought in North America.[36] It is also connected to some of the other major media companies through partnerships and alliances. For instance, in 2010 its board of directors included the late Steve Jobs, who was President and CEO of Apple as well as Disney's largest shareholder. The 2013 board included Sheryl Sandberg, Facebook's Chief Operating Officer; Jack Dempsey, Chair of the Board of Twitter; and John Chen, CEO of Blackberry, among others.

If Disney were only a TV company, its influence would still be immense. To begin with, Disney owns the ABC television network, with its 8 owned and operated stations and over 235 local affiliates that reach 99 per cent of all American TV households. ABC's stable of hit shows includes *The View, General Hospital, Desperate Housewives, Scandal, Grey's Anatomy, Private Practice, Mistresses, Jimmy Kimmel Live*, and *Dancing with the Stars*, among others. All of these signature shows are funnelled into syndication and international sales by Disney's distribution arm, Buena Vista Television. In addition, ABC's *World News Tonight, Good Morning America*, and *Nightline* have planted Disney firmly in the news business, making it a force to be reckoned with in setting the news, and hence the political agenda, in the US. Most critically in the area of TV, Disney is a partner with Fox and NBC Universal in Hulu, which aggregates TV programs and movies for distribution via the Internet.

Disney also owns a wide swath of the most valuable beachfront property in cable TV. Its cable holdings include the Disney Channel and SOAPnet, which airs same-day episodes of the major soaps, as well as sizable ownership positions in Arts and Entertainment (A&E), The History Channel, and what may be the most lucrative prize of all, an 80-per-cent share in the Entertainment Sports Network—ESPN. ESPN alone had an estimated value of $40 billion in 2013.[37] The sports broadcaster operates 8 domestic sports networks as well as a radio network that feeds programming to some 750 local stations. ESPN is so popular that cable operators pay more to carry its channels than they do for any other channel. ESPN also publishes books and magazines, produces video games, and has its own clothing line.

ESPN is also a major force internationally and is a main pillar of Canadian sports broadcasting. It is arguably the most successful and influential broadcaster on the planet. The broadcaster owns 27 international sports networks and reaches audiences in close to 200 countries. It also has a 30-per-cent equity interest in CTV Specialty Television, which owns TSN's sports channels, Le Réseau des Sports, ESPN Classic Canada, the NHL Network, and Discovery Canada. Espn.com, which offers both free access and has a paywall for *ESPN Insider*, remains one of the most popular sites on the Internet, with upward of 130 million views each month.

Disney films are part of the culture of the twentieth century. Their caravan of adorable fictional characters—Snow White, Mickey Mouse, the Little Mermaid, Aladdin, Nemo, and the Lion King—have fed the imaginations of children for generations. In the early 1990s, Disney began targeting school-age girls with its "princess" brand of characters: Jasmine, Pocahontas, Mulan, Tiana, and other princesses were added to a brand that already included Snow White, Cinderella, and Aurora. Disney owns six motion-picture studios, including Disney Studios, Touchstone Pictures, and three animation studios, the most important of which is animation and special-effects giant Pixar, created by Steve Jobs, which it acquired in 2006. In another coup, in 2012 it bought Lucas Films, which owns the *Star Wars* franchise, as well as special-effects leader Industrial Light & Magic. It is also a major force in Bollywood, owning UTV, one of the largest studios and distribution networks in India.

But Disney also moved decisively into the young adult market when it bought Marvel Entertainment for $4 billion (US) in 2009. Marvel had developed over 5,000 comic-book characters, including superheroes such as the X-Men, Spider-Man, Iron Man, Captain America, Thor, and the Fantastic Four. Interestingly, comics and graphic novels seem to have survived the onslaught of digital media in ways that other branches of the traditional media have been unable to. Age-old formulaic stories about good and evil, fantasies about possessing superhuman powers, and depictions of beauty and horror seem to strike deep chords even among digital natives. Additional factors contributing to their success include sometimes brilliant art work, a huge Internet fan culture, and outsized conventions such as Comic-Con. Disney has helped fuel the passion with a stock of blockbuster movies based on Marvel's superheroes and an avalanche of licensed products including video games, toys, action figures, and clothes.

But the boundaries of Disney's corporate empire extend even further. The company owns over 225 radio stations, 15 magazine titles, a number of publishing arms, major record labels, and the rights to thousands of musical compositions. The company also has a formidable online presence. Its bevy of Internet sites includes, most notably, Club Penguin, an online virtual world for children, and DisneyFairies.com, a site where children create fairy avatars. More than 160 million people are on Disney-related Facebook sites, a number that exceeds the population of most of the world's countries.

One of the advantages of Disney's size is that it can take and absorb risks in ways that other companies can't. Disney can afford to take calculated gambles on new products because its executives know that failures are likely to be offset by successes elsewhere and losses absorbed over time. The financial risks that Disney has taken by building a theme park in Shanghai, swallowing a company the size of Marvel or adding 2 massive, 130,000-ton ships to its cruise-line fleet would be unthinkable for any but the largest companies.

The organizational strategy that makes a conglomerate like Disney tick is that every part of the company leverages and promotes every other part. The *Pirates of the Caribbean* franchise provides a vivid example of how the Disney product cycle operates. The Pirates ride, which became the inspiration for the film series, has been a Disneyland attraction since 1967. In that time it has had over 500 million visitors. The films, which were extraordinary box-office hits, have in turn generated a small tornado of spin-off products: DVDs, games, books, clothes, and so on. Part of the franchise's success is due to Disney's ability to "flood the zone" with expensive promotions and with favourable coverage on the TV, radio, magazine, and Internet companies that it owns. In the case of Pirates, the product line came full circle as Disney remodelled the amusement ride in light of the success of the movies. The same synergies and economies of scale, the same winning formula, have been used for a whole host of products.

Comcast

While Disney commands a great deal of cultural and arguably political space, some might argue that it is far from being the most powerful or influential media giant. Comcast, although smaller than Disney, occupies key places on the media chessboard. Described by its critics as "the Dark Lord of Broadband" and the "Big Brother" of the Internet, it is the largest cable and broadband provider in the United States. These ominous descriptions come from the fact that the company was once accused of blocking file-sharing applications because they threatened to eat up too much broadband, and of handicapping competing cable channels by placing them in the upper reaches of the cable stratosphere where few viewers could find them.[38] In addition to its cable and Internet presence, Comcast owns NBC, a TV network with 10 stations and close to 200 affiliates, as well as a phalanx of top cable channels including CNBC, MSNBC, Bravo, Syfy, and USA. Other properties include Universal Studios and its theme parks, as well as arenas, ticketing and marketing companies, and sports franchises including the NHL's Philadelphia Flyers.

Perhaps Comcast's boldest move has been its attempt to capture the next great wave of TV broadcasting, namely web-based or over-the-top TV. As mentioned above, NBC is a partner with Fox and Disney in Hulu, a website that makes programs from the three networks available to users, and it has teamed with Time Warner in TV Everywhere, a service that broadcasts TV shows over the Internet to customers who also have a cable subscription. As we will see in Chapter Five, staying ahead of this particular curve will not be easy.

News Corporation

Rupert Murdoch's News Corporation (his print holdings) and his 21st Century Fox (his TV, satellite, and film arm) are the most blatantly and aggressively "political" of the major media conglomerates. Like Disney, Murdoch's world is a multi-headed giant with a vast global reach. While its principal holdings include broadcasting and satellite companies such as Fox Broadcasting, Fox News Channel, Fox Sports, Fox Studios, Star TV (the largest satellite TV service in Asia), and a 40-per-cent stake in British Sky Broadcasting, as well as strong positions in satellite services across Europe, Murdoch's most prized possessions are his newspapers: the *New York Post*, the *Sun* tabloid (London), the *Australian*, the *Times* and the *Sunday Times* (London), and the *Wall Street Journal*, among many others.

Murdoch's British tabloid the *News of the World* had long been the symbol and embodiment of lurid, sensational, highly partisan, and take-no-prisoners journalism. In political terms, it had been a guided missile aimed at his political adversaries. He has used newspaper coverage to make or break political careers, providing glowing coverage to friends such as former and current prime ministers Margaret Thatcher and David Cameron, while mocking and savaging those who did not share his views or champion his interests.[39] For over a generation, Murdoch met frequently with prime ministers at 10 Downing Street and socialized with them in private. Mired in scandal, Murdoch closed the *News of the World* in 2011, launching a new tabloid, the *Sun on Sunday*, in 2012. In the United States, Fox News has been a stalwart defender of right-wing causes and Republican politicians with little effort to provide balanced coverage or present viewers with inconvenient facts that might get in the way of its rigid ideological message. Reporting is so aggressively and brutally one-sided, that Fox News has come to be seen as an adjunct of the Republican Party rather than an independent news source.

The hacking scandal that was exposed in the UK in 2011 was arguably the low point for journalism in a democratic society. Thousands of phones, including those of then–British prime minister Gordon Brown, as well as those of crime victims and families of servicemen killed overseas were hacked by Murdoch's *News of the World* so that the most private and intimate details about people's lives could be splashed across its front pages. While the scandal deeply shook the British political establishment and led to a far-reaching inquiry, little damage seems to have been done to Murdoch's media interests in the UK or elsewhere.

Canadian Media Corporations

While Canadian media corporations are minor-league players compared to their US counterparts, the size and reach of their holdings and influence within Canada are breathtaking. For the sake of brevity we will focus on only two key players, Quebecor Media and Bell Media.

Quebecor Media

Quebecor Media, founded in 1950 by Pierre Péladeau, who was one of the most colourful and hard-charging characters in the history of Canadian journalism, has a virtual stranglehold on the media in Quebec. The conglomerate that exists today was largely put together by Péladeau's son, Pierre Karl Péladeau. Interestingly, its takeovers of broadcaster TVA and cable provider Videotron were financed in part by La Caisse de dépôt et de placement du Québec, an institution that manages the investments of public and private pension plans in Quebec. At the time, the Quebec government wanted to block Rogers from controlling cable services in Quebec.

With regard to Quebecor's hold on Quebec's media, there are few instances in the Western world where so much power in a given territory rests in the clutches of a single company. Quebecor Media owns the dominant television network, TVA, as well as a host of specialty services including an all-news and an all-sports channel. Its news programs are the leaders in every local market in the province, and 23 out of the top 30 most-watched TV shows in 2011 were broadcast by TVA.[40] Another of its arms, Videotron, dominates the cable industry in Quebec, and Quebecor is also the largest Internet provider. Just two of its newspapers, *Le Journal de Montréal* and *Le Journal de Québec*, account for almost half of the total newspaper readership in the province. In addition, the company is the largest book publisher as well as the largest wireless provider in the province. At the time of writing, Quebecor also owned roughly 200 weekly newspapers and magazines, operated stores across Canada that sell magazines, music, and videos, many of which are its own products, and had a live entertainment arm that sustains much of the Canadian concert scene. In 2013, Quebecor, through TVA Sports, made a deal with Rogers to purchase French-language broadcast rights to the NHL. Quebecor also holds the lease and arena-management contract for the new hockey arena being built in Quebec City. As one observer put it, "the dots" that would bring a Quebecor-owned NHL team back to Quebec City "are plainly visible."[41]

There can be no doubt about Quebecor's influence, especially if it chooses to aim all of its cannons on a single target. In a study based on interviews with media executives, journalists, regulators, and scholars, Colette Brin and Walter Soderlund found that while Quebecor mostly uses its considerable media reach to promote its hit TV shows and commercial products, political leaders are wary of the political impact that the company can have. As one Quebec TV executive put it, "because of Quebecor specifically, convergence is a huge threat. Not specifically convergence, in fact, but concentration of information. I'm not sure people are fully aware of the democratic impact. It's not the role of the media to determine the political agenda of a society. The Liberal Party of Quebec and the Parti Québécois can't do anything without wondering how Quebecor will spin the story."[42] It can be argued that because Quebecor controls so many platforms, the overall pool of political and journalistic views available to Quebeckers has been sharply reduced.[43] It must be noted, however, that *Le Journal de Montréal* has bloggers from all sides of the political spectrum.

Quebecor's promotion of *Star Académie*, a show originally developed in France, is a textbook example of the power of media convergence and cross-media promotion. Described as a cross between "American Idol and Big Brother," contestants live together in the same house while competing against each other onstage in a singing contest. The show is the most expensive ever produced in Quebec, and the finales draw upward of three million fans. Airing on TVA, the show is also available to cable subscribers who sign on to a video-on-demand service, and exclusive content is provided to Internet subscribers, who are given access to *Star Académie* web cams—a surprisingly popular feature. In addition, *Star Académie* stories and promotions are prominently featured in Quebecor's newspapers and magazines, best-selling souvenir books have been published, and *Star Académie* CDs, videos, and other products drape the shelves of its retail outlets. In Quebec, *Star Académie*, like Quebecor Media, is simply everywhere.[44] Or as Brian Myles, the president of la Fédération professionnelle des journalistes du Québec, has described the power of Quebecor: "It's a planet that creates its own gravity and spins in its own solar system."[45]

There was also considerable controversy when the company's largest shareholder, Pierre Karl Péladeau, decided to run for the Parti Québécois in the 2014 Quebec election. Admitting that "he had always been a sovereigntist," Péladeau insisted that he has never pressured journalists to follow a particular line.[47] However, the claim that he had been a "hands-off" boss is disputed by others. A statement issued at the time by la Fédération professionnelle des journalistes du Québec warned that the combination of high political office and media ownership had created "an explosive mix."[48]

Quebecor's influence in Quebec has been offset to some degree by the Desmarais family's Gesca, which controls seven French language dailies, including *La Presse* and *La Presse+* on mobile devices, and by the public broadcaster, Radio-Canada.

Bell Media

Our other Canadian example is Bell Media, a subsidiary of Bell Canada Enterprises, Canada's largest communications company. BCE is the example par excellence of technological convergence driving cross-media ownership. BCE's strategy is hardly a mystery: it wishes to own the entire backbone of content and delivery and to be the key provider of news, sports, and entertainment on every available screen, from laptops to smart phones to tablets.

As the owner of Bell Canada, one of the world's oldest phone companies, BCE still provides local and long-distance services. But it also serves over 7.5 million cell-phone subscribers through Bell Mobility, has over 2 million satellite and cable subscribers, and is a major Internet provider. In 2011, BCE completed a deal to buy Canada's largest broadcaster, CTV, in which it had a minority position, and maintains a 15-per-cent stake in the *Globe and Mail*. As discussed previously, in 2011, it joined forces with Rogers to buy 75 per cent of Maple Leaf Sports Entertainment (MLSE), the most powerful conglomerate in Canadian sports. (It must be pointed out, however, that neither conglomerate has outright control. Businessman Larry Tanenbaum, who owns 25 per cent of MLSE, has the swing vote.)

By Canadian standards, CTV is a colossus. In the 2013 season, the network aired six out of the top ten highest-rated regularly scheduled shows.[49] Many of the roughly 30 over-the-air conventional stations that it owned in 2014 are market leaders, giving the network a dominant position in local news. CTV Two, a boutique operation that covers a number of smaller markets, gives Bell Media an additional window in over-the-air TV. But CTV's longest shadow is cast over cable TV, where its franchises include The Sports

Network (TSN), Bravo, The Discovery Channel, CP24, Much Music, MTV Canada, Space, The Comedy Network, CTV Newsnet, the Business News Network, and the Canadian Learning Channel, among others. CTV also has a one-third stake in the Outdoor Life Network and owns or has a share in a phalanx of digital channels. Bell's controversial takeover of Astral in 2013 brought a bounty of key French-language pay and specialty channels, as well as 77 radio stations in 47 locations. These radio stations were in addition to the 33 radio stations that it owned before the takeover. Fearing an overwhelming concentration of ownership in the radio sector, the CRTC has asked Bell Media to shed ten of these stations.

While TSN is Canada's most-watched specialty channel, Bell Media failed to outbid Rogers for the Canada-wide rights to broadcast NHL games between 2014 and 2026. While this is a considerable blow, the specialty service still has many assets, including the regional rights to broadcast Montreal Canadiens, Toronto Maple Leafs, Ottawa Senators, and Winnipeg Jets games as well as rights to the CFL, curling, NCAA March Madness, the NFL, and Toronto Raptors games. Even without a big NHL deal, TSN will still be one of the great money machines in Canadian broadcasting.

In terms of political influence, Bell Media's small ownership position in the *Globe and Mail* should not be discounted. The majority owner is the Thomson family through its Woodbridge holdings. The very incarnation of grey respectability, the *Globe* is the paper most read by members of the Canadian business and political elite. Through its investigative work, in-depth articles on social and business trends, as well as its clutch of star columnists including Jeffrey Simpson, Margaret Wente, Roy MacGregor, and John Ibbitson, among others, the *Globe* still has the capacity to launch a national conversation and to set the political agenda as well. While editorial approaches are separate and arguably very different, CTV and the *Globe* sometimes join forces to conduct polls and sponsor events. There also seems to be a high wall separating the *Globe* from BCE's business interests. When in 2013 BCE joined forces with Rogers Communication and Telus to block the giant American telecom provider Verizon from entering the Canadian market, *Globe* writers lambasted BCE for its high cell-phone charges and for trapping customers in long-term contracts.

Corporate Rules: Values, Ideology, and the News

A main consequence of the domination of the media by corporate conglomerates is the triumph of consumer values. Media users are treated primarily as consumers rather than as citizens. Not only is there no escape from the daily meteor shower of commercials that rain down on us, but commercial values invade almost every aspect of programming and news production. And just as there are magazines that are little more than billboards for industries or products with ads dressed up as articles, there are now entire specialty channels that, although camouflaged as home improvement, food, music, real estate or travel, are little more than non-stop ads. To media scholar Toby Miller, we have now reached the point where consumerism has replaced citizenship as the defining characteristic of identity.[50] Consumerism is the lens through which we see the world, and it is the common culture, the experience that we all share. For many of us, happiness and identity are linked to lifestyle: buying, owning, consuming, and possessing. Consuming becomes an ideological exercise and its lessons are taught at an early age. Norma Pecora expresses it well when she says, "with the consumerism of the child comes the ideological shaping of the adult."[51]

Media conglomerates such as Disney are in the business of selling brands. As Naomi Klein has demonstrated, branding is aimed primarily at young teens and adults who are targeted wherever they turn by what amounts to a kind of saturation bombing.[52] But advertisers start the process even earlier. The average 2- to 7-year-old in the US is exposed to just under 14,000 TV ads a year, while 8- to 12-year-olds are inundated by over 30,000 ads.[53] Benjamin Barber believes that brand identities "go all the way down to the core" and that they are now so omnipresent and powerful that they can "displace traditional ethnic and cultural traits and overwhelm the voluntary aspects of identity we choose for ourselves."[54] Columbia University scholar Todd Gitlin describes the power of branding this way:

> On signs, T-shirts, caps, coffee mugs, key chains, shopping bags, and posters, in shops, private and public museums, arenas, theatres, and tourist sites, branding is now normal.... But the most extraordinary thing is the extent to which branding is voluntary, even enthusiastic, a fashion statement of affiliation. Labels affirm membership.... In an era of ever-renewed self-reinvention, when religion, region, and trade fail to provide deep identities, a brand can be a declaration....[55]

While global brands are in some cases considered symbols of cosmopolitanism, liberation, and progress (in some instances, wearing a New York Yankees baseball cap, listening to jazz, or having coffee at Starbucks can be a symbol of freedom or difference), one has to ask how healthy it is to wear a corporate logo as a badge of identity, or to believe that it represents who you really are as a human being.

Patrick Watson, a former TV journalist, producer, and chair of the CBC's Board of Directors, believes that there is a tie-in between the daily carnage that people are shown in the news and their propensity to seek happiness and indeed order and meaning by shopping and buying. He explains the connection:

> I am becoming convinced that it is very much in the interests of Global Corporatism to keep bad news on the screen. The viewer is so powerfully persuaded by the night's review of death and disaster that the opportunity for personal salvation represented by buying happiness off the shelf or at the car dealership becomes insanely seductive. The notion that one might become involved in any kind of personal, community or international action aimed at bettering the world is rendered inconceivable by the relentless display of a world that is only getting worse, a world in which comfort and assurance can be found only in a shop.[56]

While Watson's argument may seem far too conspiratorial and over-the-top, the question of whether negative news creates a sense of despondency and passivity and a search for some kind of happiness through consumption can't be so easily dismissed. Amid so much disorder, consuming provides satisfactions, ambition, and indeed order.

Moreover, corporate marketing and advertising not only try to sell us the keys to physical and psychological comfort, but they also trumpet solutions to social and political problems. Corporations make ads telling us how "green" they are, how new products will advance science and better our lives, how they are creating jobs, and giving back to the community. In some cases they even claim that they *are* the community. Patricia Cormack of St. Francis Xavier University has described how certain companies have incorporated a social mission into their brands: Becel with preventing heart disease, Dove with women's self-esteem, Loblaws with proper nutrition for children, Roots with Canadian nationalism, and Tim Hortons with helping children in need, absorbing new immigrants, and supporting Canadian troops overseas.[57] Cormack also discusses the attempt by Tim Hortons to make its shops into the new public square, a place of inclusiveness, down-home conversation, and Canadian values. She notes that while governments often treat citizens as if they were consumers, Tim Hortons has reversed the process by turning consumers into citizens.

As Thomas Frank once put it, "Dreaming of a better world is now the work of business. We used to have movements for change; now we have products."[58] This raises the issue of whether at least at some level the endless buzz of corporate self-promotion discourages citizen involvement. Why should people engage in civic life when they are being constantly reassured that corporations can be left alone to solve society's problems? To push the argument further, some contend that governments should not be involved in solving social problems because corporations are best situated to do the job.

Needless to say, the image of corporations as civic activists can be deeply misleading. It must be said, however, that after the prolonged downturn in the economy that came after the collapse of Lehman Brothers in 2008, corporate public-relations campaigns arguably encounter much greater resistance from a far more skeptical public. Presumably all of the PR campaigns and "repositioning" in the world will not make BP, Goldman Sachs, Barclays Bank, or News Corporation look like model corporate citizens.

Corporate power has altered journalism in fundamental ways. Most disturbing, perhaps, is the merging of journalism and entertainment and the degree to which accountability reporting has been weakened and jeopardized. When a film star appears on a morning news show to talk about her latest picture, when celebrities appear on the covers of news magazines, or when stories about new products, books, fashion trends, or sports figures are presented as news, it's often difficult to know where genuine news leaves off and corporate self-promotion begins.[59] News programs routinely report on which films grossed the most money at the box office over the previous weekend, and many newspapers carry the week's TV ratings as well as multiple stories about stars, TV shows, fashions, and new products. Simply put, the news has increasingly become a reflection of the products of those corporations that operate the news shows.

As a consequence, conflicts of interest seem to be growing exponentially for journalists. Christopher Waddell, former parliamentary bureau chief for CBC TV and holder of the Carty Chair in Business and Financial Journalism at Carleton University, refers to the "hall of mirrors" created by Rogers and Bell Media's ownership of MLSE and the former's ownership of the Toronto Blue Jays baseball team. Waddell asks whether sports fans should care about whether the journalist covering the story is employed by the same company as the player or team he or she is reporting on and whether both of their jobs depend on pleasing advertisers and sponsors. The danger is that reporting can descend into self-promotion, with journalists becoming little more than PR representatives for the teams, the league, and the media companies that employ them.[60]

Indeed, legendary sports writer and member of the Hockey Hall of Fame Roy McGregor believes that cable sports networks risk becoming a promotional arm of major-league sports, especially hockey.[61] Commentators avoid conflicts of interest by focusing on minutiae such as rumours about who will be traded, the prettiest goals of the week, which coach is about to be fired, or who should play right wing on the third line for a team making a playoff run. Bigger issues such as whether taxpayers should pay for new stadiums, the agony and sometimes life-long effects of concussions, doping scandals, NHL expansion, or the shocking drop in participation in amateur sports in Canada tend to be avoided. In short, the commentator's job is to promote the next game rather than to cover sports with a journalistic edge.

The problem is that the "hall of mirrors" exists in many areas. In the 2003 Lincoln Report on the future of Canadian broadcasting, the House of Commons Standing Committee on Canadian Heritage warned about the breakdown of trust that occurs when news merges into self-promotion and advertising. According to the report,

> As witnesses concerned about the perils of cross-media ownership told the committee, the danger is that too much power can fall into too few hands and it is power without accountability. Ownership of multiple media outlets ... gives corporations extraordinary power to shape the views of citizens. Under such circumstances the number and range of voices and perspectives that are available to readers and viewers can be sharply limited. Cross-promoting of one media outlet by another turns news and commentary into an advertisement or a marketing ploy. This can only have a corrosive effect on the trust that citizens place in news organizations.[62]

News organizations have also learned to tread softly when it comes to advertisers and corporate partners. These worries were famously captured in the movie *The Insider*, starring Russell Crowe and Al Pacino. Based on a true story, the film depicts how when faced with the power of big tobacco, CBS's *60 Minutes* backed away from airing a story about how the tobacco industry was hiding the fact that cigarettes were laced with addictive ingredients. Similarly, during the 2008 Olympics in Beijing, NBC reporters seemed to literally run away from stories about the repression of dissidents by the Chinese government or the wholesale removal of entire populations to make way for Olympic venues. NBC-Universal was then owned by General Electric, which was afraid of losing contracts if it offended the Chinese government. Closer to home, with newspapers now increasingly dependent on real-estate and car ads, critical stories about the shape of city development or our dependence on the automobile are few and far between. Also, very few news outlets have consumer reporters. The problem, I suspect, is that there is little to be gained by shining a spotlight on your friends, especially if they hold the purse strings.

Nervousness about offending powerful interests has migrated to the online world as well. Gatekeepers such as Apple have rejected apps that might be controversial or embarrassing. Media writer Michael Wolff believes that Apple refused to carry his app because he had written critically about the company.[63] Apple also refused to carry an app that charted US drone attacks. It deep-sixed apps by *Playboy* and the German magazine *Bild* because of what it considered to be pornography.[64] It also censored an issue on an app of the comic book series *Saga* because it showed images of gay sex. The app *Sweatshop*, a satirical game about social injustice, was also banned.[65] Brian X. Chen, an editor for *Macworld*, believes that media organizations may soon have to impose a kind of self-censorship, tailoring their app specifications and perhaps even their content so that they will be acceptable to Apple. Chen suggests that "if a Time magazine app sells better on the iPad than it does in print, then the company would likely produce content for the iPad first and then do so for print and the web. As a result, what we would potentially get as readers of all media would be the censored, 'App Store safe' version of the content."[66]

With so many "no-fly zones," self-censorship remains a persistent problem. In a survey of self-censorship in the newsroom conducted by the Pew Research Center in 2000, 35 per cent of American broadcast journalists admitted that they "commonly" avoided reporting stories because these stories might damage the financial interests of their news organizations. Roughly 20 per cent either "commonly" or "sometimes" failed to report stories that might place advertisers in a negative light.[67] A survey of journalists conducted that same year by the Pew Research Center found that over 40 per cent of journalists self-censored what they wrote.[68] According to an old joke,

> A young reporter writes an exposé, but the editor says, "I don't think we're going to run that." The second time the reporter goes to her editor, the editor says, "I don't think that's a good idea," she doesn't research and write the story. The third time the reporter has an idea. But she doesn't go to her editor. The fourth time she doesn't get the idea.[69]

Or to paraphrase one wary journalist, every reporter "knows the story they shouldn't write."[70] Still, many journalists believe that the wall between corporate interests and journalism should be both high and impenetrable—a journalistic Great Wall of China that should never be breached. Once sections of the wall get breached, journalism becomes an exercise in telling some truths while avoiding others.

The size of news organizations may not be the critical factor. One can argue that small media organizations are much more vulnerable to threats from advertisers and sponsors than are large conglomerates. Presumably local media companies think twice before they report on overcharging by local venues or flaky practices by local employers. Promoting local business and boosting civic pride are likely to bring in more advertising than negative reporting or controversies. To put it differently, big corporations can often go where small media operations fear to tread.

One of the great concerns in a democracy is when media power and partisan politics become so intertwined that they can alter the force of political gravity. It's one thing for a news organization to have a point of view that becomes part of the broader political mix. It's another when a giant media corporation is so powerful that it can block others from being heard and can distort the political system as a whole. Perhaps the most grotesque example occurred in Italy when former prime minister Silvio Berlusconi owned most of the country's media and controlled the public broadcaster as well. Issues of corruption, contempt for the law, and almost non-stop buffoonery were given a pass by journalists who feared for their careers. And, as mentioned above, in Britain, Rupert Murdoch's control over much of the media created a chill that was felt throughout the political system. As British journalist Henry Porter observed about the hacking scandal,

> This story is about the failure of an entire political class. PR people, writers and lawyers drank Murdoch's champagne, swooned in his company, took his calls, and allowed Rebekah Brooks (editor of his tabloid newspaper *News of the World*) to irradiate them with her crooked little smile. Over more than three decades, the perversion of politics by and for Murdoch became institutionalized, a part of the landscape that no one dared question. Serious crimes were committed and the police covered them up. Corrupt, or at least badly compromised, relationships became the norm and all but a very few politicians looked the other way, telling themselves this was how things were and always would be.[71]

Another reporter, Sarah Ellison, described the entire British political system as living under "a kind of permanent blackmail."[72]

The effects in the US of Rupert Murdoch's sledgehammer journalism are no less dramatic. Heavy doses of one-sided attack journalism can be extremely damaging to the political system as a whole. The public can be misled when inconvenient facts are belittled or ignored. For instance, there is evidence that viewers of Fox News are less likely than others to accept the science behind climate change. Most famously, a majority of Fox viewers believed that Iraqi dictator Saddam Hussein was behind the attacks made on the US on 9/11. Although the claim was patently false, it may have been a factor in building support for the invasion of Iraq in 2003.[73] Most concerning, however, is when political figures who take rigid ideological positions are given a great deal of airtime, in effect rewarded for their intense one-way partisanship while those who take middle-of-the-road positions, who seek compromise, are mocked or are depicted as weak.

In Canada, some of the great media barons of the past were ardent ideological warriors: Clifford Sifton, John Bassett, "Holy Joe" Atkinson, Beland Honderich, George McCullagh, and, more recently, Paul Desmarais, Conrad Black, and Izzy Asper. They called the shots in deciding key editorial positions, hired in their own ideological image, and used their news organizations to protect their political friends and lambast their opponents. Peter White, a former newspaper executive, once described Conrad Black as being "part businessman, part media figure and part politician—though without the vagaries involved in dealing with an electorate."[74] Clearly some media owners wade knee-deep into politics. According to Walter Soderlund and his colleagues, to think differently would be "naïve in the extreme."[75]

Democracy Insurance

A basic premise behind the functioning of democratic institutions is that there needs to be a check on the power of the powerful. Institutions must ensure that citizens are protected against tyranny whether the tyranny of dictators, governments, or the tyranny of a single idea. In Canada, the power of the federal government is checked by the opposition parties in the House of Commons, the power of provincial governments, the Supreme Court and the Charter of Rights and Freedoms, reports by the Auditor General, and by the exposure, criticism, and debate generated by the news media. The theory behind the separation of powers is that power has to be watched, questioned, and restrained in order to prevent abuses, to prevent tyranny.

The same reasoning applies to media power. Too much power in too few hands can endanger and distort the flow of ideas and the political process itself. As C. Edwin Baker contends in his book about media ownership and democracy, "concentrated media ownership creates the possibility of an individual decision maker exercising enormous, unequal and hence undemocratic, largely unchecked, potentially irresponsible power.… Even if this power were seldom if ever exercised, the democratic safeguard value amounts to an assertion that *no democracy should risk the danger.*"[76] In other words, every democracy needs to have some form of regulatory fire insurance.

Some will argue that the Internet has made these concerns obsolete. They believe that the web is such a vast ocean that the very notion of "control" or "monopoly" now seems absurd. Opinions can no longer be suppressed and ordinary citizens have the capacity to create their own media micro systems. In addition, media giants now face an active and "monitorial" audience. Their products and messages are continually being challenged, interacted with, redirected, and subverted. The warning issued by media guru Henry Jenkins is that, "Producers who fail to make their peace with this new participatory culture will face declining goodwill and diminishing revenues."[77] To put it bluntly, audiences have power and you neglect them at your peril.

Few would dispute that the web has spawned a participatory culture that is populist, bottom-up, innovative, edgy, and chaotic. Tweeting, interacting on Facebook, swapping music, photos or videos, blogging, web broadcasting, participating in online auctions, collaborating on encyclopedias such as *Wikipedia* or on news and opinion sites such as *Digg, Buzzfeed* or *Reddit* have become part of everyday life for hundreds of millions of people. Person-to-person and consumer-to-consumer communication has become a world of its own—dynamic, pervasive, and unstoppable.

Writers such as Clay Shirky claim that what has been created is a new "cognitive surplus" that allows all of us to widen our experiences, develop new ways of solving problems and harnessing a new collective intellectual energy.[78] *Wired* magazine editor Chris Anderson believes that the Internet has created a "long tail" and that the "power of the Top Ten has been usurped by the economics of the next thousand."[79] In another signature remark, Anderson declared that, "The ants have megaphones."[80]

While there is much euphoria that surrounds the democratic potential of web-based media, those who believe that the Internet is an open space and thus a check on media concentration are living in fantasyland. As CNN founder Ted Turner put it bluntly, "The top 20 Internet news sites are owned by the same media conglomerates that control the broadcast and cable networks. Sure, a hundred-person choir gives you a choice of voices, but they're all singing the same song."[81] While Turner may have exaggerated the degree to which the online world is dominated by major conglomerates, he is not exaggerating by much. The Project for Excellence in Journalism reported in 2010 that while a long tail of news sites existed, a handful of top sites garnered the lion's share of traffic and that the majority of users confined their searches to between two and five news sites—never venturing too far down the long tail.[82] Of the ten most visited news sites in the US in March 2011, seven were those of traditional media companies, two were aggregators and only one could be seen as independent, the *Huffington Post*. Much of what's on *Huff Po,* however, is aggregated from traditional news sources although it is slowly creating its own news production capacity.[83]

Despite the importance of the new participatory culture, the vast majority of what is discussed in cyberspace—news stories, TV shows, celebrities, musical artists, films, or sports events—is still the product of the mainstream media. What appears on blogs or *YouTube* or is tweeted only becomes part of the public debate if it is pulled to the forefront by the old warhorses of the traditional media and by the major conglomerates that control them. Indeed, a study of news on social media sites published by the Pew Research Center found that the flow of information was almost entirely in one direction. In 2010, for instance, more than 99 per cent of the stories that appeared in blogs came from the mainstream media and only a single news story that originated on social media sites was picked up by newspapers or TV.[84] Similarly, in an attempt to discover the rhythms of the "news cycle" researchers at Cornell used powerful computers to track 90 million articles that appeared on 1.6 million media sites and blogs during a 3-month period in 2008.[85] They found that only 3.5 per cent of story lines that originated in blogs made it into the traditional media.

In a study of 20 news and media websites published in 2013, Pablo Boczkowski and Eugenia Mitchelstein found that "novel, born-on-the Web" news options failed to attract much of an audience. In fact, blogs and citizen generated content accounted for just 3 per cent and a quarter of 1 per cent of news choices respectively. As Boczkowski and Mitchelstein sum up their findings, "Despite the hype about these storytelling options among some academics and practitioners, the levels of supply and demand suggest that they aren't a real competitor to traditional formats."[86] A study of the news environment in Philadelphia published in 2013 by C. W. Anderson came to the same conclusion.[87]

While I know of no similar Canadian studies, I can't imagine that the results would be much different especially considering the relative weakness of the Canadian blogosphere as compared to that in the US.

Admittedly, the direction of traffic is becoming increasingly difficult to track. This is especially the case with Twitter. During elections, journalists from the mainstream media, bloggers, campaign operatives, interest group representatives, and ordinary citizens tweet each other at a sometimes dizzying pace. It's often difficult to "credit" any one source with originating a train of thought or a fast-breaking story. But tweeting about news and politics is largely confined to a narrow circle of "super citizens" including those who are paid by conventional news organizations to be part of the circle.

One of the country's leading media scholars, Darin Barney, believes that the new participatory culture has done little to alter the balance of media power. As Barney has observed, "While everyone has the potential to be an independent producer, distributor and gatherer of information via the Internet, the fact remains that most people, most of the time, experience the medium much as they do any other mass communication medium: as an audience that is relatively powerless in relation to those who control the design, content and deployment of the medium."[88] No less an authority than the much venerated media scholar Manual Castells has cautioned that however dynamic and important the "counter-power" exercised by users might be, it is still no match for the power of the corporate giants.[89]

The problem of media concentration, of corporate "over-fishing" has been dealt with by most democracies in the Western world in two fundamental ways: the power of media conglomerates is balanced by strong public service broadcasters such as the CBC/Radio-Canada, the BBC in the UK, or the ARD and ZDF in Germany; and the size of media holdings is limited by government regulation. As we will see in Chapter Seven, the public broadcaster CBC/Radio-Canada has been diminished to the point where it may no longer be an alternative voice or even a voice that is being heard by most Canadians. At the same time, the rules governing cross-media ownership in Canada have more holes than Swiss cheese.

When it comes to rules governing cross-media ownership, Canada came late to the party, establishing regulations long after most other Western democracies had taken action. In the wake of recommendations by a House of Commons (Lincoln Report) and then a Senate committee, the CRTC finally enacted limits on media ownership in 2008.[90] But these rules are far less stringent than those found in France, Britain, Australia, or in the Scandinavian countries. This is because, as Oxford professor Robert Picard has noted, the "national champions" argument has always had special resonance in Canada. As he puts it, "If you look at media, Canada has always allowed levels of concentration that are two or three times higher than those found in Europe or the United States. And understandably so—the idea that Canada had to protect against the US certainly made sense, and it had to be competitive against the US if it was going to produce its own."[91] The question, as we will discuss in Chapter Seven, is whether putting most of our eggs in the national champion's basket has been effective given that so much of the media giant's big ticket programming is American, news budgets have been slashed, and they offer little local programming.

The CRTC limits companies to owning just two traditional platforms in a single market. So a company could, for instance, own a TV station and a newspaper, but it cannot own a radio station. Or it could own a radio station and another platform, but not all three. Also no TV broadcaster can own stations that reach more than 45 per cent of the country's total viewing audience. In radio, companies are limited to three stations in a single market, only two of which can be in the same broadcast band: AM or FM.

What's interesting is how antiquated and even quaint these rules seem in light of the realities of media shock. This is because the rules are based on ownership of the traditional media with no accounting for how the score-card of media power is calculated in a post-broadcasting and post-traditional media environment. Bell Media, which is a phone operator and an Internet provider as well as the largest TV and radio broadcaster in the country, can sidestep regulatory limits because it doesn't own newspapers in local markets and its other platforms are not included in the rules. Shaw Communications is another example of a mega-corporation that is largely unaffected by the rules governing cross-media ownership. In addition to being one of the country's major cable operators and Internet providers, it owns Global TV as well as Corus Entertainment. It operates roughly a dozen conventional TV stations, 50 radio stations, a Pay TV outlet, and a phalanx of valuable cable properties. Yet, under the CRTC's guidelines, Shaw passes the cross-media ownership test because it doesn't own newspapers.

It needs to be pointed out that the CRTC is not the only regulator attempting to ensure that competition isn't stifled. The Competition Bureau of Canada also has the power to block takeovers that it feels are injurious to consumers and damaging to the national interest. But it has rarely intervened in the media sector.

Regulators now look on helplessly as their power slowly crumbles. The CRTC has no control over "search," data mining, YouTube videos, web broadcasting, smart-phone apps, and a host of other services that have come with media shock. Even attempts to regulate broadcasting by Canadian media conglomerates to mobile devices may be beyond their reach. For instance, the agency has a policy that would prevent broadcasters from downloading content to their subscriber's smart phones and other mobile devices unless that same content is available to competitors at reasonable rates. Following these rules will undermine the strategies of virtually all of the major media companies in Canada, which is to own the entire media spinal cord from content to cable to smart phones. How the CRTC intends to navigate in these politically charged waters remains to be seen.

While media change has opened up extraordinary new avenues for citizen engagement, wide boulevards in fact, powerful mega corporations have moved quickly to dominate, close off, and monetize these spaces. The challenge posed by media shock is how to resolve the tension between corporate power and the rights of ordinary citizens. So far at least, the board is tilted in the direction of corporate power.

Notes

1 James Carey, "The Dark Continent of American Journalism," in *James Carey: A Critical Reader*, ed. Eve Stryker Munson and Catherine A. Warren (Minneapolis: The University of Minnesota Press, 1997), 160.

2 Austin Ranney, *Channels of Power: The Impact of Television on American Politics* (New York: Basic Books, 1983).

3 See Elihu Katz, Jay Blumer, and Michael Gurevitch, "Utilization of Mass Communication by the Individual," in *The Uses of Mass Communication: Current Perspectives on Gratification Research*, ed. Jay Blumer and Elihu Katz (Beverly Hills, CA: Sage, 1974).

4 Stephen Ward, Diana Owen, Richard Davis, and David Taras, eds., *Making a Difference: A Comparative View of the Role of the Internet in Election Politics* (Lanham, MD: Lexington, 2008).

5 See Nancy Baym, *Personal Connections in the Digital Age* (Cambridge: Polity Press, 2010), 45.

6 John Naughton, "Tech Giants Have Power to Be Political Masters as well as Our Web Ones," *The Guardian*, February 26, 2012, http://www.theguardian.com/technology/2012/feb/26/internet-companies-power-politics-freedom.

7 Auletta, *Googled*, 131.

8 Ibid., 252.

9 Walter Isaacson, *Steve Jobs* (New York: Simon & Schuster, 2011), xxi.

10 Wu, *The Master Switch*, 235.

11 See Jonathan Knee, Bruce Greenwald, and Ava Seave, *The Curse of the Mogul: What's Wrong with the World's Leading Media Companies* (New York: Penguin, 2009), 166–67; Edward Jay Epstein, *The Hollywood Economist* (New York: Melville, 2010), 168.

12 Robert McChesney, *The Problem of the Media* (New York: Monthly Press Review, 2004), 178.

13 Quoted in Ken Auletta, *The Highwaymen: Warriors of the Information Superhighway* (New York: Random House, 1997), 52.

14 See Ben Bagdikian, *The Media Monopoly* (Boston: Beacon Press, 2000); Ben Bagdikian, *The New Media Monopoly* (Boston: Beacon Press, 2004).

15 Andew Seidman, "Universal Music, EMI Defend Planned Merger to Keep Industry Competitive," *Globe and Mail*, June 22, 2012: B6.

16 Des Freedman, "Web 2.0 and the Death of the Blockbuster Economy," in James Curran, Natalie Fenton, and Des Freedman, *Misunderstanding the Internet* (New York: Routledge, 2012), 89.

17 Joel Kotkin, "Entrepreneurs Turn Oligarchs," *New Geography*, August 8, 2013, http://www.newgeography.com/content/003875-entrepreneurs-turn-oligarchs.

18 Ibid.

19 Kenneth J. Goldstein, email correspondence, September 14, 2011.

20 Joseph Schumpeter, *Capitalism, Socialism and Democracy* (New York: Harper, 1975).

21 The phrase "too big to fail" was coined by former US Treasury Secretary Robert Rubin. Cited in McChesney, *Digital Disconnect*, 41.

22 Wu, *The Master Switch*, 246–47.

23 Conrad Black, *A Matter of Principle* (Toronto: McClelland & Stewart, 2011), chapter one.

24 Knee, Greenwald, and Seave, *The Curse of the Mogul*, 42.

25 Laura Colarusso, "Murdoch's Political Money Trail," *The Daily Beast,* July 15, 2011, http://www.thedailybeast.com/articles/2011/07/15/how-rupert-murdoch-s -money-helps-him-makes-friends.html.

26 John Dunbar, "A Television Deal for the Digital Age," *Columbia Journalism Review* XLIX, no. 5 (January/February 2011): 38.

27 Tom Hamburger and Matea Gold, "Google, Once Disdainful of Lobbying, Now a Master of Washington Influence," *Washington Post,* April 12, 2014, http://www .washingtonpost.com/politics/how-google-is-transforming-power-and-politics google-once-disdainful-of-lobbying-now-a-master-of-washington-influence/2014/ 04/12/51648b92-b4d3-11e3-8cb6-284052554d74_story.html.

28 Kotkin, "Entrepreneurs Turn Oligarchs."

29 Friends of Canadian Broadcasting, Friends' submission to "Let's Talk TV," CRTC Public Notice of Consulation 2014-90, June 2014, 10.

30 Ibid., 11.

31 Derrick de Kerchove, *The Skin of Culture: Investigating the New Electronic Reality* (Toronto: Somerville House, 1995).

32 Jenkins, *Convergence Culture*, 11.

33 Kenneth J. Goldstein, "From Assumptions of Scarcity to the Facts of Fragmentation," in *How Canadians Communicate II: Media, Globalization, and Identity,* ed. David Taras, Maria Bakardjieva, and Frits Pannekoek (Calgary: University of Calgary Press, 2007), 3–21.

34 Wu, *The Master Switch*, 209.

35 All references to Disney holdings and finances are taken from The Walt Disney Company, *Fiscal Year 2013 Annual Financial Report and Shareholder Letter,* http://the waltdisneycompany.com/sites/default/files/reports/10k-wrap-2013.pdf.

36 Henry Giroux and Grace Pollack, *The Mouse That Roared: Disney and the End of Innocence* (Lanham, MD: Rowman & Littlefield, 2010), 19.

37 Mark Fainaru-Wada and Steve Fainaru, *League of Denial: The NFL, Concussions and the Battle for Truth* (New York: Penguin-Random House, 2013), 8.

38 Dunbar, "A Television Deal," 34–38.

39 See Carl Bernstein, "Murdoch's Watergate?," *The Daily Beast,* July 9, 2011, http:// www.newsweek.com/carl-bernstein-phone-hacking-scandal-murdochs-watergate -68411; Henry Porter, "Over More than Three Decades, No One Dared Question the Perversion of Politics By and For Rupert Murdoch," *The Guardian,* July 10, 2011, http://www.theguardian.com/commentisfree/2011/jul/10/rupert-murdoch -phone-hacking-cameron; Richard Cohen, "Just Desserts for 'Citizen Murdoch,'" *Washington Post,* July 18, 2011, http://www.washingtonpost.com/opinions/just -deserts-for-citizen-murdoch/2011/07/18/gIQAYn23LI_story.html; Paul Barrett and Felix Gillette, "Murdoch's Mess," *Business Week,* July 18, 2011, http://www.businessweek .com/magazine/murdochs-mess-07142011.html.

40 Kai Nagata, "Warnings from Quebec," *The Tyee,* September 12, 2011, http://thetyee .ca/Opinion/2011/09/12/Nagata_Quebec_Warning/.

41 Sean Gordon, "Quebec City and the NHL," *Globe and Mail,* November 28, 2013: B11.

42 Colette Brin and Walter Soderlund, "News from Two Solitudes: Examining Media Convergence Practices in Quebec and Canada," paper presented to the 16th Biennial Conference of the American Council of Quebec Studies/7th Biennial ACSUS-in-Canada Colloquium, Quebec City, November 2008.

43 Nagata, "Warnings from Quebec."

44 Konrad Yakabuski, "Beautiful Machine," *Report on Business Magazine,* September 2007, 50–58.

45 Quoted in Danika Gendron, "In Quebec, Quebecor a 'Planet that Creates Its Own Gravity': Enquête Report," *Wire Report*, November 17, 2011, http://www.thewirereport.ca/news/2011/11/16/in-quebec-quebecor-a-planet-that-creates-its-own-gravity-enqu%C3%AAte-report/23218.

46 Lawrence Martin, "Is Stephen Harper Set to Move against the CRTC?," *Globe and Mail*, August 19, 2010: A11.

47 Daniel Leblanc and Rhéal Séguin, "Peladeau the Sovereigntist," *Globe and Mail*, March 11, 2014: A6.

48 Les Perreaux and Rhéal Séguin, "Opposition Calls on Peladeau to Explain How He'll Guarantee Independence of Quebecor Media's Outlets," *Globe and Mail*, March 11, 2011: A7.

49 "What Canadians Were Watching on TV in 2013," *Calgary Herald*, December 21, 2013, http://www.calgaryherald.com.

50 Toby Miller, *Cultural Citizenship: Cosmopolitanism, Consumerism and Television in a Neoliberal Age* (Philadelphia: Temple University Press, 2007).

51 Quoted in Benjamin Barber, *Consumed: How Markets Corrupt Children, Infantilize Adults and Swallow Citizens Whole* (New York: Norton, 2007), 16.

52 Naomi Klein, *No Logo: Taking Aim at Brand Bullies* (Toronto: Knopf Canada, 1999).

53 Sachs, *The Price of Civilization*, 138.

54 Barber, *Consumed*, 167.

55 Todd Gitlin, *Media Unlimited: How the Torrent of Images and Sounds Overwhelms Our Lives* (New York: Henry Holt & Company, 2001), 69–70.

56 Patrick Watson, *This Hour Has Seven Decades* (Toronto: McArthur & Company, 2004), 479.

57 Patricia Cormack, "Double-Double: Branding, Tim Hortons, and the Public Sphere," in *Political Marketing in Canada*, ed. Alex Marland, Thierry Giasson, and Jennifer Lees-Marchment (Vancouver: UBC Press, 2012), 209–23; see also Patricia Cormack and James Cosgrove, *Desiring Canada: CBC Contests, Hockey Violence, and Other Stately Pleasures* (Toronto: University of Toronto Press, 2013).

58 Thomas Frank, "Liberation Marketing and the Cultural Trust," in *Conglomerates and the Media*, ed. Erik Barnouw, Richard M. Cohen, Thomas Frank, Todd Gitlin, David Lieberman, Mark Crispin Miller, Gene Roberts, Thomas Schatz, and Patricia Aufderheide (New York: New Press, 1997), 187.

59 McChesney, *The Problem of the Media*, 85.

60 Christopher Waddell, "The Hall of Mirrors," in *How Canadians Communicate V: Sports*, ed. David Taras and Christopher Waddell (Edmonton: Athabasca University Press, forthcoming).

61 Roy McGregor, "Troubles in the Toy Department," keynote address, How Canadians Communicate About Sports Conference, Banff, AB, November 9, 2012.

62 Standing Committee on Canadian Heritage, *Our Cultural Sovereignty*, 405.

63 Chen, *Always On*, 93.

64 Ibid., 90–91.

65 Michael Thomson, "Why Apple Shouldn't Censor the App Store," *Complex Tech*, April 11, 2013, http://www.complexmag.ca/tech/2013/04/app-store-controversial-censorship-and-the-social-conflict-behind-it.

66 Chen, *Always On*, 95.

67 Andrew Kohut, "Self-Censorship: Counting the Ways," *Columbia Journalism Review* (May/June 2000): 42–43.

68 Pew Research Center for the People and the Press, *Journalist Avoiding the News: Self-Censorship: How Often and Why*, April 30, 2000, http://www.people-press.org/files/legacy-pdf/39.pdf.

69 Trudy Lieberman, "You Can't Report What You Don't Pursue," *Columbia Journalism Review* (May/June, 2000): 44.

70 Kohut, "Self-Censorship: Counting the Ways," 48.

71 Porter, "Over More than Three Decades."

72 Sarah Ellison, "Murdoch and the Vicious Circle," *Vanity Fair*, October 2011, 172.

73 Frederick W. Mayer, "Stories of Climate Change: The Media and US Public Opinion 2001–2010," Joan Shorenstein Center on the Press, Politics and Public Policy, discussion paper (Cambridge, MA: Harvard University, February 2012); Halpern, "Mind Control & the Internet," 33–35; Aaron McCright and Riley Dunlap, "The Politicization of Climate Change and the Polarization in the American Public's Views of Global Warming 2001–2010," *Sociological Quarterly* 52, no. 2 (Summer 2011): 155–94; W. Lance Bennett, Regina G. Lawrence, and Steven Livingston, *When the Press Fails: Political Power and the News Media from Iraq to Katrina* (Chicago: University of Chicago Press, 2007), 120.

74 Quoted in John Partridge, "Citizen Black," *Globe and Mail*, July 25, 1987: D6.

75 Walter C. Soderlund, Ronald Wagenberg, Kai Hildebrandt, and Walter Romanow, "Ownership Rights vs. Social Responsibility," in *Canadian Newspaper Ownership in the Era of Convergence*, ed. Walter C. Soderlund and Kai Hildebrandt (Edmonton: University of Alberta Press, 2005), 140.

76 C. Edwin Baker, *Media Concentration and Democracy: Why Ownership Matters* (Cambridge: Cambridge University Press, 2007).

77 Jenkins, *Convergence Culture*, 24.

78 Shirky, *Here Comes Everybody.*

79 Freedman, 72.

80 Ibid.

81 Ted Turner, "My Beef with Big Media," *Washington Monthly*, July/August 2004, http://www.washingtonmonthly.com/features/2004/0407.turner.html.

82 Freedman, 89.

83 James Curran, "Reinterpreting the Internet," in James Curran, Natalie Fenton, and Des Freedman, *Misunderstanding the Internet* (New York: Routledge, 2012), 19.

84 Pew Research Center's Project for Excellence in Journalism, *New Media, Old Media: How Blogs and Social Media Agendas Relate and Differ from Traditional Press*, May 23, 2010, http://www.journalism.org/2010/05/23/new-media-old-media/.

85 Steve Lohr, "Study Measures the Chatter of the News Cycle," *New York Times*, July 13, 2009, http://www.nytimes.com/2009/07/13/technology/internet/13influence.html.

86 Pablo Boczkowski and Eugenia Mitchelstein, *The News Gap: When the Information Preferences of the Media and the Public Diverge* (Cambridge, MA: The MIT Press, 2013), 18.

87 C.W. Anderson, *Rebuilding the News: Metropolitan Journalism in the Digital Age* (Philadelphia: Temple University Press, 2013).

88 Darin Barney, *The Network Society* (Cambridge: Polity Press, 2004), 141.

89 Manuel Castells, *Communication Power* (Oxford: Oxford University Press, 2009).

90 Standing Committee on Canadian Heritage, *Our Cultural Sovereignty;* Standing Senate Committee on Transportation and Communications, *Final Report on the Canadian News Media* (Ottawa: House of Commons, 2006).

91 Simon Houpt and Steve Ladurantaye, "Is Bell Too Big?," *Globe and Mail*, September 1, 2012: 9.

Four
Me-media and Political Connectedness (or Not): Cable, Blogs, and YouTube

Media shock has produced a vast kaleidoscope of new spaces for connection and interaction. The era of media scarcity that lasted well into the 1980s has given way to a vast abundance of media choices. Not only is the endless sparkle of stars in the new media sky extraordinary, but so too is the emergence of media tools that have transformed many aspects of our social and professional lives. We are experiencing nothing less than a new culture of communication based on its own rules, rituals, and values. While many scholars identify these changes almost solely with web-based media, any discussion of the effects of the digital revolution and the hyper-fragmentation that it has produced must include the cable explosion. It was the 500-channel universe that broke the stranglehold of the conventional TV networks and created a media culture contoured to individual choices and interests. Cable also fundamentally reshaped news and entertainment in ways that have had a profound effect on the culture and on politics. While cable may have led the way in terms of media fragmentation, the changes wrought by web-based and social media have been breathtaking. Their impact would seem to support Marshall McLuhan's famous claim that changes in media penetrate deeply into the human psyche and nervous systems, altering and rewiring every aspect of our lives.[1]

The problem for scholars is that understanding the effects created by media shock is difficult and illusive. The sheer pace of change, the "acceleration of the acceleration," has made scholars into the functional equivalents of storm chasers, constantly trying to catch up to the latest storm but never quite reaching it before they see a new storm brewing just over the horizon. As Harvard professors John Palfrey and Urs Gasser have put it, "The story of the effect of Internet use on politics is just now breaking; these issues are playing themselves out, right now, in different contexts around the world. The terrain is unsettled. The scholarly field studying these issues is nascent. Empirical evidence is more or less nonexistent."[2] This is especially the case for those who have been trying to assess the political impact being made by the digital revolution. The hot new technology of one election is quickly forgotten as the next medium or device emerges. According to Yaroslav Baran, in Canada, 2004 was touted as the Blackberry election, 2006 was considered the blogging election, 2008 was supposedly the YouTube election, and 2011 was the Twitter election.[3] In each case journalists were almost euphoric about how all of media and indeed democracy was about to change—even as so much of it remained the same.

This chapter reviews some of the debates about the nature of media change first described in Chapter Two. Before beginning our travels across the many jagged edges of media fragmentation, there is one important caveat. As discussed in the previous chapter, while media shock may have ushered in a new culture of communication and even altered our basic orientations and identities, net neutrality and the openness of the media cannot be taken for granted. Corporate giants control much of the access to both cable and web-based media, and they are setting up tollbooths and check-out counters at many key stops. Citizens who can't afford to pay for subscriptions or for the micro-payments that increasingly block entry to websites, TV channels, games, books, and movies may gradually lose their footholds in the media world.

The New Debate about Media Effects

We will begin by looking at the media effects debate through a wide lens before discussing the specific effects of cable, blogs, and YouTube in this chapter, and Facebook and Twitter in the chapter that follows. In the early 1990s, when the Internet first emerged from within the tight enclaves of the scholarly and defence communities that nurtured and sustained it, some observers saw it as the gateway to a more open, inclusive, and dynamic democracy. Uncontrolled, exuberant, experimental, and populist, the Internet would give power back to the people and inspire new forms of deliberation and political activism. Leading experts had an almost unshakeable belief that democracy would be reshaped from the ground up. In 1999, Todd Gitlin boldly predicted that, "Because of technology, relentless horizontal momentum is irreversible. The vertical cannot hold.... Roll over, authorities—the culture of the next millennium is not going your way."[4] Futurist Francis Fukuyama was no less euphoric in his predictions. He claimed that "a society built around information" would value two things above all, freedom and equality, and that "hierarchies of all sorts, political and corporate, have come under pressure and begun to crumble."[5] Esther Dyson was convinced that "the great virtue of the Internet is that it erodes power. It sucks power out of the center, and takes it to the periphery; it erodes the power of institutions over people while giving to individuals the power to run their own lives."[6]

If cyber-euphoria has a king, it is the Spanish media theorist Manuel Castells. In a particular moment of hyper-enthusiasm, Castells argued that the "network" society had become so expansive, powerful, global, and instant that it had the capacity to overwhelm and sideline the nation-state.[7] He predicted that ordinary citizens would be able to participate in a vast, constantly moving, and interactive web of exchanges that would bypass formal structures and old elites. Politics, health care, and community life would all be transformed. Castells would later admit that media conglomerates now dominate many of these networks and that nation-states have a stubborn staying power, levers of control over the organization of daily life, and an emotional bond with their citizens that make them difficult to circumvent, let alone displace. But for Castells the gates are now open to a new human experience: "Our minds—not our machines—process culture.... If our minds have the material capability to access the whole realm of cultural expressions—select them, recombine them—we do have a hypertext: the hypertext is inside us."[8]

As mentioned in Chapter Two, Clay Shirky believes that web-based media have allowed us to create a "cognitive surplus."[9] New vehicles of cooperation and exchange have added to our collective intelligence, as well as to our ability to solve problems. In Shirky's famous phrase, "the Internet runs on love" because it allows people to mobilize around communities of help. Our spaces and experiences are constantly being enlarged. Shirky believes that we are moving forward one idea, one device, and one experience at a time. There are numerous sites where people collaborate, learn, trade, and interact: Wikipedia, eBay, Uber, Airbnb, Reddit, Angie's List, Ted Talks, Khan's Academy, and Kijiji, to name just a few. Then there are apps such as WebMD; IChart (EMR), an app that allows doctors to call up patients' medical charts; Couch to 10 K, an app that provides users with a running coach; Epocates, a drug interaction-site; REV to help mechanics do diagnostics; SoundBrush, which allows musicians to compose and arrange their own music; Waze, which tells drivers the best route to follow "right now"; or the Big Birds Words app, which helps children learn new words. Innocentive and Kaggle are examples of sites that bring researchers together to solve difficult engineering or scientific problems. Hence even as you are reading this, according to Shirky, "people are working hammer and tongs at figuring out the next good idea."[10]

There is also now a burgeoning scientific literature about how the new technologies of communication have altered our thinking patterns. These adaptations are changing how we learn, socialize, connect with others, and live our lives. On the positive side, commentators and scientists such as Steven Johnson, Gary Small, James Gee, Gigi Vorgan, and Jakob Nielson, among others, provide evidence that new web-based media are making us more efficient.[11] Digital natives learn to multi-task, are oriented to networks, and are able to monitor their environments in ways that those who grew up in the pre-digital media world are unable to match. It needs to be pointed out, however, that these conclusions have been sharply disputed. Some studies have found that while some people learn to multi-task well, the vast majority have difficulty juggling many tasks at once and produce slower and poorer responses to problems.[12] They also, according to a study cited by Gardner and Davis, display "cognitive processing that was less flexible and more automatic than subjects engaged in a single task."[13] In other words they are less able to think deeply about a problem.

Even if the digital revolution does not live up to the early euphoria about democratic change, one fact is certain: it is now much more difficult for tyrannical regimes of any kind to take hold. The daily onslaught of hundreds of millions of opinions, images, and interactions has made it almost impossible for any single leader or political regime to impose their views in the ways that the Nazi, Fascist, and Communist regimes did during the twentieth century. Arguably a would-be authoritarian dictator could never rise to power amid a cacophony of 24-hour cable news channels, radio hotline shows, late-night monologues, and blogs where opponents would have equal time and ridicule would be unavoidable. Authoritarian regimes can clearly succeed in environments where a strong civil society and a strong media have not yet taken hold. And while these regimes try to erect firewalls in order to prevent their citizens from being exposed to "alien" thoughts, these attempts may be futile. While blocking strategies may work in the short run, it's difficult to have anything resembling a modern economy without interactions with the rest of the world. Unlike the emperors of old China who chose to burn their ships rather than allow interaction with the rest of the world, scuttling digital media is much more difficult.

Some observers believe that web-based media have already altered the political terrain. While those who are disengaged from civic life have remained disengaged, media shock is allowing those who are already engaged to become even more engaged. While their influence may be felt most strongly at the back end of politics—organizing, fundraising and communicating within and between groups—a new era of citizen politics is already underway. Videos, petitions, citizen journalism, blogs, live tweets from the campaign trail, Facebook groups, vote mobs, and the constant monitoring of political leaders are just the beginnings of what might become a profound revolution.

But where some scholars see the dawning of a new era of democratic expression, others see dark shadows on the horizon. Nicholas Carr, for example, argues that the web is rewiring our brains and making us into "shallow thinkers."[14] The worry is that we have sunk into a state of "continuous partial attention" that impairs our ability to listen attentively to others or to read or think deeply. They worry about the deadening and addictive effects of spending too much time online and, ironically, the degree to which digital media can separate, divide, and isolate people from the very communities that should sustain them and will not be sustainable without them.

Some commentators believe that the idea that we now have greater access to information than ever before is an illusion, a fantasy that floats somewhere on an imaginary cloud. This is because the existence of many more media choices may actually reduce our consumption of news and information rather than expand it. One of the most important standard-bearers of this position is Markus Prior. In his award-winning book *Post-Broadcast Democracy*, Prior demonstrates that the rise of cable and the Internet coincided with a dramatic downturn in voting and other forms of political involvement.[15] The main reason for this collapse was that when the traditional media were dominant in the period from the 1950s to the 1980s, there were so few choices that readers and viewers could not avoid being exposed to relatively heavy doses of news. As a result they tended to follow public affairs and vote in elections. But amid the vast cornucopia of entertainment choices now available on TV and web-based media, many people choose to be "news-less"—they avoid the news entirely. This produces a domino effect. The less people are exposed to news, the less interest they have in politics and hence the lower their level of civic engagement.[16]

Robert Putnam, Cass Sunstein, a respected legal scholar and a former senior official in the Obama administration, and Eli Pariser, the director of MoveOn.Org., are among those who warn that cable and web-based media are creating and reinforcing a series of identity ghettos.[17] Their argument is a variant of the old "selective exposure" thesis: we choose to be exposed only to media that reinforce the views that we already have. Their concern is that as people congregate in their own comfortable media enclaves, the opportunity to meet and exchange ideas with those who have different views is vanishing. Gun owners, Goths, environmentalists, hockey fans, feminists, conspiracy theorists, political activists, and followers of every imaginable show, game, music video, or celebrity all gravitate not to great public spaces, but to the limited and protected confines of their own groups. As Pariser argues, "By definition, a world constructed from the familiar is a world in which there's nothing to learn." For Pariser, the danger is that "you can get stuck in a static, ever-narrowing version of yourself—an endless you-loop."[18] In the end, "the user has become the content."[19]

Some aspects of selective exposure are shaped by "search." Search engines now use algorithms that are based on what previous searches have revealed about a user's interests.[20] Two people typing in the same keywords can be directed to completely different sources. Each of us now has our own customized Google or Yahoo. As the vast majority of users never look beyond the first listings on the first page that's presented to them,[21] this invisible "filter bubble" has a remarkable ability to shape both what we know about a given topic and the nature and quality of public debate. And not only are people being segregated according to the information communities that both they and their search patterns are creating, but the psychology and emotions that go with finding "your place" have an impact as well. As Andrew Leonard, a technology columnist for *Salon*, has put it, "What I find disturbing ... is how easy the internet has made it not just to Google that fact that I need when I need it, but to get the mind-set I want when I want it."[22]

Sunstein believes that the narrowing of our information arteries is occurring in at least two ways. The first is the loss of what scholars call "by-product learning." Sunstein comments on the value of reading a hard-copy newspaper: "Your eyes might come across a story about ethnic tensions in Germany, or crime in Los Angeles, or innovative business practices in Tokyo, or a terrorist attack in India, or a hurricane in New Orleans, and you might read those stories although you would hardly have placed them in your Daily Me."[23] Through newspapers and TV news shows, readers and viewers are exposed to sights, images, and stories that they would not ordinarily encounter through a narrow Internet search. Search is now in effect a deep mining operation that rarely allows a person to move sideways. Or, to put it differently, the filter bubbles created by search and Facebook resemble "cars rather than public transit or busy sidewalks."[24]

Sunstein's second concern is that information ghettos not only expose people to a "limited argument pool," but also "to louder echoes of their own voices."[25] He cites studies that show that when people interact only with those who share their beliefs, their views often become more extreme. This is because as people invest more and more of themselves in a particular lifestyle or cause, the fears and costs of rejection increase. One way to ensure that they are accepted is by taking ever stronger and more sensational positions. In Sunstein's view, the Internet has created a new law of social and political physics: the greater the number of choices, the greater the degree of political polarization within society.

Indeed, Sue Halpern contends that online polarization is now beginning to have a dramatic effect on the nature of political debate. She points out that despite a broad scientific consensus on climate change, between 2001 and 2010 the percentage of Republicans who believed in global warming fell from 49 to 29 per cent. This decline was linked to the one-way mirror of selective media exposure. For Democrats, who were exposed to more progressive media, the percentage went up from 60 to 70 per cent. With the two sides unable to agree on a common set of facts, the possibility of a meaningful debate became non-existent.[26]

The ghettoization argument is supported by the findings of a 2008 study by Kathleen Hall Jamieson and Joseph Cappella.[27] Using multiple surveys, Jamieson and Cappella correlated viewing, listening, and reading patterns with political opinions and allegiances over a ten-year period. They found that while conservatives in the US are exposed to a variety of mainstream media, large numbers gravitate to what the authors describe as a cross-media "echo chamber" consisting of the *Wall Street Journal*, Fox News, and Rush Limbaugh's radio show. Each of these media platforms drew roughly the same ideologically charged audience and championed the same causes. Moreover, each news source tried to inoculate its audience against being "fooled" by the "liberal" media, whose views were caricatured as flabby, elitist, and wrong-headed. Presumably the same echo-chamber effect can also be found among those with liberal views who might congregate around MSNBC, National Public Radio (NPR), blogs such as Talking Points Memo, or The Huffington Post, and newspapers such as the *New York Times* or the *Washington Post*.

While a similar audience study hasn't been conducted in Canada, one can presume that conservatives tend to congregate around their own media watering holes: the Sun News Network, *Sun* newspapers, the *National Post*, Tory bloggers, and talk radio, among other sources. Arguably those on the progressive side would find comfort reading publications such as the *Toronto Star*, the *Ottawa Citizen*, *Maclean's*, the *Walrus*, Rabble.ca or *The Tyee*, and listening to CBC radio.

These divisions were confirmed by a study of blog readers conducted by Eric Lawrence and his colleagues in 2010. They found that "both sides of the ideological spectrum inhabit largely cloistered cocoons of cognitive consonance, thereby creating little opportunity for a substantive exchange across partisan or ideological lines."[28] Their conclusion was that in the blogosphere at least, "self-segregation" trumps broader interaction just about all the time. A study of the Twitterverse published in 2011 by Michael Conover and his colleagues found that the re-tweet network was highly polarized along ideological lines as well. As they note, "many messages contain sentiments more extreme than you would expect to encounter in face-to-face interactions." The study had one caveat: those who accessed the subject areas marked by hashtags were likely to encounter tweets from people who had opposing positions. They doubted, however, that this interaction had any real effect on people with hard ideological views.[29]

Furthermore, in their study of visitors to 119 large news and politics websites, Chicago Booth Business School economists Matthew Gentzkow and Jesse Shapiro found that "isolation" based on the likelihood of meeting someone from another social group or with different views was higher for users of online sites than it was for those who read and watched the traditional media.

Not surprisingly, they found that the greatest isolation was produced by users' choice of friends, co-workers, and neighbours; we gravitate to people who are like us and who share our views.[30]

But not all of the data supports the ghettoization or echo-chamber thesis. Markus Prior has presented evidence that sharply refutes the claim that people are becoming the political equivalent of shut-ins or agoraphobics, afraid to leave their safe and protected media enclaves. He discovered that people who are interested in politics tend to migrate from news program to news program, regardless of whether they are liberal or conservative. Or, to put it another way, political junkies seek out politics wherever they can find it.[31] Studies conducted by Kelly Garrett and Cliff Lampe also refute the segregation argument.[32] While to Garrett the possibility of a "cyber-balkanized" social universe exists, the evidence is hardly clear cut. Lampe found that people on social media sites are better able than others to articulate opposing viewpoints, especially as their circle of friends widens. In broad social and economic terms, however, people on Facebook are communicating with their "friends," or at the very least people with whom they are generally comfortable.

Zizi Papacharissi believes that the problem is not just that the web is populated by groups of like-minded people, but that people engage with politics from the protected cover of private spaces.[33] Social media in particular is about private rather than public space. Although people use social media to keep in contact with and monitor friends and to learn about events, parties, and get-togethers, most of the focus is on "self-performance" and the "management of impressions."[34] Even when it comes to political engagement, "the starting point and the core of all such activity" is the self.[35] Even "friends" are for display: they advertise who we are and are a signature of our social standing. To Papacharissi, digital media have only "a fleeting collective nature."[36]

One of the key questions about the power of social media is whether it gives people the illusion of involvement while failing to deliver the real thing. This is the so-called slacktivist argument. For instance, popular author and thinker Malcolm Gladwell has argued that social media "are effective at increasing *participation*—by lessening the level of motivation that participation requires."[37] People feel that they are participating when they tweet about an issue, attach a video, sign an online petition or read a news story. This gives people the feeling that they have been involved in some way, that they are making a difference. Often this illusion turns into self-deception. Hundreds of thousands of people play "Free Rice," a game whose goal is to feed the hungry, or Folding@home, a game to cure diseases—while little actually happens outside of the game.

Similarly, during the 2012 US presidential election, election turnout on Facebook's election map seemed startlingly high, and studies had suggested that Facebook could as much as "quadruple the power of get-out-the-vote messages."[38] Yet in the country as a whole, voter turnout collapsed by 9 per cent from the previous election with close to 120 million Americans not voting.[39] Clearly the Facebook numbers did not reflect and had little impact on what was happening in the real world. One of the problems for researchers is that the illusion of participation may carry over into surveys, where users enthusiastically describe how much they are engaged in issues and events—even though they never show up when heavy lifting is required. Thomas Friedman of the *New York Times* has put it even more bluntly:

> To be sure, Facebook, Twitter and Blogging are truly revolutionary
> tools of communication and expression that have brought many
> new and compelling voices to light. At their best, they're changing
> the nature of political communication and news. But, at their worst,
> they can become addictive substitutes for real action. How often have
> you heard lately: "Oh, I tweeted about that." Or "I posted that on
> my Facebook page." Really? In most cases, that's about as impactful
> as firing a mortar into the Milky Way galaxy. Unless you get out of
> Facebook and into someone's face, you really haven't *acted*.[40]

Even Clay Shirky, among the chief advocates for the Internet's ability to mobilize change, believes that the step from conversation to meaningful political activity has yet to take place for most users.[41] The irony is that the very virtues that can make online political engagement so effective—such as the ability to react instantly and spontaneously, to spread information quickly, to reach millions, and to stretch across the globe—can also be impediments to action. The conventional wisdom is that online groups are often too leaderless and amorphous to make organized decisions, are too diffuse to operate or "think" strategically, and rarely sustain themselves beyond the initial waves of excitement. Unless there is an underlying organization to begin with, political movements that start online tend to be sporadic and unpredictable, and to evaporate quickly.

On the other hand, Manuel Castells believes that the conventional wisdom misses the point. In his 2012 book *Networks of Outrage and Hope*, Castells focuses on the role played by web-based media in political uprisings and social movements, from Egypt to Spain to the Occupy Wall Street Movement in North America.[42] In his view, Twitter feeds, blogs, YouTube videos, Tumblr photos, and mini-documentaries allowed each of these movements to create their own virtual environments. They each had their own communications architecture and culture. The key to success, however, was whether the power and influence of these newly established cyber-communities could be transferred to the actual spaces where people lived and real decisions were being made. Here the results have been mixed. In Tunisia, Egypt, and Iceland, the social uprisings that occurred in 2011 and 2012 produced dramatic political changes. But in the case of the *Indignadas* movement in Spain, the Occupy movement in the United States, and the electoral triumph of Islamic parties in Egypt, conservative forces eventually overwhelmed the protesters and reclaimed the streets. In Egypt, a brutal military regime that had been ousted by mass demonstrations during the Arab Spring in 2012 was effectively reinstated by mass demonstrations by the very same people in 2013.

But to Castells the battle is not necessarily about gaining immediate political power. The battle is over who has the capacity to create "meaning" and produce the prevailing narratives in society. He believes, for instance, that while the Occupy Wall Street movement could not sustain itself for long in the real political world, it succeeded nonetheless in popularizing the notion that wealth was divided between the 1 per cent and the 99 per cent. Moreover, while these groups may often lose the battles for the public square, their defeat is temporary. In Castells's words,

> In this long journey, the tempos alternate: sometimes accelerating, and then calming down in other moments. But the process never stops, even if it remains unseen for a while. There are roots of the new life spreading everywhere. With no central plan, but moving and networking, keeping the energy flowing, waiting for spring.[43]

Moreover while critics such as Malcolm Gladwell argue that little can be achieved without strong leaders, hard-core political organization, and specific policy solutions, Castells believes that these critics miss the point. It's the very looseness and diversity of these movements, and hence their ability to create their own cyber-environments, that is the signature of their success. Specific policies can wait. My own view is that without the hard casing of specific policies and long-term organization, Castells's promised "spring" might take a long time coming—or never come at all.

One powerful Canadian example of a social movement ignited in part by the use of social media was the Idle No More Campaign in 2013. The movement, which was triggered by the general condition of Aboriginal peoples in Canada, dissatisfaction with inaction by the Harper government on a whole series of fronts, as well as wholesale discontent with the *Indian Act*, produced a small tidal wave of tweets, photos, plays, videos, and artwork. Researcher

Mark Blevis charted close to 900,000 tweets made by 113,000 people over a 2-month period.[44] While the movement succeeded in mobilizing and politicizing many, if not most, Aboriginal youth, it divided the Aboriginal leadership and had little traction within the wider society. In fact, the more Canadians learned about the movement, the less supportive they seemed to be.

As discussed in Chapter Two, elections provide an invaluable scorecard for measuring actual participation. The blunt reality, as Christopher Waddell and I have written with respect to the 2011 Canadian federal election, is that despite considerable hype from journalists about the power of social media, "Social media did not figure prominently in the campaign or its outcome. Available data supports such a conclusion on four grounds—the limited number of people who are active social media participants, the narrow range of issues those people highlighted during the campaign, the lack of impact on the issues that they raised, and the paucity of uses that were found for social media during the campaign."[45] The simple question is this: if social media can't make an impact during elections, then when can they?

Moving away from the world of politics, one of the most widely accepted assumptions about the Internet is that it is a young person's medium. Digital natives are the founding generation of media shock not only because they grew up with new information technologies, but because they were also early adopters as new technological developments took place. For the first time in history, some would argue, the flow of cultural knowledge has been reversed: the young now transfer knowledge to the old. When young people tell their parents about videos circulating on YouTube, print out a Google map, teach them to Skype, or show off the latest apps on their cell phones, the traditional hierarchies for the transmission of knowledge are being disrupted. Anyone who has visited a university recently will know that the way that information is being communicated is changing dramatically. The medical student who answers a question on rounds by showing the senior physician her smart-phone screen with an answer that she has just Googled; students whose first and last stop on a research project is Wikipedia; and Facebook groups that form their own communities within classes, in effect creating an educational space that runs parallel to the class but that excludes the professor—all of these scenarios, and more, are in the process of overturning long-established hierarchies and traditions of teaching and authority.

One extraordinary example occurred at the University of Calgary when two students, Steven and Keith Pridgen, were expelled for creating a Facebook page devoted to criticizing their instructor. A Court of Queen's Bench judgement handed down in 2010 ruled against the university. The judge reasoned that "students should not be prevented from expressing critical opinions regarding the subject matter or the quality of the teaching that they are receiving."[46] In short, professors need to be aware that the boundaries of their classrooms may now extend into the deep furrows of cyberspace, a realm over which they have no control.

While the assumption that online activity belongs to the young is undoubtedly true, middle-aged and older people are now heavy users of social media. In fact, data collected in 2011 show that while 86 per cent of Canadians between 18 and 34 use social media, 67 per cent of those between 35 and 54, and 40 per cent of those 55 and over, are users as well.[47] Moreover, when it comes to sites devoted to news and politics, older citizens make up a remarkably large percentage of users. According to one study, almost 60 per cent of those who visited political sites were 45 or older.[48] These numbers parallel other aspects of civic engagement. Just as those who are older and economically better off tend to vote, volunteer, donate, and join associations more frequently than others, so too are they more likely to visit political sites online.

What differentiates younger users, however, is texting. In fact, a Pew study found that most teenagers text at a furious pace, sending 50 or more text messages per day—and one-third send more than 100.[49] For many, texting has become addictive and also stressful, as users feel that they always have to be messaging, always have to reply immediately, and always have to be on. For some digital natives, the texting compulsion is now so great that they treat earlier tools such as email and blogging as almost prehistoric.

Facebook, together with other web-based media and, of course, smart phones, has helped create what can be described as a portable bubble, a self-enclosed media world that we carry with us wherever we go. This has led to a new phenomenon: "absence-in-presence" and "presence-in-absence." The first occurs when people are texting, checking their Facebook page, or watching videos on their smart phones while they are at business meetings, attending classes, at the dinner table, or even in face-to-face conversations. While multi-tasking has become a way of life, part of the new normal, for many people it's still a bit of a shock to be in a room where people are "absent"—meaning that their attention is elsewhere—even while they are present. What is surprising is the extent to which this continual state of partial attention and distraction seems to have become widely accepted, despite the offence that it might give to those who are being ignored. Just as we seem to have created a generation of peek-a-boo citizens, we now have peek-a-boo appearances by people whose attention is increasingly divided, sporadic, and fleeting even when they are sitting across from you at the same table. Stanford University researcher Clifford Nass believes that the result of this fixation with technology is that it diminishes both empathy toward others and the humanity of those around us. As Nass argues, "The way we become more human is by paying attention to each other. It shows how much you care."[50]

The other side of the coin is that web-based technologies allow us to maintain connections with family members or friends even when they are far away. They are in effect "present in absence." We can be at dinner tables or in classrooms or look at the sky or other features of the landscape thousands of miles away. Dhiraj Murthy believes that the "telepresence" of visitors in hospital rooms, whether through Twitter or Skype or text messaging, has given great comfort to people who would otherwise feel alone or helplessly at a distance.[51] In their multi-generational study of youth and identity, Howard Gardner and Katie Davis found that a remarkable number of young people today have never had the experience of being lost.[52] They have apps to give them directions across the city, and their parents are always in reach. They are safe unless their smart phones are lost. This may be as good as it gets in terms of the erosion of time and space—at least until we invent a transporter like the one used on *Star Trek* to beam us from one place to another in the galaxy.

In a world of glaring inequalities, wide disparities exist between those who are already socially connected and those who aren't. Robert Putnam's claim that social capital in terms of wealth, education, and engagement in community life is the "pre-requisite for, rather than a consequence of, effective computer-mediated communication" resonates through virtually all of the surveys that have been conducted on Internet use.[53] People who already have a rich social and cultural life use the Internet to become even more connected, while those without strong relationships or resources offline are unlikely to be able to find them in cyberspace. For instance, Craig Watkins's study of social media found that the young people that he surveyed did not "friend" strangers online; they "friend" friends.[54] While social media may help maintain "the strength of weak ties," in Mark Granovetter's much-quoted phrase, these ties are usually with those who already have abundant connections and resources.[55]

Certainly the divisions between the rich and the poor, and the educated and the undereducated, are as evident on the web as they are on city streets or in the workforce. This is likely to be increasingly the case as subscriptions and micro-payments become more widespread. According to surveys conducted by the Pew Internet and American Life Project in 2010, those with incomes in excess of $75,000 were twice as likely to get their news online as those with incomes that were less than $30,000.[56] A 2008 Pew study found that while 95 per cent of those with at least some graduate education were online, only 38 per cent of those who did not graduate from high school were online.[57] There is little reason to believe that these statistics would be any different in Canada.

A last point before we proceed. The Internet is also a place of danger. For all of its many wonders, the Internet is an emporium of scams, come-ons, hate and sex sites, and dangerous fantasies and addictions. Cyber-bullying has reached devastating proportions, with bullies able to remain anonymous and continue their threats and intimidation long after their victims have left the schoolyard or the workplace. Predators and con artists lurk everywhere, and the back alleys of the Internet are often nasty places where no one, especially children, should venture.

For instance, much of the web is a virtual red-light district that is difficult for even the youngest users to avoid. Psychiatrist Elias Aboujaoude reports that the average Internet user spends at least 15 minutes each day visiting pornographic sites,[58] with over 10 per cent of all web pages, 25 per cent of all searches, and 35 per cent of all downloads containing pornographic materials.[59] The amount of traffic that goes to pornography sites is at least five times larger than the audience for news and media sites.[60] The Internet is also a reservoir of hate and racism. One report published in 2011 claimed that there were as many as 15,000 hate and terror sites on the web.[61] White supremacists, jihadists, Holocaust deniers, and old-fashioned cranks and creeps, in some cases writing from prison, are all posting their own distorted versions of history and spinning webs of hate.

As will be discussed later in the next chapter, privacy has also become a major concern. Although most users don't realize it, they are the Internet's main product. Or, to put it differently, what they don't realize is that their laptops, smart phones, and tablets are spying on them. Companies have made "big data" into big business by aggregating, packaging, and selling information about the tastes, purchases, and lifestyles of their users. In fact, all major businesses buy or compile data all the time and use it to monitor their environments with the same intensity with which a wolf hunts its prey. While, on the positive side, Big Data has become an extraordinary instrument of public policy, data can be easily misused or fall into the wrong hands. Scholars are worried that society's obsession with data, and with turning every conceivable grain of human activity into those data, can rob us of our creativity, independence, and privacy.[62]

Some scholars fear that we now live in a surveillance society, where companies such as Facebook can prosper only if they are able to push back the walls of personal privacy and make public what was once private. Arguably citizens know that they have entered into an unsavoury bargain:

they have agreed to give up their privacy in exchange for the advantages that come with being online. The end result may be, as Scott McNally of Sun Microsystems famously put it, "You already have zero privacy. So get over it."[63]

The rest of this chapter will focus on three information technologies that have splintered audiences and helped create the Me-media environment. The goal is to examine the effects that cable, the blogosphere, and YouTube appear to be having on citizen involvement and the nature and quality of public life.

The Cable Explosion

The vast public squares and the nation-building experiences created by radio and then by the early days of television did not last for long. The era when TV networks could assemble mass audiences lasted from roughly the mid-1950s to the late 1980s. Although Canadians still gather on the main conventional channels for nightly news shows, popular events such as the NHL playoffs and the Grey Cup, or to watch hit shows such as *Dancing with the Stars* or *Survivor*, the explosion of cable channels that began in the 1980s ushered in a new era of narrowcasting and media fragmentation. Audiences were soon splintered along the knife edges of cable TV, and with it the era of highly customized Me-media had begun.

Because of the country's vast distances and the desire of Canadians to access popular US channels, the degree of cable penetration in Canada has been among the highest in the world. Ken Goldstein, one of the country's leading media experts, notes that subscriptions charged to customers by cable and satellite providers (broadcasting distribution undertakings [BDUs], in CRTC parlance) and then passed through to the specialty channels that they carry surpassed advertising as the main source of revenue for Canadian television in 1991, while the same tipping point was not reached in the US or the UK until 2003.[64] Canada became a subscription culture long before most other countries. Since that time the move away from over-the-air conventional TV has picked up speed. While network TV accounted for 79 per cent of all TV revenues in 1998, it fell to just 43 per cent in 2010.[65] Most Canadians now have access to between 60 to 80 channels, and in many cases hundreds more.

While much of cable is a dreary landscape—of reruns; filler shows about brides, dieters, northern pilots, survivalists, snake handlers, hoarders, swamp people, and truckers; documentaries that in some cases haven't been seen in decades; talking heads; and low-budget travel, food, and home-renovation shows—to its credit, cable has also become a place for experimentation, where off-beat and edgy shows can capture niche audiences. Cable has also created opportunities for channels such as History, Discovery, Showcase, and Arts and Entertainment, which feature highly specialized programs with loyal, if small, niche audiences. There are also a myriad of other broadcasters, such as Vision TV—the so-called Zoomer TV because it targets older Canadians—or FX Canada, which specializes in edgy, off-beat, and sometimes dark shows. In the case of the former, the programming is too staid and too yesterday; in the latter, too controversial or quirky for the conventional networks to touch.

Cable TV is divided into two very different universes: Big TV and Little TV. Beginning in the early part of this century, a handful of cable channels and online TV producers have ushered in a new golden age of mass-market TV: Big TV. In the US, the much-celebrated subscription channel HBO, owned by Time Warner, and channels such as Showtime and AMC, as well as new online broadcasters such as Netflix, have produced a new generation of hyper-serialized, edgy, brilliantly acted and scripted shows that have turned TV watching on its ear. People now engage in binge viewing, sometimes watching an entire season in a few days, pay by subscription, and follow characters that are mostly bad, violent, and greedy. Shows such as *The Sopranos, The Wire, Six Feet Under, Curb Your Enthusiasm, Homeland, Mad Men, Breaking Bad, House of Cards, Game of Thrones*, and *True Detective* are among a host of new mass audience shows in recent years. Such shows are challenging the supremacy of the over-the-air conventional networks and pose a particular threat to Canadian TV networks, which lack the budgets and arguably the skill and gumption to compete. For Canadian networks, Big TV is turning into the equivalent of an endless missile barrage against which there is little defence.

But just as cable can be big, it can also be very small. The headlong rush into cable and satellite received a strong push from the federal government and the CRTC. The idea was to flood the airwaves with Canadian content by adding countless hours of relatively cheap-to-produce sports, children's, music, and news programming. The CRTC has tried to maintain a preponderance of Canadian specialty channels, and while virtually every Canadian specialty channel is inundated with American programming, they all have had to abide by Canadian-content requirements. While the Canadian-content obligations of specialty channels are less than those for the over-the-air conventional channels, the reality is that cable is helping to Canadianize the airwaves. Indeed the viewing of English-language Canadian programs has skyrocketed since 1997 when it was only 27 per cent of total TV viewing. In 2012 it had reached close to 40 per cent.[66]

The quality of these shows is another matter. Most are inexpensive, cookie-cutter imitations of American reality shows. However entertaining, zany, or cute these shows might be, they are hardly what nationalists had in mind when they first fought for Canadian-content requirements. Some shows, such as *Ice Pilots of the NWT*, have attracted international followings, although I can't imagine that its cast of crusty characters and visuals of frozen tundra have done much to boost Canada's image abroad.

While specialty channels are supposed to boost Canadian arts and culture, Canada is often an afterthought. John Doyle, the *Globe and Mail*'s popular and insightful television columnist, was furious when Bravo!, whose offices are in the heart of the vibrant cultural scene in downtown Toronto, aired *Work of Art: The Next Great Artist*, a program that showcased up-and-coming American artists. As Doyle wrote at the time, "this is where I live, where I vote and where I spend my money. It matters, today of all days. If the corporation that owns Bravo! is considered a person, it might want to shift its rear end and just walk around outside to find its art stars. Enough with the cheap imports, already."[67] In cable land, Canadians are more often than not watching shows about pawnbrokers in Louisiana, young couples searching for homes in Houston or Cleveland, "real" housewives in Atlanta or in Orange County, murder trials in places like Florida and Utah, cuisine in Chicago, or haunted houses in New England. Rednecks are everywhere on cable; but Newfoundlanders, Québécois, and Albertans are hard to find.

There are a number of reasons for cable's extraordinary success. Perhaps the most important is that specialty channels have a stronger financial base than conventional TV. Specialty channels have two financial pillars: subscription fees and advertising. Conventional over-the-air broadcasters such as CTV or Global have had to rely on advertising as their only revenue source. The conventional broadcasters hoped that they could change the equation by forcing BDUs to pay for their signals. This led to an acrimonious battle between the main broadcasters and BDUs, with both sides airing ads to appeal to the public. Although the CRTC changed the rules to allow conventional over-the-air broadcasters to negotiate subscription fees with cable and satellite providers, the Supreme Court of Canada overruled the CRTC in a 5–4 decision issued in December 2012.

Perhaps the most potent factor in the success of specialty channels is that they allow broadcasters to offer advertisers access to readily identifiable niche audiences. Advertisers now know where to find sports and music fans, children, young mothers, older women, history buffs, pet lovers, news junkies, and businesspeople, as well as those interested in travel, fitness, violent sports, beauty products, or home improvements. Audiences can now be categorized, bundled, and delivered to advertisers in neat packages.

Cable also benefited from the fact that conventional broadcasters such as Global, CTV, and TVA have been caught in a vicious circle. The more viewers migrated to speciality channels, the more conventional over-the-air broadcast-ers tried to "re-aggregate" or "reassemble" their audiences by establishing their own key outposts along the cable frontier. Almost all Canadian specialty chan-nels are now owned by the same media conglomerates that own conventional broadcasters. Media giants are still trying to catch up to their audiences—although the scramble is now leading them to Internet TV and mobile devices.

While conventional over-the-air broadcasters have had to face the full blast of competition brought by media shock, BDUs were in the enviable position of being "too protected to fail" at least until recently. In fact, one former TV executive has described cable as "one of the all-time great business models."[68] Once the cable pioneers convinced people to pay for something that they used to get for free, the rest was easy. This is because BDUs operate more like utilities than ordinary businesses. They are shielded by laws that protect them from foreign ownership, enjoy virtual monopoly status within various regions of the country, and have captive audiences that have little choice but to accept their rates and services. As mentioned previously, cable operators have raised rates by four times the rate of inflation since 2002.[69]

In one of the great moves in Canadian business history, in 2011 BDUs were able to achieve what was in effect a reverse takeover: the lion's share of conventional TV stations were bought by companies that owned BDUs. Shaw was able to pick up the pieces after CanWest Global went bankrupt, Rogers Media took over CityTV, Bell Media owns CTV, and TVA is controlled by Quebecor Media. The once fateful line between carriage and content has been all but obliterated as TV networks are now part of much broader "vertical inte-gration" strategies. Inexplicably, however, the federal government still governs the broadcasting system as if none of this had taken place. The system operates under the canopy of two distinct acts: the *Broadcasting Act* of 1991 and the *Telecommunications Act* of 1993. While the convergence of every medium with every other medium is one of the principal realities of media shock, the federal government's media policy seems to be lost in time, around the mid-1990s.

But cable is not without its problems. In fact one can argue that it is entering an era of potentially shattering turbulence. The next waves of media shock are likely to make "cord cutting" much more popular, as online TV services such as Apple TV, Netflix, YouTube, and Hulu bring even greater variety and more affordable viewing. BDUs are well aware that online broad-casting from outside Canada could sweep them away or at the very least leave them deeply wounded. Media pundit Michael Wolff believes that cable's days at the top of the media heap are numbered. As he emphatically predicts,

> The cable programming business—running, practically speaking,
> on consumer inertia—doesn't work anymore, and shouldn't. It's too

costly and inefficient. It will die. This is easy. There will not be a cable business in five years, at least not a healthy one. This is so evident that in the media business one is not even regarded as a Cassandra to say as much, but rather a killjoy.[70]

One question that needs to be addressed is whether the CRTC's policy of binge licensing damaged the broadcasting system by weakening the major networks and lowering their ability to produce quality programming. In other words, did more channels produce less real choice? The answer is definitely yes. One can argue that there are a variety of ways in which the cable revolution has weakened the structures of Canadian television.[71] First, there is little question that the cable explosion wounded conventional broadcasters by siphoning away audiences and advertising revenues, a process that has been accelerated by the onslaught of online broadcasters. The networks have cut news divisions, invest as little as possible in Canadian drama, and have largely become "re-broadcasters" of American shows.

Local stations may have been the hardest hit by the cable explosion. Local TV news shows, which are the signposts of their stations, are easily lost amid the dense forest of 24-hour news, sports, business, weather, and celebrity channels. While local news stations may have the market cornered on reporting local events, many have been reduced to little more than shoestring operations, with few reporters and little money for investigative work. As local reporting is part of the connective tissue of community life, the weakening and possible breaking of this vital link is a critical issue. For example, when Calgary was devastated by floodwaters in summer 2013, local TV stations were a lifeline, providing vital and sometimes desperately needed information to citizens. Without this lifeline, emergency efforts would not have been nearly as effective.

Most crucially, faced with intense competition because of the proliferation of channels, the main over-the-air broadcasters have been reluctant to invest large sums of money in high-quality productions. The cost of producing a major Canadian drama is roughly $2 million an hour, with costs continually rising (compared to $3–4 million an hour and up for major Hollywood shows). Not only can Canadian broadcasters buy programs off the shelf in Hollywood for far less than the cost of producing a similar show in Canada, but Hollywood shows also benefit from having recognizable stars and expensive promotion campaigns. Given this reality, why would broadcasters undertake the financial risks associated with producing signature Canadian productions when the prospects of hitting the jackpot, of creating a hit series, in a 500-channel Me-media universe are relatively small?

Unfortunately, this has become a Catch-22. The less money is invested in Canadian shows, the less likely these programs are to attract large audiences. The circle of taking few chances and getting few rewards rarely gets broken. Why Canadian TV continually fails to produce great dramas—the equivalent of what HBO, the BBC, or Showtime produce on a regular basis—is hardly a mystery. The simple and perhaps brutal reality is that Canadian broadcasters have decided, with some exceptions perhaps, that they can no longer compete. There is one major exception—and that is in Quebec, where French-language drama remains popular, creative, and successful. This is largely because language limits the appeal of Hollywood TV, but also because the TV networks have been able to tell meaningful Quebec stories.

The cable revolution has been especially damaging to the CBC. The licences for sports, music, and children's channels are the most coveted and lucrative spaces in the cable universe, and these licences have all been awarded to private broadcasters. In Europe, public-service broadcasters such as the BBC in the UK, and ARD and ZDF in Germany were granted valuable footholds on the mountaintops of cable TV when licences were being awarded. Aside from its all-news channels—CBC News Network and Réseau de l'information de Radio-Canada—and a smattering of niche operations such as Bold, Documentary, and ARTV which are not on basic cable packages, the CBC has been cut out of the action. Had the CBC been given even one or two of the more lucrative licences, it could have enjoyed increased and more dependable revenues, as well as greater economies of scale. In retrospect, one can argue that it was the denial of the prime spaces on cable that inflicted the deepest wounds on public broadcasting.

Canadians now have access to an ever expanding kaleidoscope of general sports channels, each of which broadcasts games, provides highlight packages, and offers lively banter about stars, coaches, referees, scandals, and trades. In sports television the buzz never stops. These channels have impressive websites that feature game updates, highlights, and re-broadcasts, host fantasy leagues, invite fan comments, and contain galleries of photos. In addition to general sports channels, ESPN offers a fleet of its own channels, and there are also specialty channels for football, racing, golf, or soccer aficionados, as well as team and league channels such as Leafs TV, the NHL Network, or NBA TV Canada. There are also specialty channels in the upper reaches of the cable stratosphere devoted to sports legends, classic games, college, and even local amateur sports. Ticket packages such as "Centre Ice" or "NFL Ticket" on pay-per-view channels are available for the playoffs or for entire seasons. One TV channel, NFL Red Zone, covers all of the games on a given Sunday by showing every key play in real time. And this is just the tip of the sports iceberg. With the advent of web TV, as well as the proliferation of applications designed for smart phones and tablets, fans have access to scores, shows, games, and highlights on any screen and from wherever they may be.

The Bell Media/Rogers takeover of the Maple Leafs was driven largely by the need to control live sports entertainment. The theory is that live sports will keep customers from cord cutting and will attract smart-phone and tablet users. Live sport is seen as the strategic high ground of media power: control sport and, as in the movie *Field of Dreams*, "they will come." This was certainly Rogers's motivation in inking a $5.2-million, 12-year deal with the NHL for exclusive broadcasting rights to Canada-wide games. Sports is now so central that in 2012–13, 23 out of the top 25 rated shows in all of US television were NFL games.[72] Interestingly, aside from the Olympics, the largest audiences for sports in Canada have been for either World Junior Hockey Championship Games or the Grey Cup.

What has emerged is a "sports on demand" culture, an enormous and relentless engine that is in continuous forward motion, always looking ahead to the next game, the next tournament, the next week, always breathlessly in suspense. The centrality of sports culture raises important societal issues. One of them is the phenomenon of the "deep" fan and what Umberto Eco calls "sports 'cubed.'"[73] For some fans, sports have become so available and so all-consuming, and their knowledge of sports so integral to their identity, that they have few reference points outside of it. Eco believes that the joy and innocence of sports are now overshadowed by a professional sports entertainment complex that endlessly promotes, refers to, and feeds off itself. At the same time, participation in amateur sports in Canada is spiralling downwards.[74]

Fantasy leagues are now at the heart of the "sports cubed" phenomenon. Based primarily on the NFL, close to 50 million people now manage teams in fantasy leagues of one kind or another. Fantasy leagues are promoted by a barrage of websites, sports channels, and the leagues themselves. The effects on the media and sports culture have been dramatic. Where most fans used to follow one team exclusively, either their hometown team or another team that appealed to them based on memories or favourite players, loyalties are now scattered across a spectrum of teams as fans now follow their fantasy choices. As a result, TV viewing is up because fans have a stake in more games. The networks now schedule games featuring teams that have players who are popular in fantasy leagues as much as they choose games that might be crucial in determining which teams actually make the playoffs. In the end they have a mix of both.

The third and perhaps biggest change is that cable has altered the boundaries of taste and morality. Faced with intense competition, cable programming has become increasingly sensational, desperate, and bizarre. Extreme fighting, the glamorization of gambling (especially poker), makeover shows that promote plastic surgery, bounty hunters, tattoo artists, mob wives, multiple programs about ghosts, sadistic reality shows that bring pain and humiliation, and an endless parade of celebrity villains have become the steady diet of cable TV. While aliens from other planets may not have shown up in your neighbourhood, they are everywhere on cable TV. In effect, behaviours and interests that were once considered eccentric and marginal have become central, at least on cable.

Cable TV has helped create what can best be described as a shock culture. There may be little that can shock us because all of the previous thresholds have been broken, but cable TV continues to lower the bar. Shows about psychic children who communicate with the dead, inmates on death row, UFO hunters, teen moms, midget wrestlers, gypsy weddings, and the world's most dangerous police chases are meant to provide voyeuristic thrills, however gruesome and outlandish they might be. At one point there was even a trio of shows—*Half-ton Dad*, *Half-ton Mom*, and *Half-ton Teen*—about people who are so grotesquely overweight that they could no longer leave their beds. Presumably some viewers find such sad and horrifying displays of human suffering to be pleasurable in some way.

Some shows allow us to mock the rich, while others allow us to supposedly feel better by showing us people who are experiencing the worst moments in their lives: being arrested, rejected by lovers, or having their homes and cars repossessed while their neighbours are looking on. Among the most shocking shows are programs that up the ante in terms of their veneration for violence. One show, *Deadliest Warriors*, portrays the arsenals of weapons used by various groups in history such as samurai warriors, the Incas, the Navajos, and Roman gladiators, and the damage that they can do to opponents. The show revels in displays of blood and carnage. Whatever its merits as a history show, the program is a seminar on how to kill efficiently. *1000 Ways to Die* is, if anything, even more grotesque. Under the guise of informing people about medical and safety issues, the show depicts the hideous circumstances in which people who are inevitably described as born losers or too stupid to save themselves meet their untimely ends. But even these shows pale next to programs about hospital emergency rooms where dying patients are shown in their final moments. A more grotesque violation of people's dignity and privacy is hard to imagine.

Interestingly, Canadian satellite and cable operators seem to have few qualms about carrying the specialty channels that air these shows. Surprisingly, and perhaps shamefully, Canadian educators and commentators have had little to say about this race to the bottom. The CRTC has all too predictably done nothing.

Another profound change brought by cable has been to news and public-affairs programming. On the surface at least, Canadians now have access to a veritable smorgasbord of news shows. In addition to over-the-air broadcasters, Canadians can now watch CBC News Network, CPAC, RDI, the Sun News Network, Le Canal Nouvelles, BBN, APTN, and a myriad of ethnic broad-casters. Canadians also have access to copious amounts of news and political punditry from foreign sources such as the BBC, Fox News, MSNBC, TV 5, Al Jazeera, CNBC, and CNN, including broadcasts from countries as diverse as India, Italy, and France. We live in an "all-news, all the time" culture, a 24-hour—and some would argue 24-minute—news cycle.

The irony of this proliferation of news programs, however, is that more news may be producing less information. Cable broadcasters have found that they can make money by endlessly re-broadcasting stories, appealing to small niche audiences, and filling the screen with pretty faces and panels of obscure experts and party mouthpieces. In fact, broadcasters such as Fox or MSNBC in the US, and Sun News Network in Canada, have found that appealing to a small sliver of the ideologically faithful can be profitable. Hence some all-news channels have become continuous 24-hour pep rallies for one par-ticular point of view, with no pretense of objective reporting, giving a fair hearing to another point of view, or reaching out to a wider audience. The worst part of this hyper-partisanship is that it turns the normal forces of political gravity on their head. Politicians and pundits who take strong ideo-logical positions are rewarded with even greater coverage, while those who seek compromises or take a middle-ground position are mocked and vilified. Not only has this changed politics by exacerbating political divisions, but the very idea of the news media as a source of neutral and trusted information has broken down.[75] Journalists no longer have to be accountable to standards that have been the bedrock of journalism for generations.

Moreover, cable news executives have had to adapt to the shock cul-ture that permeates almost all of cable TV. This is especially the case in the American cable universe, where the obsession with crime and celebrities has reached epidemic proportions, and where such stories are routinely given more airtime than news about government policies, health care, the economy, the environment, or global politics. High-profile murder trials, for instance, can dominate coverage for months, sidelining other news stories regardless of how important they may be for the economy or the functioning of govern-ments. In addition, news broadcasts are constantly being interrupted by "fast breaking" stories, most of which are little more than "snowflake news"—stories that disappears from sight almost as soon as they are reported. The latest news, regardless of how trivial it might be, constantly replaces other news, regardless of how important it may be. There is always a murder, a trial, a fire, or a weather alert occurring somewhere in North America that demands immediate attention. The idea is to provide viewers with a steady supply of jolts and maintain the illusion that news organizations are "on top" of the latest stories.

Even when serious public policy issues are discussed, the formats are designed to create and enhance the spectacle of conflict rather than provide deeper analysis and discussion. The guiding philosophy on many shows is that viewers want to see the verbal equivalent of car crashes, and that personal attack, rudeness, interruptions, outrageous comments, and hyper-partisanship will attract viewers. Hence panels usually have a pro-con, for-and-against structure, and the guests who appear are invited on because of the verbal pyrotechnics that they all too willingly provide. Interestingly, a University of Pittsburgh study found that politicians with extreme views were quoted far more often than those with moderate views.[76] Tom Friedman of the *New York Times* has described the degeneration of political debate on television in the US in this way: "the rise of cable TV has transformed politics in our country generally into another spectator sport, like all-star wrestling. C-Span is just like ESPN with only two teams. We watch it for entertainment, not solutions."[77]

Fed up with shows that, while masquerading as journalism, were nothing more than screaming matches, Jon Stewart of Comedy Central attacked the hosts of CNN's *Crossfire* when he appeared on the show in 2004. He scolded the hosts for a format that was based on "partisan hackery" and for abandoning any responsibility for the quality of public discourse.[78] The show was cancelled soon after Stewart's demolition job but was resurrected in 2013. For-and-against formats have continued to thrive because they are cheap and easy to produce, and news managers believe that confrontation sells.

Nor is Canada immune to the values of the cable news culture. Although cable news shows in Canada provide far less theatre, the Sun News Network follows the Fox News formula of "total partisanship." While touting itself as the network that fights for ordinary people against established power, it neglects to inform its viewers that it is owned by media giant Quebecor, the very embodiment of Big Media. While the other news channels are not as ideological as Sun TV, they are dominated by a steady stream of "talking heads" who are usually journalists or political operatives chosen because they are on different sides of an issue. Investigative reports, deep background, and discussions with real experts on any topic are increasingly rare.

None of this takes away from the fact that there are pockets of real excellence in cable news. *Morning Joe* on MSNBC is a breakthrough show both in its use of an informal breakfast table style and in its long and substantive political discussions. C-Span offers exceptional programming, as do the multitude of documentary channels that provide searing glimpses into the world's problems and injustices. The BBC's long-form news reports and coverage of world events are impressive. CBC News Network and CPAC, the Cable Public Affairs Channel, broadcast Question Period in the House of Commons, and CPAC airs oral arguments made before the Supreme Court of Canada. Admittedly, however, the audiences for Question Period and for oral arguments before the court are so minuscule that one wonders how they could possibly get smaller.

Another byproduct of the dominance of cable TV has been the off-loading of politics from the main channels to the back alleys of cable TV. With obvious exceptions such as CBC's *The National's* much-watched and excellent "At Issue" panel, an equivalent panel on Radio-Canada's *Le Téléjournal,* investigative shows such as the CBC's *The Fifth Estate* and Radio-Canada's *Enquête,* CTV's *W5,* and a few dismal Sunday news shows that attract tiny audiences, political debate and discussion have all but vanished from the main over-the-air conventional channels. This devaluing of political discussion has deprived the political system of the oxygen supply that comes with access to larger audiences, but more subtly it sends a message that political issues are just not important.

As previously mentioned, Markus Prior, a survey researcher at Princeton University, provides statistical evidence to back up concerns about the role played by cable TV in the decentring of political life in the US.[79] After an exhaustive study that correlated audience trends with voter turn-out, Prior concluded that media fragmentation was almost single-handedly to blame for reducing voter turnout in elections and for triggering a downward slide in civic knowledge. As discussed above, he found that during the 1960s and 1970s when there were far fewer channels, large numbers of people watched news programs (because they couldn't avoid them), and as a consequence, people knew more about public affairs and were highly motivated to vote. Following the explosion of specialty channels and with far more choices available to them, viewers could avoid news shows entirely, and the number of people who voted dropped dramatically. Prior asks a simple but disturbing question: "When media users get what they want all the time, does anyone get hurt?"[80] His troubling answer is that "their new found freedom may hurt both their own interests and the collective good."[81]

Cable has arguably also done little to improve our knowledge of Canadian history. One of the reasons that Canadians may have little knowledge about their history is that it's been largely erased from network television. While there have been extravaganzas such as CBC's *Canada: A People's History* or *The Greatest Canadian* contest, and a wide range of mini-series on events such as the Halifax explosion or the Diefenbaker government's decision to cancel the Avro Arrow jet fighter, and on political leaders such as Louis Riel, Maurice Duplessis, Pierre Trudeau, and René Lévesque, history-based shows are now few and far between. History in effect has been relegated to specialty channels such as the History Channel, which has widened its mandate to include almost any movie made before 2010 and shows about pickers, pawn-brokers, and alien invasions. These shows "drive by" rather than visit history.

Aboriginal Canadians are also missing from network TV. While the goal in creating the Aboriginal Peoples Television Network was to provide a larger showcase for Aboriginal life, it may have played a role in creating a smaller showcase on the main channels. This is because it relieved the networks of the responsibility to deal with native issues and cultures. I could not help but think, after reading Mary Jane Miller's remarkable book *Outside Looking In*, about the depiction of Aboriginal peoples in prime-time Canadian TV dramas, that it is unlikely that programs on the scale of *Spirit Bay*, *The Rez*, or *North of 60* will ever be made again. As mentioned earlier, big dramas have become too expensive and hence too risky for broadcasters to produce, and a show dealing with Aboriginal Canadians may be even riskier still.[82] There are notable exceptions, however, for example CTV's *Corner Gas* and CBC's *Arctic Air* have had strong Aboriginal characters.

In the end, one is left wondering whether governments and regulators should have taken more seriously the warning issued by the distinguished media scholar Elihu Katz before they opened the floodgates to hyper-fragmentation. As Katz predicted:

> Why are governments contributing to the erosion of nation-states and national cultures? Why don't they see that more leads to less to insignificance ... to endless distraction, to the atomization and evacuation of public space? Why don't they see that national identity and citizen participation are compromised? Why don't they realize that they're contributing directly to the erosion of the enormous potential which television has to enlighten and unite populations into the fold of national cultures?[83]

While television systems around the world have travelled down these same paths, not all Western countries have opened the door to the almost unlim-ited expansion that Canada has. While there is much that is good in the cable and satellite universe, there is also a great deal to be concerned about. In 1961, Newton Minow, a former head of the Federal Communications Commission in the US, referred to television as a "wasteland."[84] Much of that TV wasteland can still be found on cable.

The Blog Hierarchy

A blog (short for weblog) is a webpage on which people can post observations, gossip, news, advice, videos, photos, and advertisements. In most cases they are unedited and unsupervised by others. Posts are archived and appear in reverse chronological order so that visitors can follow a blogger's thoughts over time. Most critically, bloggers usually invite and receive comments from their readers so that successful bloggers attract a continuing flood of responses. Bloggers also create a "blogroll" linking their sites to other websites or blogs that have similar interests or views, with the result that they are then bound together in what superblogger Andrew Sullivan has described as "a seamless and endless conversation."[85]

In the Canadian political blogosphere, bloggers have created distinct blogging communities where bloggers continually react to, promote, and reinforce each other's views. Conservative bloggers have formed the Blogging Tories, Liberal bloggers the Liblogs, New Democrats the Blogging Dippers, and Green bloggers, Quebec bloggers, and Saskatchewan bloggers—to name just a few groups—have formed similar communities. The entire political blogosphere probably contains about 300 hard-core blogs, although blogs come and go with relative frequency, and their levels of activity vary widely.

Beyond politics, a constellation of Canadian blogging communities has formed around topics as diverse as hockey, wine tasting, organic farming, spirituality, the music scene, and urban issues. Then there are blogs that are basically corporate public relations in another form—business executives, magazine editors, political leaders, directors of organizations, and so on, who blog because they feel that it makes them appear more approachable, engaged, and digitally savvy. Some top bloggers have been bought out by large media companies or appear on corporate sites.

However, one must be careful about how the term *blog* is defined. As mentioned in Chapter One, there is a new breed of hybrid media that is a kind of blog in that it aggregates other media, but it is also part magazine, part newspaper, part photo gallery, and part video-production centre. These hybrids have morphed into large-scale news organizations with sizable staffs and resources and can no longer be considered blogs, although they host many of them. Media organizations such as The Daily Beast, The Huffington Post, and Politico can be compared to blogs in the same way that an aircraft carrier and a small dinghy are both considered boats.

Tumblr blogs, taken over by Yahoo in 2013, are a form of microblogging that resembles a series of picture books. They are, according to Winston Ross, a caravan of photos, jokes, music clips, and a great deal of amateur pornography.[86] They are less about storytelling and more about expressing off-beat emotions. There is usually little political content.

It is difficult to pin down exactly how many active blogs there are in the world today. Estimates fluctuate wildly, varying from 150 to 450 million. There were over 200 million Tumblr blogs in 2014. A survey conducted in Quebec estimated that 16 per cent of the population had either kept a blog or posted comments on one in 2009–10.[87] An American survey estimated that approximately 14 per cent of adults in the US were writing blogs in 2010.[88] What makes counting difficult is that the blogosphere is in constant flux, with blogs coming and going relatively quickly. Most bloggers eventually stop posting because they find that maintaining their blogs is too time consuming or that the passions that led them to blog in the first place have cooled. Many former bloggers have joined Facebook or Twitter or Pinterest where, in effect, they continue to blog but in a different form. Hence there are now tens of millions of abandoned blogs littering the blogosphere like so many cars left on the side of the road. The Japanese, with their great flair for poetic descriptions, refer to abandoned blogs as *ishikoro*, or "pebbles."[89]

Comedian Stephen Colbert once defined a blogger as "someone who has a laptop, an axe to grind and their virginity,"[90] and others have used the term "the pyjamahadeen"[91] to describe bloggers who sit in their pyjamas in front of their computers, surrounded by empty pop cans and pizza boxes, and rarely see daylight. Cynics see them as the same people that you might otherwise see at *Star Trek* conventions wearing goofy hats, glued-on ears, and strange-looking glasses. Another wit described blogging as "karaoke for shy people."[92]

The truth is that while the blogosphere appears at first glance to be an amorphous and shapeless sea, a distinct hierarchy exists. Political scientist David Perlmutter describes the blogosphere as being shaped like "a narrow, tall spike (the top blogs) and then a very long 'tail' formed by the many other blogs." The small numbers of bloggers who have made it to the top of the pyramid are, in Perlmutter's words, "blogging royalty."[93] While it is always difficult to measure influence—and this is especially the case with a community as diverse, volatile, fleeting, and hard to grasp as the blogosphere—the gulf between superstar bloggers such as Heather Armstrong of Dooce.com or Glenn Reynolds of Instapundit.com, who have attracted hundreds of thousands of readers daily, and a grade 8 student writing for his friends couldn't be wider. While most top bloggers may have started as lone-wolf operations, they are now established institutions with advertising, staff, and the ability to post continually throughout the day.

A sharp distinction needs to be drawn between the Canadian and American political blogospheres. In their survey of Canadian bloggers,

Thierry Giasson and his colleagues found that while a majority of political bloggers believed that they influenced other bloggers, they had little or no impact on public opinion or on the traditional media.[94] In other words, while the storms brewing within the Canadian political blogosphere may be interesting to observe, in terms of affecting the political system as a whole they rarely reach landfall. In the US, however, the top bloggers have made much more of an impact, the storms they create reaching landfall almost all the time. As Simon Houpt of the *Globe and Mail* observed about the differences between the Canadian and American blogospheres, "By comparison, our blogosphere is tame and ignorable. For it is the very rare Canadian politics or news blog that manages to grab a critical mass of eyeballs and break out of its tiny community of like-minded people; and almost none that sets the agenda."[95]

To some degree, then, the US blogosphere is a model for what the Canadian blogosphere might become. According to Richard Davis, perhaps the leading expert on political blogs in the US, blogs there have become part of a new political/journalistic routing system whereby political operatives, journalists, and bloggers feed each other with the latest snippets of information or float ideas that are not ready for the mainstream media.[96] As will be discussed in the next chapter, Twitter also occupies much of the high ground in terms of sparking and propelling opinion on any given day.

Leading bloggers have been influential in the US because they enjoy what scholars refer to as "first mover advantage." Bloggers have the ability to respond quickly to fast-breaking events and hence to "define" or "frame" the story. By the time traditional news organizations have caught up, the blogosphere may have already rendered a judgement. If the old adage that "journalism is the first draft of history" is true, then it may also be the case that "blogs have become the first draft of journalism."[97] The problem for bloggers is that while they may have an early advantage, they rarely have the capacity to sustain a story over time. Once big news organizations with their sizable staffs and resources, as well as access to credible news sources, decide to run with a story, the influence of bloggers tends to fade. One effect, however, is that once a story is in the blogosphere—and of course on Twitter—there is enormous pressure on traditional news organizations to leap on the story. Where they once had the luxury of waiting to see where the chips would fall, they can no longer afford to delay.

Many bloggers are one-note wonders, confining their thoughts to only a single topic or cause. They develop great expertise in a particular area and cling to that topic with an almost fanatical passion. Arianna Huffington once remarked that, while "print has ADD, blogs have OCD"—referring to attention deficit disorder and obsessive compulsive disorder.[98] In fact, after the financial meltdown that came with the fall of Lehman Brothers in 2008, it was bloggers that provided the analysis that was often missing from the mainstream media. Armed with dogged determination, considerable expertise, the time and space not available to most journalists, as well as a fearlessness that comes from not being afraid to offend powerful interests, blogs such as Calculated Risk, Baseline Scenario, Naked Capitalism, and Zero Hedge were able to fill in gaps left by the mainstream news media.[99]

Perhaps the main reason for the influential nature of A-list bloggers in the US is the quality of their readership. Their readers are for the most part educated, affluent, likely to vote, and disproportionately made up of people who influence other people.[100] Many leading business executives and investors, policy analysts, and military and religious leaders undoubtedly follow, at least to some degree, the debates that are heating up the blogosphere on the topics that are most vital to them. Perhaps the best example is Mike Allen's *Playbook* on Politico. *Playbook* is arguably one of the most influential tip sheets in American political life and is daily reading for virtually anyone who follows politics. The *New York Times*'s Mark Leibovich believes that *Playbook* also sets the media agenda.[101] There are similar blog-like tip sheets in business, finance, and global affairs.

ChinaSmack, which offers English-language users a look at the hot topics on online sites in China and tries to capture the tempo of everyday discussion in offices and student dorms, has attracted a wide following among those who need to stay close to developments in that country. In the UK, blogs aligned with political parties, such as Conservative Home and Labourlist, and those published by Iain Dale and Guido Fawkes have sizable followings.

If we believe in Lazarsfeld and Katz's famous theory that the media's influence is indirect—that their messages are absorbed mostly by respected opinion leaders in the community and then transmitted to the broader public indirectly through these leaders—then one can argue that the influence of blogs is based on this same type of cascading effect.[102] Interestingly, in their study of the Canadian political blogosphere, Thierry Giasson and his colleagues found that political bloggers tend to be "hyper-citizens" who are deeply involved in a variety of political and community activities and causes.[103]

Most critical to their success and influence, perhaps, is that blogs are part of the daily oxygen supply for a large number of journalists both in Canada and the US. One survey of American journalists found that a majority of news workers consult blogs on a regular basis.[104] Many journalists begin their day by reading blogs, and many have blogs of their own. But the relationship between bloggers and journalists is not without its problems. While they might read blogs for ideas and as a way of gauging the public's reaction to stories, blogs are rarely quoted in daily newspaper or TV news accounts. They remain as a kind of background noise and are rarely acknowledged, perhaps because so much of what appears in blogs is rumour and speculation that can't be readily verified.

While blogs can be placed into quite a number of categories, I will highlight just four. First, there are celebrity bloggers such as Andrew Sullivan, Matthew Drudge, Nate Silver, Heather Armstrong, Ree Drummond, Jason Kottke, Perez Hilton, Ariana Huffington, Michelle Malkin, and Joshua Micah Marshall, who have made their names and created followings almost exclusively because of their online activities. (I'm excluding for the moment video bloggers [vloggers] such as Lonely Girl 15, Peter on Geriatric 1027, and Chris Crocker, whose video diaries made them YouTube celebrities.) According to Mark Tremayne, the power of star bloggers comes from their being seen as "outsiders" with respect to the mainstream media: irreverent, caustic, populist, and willing to challenge conventional wisdom.[105] While getting to the top of the blogging hierarchy is often giddy and intoxicating, staying at the top is another matter. As Sarah Boxer, art critic for the *New York Times*, warns,

> Bloggers are golden when they're at the bottom of the heap, kicking up. Give them a salary, a book contract, or a press credential, though, and it just isn't the same. (And this includes, for the most part, the blogs set up by magazines, companies and newspapers.) Why? When you write for pay, you worry about lawsuits, sentence structure and word choice. You worry about your boss, your publisher, your mother and your superego, looking over your shoulder. And that's no way to blog.[106]

For whatever reason, Canada has had only a smallish cadre of such celebrity bloggers. For example, Lainey (of Lainey Gossip) has a wide following and appears regularly on TV—although she rarely focuses on Canadian celebrities. One extraordinary blog is Vancouver policeman Steve Addison's Eastside Stories: Diary of a Vancouver Beat Cop. Addison provides a harsh, unfiltered view of life on Vancouver's skid row. He captures the daily turmoil experienced by those who live on its streets and the dangers faced by police officers on patrol. On a completely different topic, investor Paul Kedrofsky's Infectious Greed is known for its in-depth analysis of business trends and statistics. It's must reading for those who believe that numbers speak. In Quebec, *Le Journal de Montréal* and *Huffington Post Quebec* have both spawned a flotilla of bloggers, some of whom have substantial followings. Drunk Blue Jays Fans and The Checking Line are among a number of sites that have followings among sports fans. University of Alberta professor Andrew Leach's Rescuing the Frog is must reading for those interested in climate, energy, and the oil sands. Sean Holman's Unknowable Country deals with democratic rights and generates much debate. No Strings Attached: Laila Yuile on Politics and Life in BC has a devoted following. And Saskatchewan Conservative blogger Kate McMillan's Small Dead Animals has won a number of awards.

A second category of blogs can be classified as aggregators. Aggregators such as Bourque Newswatch, National Newswatch Canada, Google News, Reddit, Flipboard, The Huffington Post, Boing Boing, Digg, and RealClearPolitics cherry-pick the best stories and opinion pieces from newspapers, magazines, and blogs around the country and the world. While aggregators may be convenient one-stop shopping for newsaholics, allowing them to make the daily rounds of stories, opinion pieces, and gossip with little effort, media mogul Rupert Murdoch has famously described aggregators as modern-day pirates who endanger the safe waters once enjoyed by the traditional print media. Aggregators place newspapers and magazines in a prisoner's dilemma. If the print media prevent aggregators from showcasing their articles, then these articles might never be seen by most of the reading public. News organizations would also lose the click traffic that comes when users read one of their articles or columns. The impact would be felt most by the star columnists that make up the heart of a newspaper. Their influence comes from having a large and influential readership, and without readers, their star power would quickly diminish. Without a large readership, their access to sources would dry up, as would the appearance and speakers' fees on which they depend for the good life. If, on the other hand, news organizations allow their valued products to be pillaged by aggregators, then they risk losing the readers that count the most: those who pay. But then why pay at all if so much is available on aggregators for free? I will discuss this conundrum at greater length in Chapter Six.

A third category of bloggers is composed of people who have been able to translate their celebrity or professional standing in society into an online presence. These bloggers are the reverse of the bloggers in the first category, who are cyber-celebrities but are hardly recognizable in the outside world. Leading bloggers have included comedian Rick Mercer, musician Matthew Good, *Maclean's* journalist Paul Wells, pollster Allan Gregg, Sun News TV host Ezra Levant, prominent legal scholar and newspaper columnist Michael Geist, *Calgary Herald* columnist Don Braid, and Liberal party strategist Warren Kinsella. The ranks of prominent Canadian bloggers, however, have been thinned by a migration to Twitter. As we will see in the next chapter, blogging and tweeting require different skills—and it's hard to do both.

An important subdivision of this category comprises journalists. As mentioned, a great many journalists maintain blogs as part of their jobs. The idea is to keep readers engaged with tidbits of information or speculation that didn't make it to print, and to give journalists the chance to expound on topics of their choice. While turning journalists into bloggers might seem like a good idea on the surface, it also poses troubling questions. First, there is the danger that the line between reporter and columnist, between those who are paid to write factual stories and those who are paid to write opinion pieces, is being extinguished. Can readers then trust journalists to write objective and factual stories, when strong points of view are clearly evident in their posts? Second, blogs mean more work at a time when newsrooms are sometimes stretched perilously close to the breaking point. Time spent blogging is time not spent doing the extra research and interviews that sometimes make all the difference in pushing a story forward. The same can be said for tweeting.

While Canadian journalists may feel at home in the blogosphere, it has generally been inhospitable ground for Canadian politicians. While party leaders and candidates sometimes write blogs during election campaigns, their passion for blogging seems to evaporate once they are elected and have to face the harsh and unforgiving constraints of party discipline. According to the University of Guelph's Tamara Small, the Canadian parliamentary blogosphere is almost non-existent. The experience of former Conservative MP Garth Turner is a case in point. Turner attracted a great deal of attention when he began blogging from the Tory government backbenches in 2006. However, the outspoken author of Garth Turner Unedited soon ran afoul of the tight controls that the Harper government imposed on caucus members and was eventually expelled. As Turner pointed out when he was still a Tory, "I think that I am the only MP that does this because most people think that they are going to get their asses shot off … because they are opening themselves up to profound criticism and profound comment. And most times that really scares people; it really frightens politicians because the negative is something you are always trying to avoid."[107]

The Turner episode raises the issue of whether Parliament's rigid system of party discipline allows MPs the freedom that is necessary to express their views and engage with their constituents online. The answer so far is decidedly no. As Small has pointed out, parties want to be able to control the message, so online communication by parties tends to be a one-way street.[108] Parties use blogs, Facebook, and Twitter as "broadcast" sites rather than as sites for engagement and conversation. They don't want their sites to be turned into free-fire zones where party messages will be disputed by opponents, or policies challenged and ridiculed. Hence the "party and message" discipline that is the basic rule of federal and provincial politics extends to online communication as well.

A fourth group of bloggers is the vast army of ordinary people who are trying to reach a larger audience. In terms of influence, they are at the end of a very long tail. According to Boxer, many of them are not so much writers as "curators" or "impresarios" who collect and comment on interesting videos, articles, or photographs that they have gathered from across the great expanse of the web.[109] Tumblr blogs are particularly effective for such archival work. In some sense these blogs are living museums or works of art that can be visited by anyone in the world at any time of the day. Scattered among the millions of blogs in the online sky are examples of extraordinary life writing: soldiers in war zones who for the first time in history are able to provide immediate eyewitness accounts of the fighting, women in Iran describing what their lives are like living behind the veil, African political refugees writing about their experiences as outcasts in distant lands, or cancer survivors recounting their terrifying experiences while providing solace for those who are stricken. Bloggers are telling simple but poignant stories about love, death, families, companionship, and getting old.

In reality there are many shades of blogging; some blogs are no doubt cries in the wilderness from those who are powerless and melancholy and have few other means of expression. But it's also the case that leading bloggers have become part of the mix of media and politics and are able on occasion to break stories, reach influential readers, frame events, and stir controversy. This is particularly the case in the US. The key question is whether blogs invigorate the public sphere by adding fuel to policy discussions and involving more people in active politics. The verdict so far is sometimes, perhaps, and it depends...

YouTube and Video Politics

In order to understand the impact that YouTube has had on power relations, it's important to reflect on some of Joshua Meyrowitz's ideas about the influence of a much older medium: television. In his classic book, *No Sense of Place*, Meyrowitz argued that TV's influence comes from the fact that it creates a shared arena.[110] For the first time in history, TV took people to places that had previously been shielded from public view: non-Christians could see how Christmas was celebrated or how a Pope was chosen; the poor and disenfranchised could enter the homes of the wealthy and see the spectacles of consumption that they indulge in; women who were excluded from the male-dominated worlds of business, law enforcement, or sports could peer into the inner confines of male power; and viewers who might not encounter Blacks or Jews or gay people in everyday life could "meet" them on TV. Cameras take viewers inside police cars, prisons, and hospital emergency rooms, behind the scenes at sports events, and on patrol with soldiers in war zones. Moreover, talk and advice shows, which are the staple of daytime TV, are usually about deeply private topics that had previously been out of bounds: sexual or spousal abuse, betrayal and infidelity, or various kinds of addiction. As Meyrowitz observed, "Television enhances our awareness of all the people that we cannot be, the places we cannot go, the things we cannot possess."[111]

Meyrowitz's main argument is that TV's populist and levelling power helped trigger a vast social revolution. Where there was once an educational ladder that children had to climb one protected step at a time, TV threw the doors of the adult world open to children, exposing them to everything that adults were exposed to. The result was that children assumed adult behaviours at earlier ages and childhood was less protected. TV helped convince women that there was nothing that men did that they couldn't do, and that they had just as much right to be in boardrooms or courtrooms as men. According to Meyrowitz, the cold and unforgiving glare of the TV camera also transformed political life. Where political leaders were once seen at a distance and were therefore shrouded in mystery and unreachable authority, TV created a withering intimacy where off-hand comments, nervous gestures, and false smiles were captured for all to see and could be stored, catalogued, and aired again and again.

If we accept Meyrowitz's perspective, then YouTube is television on steroids. First, the sheer volume of YouTube's content is staggering. It is the world's largest archive of video history and the largest "living" archive of contemporary culture. Every week the equivalent of 180,000 feature films are loaded on to YouTube.[112] There are as many videos watched in a given week as there are people on the planet. As mentioned in the introductory chapter, if you took all of the TV programs aired by all of the major networks in North America over the last 60 years, this entire avalanche of programming would add up to the amount of visual material watched on YouTube in only a two- or three-week period. As is the case with TV, YouTube has the ability to assemble mass audiences and penetrate into private spaces in unprecedented ways. It is, in effect, a non-stop tour through virtually every corner of the human landscape or, as Michael Strangelove has described the YouTube experience, it's "like channel surfing through 100 million lives."[113]

While Meyrowitz made much of the fact that TV allowed viewers to be taken "backstage" to places where they had previously been prevented from going, TV remains highly regulated, and TV viewing, even on the wackiest cable channels, pales in comparison with what viewers can watch on

YouTube. Despite claims by YouTube that it removes offensive materials, and many videos are in fact removed, the reality is there is almost nothing that is off limits: there are videos instructing people on how to make bombs, and scores of videos depicting vomiting teenagers, drunken parents, and people in bathrooms. One of the most popular videos teaches viewers about how best to perform oral sex. There are also scenes of violence from wars and crime scenes that would shock Jerry Springer. In many ways it is the last outpost on the media frontier—a kind of Wild West before the law showed up. A tamer description is offered by Jean Burgess and Joshua Green, who have described YouTube as "massive, heterogeneous ... accidental and disordered."[114]

YouTube is owned by Google and is part of its mammoth advertising machine. Every video that is watched provides more data for Google's algorithms and is used to target specific audiences with advertising. Interestingly, more searches are made on YouTube than on any other search engine—except, of course, for Google itself. But YouTube has also become a TV production hub. The website has helped finance and has incubated close to 150 new TV channels, including Awesomeness TV, Machinima (which is aimed at gamers), DreamWorks Animation, and Epic Rap Battles of History.

YouTube is a vast culture-making machine and perhaps the best example of what Clay Shirky refers to as "the cognitive surplus." The great university lecture, science channels, videos on how women can check themselves for breast cancer, original characters such as Peter Oakley teaching elderly people how to use a computer, and videos on everything from how to throw your opponents in judo to documentary accounts by former child soldiers—all of these, and more, have turned YouTube into one of the planet's greatest teaching tools. One of the most viewed videos is one in which the rapper Soulja Boy teaches viewers to do "The Superman Dance." While hardly as entertaining as Soulja Boy, at least to most people, I have used YouTube in my own classes to introduce students to recent Canadian political history: scenes of John Diefenbaker in full spellbinding rhetorical flourish denouncing Lester Pearson's Liberal government for trying to replace the Red Ensign with a new Canadian flag, René Lévesque's tearful tribute to his friend Pierre Laporte after he hears that he has been murdered by the FLQ, and Pierre Trudeau's "bleeding hearts" speech after he brought in the *War Measures Act* during the October Crisis are just some examples of what is now just a click away. My students have also watched political ads until they are blue in the face.

YouTube is also a Me-media machine par excellence. While the audience for the most popular videos can be massive, viewing is scattered across a vast sea of tastes and interests. Users have complete freedom to roam and to choose when, where, how often, and for how long they will watch. Viewing is often chaotic and impulsive, with one unexpected choice leading to another. Friends, co-workers, and family members also provide links to their favourite videos, creating a mushroom effect as these links are passed along.

In fact, YouTube is at its heart a profoundly schizophrenic medium. While it is at once bottom-up, subversive, authentic, and participatory, it is dominated mostly by corporate products and messages. Although Burgess and Green acknowledge YouTube's disruptive capacity and note that "participatory culture is not a gimmick or a sideshow," they found that corporate and commercial interests have taken over the medium. In a 2007 survey of the most viewed, most favourite, most responded to, and most discussed videos, they found that only a small percentage of user-created videos were able to break through the popularity threshold. Despite the "myth" of user power, very few "slice of life" or cat videos attracted large audiences. Of the ten most watched videos, seven were clips from videos provided by major music labels.[115] Of the 30 most watched videos taken from a list published in 2013, every single one featured an established artist such as Justin Bieber, Eminem, Jennifer Lopez, Katy Perry, Carly Rae Jepson, Lady Gaga, Shakira, or Rihanna. In addition to the stratospheric popularity of music videos by major stars, viewing is dominated by celebrity interviews, highlights from TV shows, sports clips, and footage from films produced by the major studios as well as by independent producers. In other words, the products of the traditional media account for the lion's share of viewing.

Indeed, to a large degree YouTube has become an adjunct of big media. Virtually all of the major entertainment stars have their own YouTube channel, because the basic reality is that if they aren't watched on YouTube, they aren't in the culture. TV shows such as *The Daily Show* or *Saturday Night Live* have been masterful in using YouTube as a form of continuous advertising. Teasers clips are always up so that users can be enticed to watch the full show later on or to bounce it to their friends so that they get a laugh. In effect, these shows get a double or triple hit from the same skits or gags. As mentioned in Chapter Three, various networks and studios have ironed out special arrangements with YouTube so that the studio promotion machine never stops churning.

Most pointedly, however, the goal for most of the singers, comedians, dancers, actors, and producers who are posting on YouTube is to be discovered by big corporate media. While YouTube provides a platform that allows amateurs to be noticed, being a one-video wonder on YouTube never adds up to very much. The real goal is to get noticed by powerhouse studios, promoters, and distributors. Famously, YouTube was instrumental in placing Canadians such as singers Justin Bieber and Maria Aragon, comedian Russell Peters, and cooking show *Epic Meal Time* into the professional limelight. In effect, YouTube has become a 24-hour-a-day, never-ending talent show, and sometimes, just sometimes, the audience falls in love with the magic—and so do the studios.

In the area of news, a study conducted by the Pew Research Center's Project for Excellence in Journalism looked at the most popular news videos to appear on YouTube from January 2011 to March 2012.[116] Researchers found that YouTube could produce what I term "news moments" especially during natural disasters or political upheavals. Videos taken by eyewitnesses after the earthquake and tsunami that ravaged much of northern Japan in 2011 reached an audience of close to 100 million viewers and made it onto TV newscasts as journalists couldn't reach the affected areas beacause of the devastation that was caused. Rarely have scenes of nature's overwhelming power and wrath been captured so vividly. Videos about the killing of Osama bin Laden and of a horrific motorcycle accident also reached large audiences. The study noted that on any given day, news videos could be more popular than even the most popular entertainment videos and that citizen-produced videos played a "substantial role in supplying and producing footage" used by TV news shows.

This is precisely what excites scholars such as Michael Strangelove. The importance of YouTube to Strangelove is that part of it remains a bottom-up, populist, and mostly non-commercial space. Moreover, while corporate messages and products are everywhere, they are often altered and subverted, mocked and twisted into popular forms. What is taking place is nothing less than a "large social shift" in favour of amateur production. According to Strangelove, "What must be recognized is that there has been a vast increase in the volume of amateur video production, a vast growth in the number of amateur videographers, a vast increase in the size of alternate media's audience and a significant increase in the technical capabilities of amateur videos."[117] For Strangelove, YouTube is the final step in "the democratization of the lens."[118]

YouTube's greatest impact, in fact, may be in the realm of mobilizing citizen participation and responses. YouTube videos played a major role in triggering and publicizing the revolutions that erupted throughout the Arab world in 2011, bringing down regimes in Tunisia, Egypt, and Libya and shaking others to their core. A contagion effect seems to have been created as demonstrators used Twitter, Facebook, and YouTube-posted videos to transmit messages about what was happening on the streets to each other and to the world beyond. Ultimately the old regimes could not withstand or refute the power of these images.

One of the most haunting and powerful videos produced by citizen journalists was of a beautiful young woman, Neda Agha-Soltan, slowly dying after being gunned down by government thugs on the streets of Tehran because she had protested the bogus election of then-Iranian president Mahmoud Ahmadinejad. Through the video, which first appeared on Facebook, she became a symbol of freedom and indeed of women's rights around the world. Evgeny Morozov, one of the leading skeptics about Internet freedom, believes that in the case of Iran at least, YouTube, smart phones, and Facebook have become double-edged swords. The regime used these technologies to spy on protesters, find out about and disrupt their plans, and chase down and arrest dissidents.[119] The Iranian government also used web-based media to distribute their own propaganda videos.

Among the most powerful examples of citizen journalism are the videos that depict police brutality or misconduct. In these instances, smart phones, YouTube, Facebook, and Twitter are all part of the same instrument of exposure. With alarming frequency, police in Canada are shown shoving, kicking, harassing, or tasering innocent victims. One of the most notorious incidents was a video of RCMP officers killing a Polish tourist, Robert Dziekanski, at the Vancouver airport in 2007. The British Columbia government was forced to hold an inquiry after horrific images of his death were picked up by television news shows and then shown around the world. Similarly, videos obtained from citizens led to the identification of a police officer who allegedly brutally beat an innocent demonstrator, Adam Nobody, during the G20 summit held in Toronto in 2010. The videos forced a Special Investigations Unit to re-open an examination of the incident. Another shocking incident occurred in Toronto in 2013, when 18-year-old Sammy Yatim died after being shot eight times by police after he threatened passengers on a streetcar with a knife. Videos of the incident soon went viral. One of the officers, James Forcillo, was charged with second-degree murder, the Ontario Ombudsman initiated an investigation into police procedures, and the Toronto Police Service carried out an internal investigation.

YouTube videos were also used to record and then prosecute rioters in downtown Vancouver following the Vancouver Canucks' loss to Boston in the seventh game of the Stanley Cup finals in 2011. While invaluable to the police who used video images to charge those who had committed these disgraceful and cowardly acts of vandalism, online vigilante groups also used videos to expose and then carry out their own brand of justice against the perpetrators. The Vancouver riots set a dangerous precedent because they ignited and mobilized what were, in effect, online mobs acting on their own outside of the justice system. But probably the most poignant and powerful image posted during the riots was of "the kiss." The image of two lovers kissing while lying on the street as police chased rioters in the distance resonated across the globe.

Arguably we have now reached the point where we see each other through a two-way lens. The police use video cameras and sometimes YouTube videos to watch the public, even as the public has an increasing capacity to watch the police. A similar two-way mirror applies to politicians. Many politicians have yet to learn that with citizen journalists and political opponents potentially everywhere, a misplaced remark, an unthinking moment, or an appearance with the wrong people can make headlines. When George Orwell described his nightmarish vision of the surveillance society in his futuristic novel *Nineteen Eighty-Four*, he believed that modern technology would be used by governments to spy on and intrude into every aspect of people's lives. Ordinary citizens would be unable to escape the government's penetrating gaze. One can argue that today's political leaders have to endure a similar kind of scrutiny. Virtually wherever they go, someone is watching and most likely recording.

There are countless examples of YouTube video "bombs" exploding unexpectedly during political campaigns. Time and time again political leaders, parties, and strategists lose control of the agenda because a YouTube bomb thrown from the sidelines has torn a hole in their game plans. Perhaps the most notorious example of political death by video took place when one-time presidential hopeful, Virginia Republican Senator George Allen, spotted a Democratic campaign staffer at one of his re-election rallies for another term in the Senate. He referred to the dark-skinned Asian man as a "Macaca"—a racial slur used in North Africa. But equally as telling were his smirk and arrogant manner. Allen never recovered from the YouTube moment and lost his re-election bid.

During the 2008 race for the US presidency, Barack Obama's campaign was shaken by YouTube videos featuring his former preacher Jeremiah Wright, an incendiary speaker who seemed to delight in stoking racial fires. The videos, which dominated news coverage for weeks, undermined Obama's image as a moderate and transcendent politician who could heal racial wounds. Obama responded by giving a major speech on race. The speech, which generated massive news coverage and a sizable YouTube audience, was the political equivalent of an emergency room operation. Luckily for Obama, the speech repaired much of the damage.

Four years later, during the 2012 presidential race, a video of Republican candidate Mitt Romney speaking at what was supposedly a closed-door fundraiser was leaked to *Mother Jones*, a liberal magazine, which then sent it viral. Romney famously told those attending the $50,000-per-person dinner that since 47 per cent of Americans didn't pay income tax, they would probably support President Obama because "they believe that they are 'victims' who are entitled to health care, to food, to housing, you name it. So my job is not to worry about those people. I'll never convince them that they should take personal responsibility and care for their lives." Writing off almost half the population as "victims" reinforced the image that the public had of Romney as a cold and uncaring plutocrat. The video produced a media echo that lasted throughout the campaign. Obama barely survived a similar video incident in 2008 when he was shown telling guests at a fundraiser that people in small towns cling to guns and religion. His opponent in the primaries, Hillary Clinton, feasted on the video like a pit bull tearing into a steak.

A more pleasant YouTube surprise for the Obama campaign in 2008 was the thrilling "Yes We Can" video, which featured a collage of words and music from rock and movie stars inter-spliced with video from his speeches. The video, which was put together for $30,000 by singer/producer will.i.am, was made over a single weekend. "Yes We Can" won an Emmy award, attracted 20 million views, and was aired repeatedly in the mainstream media. While coming from outside the campaign, and hence outside the laws governing election spending, the video nonetheless had a dramatic effect in galvanizing younger voters. The same was true for "Obama Girl: I've Got a Crush on You," performed by Amber Lee Ettinger. The video attracted over 20 million views and spawned a cottage industry of copycat videos.

Perhaps the best Canadian example of a political video bomb is the "Culture en péril" video that was posted on YouTube during the 2008 federal election campaign. The video was created by a group of Quebec artists in order to protest the cuts that the Harper government had made to arts funding. In the video, musician Michel Rivard faces a panel of federal bureaucrats who question him about a funding application. The bureaucrats are offended by his hit song, "La complainte du Phoque en Alaska," because they mistake "phoque," which means "seal" in French, for a more graphic word. He is also peppered with questions about whether he is a homosexual or believes in God. Rivard is bewildered by the assault and his grant application is refused. The video, which attracted over a million views, benefited the Bloc Québécois, which was then able to make the fight against the Harper government's arts cuts into a *cause célèbre* in Quebec.

Interestingly, there was no equivalent to "Culture en péril" during the 2011 federal election campaign. The closest perhaps was the "Just beat it" video produced by an Ontario anti-poverty group. Performed to the tune of the famous Michael Jackson hit, the video featured a dozen or so people from various ethnic groups mocking Conservative party attempts to win over ethnic communities. The message was that they "Don't wanna be an ethnic, be

Canadian." A video of a Rick Mercer TV rant meant to rally young people to vote seemed to make little impression, although it attracted over 100,000 hits. At the provincial level, during the 2012 Alberta election, a video made in 48 hours for $3,000, entitled "I never thought I'd vote PC," showed hip young people urging voters to shelve their prejudices against the ruling Tories because the insurgent Wildrose Party would be even worse. The message seemed to capture the feelings of many voters and helped legitimize their choice.

To be effective, videos have to be funny, poignant, entertaining, or sensational in some way. With hundreds of millions of videos posted every week, getting a single tree noticed in the massive forest of YouTube is not easy. Gaffes, miscues, and embarrassing situations will get noticed largely because they will be picked up by the mainstream media. The feedback loop is such that hot videos produce hot stories, which produce an even larger audience for those same videos. Sadly for politicians seeking to be YouTube stars, routine speeches, self-serving campaign promos, and ads that come across as just another ad are unlikely to attract many viewers.

The Politics of Me-media

There is no question that cable, blogs, and YouTube have given audiences far more media choices and means of expression than could have been imagined just a generation ago. One of the most profound changes has been the ability of each person to create what is in effect their own hyper-individualized media environment. Not only can we choose which media to read or watch and when, but each person can also become his or her own production centre—posting, redacting, blogging, tweeting, making videos, and so on. Even ads are highly targeted. We can now live in our own media orbits, seldom seeing or hearing what we don't want to.

However, just when we thought that the mass-media society was evaporating, that the ability to assemble mass audiences was a thing of the past, Big TV has reinvented it. What's fascinating is the degree to which, even in a Me-media world, many people make the very same media choices: they listen to the same music, watch the same serialized TV programs, follow the same sports events, and watch the same YouTube videos. The reality, as discussed in Chapter Three, is that powerful conglomerates have created a common culture even amid the chaos of so much choice.

Each of the media tools described in this chapter has a different relationship to corporate and political power. As I have shown, cable has both transformed and diminished news and politics. As audiences have splintered, news has become both more ideological and more sensationalized. The news cycle now moves at break-neck speed, with fast-breaking stories always available, always at the ready even if they are little more than "snowflake" news. In addition, political debates and discussions have largely been relegated from the main channels to cable—signalling to viewers and even to journalists that politics doesn't sell and isn't important. We must also remember Prior's conclusions that greater choice has led to less political knowledge and less citizen involvement, including lower voter turnouts, because cable is mostly about entertainment—and for most people, entertainment trumps news almost every time.

Blogs create a different effect. While they are a great instrument of expression and life writing, there is a distinctive hierarchy of power, with a few bloggers who are at the top of the pyramid wielding considerable influence while the vast majority of bloggers are stranded with few people reading or caring what they write. If you are Jeffrey Goldberg of Goldblog, or Andrew Sullivan of The Dish, you have won the blogging sweepstakes and are part of the political culture. Top bloggers enjoy what in effect are the blogging mansions by the ocean. However, in Canada, unlike in the US, bloggers remain at the peripheries of power.

YouTube has the capacity to both legitimize and disrupt power. One cannot forget that YouTube is owned by one of the most powerful corporations in the world, Google. YouTube tracks choices and tastes, feeds the Google algorithm monster, and matches individuals with ads. It is also a vehicle for promoting rock stars, TV programs, and celebrities that are largely the products of traditional media. Thus YouTube promotes and re-imposes the power of established media and corporate culture. Yet at the same time it has created remarkable spaces for personal expression, for eyewitness accounts, and for the citizen's lens. Citizens can, on occasion, have a news-making capacity and act as a check on the power of the powerful, be they political leaders, the police, or school bullies.

Taken together, cable, blogs, and YouTube have deeply transformed both media and politics. It is far too early to answer the question raised in the introduction to this chapter about whether media fragmentation is ushering in an era of radical and progressive democratic change or is producing a darker world where we are increasingly cut off both from one another and from the world around us. There are examples of powerful political moments that have been propelled by cable and YouTube when the public square is alive with ideas, exchanges, and learning. At the same time, Eli Pariser's view is that "personalization has given us ... a public square sorted and manipulated by algorithms, fragmented by design and hostile to dialogue."[120] The dilemma, perhaps, is that both are true. In the next chapter we will see whether this dichotomy exists in social media as well.

Notes

1 Marshall McLuhan, *Understanding Media: The Extensions of Man* (New York: Mentor Press, 1964).

2 John Palfrey and Urs Gasser, "Activists," in *The Digital Divide*, ed. Mark Bauerlein (London: Penguin, 2011), 192.

3 Baran, "Social Media in Campaign 2011," 85.

4 Quoted in Vincent Mosco, *The Digital Sublime: Myth, Power and Cyberspace* (Boston: Massachusetts Institute of Technology, 2004), 99.

5 Quoted in ibid., 57.

6 Quoted in Eli Pariser, *The Filter Bubble: What the Internet is Hiding from You* (New York: Penguin, 2011), 59.

7 Manuel Castells, *The Rise of the Network Society* (Malden, MA: Blackwell, 1996).

8 Jenkins, *Convergence Culture*, 129.

9 Clay Shirky, *Cognitive Surplus: Creativity and Generosity* (New York: Penguin, 2010).

10 Clay Shirky, "Gin, Television and Social Surplus," in *The Social Media Reader*, ed. Michael Mandiberg (New York: New York University Press, 2012), 236–41.

11 See selections from Mark Bauerlein, ed., *The Digital Divide* (London: Penguin, 2011).

12 Chen, *Always On*, 122–25.

13 Gardner and Davis, *The App Generation*, 146.

14 Nicholas Carr, *The Shallows: What the Internet Is Doing to Our Brains* (New York: Norton, 2010).

15 Prior, *Post-Broadcast Democracy.*

16 It's important to acknowledge the earlier work done on this topic by German scholar Christina Holtz-Bacha. See Christina Holtz-Bacha, "'Videomalaise' Revisited: Media Exposure and Political Alienation in West Germany," *European Journal of Communication* 5, no. 1 (March 1990).

17 Cass Sunstein, *Republic.com 2.0* (Princeton, NJ: Princeton University Press, 2007); Putnam, *Bowling Alone*; Pariser, *The Filter Bubble.*

18 Pariser, *The Filter Bubble*, 16.

19 Ibid., 47.

20 Ibid., 2.

21 Matthew Hindman, *The Myth of Digital Democracy*, 69.

22 Quoted in Jenkins, *Convergence Culture*, 237.

23 Sunstein, *Republic.com 2.0*, 9.

24 Ethan Zuckerman, *Rewire: Digital Cosmopolitans in the Age of Connection* (New York: Norton, 2013), 223.

25 Sunstein, *Republic.com 2.0*, 61–62.

26 Halpern, "Mind Control & the Internet," 33–35; McCright and Dunlap, "The Politicization of Climate Change," 155–94.

27 Kathleen Hall Jamieson and Joseph Cappella, *Echo Chamber: Rush Limbaugh and the Conservative Media Establishment* (New York: Oxford University Press, 2008).

28 Eric Lawrence, John Sides, and Henry Farrell, "Self-Segregation or Deliberation? Blog Readership, Participation and Polarization in American Politics," *Perspectives on Politics* 8, no. 1 (March 2010): 152.

29 Michael D. Conover, Jacob Ratkiewicz, Matthew Francisco, Bruno Goncalves, Filippo Menczer, and Alessandro Flammini, "Political Polarization on Twitter," *Proceedings of the Fifth International Conference on Weblogs and Social Media*, sponsored by

the Association for the Advancement of Artificial Intelligence, 2011, 89–96, http://www.aaai.org/ocs/index.php/ICWSM/ICWSM11/paper/view/2847/3275.

30 Zuckerman, *Rewire*, 99–102.

31 Prior, *Post-Broadcast Democracy*, 273.

32 Quoted in Rory O'Connor, "Word of Mouse: Credibility, Journalism and Emerging Social Media," Joan Shorenstein Center on the Press, Politics and Public Policy, John F. Kennedy School of Government (Cambridge, MA: Harvard University, February 2009).

33 Papacharissi, *A Private Sphere*.

34 Ibid., 141.

35 Ibid., 157.

36 Ibid., 159.

37 Gladwell, "Small Change"; emphasis in original.

38 Maria Vultaggio, "Young Voter Turnout High on Facebook's 2012 Election Map," *International Business Times*, November 6, 2012, http://www.ibtimes.com/young-voter-turnout-high-facebooks-2012-election-map-862118.

39 *Press TV*, "Voter Turnout in 2012 US Presidential Elections 9% Lower than 2008," November 7, 2012, http://www.presstv.com/detail/2012/11/07/270958/voter-turnout-in-2012-us-presidential-elections-9-lower-than-2008/.

40 Thomas L. Friedman, "Facebook Meets Brick-and-Mortar Politics," *New York Times*, June 9, 2012, http://www.nytimes.com/2012/06/10/opinion/sunday/friedman-facebook-meets-brick-and-mortar-politics.html?adxnnl=1&adxnnlx=141519 9813-pHqKER3I37iM8GPvyIRMQA.

41 Shirky, *Here Comes Everybody*.

42 Castells, *Networks of Outrage and Hope*.

43 Ibid., 144.

44 Joe Friesen, "At the Crossroads: The Idle No More Campaign," *Globe and Mail*, January 25, 2013: A6–7.

45 Taras and Waddell, "The 2011 Federal Election," 96.

46 *Pridgen v. University of Calgary*, Court of Queen's Bench of Alberta [2010].

47 Les Faber, "Canadian Social Media Statistics 2013," *WebFuel*, July 20, 2011, http://www.webfuel.ca/canada-social-media-statistics-2011/.

48 Hindman, *The Myth of Digital Democracy*, 68.

49 Hilary Stout, "Antisocial Networking?," *New York Times*, May, 2, 2010, http://www.nytimes.com/2010/05/02/fashion/02BEST.html?pagewanted=all.

50 Quoted in Matt Richtel, "Attached to Technology and Paying the Price," *New York Times*, June 7, 2010, http://www.nytimes.com/2010/06/07/technology/07brain.html?pagewanted=all.

51 Dhiraj Murthy, *Twitter* (Malden, MA: Polity Press, 2013).

52 Gardner and Davis, *The App Generation*, 84.

53 Putnam, *Bowling Alone*, 177.

54 S. Craig Watkins, *The Young and the Digital: What the Migration to Social-Network Sites, Games, and Anytime, Anywhere Media Means for Our Future* (Boston: Beacon, 2009), 54.

55 Ibid., 69; Zuckerman, *Rewire*, 177–80.

56 Charles Murray, *Coming Apart: The State of White America, 1960–2010* (New York: Crown Forum, 2012), 244–45.

57 Kay Schlozman, Sidney Verba, and Henry Brady, "Weapons of the Strong? Participatory Inequality and the Internet," *Perspectives on Politics* 8, no. 1 (June 2010): 490.

58 Aboujaoude, *Virtually You*, 181.

59 Ibid.

60 Hindman, *The Myth of Digital Democracy*, 60–61.

61 Curran, "Reinterpreting the Internet," 10.

62 Mayer-Schonberger and Cukier, *Big Data*.

63 Quoted in Daniel J. Solove, "Speech, Privacy, and Reputation on the Internet," in *The Offensive Internet*, ed. Saul Levmore and Martha C. Nussbaum (Cambridge, MA: Harvard University Press, 2010), 20.

64 Slides used in address by Kenneth J. Goldstein, "2012: The End of the Future of the Mass Media," University of Calgary, Calgary, February 6, 2008.

65 Grant Robertson, "TV Networks Losing Ground to Rival Services," *Globe and Mail*, July 9, 2008: B4; CRTC, *Communications Monitoring Report*, 2011 (Ottawa: Government of Canada, July 2011), 30, Table 4.1.1, http://www.crtc.gc.ca/eng/publications/reports/policymonitoring/2011/cmr2011.pdf.

66 Friends of Canadian Broadcasting, Friends' submission to CRTC, 9.

67 John Doyle, "One More Time Can We Please Have Canadian Arts on Canadian TV, Please?," *Globe and Mail*, October 6, 2011: R3.

68 Robert Levine, *Free Ride: How Digital Parasites are Destroying the Culture Business, and How the Culture Business Can Fight Back* (New York: Doubleday, 2011), 141.

69 Friends of Canadian Broadcasting, Friends' submission to CRTC, 10.

70 Michael Wolff, "Cable's on a Fast Train to Oblivion," *USA Today*, February 18, 2013: B1–2.

71 This entire discussion owes and borrows a great deal from Kenneth J. Goldstein, "From Assumptions of Scarcity," 3–21.

72 Fainaru-Wada and Fainaru, *League of Denial*, 6.

73 Umberto Eco, "Sports Chatter," in *Travels in Hyperreality*, trans. W. Weaver (Orlando: Harcourt Brace Jovanovich, 1986).

74 Gruneau, "Goodbye Gordie Howe."

75 Thomas Patterson, *Informing the News* (New York: Vintage, 2013), 5.

76 Ibid., 36.

77 Thomas L. Friedman, "The Fat Lady Has Sung," Sunday Opinion, *New York Times*, February 21, 2010: 8.

78 Quoted in Sean Hebert, "Jon Stewart, Stephen Colbert and the Evolving Role and Influence of Political Satirists in Twenty-First Century America" (Master's thesis, University of Calgary, 2012), 64.

79 Prior, *Post-Broadcast Democracy*.

80 Ibid., 266.

81 Ibid., 271.

82 Mary Jane Miller, *Outside Looking in: Viewing First Nations Peoples in Canadian Dramatic Television Series* (Montreal: McGill-Queen's University Press, 2008).

83 Elihu Katz, "And Deliver Us from Segmentation," *Annals of the American Academy of Political and Social Science* 546 (July 1996): 22–33.

84 Address by Newton Minow, "Television and the Public Interest," *National Association of Broadcasters*, Washington, DC, May 9, 1961.

85 Quoted in Zizi Papacharissi, "Audiences as Media Producers: Content Analysis of 260 Blogs," in *Blogging, Citizenship and the Future of Media*, ed. Mark Tremayne (New York: Routledge, 2007), 21.

86 Winston Ross, "The Old Person's Guide to Tumblr," *The Daily Beast*, May 20, 2013, http://www.thedailybeast.com/articles/2013/05/20/the-old-person-s-guide-to -tumblr.html.

87 Thierry Giasson, Harold Jansen, Royce Koop, and Ganaele Langlois, "'Hyperciti-zens': Blogging, Partisanship and Political Participation in Canada" (paper presented, Canadian Political Science Association meetings, Edmonton, June 2012).

88 Curran, "Reinterpreting the Internet," 18.

89 Ibid.

90 David D. Perlmutter, *Blogwars* (New York: Oxford University Press, 2008), 34.

91 Warren Kinsella, "Blogging and the Rise of the Pyjamahadeen," *Literary Review of Canada* 15, no. 7 (September 2007): 27–28.

92 Quoted in Sarah Boxer, "Blogs," *New York Review of Books*, 55, no. 2 (February 14, 2008):17, http://www.nybooks.com/articles/archives/2008/feb/14/blogs/.

93 Perlmutter, *Blogwars*, 27.

94 Giasson, Jansen, Kopp, and Langlois, "'Hypercitizens.'"

95 Simon Houpt, "Lament for a National Blogosphere," *Globe and Mail*, May 23, 2012: R1.

96 Richard Davis, *Typing Politics: The Role of Blogs in American Politics* (New York: Oxford University Press, 2009).

97 Ibid., 129.

98 Ryan Chittum, "Missing the Moment," in *Bad News: How America's Business Press Missed the Story of the Century*, ed. Anya Schiffrin (New York: New Press, 2011), 90.

99 Chittum, "Missing the Moment," 90–91.

100 Perlmutter, *Blogwars*, 31.

101 Mark Leibovich, *This Town* (New York: Penguin, 2013), 5–7.

102 See Elihu Katz and Paul Lazarsfeld, *Personal Influence: The Part Played by People in the Flow of Mass Communication* (New York: Free Press, 1955).

103 Giasson, Jansen, Koop, and Langlois, "'Hypercitizens.'"

104 See Davis, *Typing Politics*, chapter 6.

105 Mark Tremayne, "Introduction: Examining the Blog-Media Relationship," in *Blogging, Citizenship and the Future of Media*, ed. Mark Tremayne (New York: Routledge, 2007), xvi.

106 Boxer, "Blogs," 18.

107 Tamara A. Small, "Blogging the Hill: Garth Turner and the Canadian Parliamentary Blogosphere," *Canadian Political Science Review* 2, no. 3 (2008): 103–24.

108 Tamara A. Small, David Taras, and David Danchuk, "Party Web Sites and Online Campaigning during the 2004 and 2006 Canadian Federal Elections," in *Making a Difference: A Comparative View of the Role of the Internet in Election Politics*, ed. Ste-phen Ward, Diana Owen, Richard Davis, and David Taras (Lanham, MD: Lexington Books, 2008), 113–31.

109 Boxer, "Blogs," 16.

110 Meyrowitz, *No Sense of Place*.

111 Joshua Meyrowitz, "The Shared Arena," in *Seeing Ourselves: Media Power and Policy in Canada*, ed. Helen Holmes and David Taras (Toronto: Harcourt Brace Jovanovich, 1992), 229.

112 McChesney, *Digital Disconnect*, 1.

113 Michael Strangelove, *Watching YouTube* (Toronto: University of Toronto Press, 2010), 10.

114 Jean Burgess and Joshua Green, *YouTube* (Cambridge: Polity Press, 2009), 88.

115 Levine, *Free Ride*, 3.
116 Pew Research Center's Project for Excellence in Journalism, *YouTube & News: A New Kind of Visual News*, November 2013.
117 Strangelove, *Watching YouTube*, 177.
118 Ibid., 177–78.
119 Evgeny Morozov, *The Net Delusion: The Dark Side of Internet Freedom* (New York: Public Affairs, 2011).
120 Pariser, *The Filter Bubble*, 164.

Five
Connecting and Disconnecting on the Social Media Frontier

This chapter will continue the discussion of media fragmentation by focusing on the two most influential social media sites, Facebook and Twitter. Together with a host of other social media sites such as LinkedIn, Google+, Pinterest, Snapchat, and arguably Reddit, they have transformed how we learn, socialize, and conduct business. What Facebook and Twitter have in common is that they have become public squares, places where people gather to connect, learn, and on occasion sort out political issues. While they fall far short in terms of engaging large numbers of people in politics, mostly because politicians tend to use social media for one-way, top-down communication, they are nevertheless changing the way in which journalists in particular interact with each other and their publics. Both of these social media sites are also gateways to other media, and perhaps most significantly they collect data on users that they then package and sell, although Twitter is not nearly in the same league as Facebook in "discovering and tracking" data.

While they tend to be mentioned in the same breath, Facebook and Twitter are very different instruments and have had very different effects on politics. Facebook is a closed or bounded system where communication takes place almost exclusively among a coterie of chosen friends. Twitter, on the other hand, resembles broadcasting in that tweets can be seen by a mass audience.[1] Tweeting also resembles blogging: with a maximum of only 140 characters per tweet, Twitter is in effect a micro-blog—a blog with abbreviated messages instead of long observations and narratives.

At the time of writing, Facebook had over a billion users. Twitter claimed 215 million monthly users when its initial public offering was filed in 2013. Close to 90 per cent of Canadians who were online in 2012 had a Facebook account, while roughly 20 per cent of Canadians had a Twitter profile.[2] The two sites have also had different uses with regard to politics. Facebook has been far more about connecting, buying, and being entertained than it has been about politics—although its influence on politics has sometimes been extraordinary. Twitter is more kinetic and turbulent and has become more critical to journalism and to political agenda-setting. According to Peter Hamby of CNN, it is now, in the US at least, "the central news source for the political establishment."[3]

I will argue that privacy is the main public-policy issue raised by Facebook. Facebook is at the very centre of concerns about whether people's thoughts and past actions can be protected from prying eyes and whether people are leaving digital tracks that can never be erased. Facebook has been under fire over privacy issues for years, yet despite numerous public-relations twists and turns and efforts to reassure users that their information is safe, the company always seems to arrive back at the very same place that it started— as a storehouse for personal data. It is, next to Google and the US government, the largest and most voracious data collector on the planet. The simple truth is that without access to copious amounts of private information about its users, Facebook could not be in business. It has an enormous stake in ensuring that the cloak of privacy that once shielded people from unwanted scrutiny is as thin and porous as possible.

Our examination of Twitter will concentrate on how it has changed the landscape of media and politics. As is the case with videos on YouTube, conversations on Twitter are dominated by entertainment and popular culture and help reinforce the power of established media. Justin Bieber, Lady Gaga, and Justin Timberlake have massive Twitter followings, and their tweets often make news in the traditional media. But Twitter also has a political zone where journalists, politicos, scholars, policy wonks, and super-citizens are continually jousting for influence and trying to set the political agenda. There is little doubt that Twitter has moved to the centre of the political–journalistic relationship, becoming the new town hall for sorting and sifting the latest news, theories, and gossip, and for floating trial balloons.

But the problem, as Liz Sidoti of the Associated Press in the US has observed, is that Twitter may be "a great measure of what a narrow band of people are talking about"—and little more.[4] In fact, a study undertaken by the Pew Research Center in 2012 found "a startling disconnect" between how Twitter users viewed major events and how those same events were viewed by the general public.[5] Critics contend that Twitter has created a groupthink among journalists and promotes and furthers a distorted picture of reality.

Is Facebook Your Friend?

When Facebook was created by Mark Zuckerberg when he was a 19-year-old student in 2004, he saw it as a tool to manage relationships within a limited and controlled environment, such as a university dorm. His later goal in launching Facebook Connect, the Social Graph, and then Graph Search was to make Facebook a substitute for the web as a whole, to allow users to access the web yet remain within Facebook's architecture. The magic of Facebook is that it allows users to create private islands within the vast, chaotic, and often psychologically overwhelming ocean of the web. Users create what is in effect their own mini-web, where they can control entry by others, catch up quickly on what they need to know about people and events in their immediate circle, and manage access to other sites.[6] Facebook, which is now the homepage for most Canadians, is the very embodiment of Me-media. Castells describes social media such as Facebook as "mass self-communication."[7]

There can be no doubt that Facebook has become one of the most powerful means of communication in history. Virtually every major company in the world uses the site for "relationship marketing." Many companies are now engaged in what amounts to a never-ending series of focus groups with their customers. Companies such as Jaguar scour the Internet looking for complaints about their products and then publicly respond to those complaints.[8] Analysts at Four Seasons hotels peruse Facebook sites for feedback and seek information on the needs of prospective guests.[9] Food trucks canvass their customers on Facebook. Some companies have even been bold enough to allow users to offer advice on and even choose their next line of products: Ben and Jerry ice cream flavours, the next Barbie doll, the next Super Bowl ad for Frito-Lay, colours for the next car model and so on. The great advantage is that companies can directly identify and target their customers in a way that was unimaginable even a short time ago. The great disadvantage is that customers expect to be listened to and can quickly turn away if they feel that their feedback is being ignored. The stakes are brutally high: close to 70 per cent of millennials report that they consult with friends on social networking sites before making a purchase or even choosing a restaurant.[10]

And just as social media can make or break companies, they can also make or break other media. *The Washington Post*, the *Sporting News*, the *Guardian*, and Zynga are all examples of how Facebook apps can drive traffic to other media and most critically deliver young users. Of course, Facebook is not a benevolent supporter of other media: it normally takes 30 per cent of the revenue from the apps that it hosts on its site.

Facebook's impact on politics is somewhere between astonishing and negligible, depending on circumstances. As Castells reminds us, Facebook played an integral role in the explosions that ripped through the Middle East in 2011.[11] It helped opposition forces overthrow brutal dictatorships in Tunisia and Libya and shake the military regime in Egypt to its core. It also played a role in organizing mass demonstrations that ultimately led to the toppling of governments in Iceland and Spain, among other countries.

Perhaps the most successful example was the use of social networking by Barack Obama's campaign during the US presidential races in 2008 and

2012. While some of his opponents during the 2008 race were still trying to figure out how to use their keyboards, the Obama campaign used social media as one way of building and coordinating a vast election machine. Ordinary supporters, who in an unprecedented step were given access to the campaign's voter database, were able to connect with others online to ask for donations, organize house parties and speaking events, mobilize volunteer activities, and get their contacts to the polls. The results were stunning: more than 3 million people donated money online, at least 8,000 web-based affinity groups were established, more than 1.5 million web volunteers were mobilized, and they in turn organized tens of thousands of local events and helped coordinate a highly effective get-out-the-vote campaign.[12] In addition, a band of online fact-checkers kept an eagle eye on Obama's opponents and would contact the campaign almost instantaneously if they noticed errors or discovered background information that could be used in the campaign.

According to political consultant Joe Trippi, who masterminded presidential candidate Howard Dean's much heralded 2004 web campaign, "We were like the Wright brothers. The Obama campaign skipped Boeing, Mercury, Gemini—they're Apollo 11, only four years later."[13] By the time of the 2012 election, however, the pace of media shock had accelerated even more. Smart phones had become commonplace, and Facebook had expanded its reach even further. Obama's campaign organization, Obama for America, stayed in the field after the 2008 election and had organized some 10,000 neighbourhood groups by the time the 2012 election came around. The campaign also turned to Google's Eric Schmidt for advice on how and where to place ads and how to re-engineer its Facebook campaign.[14] It developed a "targeted sharing" strategy that allowed Facebook users to provide the campaign with access to their "friends." The campaign would then use its own database to identify which of these friends were likely to vote, for whom, and the best ways that they could be contacted. The system also ensured that the names of friends who the databases showed were likely to be interested in certain topics would pop up when messages on these topics were sent to Obama supporters. On the click of a "share" button, this information would then go out to the "right" friends.[15]

How the Obama campaign used analytics will be dealt with in Chapter Eight. To some degree, campaigns are only as good as the algorithms that drive their get-out-the-vote operations—and in 2012 the Obama campaign created a new model for political campaigning.

By contrast, Facebook's impact on the 2011 Canadian election was negligible. While Facebook was used to raise money, to spur vote mobs, and for one-way messaging by party leaders, it was an adjunct to the campaigns, a sideshow rather than a main event.[16] In her study of Facebook use, Tamara

Small, perhaps the country's leading authority on online politics, found that while political parties added new content to their Facebook walls every three days on average during a sample period in 2010, content differed little from ordinary press releases.[17] In fact, Facebook was merely another venue for the same press releases that had been issued through other media. While the parties used Facebook to build databases so that they could target users for money, recruit them as volunteers, and to ensure that their messages could go viral quickly if they needed them to, they almost never responded to comments posted on Facebook.

The principal reason for this lack of responsiveness is that Canadian political parties operate in an environment that rewards tight party discipline and where losing control of the message is seen as a disaster. Simply put, the parties don't want their sites to be hijacked by opponents or their messages sidetracked or disrupted by uninvited visitors. Little wonder, then, that the Conservatives deleted over 300 messages from Stephen Harper's Facebook page in 2011 after critics used the page to skewer his policies and introduce issues that the party did not want to discuss, such as abortion, the lack of benefits for military veterans, and Canada's Middle East policy.[18]

Small found in her examinations of party websites, Facebook walls, and Twitter feeds, that while Canadian parties maintained the "façade of interactivity," their communication was inevitably top-down with little or no two-way traffic.[19] This tendency is even more pronounced when it comes to Twitter. Simply put, in the rapid-fire back-and-forth that Twitter requires, it's all too easy for politicians to say the wrong thing, for what they thought was a witty remark to blow up in their faces, and worst of all—to be drawn off message. As a former communications director for the Conservative Party, Yaroslav Baran, has warned about Twitter: "This new medium does, therefore, reinforce the need for message discipline by political parties. Woe to those who stray from their ballot question to chase a microblogging-hyped 'story' that the real world may not care about in the least—or will not have even heard about."[20] Tom Flanagan, a former chief of staff to Stephen Harper and a leading political scientist, explains the difference between how Canadian and American politicians use social media:

> ... differing constitutional frameworks have spawned different types of political parties. American parties are loose coalitions without party discipline.... They don't have Canadian style leaders, they rarely expel dissidents and no one expects their campaign platforms to be implemented because the president isn't capable of imposing party discipline on Congress, even on members of his own party.

> The looser organization of American parties has allowed
> Mr. Obama to use social media to foster horizontal links among
> voters. His messages have encouraged Democrats to form local
> discussion groups, to hold coffee parties to recruit potential
> supporters, to organize rallies, to make telephone calls and to
> raise money.... Such spontaneity would be a mortal threat to any
> Canadian political party that actually aspires to win power. Our
> media, conditioned to expect rigid party discipline, would seize on
> a Conservative pro-life, or an NDP pro-oil patch, coffee club as
> evidence of—gasp!—dissension.[21]

A sharp distinction needs to be drawn, however, between the back and front ends of politics. While, as the Obama campaigns demonstrate, social media may be effective for fundraising, organizing, and getting out the vote (the back end), they are often less effective as instruments of persuasion (the front end). It's when users are already convinced about an idea or a cause that social media can be used to mobilize action. But front-end politics is another matter. Television is still the dominant medium of politics, and appearing on TV is still the oxygen supply for political leaders or campaigns. Facebook does not have the same primacy, largely because the audience for political news is small.[22] For the vast majority of people, Facebook is about diversion, catching up with friends, and play time rather than debating ideas or promoting causes. In Canada only 4 per cent of voters between ages 18 and 34 discussed policy or political issues online in 2012. Among older Canadians, the figure was only 9 per cent.[23] According to a Pew Centre study of American users conducted in 2012, no more than 10 per cent regularly paid attention to news recommendations on social media sites.[24] On Twitter, only 3 per cent of users "regularly or sometimes tweet or re-tweet news or news headlines."[25] To a surprising degree, hard news is a foreign land for the vast majority of Facebook and Twitter users. It's a place where they rarely go or have never been.

While Facebook is about public space, it is also about the politics of the personal. There can be little doubt that as a tool for personal expression and relationship management, Facebook is a revolutionary instrument. For instance, social scientists are only beginning to document the impact that is being made by what researchers call "ambient awareness."[26] While daily exchanges of information about jobs, friends, get-togethers, videos, games, or purchases may not amount to much, over time, as one software specialist put it, "the little snippets coalesce into a surprisingly sophisticated portrait of your friends' and family members' lives, like thousands of dots making a pointillist painting."[27] Or, as Steven Johnson has commented, "the screen is not just something you manipulate, but something you project your identity onto, a place to work through the story of your life as it unfolds."[28]

While it's too early to really know the long-term effects of continuing involvement with social media, there is evidence that even a shoestring of weak ties can make people feel less isolated and less alone. Social networks are surprisingly effective in helping people solve problems such as where to look for jobs, how to deal with relationships, which products to buy or stores to go to, or how to manage assignments at school. Moreover, not joining a social network site means being cut off from the action. While there may be a growing fatigue among users who don't wish to be always on, always responsive, always checking in, logging off means losing vital contacts and never finding out about events, parties, or meet-ups. FOMO—the fear of missing out—is profound. Those who don't join risk disappearing into a kind of social Bermuda Triangle where they may be "lost" forever.

The *New York Times* film critic A.O. Scott once described the web as being "a wild social ether where nobody knows who anybody is."[29] Nothing could be further from the truth. According to the Pew Internet and American Life Project, almost 95 per cent of Facebook friends are people that we know either from high school or college, are family members or people from work.[30] Few people outside the circle are allowed in.

To Ira Wagman at Carleton University, Facebook is about narcissism, diversion, and surveillance.[31] Let's begin with narcissism, because it is a theme that resonates through much of the first wave of psychological literature about Facebook.[32] According to Mark Leary, Facebook is largely a "self-presentational vehicle" in which people both objectify and merchandise themselves.[33] A Facebook profile is a never-ending ad for the product that you love the most: yourself. Even your "friends" are a vehicle for self-promotion; they are a testament to your popularity and social status. They are social currency.

What's disturbing to some experts, however, is not the falseness of the face that people are presenting to others, but the very opposite—its accuracy. In promoting ourselves we also reveal a great deal, and often we reveal far too much. Psychiatrist Elias Aboujaoude worries about the lack of inhibition that many of his patients display: people "pour their souls out, express their worst fears, hate their mothers, and kiss and make peace"[34] in a way that takes them well beyond boundless self-promotion and into revealing their most private thoughts—including their fantasies and delusions.

Indeed, *New York Times* columnist Frank Bruni believes that cyberspace creates "a reckless velocity" based on the "speed of our impulses." Thinking that we are alone and protected, we give full vent to indiscretions, mischief, and games of pretend that would be unimaginable in any public setting.[35]

In one experiment conducted at the University of Lethbridge in 2010, a student group created an imaginary profile of an attractive female, only to find that this made-up person was able to attract "friends" within a matter of minutes and had complete strangers revealing their most inner thoughts and secrets within a day.[36] Strangely, too many people seem to be profoundly and even desperately lonely, despite having so many "friends." Friends, however, can be a loose term. As Calgary playwright Eugene Strickland observed when he first went on Facebook, "I've been on a few weeks now, and I have 120 friends. Just the other day, I was wondering if I were to die suddenly, do I even have six friends to help get me in the ground? Apparently I do, 120 friends."[37]

Wagman also discusses the power of diversion, or, as he puts it, the way in which we "log on, goof off and look up."[38] What's astonishing is the degree to which Facebook has become the place that we go to for "play" and for a break from stress. Checking in to social media is now part of our daily routine—the same as brushing our teeth, drinking coffee, and being caught in traffic. Well over 20 per cent of time spent online by Americans in 2010 was on social media sites.[39] For many people Facebook and Twitter is the first place they go to when they wake up in the morning and the last place they visit before falling asleep at night.

What seems to give Facebook its addictive, compulsive, quality is that there is always something new, something to check in on: new news, new pictures, new friends, and so on. There is even evidence that Facebooking can kick up endorphin levels, providing a quick jolt of adrenalin in the middle of the day.[40] One user described it as "Grade 11 all over again"—with all of the hope, enthusiasm, and voyeurism that this entails.[41] Moreover, to be messaged is flattering—it gives people a sense of belonging and importance, even if many of their "friends" are not really "friends" at all. In fact, some people report that much like being on a sugar high, Facebook can produce a yo-yo effect, as the high quickly drops off. My students complain that after a while they get bored, feel that they are wasting time, and sometimes feel sad or left behind as they watch more popular or successful people live their lives.[42] And that is the irony: despite the torrent of online connectedness, so many digital natives feel lonely and disconnected. You can check into Facebook all day long, spend hours managing your fantasy league teams, play a video game against people from across the world, and see and talk to friends on Face Time—and still feel deeply alone. In fact, digital natives may be the loneliest generation of all.

But Facebook's distraction economy has profound political effects. Even if political attachments are important for some users, these concerns tend to get lost as Facebook offers a never-ending cornucopia of distractions and always and inevitably returns to the personal. The situation is exacerbated by yet another problem: the extent to which Facebook may give people the illusion of involvement without its substance. As discussed at the beginning of Chapter Four, Malcolm Gladwell argues that Facebook makes minimal involvement easy because "Facebook activism succeeds not by motivating people to make a real sacrifice but by motivating them to do the things that people do when they are not motivated enough to make a real sacrifice."[43] Just as Facebook may give some people a false sense of friendship, it may also give them a false sense of involvement.

But it may also be that social media by their very nature discourages political discussion. Unless users have joined a site devoted to a political cause, where they will meet like-minded people, users are often reluctant to show their political stripes when they know that the pushback from those who disagree can be immediate, nasty, and damaging. As Elisabeth Noelle-Neumann demonstrated in one of the most famous studies of public opinion conducted in the postwar era, those who are in the minority fear the isolation and mockery that comes from disapproval and tend to remain silent—producing what she has called "a spiral of silence."[44] Presumably the spiral of silence is evident in online relationships as well. While Facebook sites may be bursting with energy and vitality and are a transmission belt for vital day-to-day information, their very openness may discourage political discussion. In fact, in their multi-generational study of youth and identity, Howard Gardner and Katie Davis found that the "app generation" is far more risk-averse than previous generations—the reason being that on Facebook having the wrong views or failing at something is "witnessed" by scores of people and can become part of "one's permanent digital footprint."[45]

The well-known theory articulated by Paul Lazarsfeld and his colleagues Bernard Berelson and Hazel Gaudet that public opinion forms through a two-step flow of communication may be relevant to understanding the impact being made by Facebook. In a study of voters conducted in Erie, Ohio, during the 1940 US presidential election, Lazarsfeld and his colleagues found that people were rarely influenced directly by what they read or saw in the mass media.[46] Far more influential were conversations about the news that voters had with people that they respected in everyday life—teachers, parents, church leaders, and close friends. Ethan Zuckerman speculates that this two-step approach may be repeating itself on Facebook.[47] Influential Facebook friends can signal the importance of an event and legitimize one opinion over another.

The third characteristic that Wagman identifies is surveillance. Surveillance takes place on two levels: we are able to track the lives of our friends, and

Facebook, in turn, is able to track us. Facebook acts as a kind of GPS system that allows users to constantly monitor what friends are thinking, watching, playing, wearing, and buying and where they are going and with whom. It legitimates voyeurism and gives it a social outlet.

On a macro level, however, Facebook is the peeping tom. This is because Facebook's real product is the people who use it; to quote law professor Lori Andrews, "Unlike Vegas, what happens in Facebook doesn't stay in Facebook." Information about users is Facebook's property and is stored, packaged, and sold to third parties or used to target users with customized ads. The photos of family, friends, parties, and trips that appear literally by the billions every week are owned not by the people taking the pictures but by Facebook. Facebook also owns Instagram, the world's most popular photo-sharing site. It is interesting to note that the Occupy Wall Street movement avoided using Facebook because of the facial recognition software that automatically tags people in photographs, whether they wished to be identified or not.[48]

As a result of running battles with the Canadian Privacy Commissioner, as well as with agencies in the European Union, the company has made many changes to its privacy policy. But, as mentioned above, despite these changes, default settings still encourage users to share personal information and can be reset without notice. In 2011, the Federal Trade Commission in the US ruled that Facebook had to obtain permission from its users before using their data for advertising. Two years later the FTC was still waiting for any signs of compliance.[49] Lori Andrews has used a time chart to display how Facebook's privacy policies seem to always revert back to the same starting point: namely Facebook's need to maintain access to as much of our personal information as possible.[50]

As mentioned above, Facebook and other social media sites can be profitable only if they can own what was once considered part of the private sphere. By signing on to Facebook we give up our right to be left alone and determine how our thoughts and actions should be communicated to the world. Mark Zuckerberg's self-serving argument is that social norms have changed to the point where "people have really gotten comfortable not only sharing more information and different kinds but more openly and with more people, and that social norm is just something that has evolved over time."[51] But have they really? Or is it that many users remain naïve about how exposed their lives have become to employers, university admissions officers, or those that would do them harm? They might not also realize, as Lori Andrews has pointed out from a legal perspective, that "anything you post can and will be used against you."[52] Institutions, corporations, and courts all consider Facebook to be a public rather than a private space and have acted accordingly. In her book *I Know Who You Are and I Saw What You Did*, Andrews chronicles case after case in which employees who describe their jobs as boring, complain about the stupidity of supervisors, or are angry about discourteous customers have lost their jobs, and, worst of all, how privacy settings have sometimes been changed without warning, leaving what users thought were private comments exposed to public scrutiny.

According to some observers, even professionals have difficulty explaining the ins and outs of the new surveillance economy, especially the ways in which companies can identify the same digital signatures across various devices—meaning that they can track you on whatever device you are on— and know that it's you.[53] Al Gore believes that "do not track" options are all but useless. Pressure from the advertising industry is such that tracking will often continue, even after you think that you have opted out.[54]

Some of the invasions of privacy that are now occurring are quite startling. As mentioned previously, there are now private investigation firms such as Spokeo or PeekYou, which, for little cost, will scour the web for information about careers, incomes, religious and political beliefs, and provide photographs of where people live and work. People's lives are effectively put under a CAT-scan, and the results made available for the world to see. While there are "reputation" services that specialize in removing harmful information from web-based media, they are expensive, and some of the information is hard, perhaps even impossible, to remove. This is especially the case where people appear in photos taken by others. Photos are strewn like leaves across the vast expanse of the Internet and are hard to keep track of.

It's also the case that people's sense of privacy and dignity changes with age and circumstances. Many young people seem to have little compunction about posting photos of themselves or their friends being visibly drunk, provocatively dressed, or in compromising situations. In fact, one study found that over 50 per cent of college students in their sample had an alcohol-related image on their Facebook profile.[55] As people get older, however, and take on professional and family responsibilities, many of the same people who posted photos of themselves lying on the floor plastered want these pictures removed. This seems to be especially the case for women. One way around the problem for some is to use the Snapchat app. Snapchat allows users to send pictures and short videos of themselves, with the images lasting only seconds before dissolving. It is not clear, however, that these images are not being collected at least somewhere in cyberspace.

Law professor Jeffrey Rosen fears that "the web means the end of forgetting."[56] The young woman who had a photo taken of her as a "drunken pirate" at a Halloween party and subsequently lost her teaching job should have had the right to have the photograph removed to ensure that it didn't damage her career any further, becoming a shadow that would follow her wherever she went. The problem for many people is even remembering that "incriminating" photos exist. Rosen's argument is that "the permanent memory bank of the web increasingly means there are no second chances— no opportunities to escape a scarlet letter in your digital past. Now the worst thing that you've done is often the first thing everyone knows about you." In asserting "a right to delete," he contends that our right to dignity is at least as important as Facebook's right to publish. It's not clear, however, how or even if these two rights can co-exist.

A number of scholars have suggested ways out of this dilemma. Oxford professor Viktor Mayor-Schonberger is haunted by how census information compiled by the Dutch government was then used by the Nazis to round up Jewish citizens during World War II. The Nazis were able to track down the vast majority of Jews in the Netherlands and transport them to death camps because the government's record keeping was so precise. In Belgium, where census gathering was less efficient, the Nazis were less successful in hunting down Jews. Today, people would have no defence against an oppressive government, as every opinion, every friendship, and every movement could be observed. As a consequence, Mayor-Schonberger wants to "reintroduce forgetting" by placing expiration dates on information. At the very least, governments and corporations would have to demonstrate why they needed to keep certain data.[57] He would also impose "speed bumps" at various points in the collection process to make collecting data slower and more difficult.

Legal scholar Daniel Solove believes that the emphasis should be on people's ability to protect their reputations rather than on the rights of corporations to collect personal information, and that information that can be used in damaging ways should be safeguarded. Another legal scholar, Lawrence Lessig, would give citizens the right to deny permission to companies to use information if they had doubts about how that information would be used. The solution would be to create "infrastructures of denial" so that information would not be so readily available.[58] For her part, Lori Andrews has proposed a "Social Network Constitution" that would ensure that Facebook remains a private space and that "the right to privacy in one's social networking profiles, accounts, related activities, and data derived there from, shall not be abridged."[59]

In a 2014 ruling, the Supreme Court of Canada argued that Canadians expect and have a right to online anonymity. The judgement ordered police departments to obtain a warrant if they wished to gain access to the records of Internet service and phone providers. Unauthorized phishing expeditions were unacceptable.

The debate about the right to be forgotten boiled over in 2014 with a decision against Google by the European Union Court of Justice, the

European Union's highest court. The court ordered Google to remove links that users found to be embarrassing or cast them in a negative light. Google now deals with approximately 1,000 requests to remove information each day. Critics argue, however, that in complying with the judgement Google has gone overboard. It has removed much valuable information and is, in effect, destroying information that should be part of the public record. The order applies only within the EU; the information can still be found on Google's American site. One can only imagine the chaos that would be created if a similar ruling were made against Facebook.[60]

"Put Down Twitter and Slowly Back Away?"

The title of this section comes from a study on the use of Twitter by journalists during the 2012 US presidential election by Peter Hamby, a reporter with CNN. Based on interviews with 70 journalists, the study is deeply critical of the distortions produced by the Twitter culture.[61] To Hamby, Twitter has made small incidents into major stories, increased the negativity and cynicism of campaign journalism, and implanted an ethic of "shoot first, update later" among journalists. We will return to Hamby's critique later in this section, but what is perhaps most significant in his study is the finding that Twitter "has become the gathering place of the political press."[62] Some would argue that Twitter has become "a national news room" where the "gatekeeping" functions of journalism now take place.

There can be little doubt about why Twitter has been so effective. Its 140-character limit is ideal for messaging on mobile devices, users can click on any topic and become part of a conversation in "real-time," and its algorithms are able to measure "trending topics" so that users (not to mention news managers) can know in an instant which stories are emerging, have gained traction, or are losing steam. Its power also comes from the fact that, in the words of Brittany Richards, Twitter "transmits 'massively shared experiences' from people in the heart of the moment," or, as Dhiraj Murthy has put it, tweets give people a "sense of being there."[63]

Like other social media, Twitter can be intoxicating. Virginia Heffernan, a reporter for the *New York Times* who specializes in digital and pop culture, likens Twitter to a game in which the best players live "in the flicker between personal and public,"[64] form alliances with other players, and put points on the board by being witty, edgy, and controversial. Moreover, the Twitter game never rests: it's a game played best by "speed freaks"; it's in continual overdrive. Indeed, Heffernan warns that because the game as played at a high level requires skill and intensity, it's all too easy for players to fall behind by being slow on the uptake or by being boring—the ultimate sin. As Heffernan observes, "Like other immersive games—including tennis, fantasy football and chess—Twitter is spellbinding when you're in it, and seems nuts and like a sicko waste of time when you're not."[65] Even Dick Costolo, Twitter's chief executive officer, admits to being confused by the speed and edginess of the Twitter art form.[66]

One of the best players is Canadian Kelly Oxford, a Calgary mother of three, who at one point had more than 350,000 followers, including a number of Hollywood actors and producers. The key to the kingdom for Oxford, who now lives in Hollywood, is that she is fast, punchy, and funny—and like a *Seinfeld* show she turns ordinary events into fodder for acute and often cutting observations about life. Another master player is Calgary mayor Naheed Nenshi. His opinions and reactions to events reach well over 100,000 Canadians. Twitter allows Nenshi to always have the last word. But Twitter has its dangers even for a savvy user such as Nenshi: while he is in control of the Twitter game most of the time, the medium has at times become a contested space, with opponents lying in wait. Nenshi's skill at fending off critics with barbed one-liners has only added to his following.

Nenshi has also made use of Reddit's "Ask Me Anything" forum, as have Liberal leader Justin Trudeau and astronaut Chris Hadfield. AMAs have become a signpost of popularity and availability. When asked whether he "would rather fight 100 duck-sized horses or one horse-sized duck?" Nenshi remarked in his imitable style: "The premise of the question is incorrect, I believe. We need to make peace with duck-horses. (But not the horse-ducks. They're jerks)."[67] Sun TV news host Ezra Levant, another Twitter aficionado, has done combat with Nenshi on Twitter on several occasions and carried the battle with Nenshi off-road to other media. Levant uses Twitter as a kind of shooting gallery, in which he fires away at one ideological opponent after another. Those under attack either respond or, wisely perhaps, duck away.

Elsewhere on the Canadian political scene, in February 2013 Stephen Harper experimented with a "day in the life" Twitter initiative. The prime minister took his followers through an entire day of meetings, limo rides, meals, Cokes, and cats. The goal was to bring people symbolically and perhaps emotionally inside the prime minister's world, even if the connection was fleeting and the view contrived and filtered. Liberal MP Carolyn Bennett logged the most tweets of any MP in 2013, averaging 29 per day.[68] Bennett is a Twitter addict—even by the standards of other Twitter addicts. Cabinet minister Tony Clement had one of the largest followings in 2013. Evidently there are thousands of people interested in his squash games and what he ate for breakfast. At the other extreme, the NDP's Pat Martin is an example of a Canadian politician who has used Twitter poorly. The Manitoba MP's frequent online blowups and vivid language, such as his analogy that putting an end to the Canadian Wheat Board was "the equivalent of the Canadian beaver biting off his own testicles," attracted a wide following among politicos.[69] In late 2012, however, he was apparently made to hang up his Twitter skates after tweeting that he was "fed up" with some of the "rat faced whores" in the Conservative party.[70] His ready-fire-aim style had become too much for the party.

Similarly, Senator Patrick Brazeau used Twitter frenetically in the days before he was arrested for assault and expelled from the Conservative caucus in 2013. The Brazman, as he called himself, fought a running and abusive Twitter battle with members of the press and against a number of Native leaders. Jonathan Kay of the *National Post* saw the Twitter feed as a warning sign that things were going terribly wrong in Brazeau's life. As Kay observed, "In the Twitter universe, everyone is too busy madly scrolling through their feed, looking for something amusing to retweet, riff on, or use to score political points. In this dehumanized space, it's easy to forget that the little Twitter icons identify actual human beings. There's a fine line between re-tweeting someone, and enabling them."[71]

The 2011 federal election revealed a great deal about Twitter's effectiveness as an instrument of citizen inclusion. While on the surface at least there was a great deal of activity, with over 400,000 Canadians following the party leaders by the end of the campaign, the actual size of the election Twitterverse was much smaller.[72] In Mark Blevis's analysis of Twitter use during the 2011 Canadian election, he found an average of roughly 16,000 daily election-related tweets. But as this number includes retweets, the actual number of those following the campaign was much less than 16,000 and perhaps as few as 5,000.[73] In fact, former Conservative Party communications director Yaroslav Baran believes that Twitter's impact on the campaign was negligible: "It hardly touched the public. Where it did, it was primarily a broadening of the political class to a large outer ring of partisan, or more highly politically aware, members of the public whose political opinions are more likely to be pre-established. Revolutionary—in a macro sense—Twitter was not."[74]

A study of tweets about Canadian politics conducted by Samara in 2011 found that the top 100 tweeters tended to be the same pundits, politicians, and activists that dominate conversations in other media.[75] In effect, the Ottawa media bubble had superimposed itself onto Twitter. The same people were recirculating their views across various media. Furthermore, studies conducted by scholars at Cornell University and Yahoo suggest that Twitter is dominated by a very few players—half of all tweets are sent by 20,000 or so "elite users," who are mostly celebrities or people who work for media organizations.[76] In addition, users tend to divide into sub-species such that celebrities follow celebrities, reporters follow reporters, and bloggers follow bloggers.[77] Few Twitter followers ever cross the streams, to use an old expression from the first *Ghostbusters* movie. Not surprisingly, the audience for the politics stream tends to be relatively small.[78]

One of the reasons for this is that political parties tend to use Twitter as a vehicle for one-way communication. In her analysis of Twitter use by party leaders during the 2011 federal election, Tamara Small found that leaders suffered from "Twitter-phobia," a fear of saying the wrong thing or losing control of the message. Aside from a brief dustup between Stephen Harper and the Liberal leader Michael Ignatieff over their willingness to debate each other, the main party leaders used Twitter almost exclusively for "broadcasting their messages of the day," rather than for interacting with the public. Most of their tweets were a kind of happy bafflegab: how committed they were to the environment or better health care, how pleased they were to be attending a particular event, or to have arrived in Saskatoon or Sarnia, how delighted they were to be giving out an award or to have met someone. They rarely responded to questions or comments from Twitter followers or reacted to tweets from other leaders. Small's argument is that when it comes to Canadian politics, at least, Twitter is a "not-so-social network."[79]

However, Twitter's effect on journalism has been more dramatic. Journalists such as the CBC's Kady O'Malley and Rosemary Barton, David Akin of Sun Media, Andrew Coyne of *Maclean's*, and Susan Delacourt of the *Toronto Star* played an agenda-setting role during the 2011 election by passing on and hence legitimizing the latest insider information or interpretations of events. While Canadian journalists seem to be proud of their posting prowess and offer few critiques of the Twitter culture, this is not the case in the US. As mentioned above, in Peter Hamby's study of journalists on the campaign trail during the 2012 US presidential election, he found that journalists were worried that Twitter had helped to create a groupthink that had dangerous implications. To Liz Sidoti, Twitter is

> a good tip sheet, but one that has no standard and has a lot of opinion and snark. What it's done, it's created a groupthink, and the groupthink component of it is really kind of scary. It means we're all reporting the same thing, and only half of it may be right.
>
> We are thinking the same way. It's become the new conventional wisdom setter, and that conventional wisdom gets amplified as well, because you have editors sitting in bureaus watching this stuff. When everything is in 140 characters, it gives a skewed version of reality, and that impacts how editors think about what reporters should be covering, and it impacts what reporters think is important.[80]

Mostly, however, according to Hamby, Twitter seemed to affect how politicians behaved toward journalists. Most of all they were reluctant to talk to reporters when they knew that even the slightest error or miscue could become an instant disaster. Twitter removed the "filters" that once existed between political candidates and reporters. There was no editorial process, no time for news organizations to ponder whether stories should be published, no second chance for politicians to revise statements. The "speed freaks" were in control.[81] The general rule was "shoot-first-and-update later" (Hamby p. 95). The main critique, however, was with Twitter's capacity to set a journalistic agenda, even if the conventional wisdom on the buses and planes was far removed from what was really happening in the race or from issues facing the country. The press was obsessed with trying to figure out who was winning the day or the news cycle, although all too often these were products of their own invention.

In addition, trivial issues could be blown out of proportion. As Hamby observed, "Embeds [those reporting from the campaigns] were tweeting that the food has not been delivered yet, the bus driver wasn't good, the temperature in the press tent was too hot, the WiFi is slow, or that they weren't happy with the placement of priority seats on the plane." In short, too many tweets were little more than "self-involved chatter."[82] This was largely because candidates stayed away from reporters, leaving them with little to write about but themselves. In addition, Twitter created blind spots for journalists. It was far easier to listen to or read each other, or to follow the issues or stories that were "trending," than to do investigative work, follow up on stories, or provide real analysis. All too often, Twitter became the easy and lazy way out. For most journalists, however, turning off Twitter is now next to impossible. For example, during the 2012 Alberta provincial election, Jen Gerson of the *National Post*, an outstanding journalist with a great feel for politics, felt that she had to be on Twitter in order to be in touch with the daily flow of the campaign. She believed that her brand and career were helped by being part of a "national bulletin board" and by the significant following that she had developed among her colleagues. On the other hand, she felt that having her work constantly on display and commented on by others could be time-consuming and exhausting.[83]

Of course, the effects on journalists can be far more dramatic if it's the boss that's tweeting. Media mogul Rupert Murdoch continually posts comments on his Twitter feed about the news of the day.[84] Presumably these "thumbs up" and "thumbs down" judgements are noticed by the many thousands of journalists who work for him and who work in an environment where, to put it mildly, the boss's views count. One can only imagine the effects on news managers had Conrad Black or Izzy Asper been able to post editorial advice on Twitter three or four times a day.

None of this takes away from the great potential that both Facebook and Twitter have as instruments of democracy. Facebook in particular has demonstrated an extraordinary capacity to marshal the back end of politics, and Twitter has become a centre of gravity for political journalists. But for those who are disengaged, social media seem unlikely to make a difference. This is largely because political leaders and political parties largely refuse to use social media to actually *interact* with the public. They refuse to step into the better future that these technologies were supposed to create.

Welcome to the New World

The issue of privacy haunts all of web-based media. While there are many innovative solutions to the problem of continual surveillance, corporate giants such as Facebook and Google show little interest because their survival depends on ensuring unfettered access to as much data as possible. The US government, which also collects massive amounts of data both on its own citizens and on citizens in other countries, supposedly for reasons of security and crime prevention, and which is routinely given access to data collected by both Facebook and other sites, also seems unwilling to provide greater protection for people's privacy. The magnitude of surveillance is such that on a typical day the National Security Agency in the US collects up to 500,000 buddy lists and inboxes—close to 90,000 of which are from Facebook.[85] Canada has its own electronic surveillance system operated by a federal government agency, the Communications Security Establishment Canada. While the agency is currently being sued by the British Columbia Civil Liberties Association for illegally seizing citizens' communications and thus violating the Charter of Rights, the public seems either unaware or unconcerned about whether they are being "watched" by governments.

In the end, users are left with a devil's bargain. We are forced to give up at least some of our right to privacy in exchange for the many benefits that the Internet provides. Google, Facebook, smart phones, the social surplus, and apps give us far too much to ever turn back. While some may believe that they are protected because companies such as Facebook could not remain in business if they behaved irresponsibly, there are others who believe that we are not as protected as we might think, and that misuses of power are as inevitable as snow during a Canadian winter.

One of the important consequences of media shock is the extent to which fragmentation is creating new communities and relationships while breaking apart old ones. While we are only at the beginning of the journey in terms of understanding the new worlds that these networks are creating, the importance of their impact is beyond dispute. The eminent scholar Ithiel De Sola Pool, who died before the Internet became so central to our way of life, was prescient nonetheless in envisioning the issues that hyper-fragmentation might raise for society. According to Pool,

> We are likely to hear complaints that the vast proliferation of specialized information serves only special interests, not the community. That they fractionate society, providing none of the common themes of interest and attention that makes a society cohere. The critics will mourn the weakening of the national popular culture that was shared by all within the community. We will be told that we are being deluged by undigested information on a vast unedited electronic blackboard and that what a democratic society needs is shared organizing principles and consensus in concerns.... These criticisms will be only partly true, but partly true they may be.[86]

While much remains to be written about the impacts being made by each of the new web-based media that we have examined in this chapter, it's more difficult to discern what hyper-fragmentation and me-media as a whole will mean for the relationship between citizens and the great institutions of public life. Some believe that the Internet is so vast, so chaotic, and so amorphous that a national conversation will become almost impossible. Perhaps we will be unable to hear each other amid so much media noise. As one observer, Howard Voss-Altman, has expressed it,

> In these times, our national consciousness is so disjointed, so pulled apart, so utterly chaotic, that we are in danger of losing our sense of nationhood, as each citizen turns inward to a private virtual world of Facebooks and Twitters, cell phones and Blackberrys, video games, DVDs and Ipods....
>
> With the proliferation of voices drowning each other out, and the ease that one can change the channel or close a link, our ability to unite for change has been severely impaired. The feelings of political connection on a screen can never replace the sense of engagement one feels when we join each other in the same time and space.[87]

Media guru Todd Gitlin, for his part, believes that the threat to public participation and dialogue comes not from the volume of traffic as much as from
the pleasures, the sensuous impulses, and the jolts of feeling that web-based
media create. According to Gitlin,

> The ceaseless quest for disposable feeling and pleasure hollows out
> public life altogether. If most people find processed images and
> sounds more diverting, more absorbing, than civic life and self-
> government, what becomes of the everyday life of parties, interest
> groups, and movements, the debates, demands, and alliances that make
> democracy happen? ... We expect some usable curiosity, some jolt of
> feeling, to await us.... Can we say the same of public life?[88]

As Markus Prior pointed out in his study, for many the Internet has become
a giant entertainment and diversion machine, sidelining and suffocating
interest in news, public affairs, and citizenship.

These arguments ignore the energy and imagination that have gone into
creating "cognitive surpluses" and the potential that exists for building community and national conversations through social media. But despite remarkable political moments, and the power of Twitter in particular to influence
the journalistic agenda, social media platforms are still in their infancy. These
arguments about being lost in an endless media sea also ignore the fact that
the traditional media can still command large audiences and allow us to share
great collective moments together. In fact, without the products produced by
the traditional media, social media would not be able to survive. But those
who worry that our ability to communicate with each other as Canadians
is in jeopardy may not be entirely wrong. Perhaps we will reach the point
where there is just too much media fragmentation, too many mosaics, to
allow a common civic identity to form. We turn in the next chapter to the
question of whether the traditional media of newspapers, conventional TV
networks, and radio stations will be able to survive the assault of web-based
and social media.

Notes

1 Murthy, *Twitter*, 19.
2 Tamara A. Small, "Social Media & Canadian Politicians" (paper presented, the School
   of Public Policy University of Calgary, May 2013).
3 Peter Hamby, "Did Twitter Kill the Boys on the Bus? Searching for a Better Way
   to Cover a Campaign," Joan Shorenstein Center on the Press, Politics and Public
   Policy, John F. Kennedy School of Government, discussion paper (Cambridge, MA:

Harvard University, September 2013), http://shorensteincenter.org/wp-content/uploads/2013/08/d80_hamby.pdf, 4.

4   Ibid., 27.

5   Ibid., 36.

6   Michael Hirschorn, "About Facebook," *Atlantic*, October 1, 2007, 152.

7   Castells, *Networks of Outrage and Hope*, 7.

8   Murthy, *Twitter*, 13.

9   Craig Offman, "'Room with a View': Hotels Mine Social Media to Win over Guests," *Globe and Mail*, October 14, 2013: A1, 10.

10 Zuckerman, *Rewire*, 108.

11 Castells, *Networks of Outrage and Hope*.

12 Brian Stelter, "The Facebooker Who Befriended Obama," *New York Times*, July 7, 2008, http://www.nytimes.com/2008/07/07/technology/07hughes.html?pagewanted=all; Bret Swanson, "Obama Ran a Capitalist Campaign," *Wall Street Journal*, November 7, 2008, http://online.wsj.com/articles/SB122602757767707787.

13 Quoted in ibid.

14 Dan Balz, *Collision 2012: Obama vs. Romney and the Future of Election in America*, ed. James Silberman (New York: Viking, 2013), 40.

15 Ibid., 78–79.

16 Taras and Waddell, "The 2011 Federal Election," 71–107.

17 Tamara A. Small, "Are We Friends Yet? Online Relationship Marketing by Political Parties," in *Political Marketing in Canada*, ed. Alex Marland, Thierry Giasson, and Jennifer Lees-Marshment (Vancouver: UBC Press, 2012), 193–208.

18 Glen McGregor, "Critical Posts on PM's Facebook Page Deleted," *Calgary Herald*, November 12, 2011: A6.

19 Small, "Are We Friends Yet?," 208.

20 Baran, "Social Media in Campaign 2011," 83.

21 Tom Flanagan, "Social Media Change Our Politics? They Haven't Yet," *Globe and Mail*, May 6, 2013: A11.

22 Small, "Social Media & Canadian Politicians."

23 Ibid.

24 Amy Mitchell and Tom Rosenstiel, "What Facebook and Twitter Mean for News," *The State of the News Media 2012*, The Pew Research Center's Project for Excellence in Journalism.

25 Hamby, "Did Twitter Kill the Boys on the Bus?," 36.

26 Clive Thompson, "I'm So Totally Digitally Close to You," *New York Times Magazine*, September 7, 2008: 45.

27 Ibid.

28 Steven Johnson, *Everything Bad Is Good for You* (New York: Riverhead Books, 2006), 119.

29 A.O. Scott quoted in Frank Rich, "Facebook Politicians Are Not Your Friends," *New York Times*, October 9, 2010, http://www.nytimes.com/2010/10/10/opinion/10rich.html.

30 Zuckerman, *Rewire*, 110.

31 Ira Wagman, "Log On, Goof Off, and Look Up: Facebook and the Rhythms of Canadian Internet Use," in *How Canadians Communicate III: Contexts of Canadian Popular Culture*, ed. Bart Beaty, Derek Briton, Gloria Filax, and Rebecca Sullivan (Edmonton: Athabasca University Press, 2010), 57.

32 Aboujaoude, *Virtually You*.

33 Ibid., 74.

34 Ibid., 81–82.

35 Frank Bruni, "Our Hard Drives, Ourselves," *New York Times*, November 18, 2012, http://www.nytimes.com/2012/11/18/opinion/sunday/Bruni-Our-Hard-Drives -Ourselves.html.

36 Valerie Fortney, "Facebook Prank a Lesson in Privacy," *Calgary Herald*, February 6, 2010: B5.

37 Eugene Strickland, "You'll Always Have a Friend with Facebook," *Calgary Herald*, June 2, 2007: C8.

38 Wagman, "Log On, Goof Off."

39 Zuckerman, *Rewire*, 107.

40 Richtel, "Attached to Technology."

41 Alyssa Schwartz, "Grownups Get their Facebook Fix," *Globe and Mail*, March 31, 2007: L9.

42 Gardner and Davis, *The App Generation*, 101–2.

43 Gladwell, "Small Change."

44 Elisabeth Noelle-Neumann, *The Spiral of Silence: Public Opinion—Our Social Skin* (Chicago: University of Chicago Press, 1993).

45 Gardner and Davis, *The App Generation*, 77–78.

46 Paul Felix Lazarsfeld, Bernard Berelson, and Hazel Gaudet, *The People's Choice: How the Voter Makes Up His Mind in a Presidential Election* (New York: Columbia University Press, 1944).

47 Zuckerman, *Rewire*, 111.

48 Castells, *Networks of Outrage and Hope*, 175.

49 Vindu Goel, "Facebook Eases Privacy Rules for Teenagers," *New York Times*, October, 17, 2013, http://www.nytimes.com/2013/10/17/technology/facebook-changes -privacy-policy-for-teenagers.html?pagewanted=all.

50 Lori Andrews, *I Know Who You Are and I Saw What You Did* (New York: Free Press, 2011), 126–28.

51 Quoted in Rosen, "The Web Means the End of Forgetting."

52 Andrews, *I Know Who You Are*, 137.

53 Claire Cain Miller and Somini Sengupta, "Selling Secrets of Phone Users to Adver- tisers," *New York Times*, October, 6, 2013, http://www.nytimes.com/2013/10/06/ technology/selling-secrets-of-phone-users-to-advertisers.html?pagewanted=all.

54 Al Gore, *The Future: Six Drivers of Global Change* (New York: Random House, 2013), 81.

55 Cited in Gardner and Davis, *The App Generation*, 83.

56 Rosen, "The Web Means the End of Forgetting."

57 Viktor Mayer-Schonberger, *Delete: The Virtue of Forgetting in the Digital Age* (Princeton, NJ: Princeton University Press, 2009).

58 Ibid., 145–46.

59 Andrews, *I Know Who You Are*, 189–91.

60 See "Forget Me, Forget Me Not," *Globe and Mail*, July 12, 2014: F9.

61 Hamby, "Did Twitter Kill the Boys on the Bus?"

62 Ibid., 81.

63 Murthy, *Twitter*, 39.

64 Virginia Heffernan, "The Game of Twitter," *New York Times*, June 12, 2006.

65 Ibid.

66 Ibid.

67 *Huffington Post*, "Nenshi AMA: Reditt Peppers Calgary Mayor with Questions During 'Ask Me Anything,'" October 10, 2013, http://www.huffingtonpost .ca/2013/10/10/nenshi-ama-reddit_n_4080833.html.

68 Fullduplex, *Peace, Order and Googleable Government 2013*, 4, http://fullduplex.ca/wp -content/uploads/2014/02/POGG2013.pdf.

69 *Winnipeg Sun*, "'F---you,' Winnipeg MP Tweets," November 16, 2011, http://www .torontosun.com/2011/11/16/f----you-winnipeg-mp-tweets.

70 Joanna Smith, "NDP MP Pat Martin 'Signs Off' after Calling Tories 'Rat Faced Whores,'" *Toronto Star*, December 20, 2012, http://www.thestar.com/news/ canada/2012/12/20/ndp_mp_pat_martin_signs_off_from_twitter_after_calling_ tories_rat_faced_whores.html.

71 Jonathan Kay, "Warning Signs of Patrick Brazeau's Unravelling on Twitter for Every-one to See," *National Post*, February 7, 2013, http://fullcomment.nationalpost. com/2013/02/07/jonathan-kay-warning-signs-of-patrick-brazeaus-unravelling-on-twitter-for-everyone-to-see/.

72 Small, "Social Media & Canadian Politicians"; Amber Hildebrandt, "The 'Twitter Campaign,' but Who Cares?," *CBC News*, April 1, 2011, http://www.cbc.ca/news.

73 Taras and Waddell, "The 2011 Federal Election."

74 Baran, "Social Media in Campaign 2011," 85.

75 Samara, *The Neighbourhoods of #cdnpoli*, 2011, http://www.samaracanada.com/ research/current-research/the-neighbourhoods-of-cdnpoli.

76 Shaomei Wu and Jake M. Hofman, Cornell University / Yahoo Research, "Who Says What to Whom on Twitter," https://iriss.stanford.edu/sites/all/files/dsi/Duncan%20 Study%201.pdf.

77 Citing the Cornell University and Yahoo Research Study in Hildebrandt, "The 'Twitter Campaign.'"

78 See also Baran, "Social Media in Campaign 2011," 82.

79 Tamara A. Small, "The Not-so Social Network: The Use of Twitter by Canada's Party Leaders." This citation is from an essay/chapter for a forthcoming book that was provided to me by the author.

80 Hamby, "Did Twitter Kill the Boys on the Bus?," 27.

81 Ibid., 37.

82 Ibid., 52.

83 Jen Gerson, "Twitter and the Alberta Election" (presentation, University of Calgary School for Public Policy, May 2012).

84 Lisa O'Carroll and Helene Mulholland, "Mayor's Love-in with Murdoch May Yield Backing for Tory Job," *Globe and Mail*, August 3, 2012: A3.

85 Robert X. Cringely, "Hard Numbers, Chilling Facts: What the Government Does with Your Data," *Info World*, October 17, 2013, http://www.infoworld.com/article/ 2612703/cringely/hard-numbers--chilling-facts--what-the-government-does -with-your-data.html.

86 Ithiel de Sola Pool, *Technology without Boundaries: On Telecommunications in a Global Age* (Cambridge, MA: Harvard University Press, 1990), 261–62.

87 Quoted in Don Braid, "Polls Need Personal Touch," *Calgary Herald*, October 16, 2008: A3.

88 Gitlin, *Media Unlimited*, 165.

Six
Falling Stars: The Future of Newspapers and Conventional Broadcasting

One of the great questions hanging over the future of both journalism and democracy is whether the traditional media will be able to withstand the devastating force of media shock. By traditional media I am referring to newspapers, conventional over-the-air TV networks, local radio stations, books, and magazines. The assault on their very existence is coming from several directions at once. First, the merger of every medium with every other medium has meant that old media forms exist in a kind of half-life, a kind of limbo state between what they are now and what they are about to become. As mentioned previously, the existence of a new kind of hybrid media such as The Huffington Post, Reddit, or The Daily Beast that is part newspaper, part blog, part broadcaster, part magazine, part photo gallery, and part social media site, is altering and transgressing all of the old boundaries. Second, the easy availability of free media, whether it be music, news, or TV programs, is a dire threat to many of the traditional media. Getting people to pay for products that they can now get for free—in other words changing the habits and expectations of an entire generation—will be a Herculean task. Third, we have seen a transfer of power to gatekeepers such as Apple, Facebook, and Google, which, through apps and online services, can determine the access that people have to other media. What makes this last development so critical is that this new media infrastructure is largely beyond the control of the federal government or the CRTC, which have acted as protectors of the current media for decades.

Media guru Clay Shirky has little patience for those who pretend that nothing has really changed, who don't understand that the old institutions and assumptions are crumbling. As Shirky has put it with regard to newspapers in particular,

> When someone demands to know how we are going to replace newspapers, they are really demanding to be told that we are not living through a revolution. They are demanding to be told that old systems won't break before new systems are in place. They are demanding to be told that ancient social bargains aren't in peril,

that core institutions will be spared, that new methods of spreading information will improve previous practice rather than upending it. They are demanding to be lied to.[1]

Even if one doesn't accept Shirky's dire assessment, we have now reached the point where even the optimists have had to take a deep breath. Some of the great newspapers of the twentieth century have gone bankrupt, and others have been reduced to shadows of their former selves. The music industry has lost well over half of its revenue since 2000, movie attendance reached a 16-year low in 2011, and most tellingly perhaps, during Comcast's takeover of NBC/Universal, the once indomitable TV network was given a book value of zero, as in $0,[2] even though Comcast's bid was for other parts of the NBC/Universal package and had little to do with conventional television. Much of the magazine industry is also floating in a sea of red ink. The circulation of Canada's largest news magazine, *Maclean's*, plummeted by 7.3 per cent between 2007 and 2011.[3] Everyone is bleeding. Most pointedly, the Canadian Media Guild estimates that 10,000 media jobs, including journalists, technicians, and managers, were lost between 2008 and 2013.[4] Many in the traditional media now seem to be waiting for the next shoe to drop—and shoes are dropping all the time.

The conventional wisdom has always been that when faced with the arrival of a new type of media, old media forms find new niches, play to their strengths, and reinvent themselves in unforeseen ways. The golden age of radio may have receded from memory, but radio has remained vibrant and prosperous, in part perhaps because young people can now take their music with them and Canadians spend more time trapped in their cars on long commutes than was the case a generation ago. Films did not disappear with the advent of TV, but the industry adjusted by finding new windows—the multiplex, cable channels, pay-per-view, DVDs, and online sources such as Netflix, Amazon Prime, and Crackle. Cable was the new medium in the 1970s and 1980s and has managed to hold onto its customers despite, and perhaps because of, changes to other media. As described in Chapter Four, cable programming has become more lurid, shocking, and extreme, and cable channels such as HBO and Showtime have led the way in producing Big TV: the new generation of serialized shows such as *Mad Men*, *Breaking Bad*, *Homeland*, and *Game of Thrones* that are remaking television and recapturing mass audiences.

It's not clear, however, that the old patterns of challenge and adaptation will continue to work as they have in the past. The harsh reality is that while some aspects of the traditional media will survive by changing their forms, others may not survive at all. Clearly there are a number of news organizations that exist today that will not be operating in five or ten years. They are nearing the end of the road.

This is not just a ho-hum, it-really-doesn't-matter problem. With their ability to assemble mass audiences and help set the political agenda, newspapers, TV networks, and local radio stations have played a crucial role in giving Canadians a sense of both community and national belonging. They have allowed Canadians to see the same images, watch and read about the same issues and personalities, listen to the same sounds, and live together in what Benedict Anderson has described as "an imagined community."[5] While most Canadians have never visited Parliament Hill, seen the Prime Minster or other party leaders in person, been to the Gaspé, seen the Canadian North or walked the streets of East Vancouver, the mass media have been able to take us on these journeys. TV was, and remains, the great nationalizing force in Canadian life. If the traditional media are washed away or deeply disfigured, then the main public squares on which Canadian public life has taken place will be much smaller—or not exist at all.

As discussed earlier, creating and maintaining a national communications system against the backdrop of vast distances, sharp linguistic divides, and the endless flood of American mass culture have taken considerable will and imagination. One of the founders of public broadcasting in Canada, Graham Spry, once remarked that Canada's alternatives in broadcasting were either the "state or the United States."[6] Without strong support and incentives from governments, the Canadian media system would have been absorbed by the American media system decades ago. The development of a communication system that could offset at least to some degree the gravitational pull of the American media came in a wide range of forms: the creation of the CBC and other public broadcasters; tax laws that discouraged companies from advertising in foreign publications, along with an array of tax breaks or other financial incentives; rules limiting foreign ownership; Canadian-content provisions for TV, music, films, and magazines; simultaneous substitution; and lenient licensing requirements for Canadian BDUs and broadcasters.

Another reason why the traditional media are so crucial is that newspapers and TV newsrooms are still the main producers of news. As mentioned in Chapter Three, virtually 95 per cent of what appears in blogs or is discussed on social media sites such as Twitter is produced by the traditional media. The vast majority of news workers are employed by newspapers, while others work for TV stations or for wire services such as Canadian Press or QMI. To put it differently, the news about political events, celebrities, scandals, crimes, and disasters that is "trending" or being debated online is being paid for by subscribers to and users of the old media. If the traditional media continue to weaken, web-based media will be weakened as well. The health of one is directly linked to the health of the other.

Moreover, we have relied on the traditional media and the journalists that they employ to carry out functions that are critical to democracy. Aside from being the great conveyer belt of daily information, they provide "accountability news."[7] As discussed previously, journalists are entrusted with the famous "watchdog" role of holding those in power accountable for their actions. Without a conscientious press, the basic work of a society—of identifying and overcoming problems and making lives better—would never get done. According to media critic Tom Rosensteil, without credible news organizations much of our public life "would occur in shadows. We won't know what we won't know."[8] Or as Alex Jones of Harvard University has put it, "if truth is in shorter supply," then "that would be a terrible blow to all of us."[9]

Simply put, a courageous press is society's surest guarantee against the abuse of power. Jones gives the example of a famous scene in the classic movie *Deadline USA*, where a news editor played by Humphrey Bogart holds up a telephone to a mob boss who is trying to prevent the paper from exposing large-scale bribery and corruption. "What's that sound?" the boss demands to know. Bogart replies, "That's the press, baby, the press! And there's nothing that you can do about it. Nothing!"[10]

Referring to the state of American journalism, the late James Carey believed that although "the weaknesses of modern journalism have become increasingly apparent and debilitating," he was also convinced that

> despite the heavy weather one can bring to bear on modern
> journalism, the truth is also that the press has been a bulwark
> of liberty in our time and no one has come up with a better
> arrangement. The watchdog notion of the press, a press independent
> of all institutions, a press that represents the public, a press that
> unmasks interest and privilege, a press that shines the hot glare of
> publicity into all the dark corners of the republic, a press that searches
> out expert knowledge among the welter of opinion, a press that
> seeks to inform the private citizen, these are ideas and roles that have
> served us well though some dark times. Not perfectly, not without
> fault, but well.[11]

Given that almost all news organizations have had to sharply reduce their budgets and staffs and have had fewer resources for investigative work, Carey's assessment may now be too optimistic. But it's not too much to say that on its best days, at its best moments, Canadian news organizations still make an extraordinary difference to the quality of Canadian democracy.

This chapter will examine the challenges being faced by newspapers, over-the-air TV networks, and local radio stations in Canada. The chapter will not deal with magazines, films, or book publishing, although the dark clouds of a deepening crisis hangs over these media as well. The irony is that while more people are reading newspapers and watching TV than ever before, the business models that have sustained the Canadian media for generations are quickly collapsing.

The following chapter is not meant to read like an autopsy report; there is much life in many of our best media institutions. But it may come across as if it were written in a hospital emergency room with too many of the patients waiting for treatment and uncertain if they will make it.

"Every Newspaper Reader That Dies Leaves No Heir"

The newspaper industry has fallen on hard times. Canadian newspaper revenues tumbled from roughly $5.7 billion in 2000 to $4.1 billion in 2012.[12] There is also little indication that this downhill trend will level off any time soon. While some of the losses were no doubt due to the recession that hit with such devastating force beginning in 2008, the economic downturn merely compounded a crisis that was already underway largely due to the forces unleashed by media shock. In what Robert McChesney and John Nichols have called "the great disassembling," major newspapers have closed, jobs have been cut en masse, stock prices have been battered, bureaus have been shuttered, salaries have been chopped, Sunday editions have been scrapped, and papers have shrunk in size.[13] In the US, prominent newspapers such as the *Chicago Tribune*, the *Los Angeles Times*, and the *Philadelphia Inquirer*, which were once thought to be invulnerable, the very pillars of their communities, have had to declare bankruptcy. The downward toboggan ride has gained such speed that the *Philadelphia Inquirer* was sold in 2012 for just 10 per cent of its 2006 sale price.[14] Some newspapers, such as the *Seattle Post Intelligencer*, have vacated print entirely and only have online editions. Even the *New York Times*, which continues to be among the most-read newspapers on the planet with close to 30 million digital readers, required a $250-million lifeline from Mexican billionaire Carlos Slim in order to stay afloat. It continues to limp from crisis to crisis.

In Canada, the most spectacular casualty has been CanWest Global, which owned Global TV as well as a stable of newspapers that included such venerable titles as the *National Post*, the *Gazette* (Montreal), the *Vancouver Sun* and *Province*, the *Calgary Herald*, the *Ottawa Citizen*, and the *Edmonton Journal*. The newspaper group, which has been resurrected as Postmedia, is now under new ownership. The company was still burdened by over $450 million in debt in 2012, continues to cut jobs, has stopped publishing Sunday papers, and is deflating the size of its hard-copy editions. Editing is done in central-ized locations, and some of it is done overseas.

Some observers argue that these newspapers would have prospered if it weren't for the brutal debt loads that their owners had assumed when they went on buying sprees in the early 2000s. While there is much truth in this, the car-nage experienced by the newspaper industry across North America has been deep, widespread, and unrelenting. There are few newspapers with their heads above the waterline, regardless of their previous corporate histories and debt loads.

The quotation that forms the title of this section, "every newspaper reader who dies leaves no heir," is taken from a speech by Florian Sauvageau, one of Canada's leading media experts.[15] But Sauvageau is hardly alone in his pessi-mism. The American journalist Philip Meyers forecasts that at the current rate of migration away from newspapers by young readers, newspapers will run out of readers by 2043. But even that date may be too optimistic. Although newspapers are relatively cheap and portable, and gather and organize infor-mation effectively, circulation in Canada has declined steadily for decades. In 1950 over 100 per cent of Canadian households received at least one newspaper (explained by the fact that many households subscribed to both the morning and evening papers that thrived in many Canadian cities). By 2012, paid subscriptions had dropped to about 27 per cent of households.[16] In other words, 70 per cent of circulation has evaporated. This downward spiral in circulation has been more dramatic than the losses experienced by the newspaper industry in virtually all other Western countries although not by a great margin. In the US, for instance, almost 33 per cent of households and in the UK over 30 per cent of households still subscribed to a daily newspaper in 2012.[17] In most European countries, however, newspaper reading remains a way of life, although some of the leading papers are begin-ning to experience substantial drops in circulation.

The experience of the country's largest-circulation newspaper, the *Toronto Star*, is typical.[18] Despite being the market leader in Canada's largest metro-politan area, circulation plummeted by 41 per cent from 2007 to 2011. Postmedia's flagship paper, the *National Post*, also faced strong headwinds, with print readership tumbling from an average weekly readership of 1,337, 800 in 2000 to only 814,898 in 2011. Montreal's *La Presse* was in a similar predicament; weekly print circulation nosedived by 14 per cent between 2007 and 2011. The *Calgary Sun*'s losses were even more devastating: its weekly print circulation fell from an average of 428,648 in 2007 to just 207, 385 in 2011—a drop in readership of 51 per cent.

While some observers may take heart from the fact that online reader-ships have grown, this is not necessarily good news. First, given that almost all newspapers in Canada erected pay-walls around their websites and digital editions in 2012, it is too early to say how reliable their earlier readership numbers are. Second, while digital editions can be produced for at least half of what it costs to produce a hard-copy edition because papers don't have to worry about newsprint and distribution costs, the hard reality is that an online subscriber is worth only a fraction, one-fifth or less by some esti-mates, of the value of a print subscriber. Alex Jones pegs the value at only a tenth.[19] This is because there is so much competition, so many stars in the Internet sky for advertisers to choose from, that the prices that newspapers can charge for advertising online is far less than they can charge for print ads. In addition, as Robert McChesney reports, as much as 80 per cent of digital newspaper advertising is placed through brokers that take as much as 50 per cent of the revenue.[20] The industry consensus is that "print dollars are being replaced by digital dimes." The irony for most newspapers is that as they invest more in their online editions, they are likely to lose even more money, further sealing their fate.

While there has been a breathtaking decline in paid circulation, it's the disappearance of younger readers that is causing newspaper executives the biggest headaches. Most newspaper readers are now 55 and over, with digital natives largely vanishing as subscribers.[21] A study conducted in 2009 by the Centre d'études sur les médias at Laval University found that a little over one-third of those between 18 and 35 were daily newspaper readers, com-pared to close to 60 per cent of those over 50.[22] Go to any of the down-town apartments where many young people live in our major cities and you will be hard pressed to find a hard-copy newspaper in front of anyone's door in the morning. While they might glance at headlines at coffee shops or on public transit, for most digital natives newspaper reading no longer seems to be a part of daily life. As veteran journalist Russell Baker has described the situation, "Surveys showing that more and more young people get their news from television and computers breeds a melancholy sense that the press is yesterday's thing, a horse drawn buggy on an eight-lane interstate."[23]

The hard fact is that newspapers have none of the attributes that young people want when they are searching for news. They expect news to be con-tinual, immediate, interactive, and, most important, free. According to Florian Sauvageau, digital natives have become accustomed to digesting news "snacks" rather than eating full meals. They are used to the jolts that come with news flashes, Twitter feeds, brief headlines, and short bursts of information. Print newspapers are the very opposite of what young people have become used to; they are static, have longer stories, and are published only once a day.

The reality may be even grimmer than Sauvageau, Philip Meyers, and Russell Baker suggest. This is because many digital natives seem to be "newsless"—they are not interested in the news, regardless of where it appears. A survey conducted by the Pew Research Center in 2012 found that almost 30 per cent of those 25 or younger received no news from any platform on a typical day, while almost 20 per cent of those between 25 and 39 fell into this category.[24] News consumption among digital natives was almost half that of those 65 and older. In fact, audiences for TV news shows and radio hotline programs are dominated by seniors. Even news blogs tend to attract an older readership. At some point many of the current genres will die simply because their audiences will themselves have died off.

To make matters worse, digital natives are part of what Sauvageau describes as a "freebie culture."[25] News is something that young people have never paid for—and presumably never intend to pay for. A 2011 study conducted by the Canadian Media Research Consortium found that over 80 per cent of those interviewed would refuse to pay for news, while only a meagre 4 per cent said that they would, with 15 per cent undecided.[26] Pushing back the prevailing culture, making headway against what Robert Levine calls "the free ride," will not be easy for newspapers.[27]

While many of the fundamentals of the newspaper industry have gone wrong, the greatest challenge has undoubtedly come from online competition. The online assault has come from many different directions, but the most devastating has been on the advertising front. According to estimates tabulated by IAB Canada, an industry think tank for the digital marketing and advertising sectors, advertising on web-based media surpassed newspaper advertising in Canada for the first time in 2010.[28] Until recently, advertising accounted for roughly three-quarters of the revenue of Canadian newspapers, with classified ads accounting for roughly one-third of the total.[29] To put it mildly, we have come a long way from the old days when local department stores or car dealerships were dependent on newspapers, and as a result had no choice but to accept high advertising rates. Now, not only are they less dependent on newspapers, but some avoid them almost entirely.

Here a number of problems have congealed at the same time. The first is that with so many sites to choose from, advertisers are spending less money on any one site. The most popular sites for advertisers are search engines such as Google and Yahoo, where advertising is highly customized and feedback to advertisers is almost instantaneous. The complete absence of any e-strategy during the early stages of the Internet means that most newspapers haven't developed the sophisticated databases and algorithms necessary to target digital readers with customized ads to nearly the degree that Google, Amazon, Facebook, or Apple has. As Robert Levine explains, "The airline ad budget doesn't go to the publication with the most appropriate content … it goes to the site where users are searching for 'flights to Paris.' The incentive to produce compelling journalism has been replaced by one to track readers."[30] It's also the case that cutting coupons out of newspapers just isn't what it used to be. Newspapers now have to compete against web-based behemoths such as Groupon and Priceline that dominate the discount shopping business. While Canadian newspapers have entered the online discount business, with Postmedia's *Swarm Jam* being one example, it remains to be seen whether these late arrivals stand much of a chance.

Another devastating blow is that revenues from employment, real estate, and other classified ads, a key driver of newspaper profits, have been savaged by a host of online competitors such as Kijiji, Craigslist, and Monster.com, which offer similar services but for free. In addition, as discussed in Chapter Five, most users of social media sites now rely on recommendations from friends before buying a product or choosing a restaurant.

For decades the art of the newspaper was the art of bundling. The newspaper could bundle weather, sports, news from city hall, entertainment, and business news in a convenient and relatively cheap package. Today there is no part of the bundle that can't be found online. Or, to put it differently, newspapers now face deadly rivals at every turn. The *Toronto Star*, for instance, once competed almost exclusively against its hometown rivals, the *Toronto Sun* and the *Globe and Mail*, with each newspaper catering to a different slice of the social, economic, and political pie. The *Star* now has to compete in specific areas, such as financial news, sports, entertainment, and world affairs against a myriad of specialized websites, blogs, aggregators, and other newspapers from around the world. Newspapers have to be so much better than they used to be just to be in the game at all.

Moreover, how the online chips have fallen has also harmed newspapers. The Internet, as Matthew Hindman has demonstrated, is a "winner-take-all" environment in which there are a few large whales swimming in the same ocean with millions of smaller fish.[31] In terms of news, this means that big brand news organizations such as Yahoo, the BBC, CNN, the *New York Times*, the *Huffington Post*, the *Wall Street Journal*, and the *Washington Post* attract the lion's share of traffic. Instead of showcasing smaller publications, the Internet has made the powerful even more powerful.

If this weren't enough, there is now an additional layer of competition. New Canadians have the capacity to connect with media in their former homelands in ways that were unimaginable to previous waves of immigrants. As a study of the media habits of Italians, North Africans, and Haitians living in Montreal suggests, immigrants now live dual media lives—one in Canada and the other by maintaining contact with media from their countries of origin.[32] Among new Canadians, the degree of exposure to Canadian news varies from person to person and group to group. In some cases it may not be very much at all.

Last, and perhaps most threatening, is the competition that comes from online aggregators such as National Newswatch Canada, Bourque. com, Google News, The Huffington Post, Reddit, and RealClear Politics. Aggregators scoop up articles, editorials, and opinion pieces from across a wide spectrum of newspapers, magazines, and blogs without paying for them. Basically the work done by the *New York Times*, with its small army of Pulitzer prizes, dozens of national and international bureaus, and over 1,000 mostly seasoned reporters, appears for free on a website operated by someone else, who then presents this treasure chest of articles as their own product. To add insult to injury, not only do aggregators pursue the same advertisers that newspapers do, but they have an inherent advantage. In what Matthew Hindman describes as "rule by the most heavily linked," sites that have a greater number of links rank higher in Google search results, so that users are directed to aggregators before they are directed to newspapers.[33] So readers' attention is drawn to Reddit, Google News, The Huffington Post, or Digg rather than to the newspapers and other media from which these aggregators have culled their stories. To Alex Jones, aggregators are "parasite sites,"[34] while Rupert Murdoch refers to them as "pirates."[35]

As discussed in Chapter Four, newspapers and magazines are caught in a Catch-22. If they don't allow their articles to appear on these sites, then they risk losing readers. There is still some advantage, after all, to having readers pass through their sites. Some readers might stay, and the higher view count might impress advertisers. On the other hand, if they allow their best work to be heisted by aggregators, then their own business models can't possibly work. The great irony is that by showcasing the very best in print journalism, aggregators are killing off the very news organizations on which their own business depends. In 2013, lawmakers in Germany, France, and Italy, among a host of other countries in the European Union, were proposing changes in copyright legislation that would compensate newspapers and magazines when Google and other aggregators used their materials. Some observers were worried, however, that establishing such a toll would hinder what had been the free flow of information and with it people's ability to find the information that they need. Critics argued that the legislation would harm the economy, cost jobs, and still not save newspapers, many of which were already beyond saving.

The fierceness of online competition aside, some observers believe that the industry's deepest wounds have been self-inflicted. Not only were newspaper owners almost completely unprepared for the e-revolution that was about to swamp them, but they systematically devalued their own products. For instance, Christopher Waddell argues that part of the problem is that both newspapers and TV networks started cutting long before the onset of the current crisis.[36] During the 1990s, at a time when profit margins were high, gluttonous owners squeezed as much revenue as they could from what they saw as lucrative cash cows. The situation was compounded when newspapers were taken over by larger, debt-laden corporations that looked for fat to trim only to find that little existed. For a variety of reasons the cuts were too deep. Doing more with less meant fewer reporters, less time for investigative journalism, a younger and less experienced workforce, and lower salaries. The more expensive certain types of stories became to produce, the more likely it became that those stories would not be covered at all. As a consequence, the quality of journalism dropped significantly. Even when it came to local news, where newspapers and local TV stations have a natural monopoly, they were increasingly unable to deliver much more than car chases, crime, weather, and sports. As Waddell points out,

> People do want to read about and see what is happening in their
> communities, yet newspapers and TV in Canada have largely
> forgotten that they replaced specialists with generalists and
> stopped covering things like school boards and much of municipal
> government and in most cases have even abandoned putting reporters
> at provincial legislatures.[37]

As a result, accountability news, which Alex Jones and others see as the most essential task of journalism, increasingly fell by the wayside because it became too expensive to produce.

One new wrinkle involves the free "bullet" newspapers that are available in most major cities in Canada. These freebies allow companies to compete in markets where they don't own a major newspaper and attract advertisers who want to reach a younger, fast-moving crowd that only has time for a quick glance at the news. *24 Hours* and *Metro* are the most prominent titles. *24 Hour* is owned by Quebecor, and the Canadian edition of *Metro* is majority owned by Torstar, which owns the *Toronto Star* as well as a number of other newspapers. In Montreal, *Metro* is majority owned by *La Presse*. *Metro* is part of a large international chain of newspapers headquartered in Sweden. These bullet papers have garnered sizable readerships—*Metro Vancouver* had a daily circulation of over 155,000, *Metro Toronto* close to 260,000, and *Montreal 24 Heures* almost 180,000 readers in 2012.[38] While they produce original stories and often do outstanding work, critics point out that they are not newspapers in the traditional sense. Thin, dripping with ads, and targeted at

frantic commuters, they are little more than a "mini-me" version of traditional newspapers.

Strangely these micro-papers in some cases compete against the larger
print editions of papers owned by the same corporations. The strategy may
not make much sense. While they attract younger readers who have largely
abandoned conventional newspapers and hence constitute a valuable target
market, bullet papers may discourage these same readers from paying for the
main newspaper because they may feel that they have already read the paper.
The more difficult conundrum for the industry is that these papers perpetuate and reinforce the culture of "free news" that has become so deeply
entrenched. But they raise an even larger issue: as successful as they are in
providing headlines, the problem from the perspective of accountability journalism is that these micro-papers have stripped away much of the editorial
and journalistic content that gives newspapers their character and arguably
their purpose. Perhaps we are approaching the point now where we have
newspapers without journalism.[39]

More than a few analysts believe that newspapers need to break the back
of the freebie culture and establish a price for news if they are to survive. But
getting people to pay may be the functional equivalent of trying to nail Jell-o
to the wall. Those in favour of creating pay-walls argue that users are more
than willing to pay for some forms of media. They pay their cable and smart-
phone bills. They subscribe to Netflix, make micro-payments for iTunes,
video games, books, and apps, and pay for concerts, movies, and pay-per-view
sports events. But news has been different. Paying for news would cut against
the grain in a number of ways. First, as discussed earlier, the vast majority of
digital natives have never paid for news, and, as we have seen from surveys,
they may continue to refuse to pay. But more critically, many Canadians are
the proverbial one paycheque away from falling over a financial cliff. Even
if they are willing to pay for a subscription or two, there are limits to how
much else they will pay for.

By 2014, virtually all of the major English Canadian newspapers were
behind a pay-wall. In Quebec, however, with the exception of *La Presse*,
almost all papers remain free online. It's too early to say whether these pay
moats will be successful. But there is reason for concern. Re-establishing a
payment culture can work only if papers band together, create a "ring of fire,"
to ensure that there are as few places that people can go to get free news
as possible. But not every news organization will want to play ball. News
organizations such as the CBC, the BBC, and certainly powerful aggregators
such as Google, Yahoo, or The Huffington Post or Reddit are unlikely to
go along. In the case of public broadcasters, setting up a pay-wall would

contravene their public-service mandates, and aggregators need the "freebie" culture in order to survive. On an ideological level, some believe that paying for news violates one of the web's essential characteristics, that it must remain a place for free expression and exchange. Paying for news would destroy net neutrality and the very spirit on which the web is based.

But there is another key question: whether pay-walls and micro-payments will generate enough revenue to stop the financial tidal wave that's currently crashing down on newspapers. It's not clear that the math adds up—newspapers will have to sell a great many $19.99-a-month subscriptions to make a big difference.

The *Wall Street Journal* is perhaps the best example of a paper that maintains high subscription rates and still attracts a large readership. It attracts an elite audience that can easily afford to pay, and offers highly specialized and arguably vital information and analysis for the financial industry. For many, doing without the *WSJ* is far more costly than not having a subscription. The same can be said for the *New York Times*. The *Times* first tried a pay-wall in 2005 but removed it when it became clear that most of its readers were turning elsewhere for news and commentary. The *Times* now makes some of its articles available for free each month, after which a subscription is imposed. But not all newspapers have the same value to their readers as the *Wall Street Journal*, the *New York Times*, and arguably the *Globe and Mail*. When New York's *Newsday* set up a pay-wall, it attracted only 35 subscribers in the first 3 months.[40] In effect the emperor had no clothes, or at least no clothes that anyone wanted to pay for. Online traffic to the *Times* of London fell by more than half after its pay-wall went up.[41] It didn't take long before ad revenue crumbled as well. A study of three dozen American papers found that only 1 per cent of users continued to pay after a pay-wall was enforced.[42] For newspapers that are not seen as absolutely essential, a pay-wall may be the ultimate self-inflicted wound.

Nor are apps much of a solution. Only 11 per cent of Americans subscribed to a news app in 2011, but close to 90 per cent of them received the apps for free.[43] Paying for apps is another matter, and it must be remembered that hosts such as Facebook and Apple can take a large cut of the revenues.

One of the boldest experiments in Canadian journalism is being undertaken by *La Presse*, Montreal's most popular newspaper. *La Presse* invested over $40 million in a new tablet edition of the newspaper, *La Presse+*. The paper beefed up its staff and has created a hybrid medium with videos, multiple links, and photo blogs that has attracted a large number of subscribers. The tablet edition now brings in close to 30 per cent of all revenues. The gamble is that by investing money and improving quality, *La Presse+* will become the must-read paper in Quebec.

Among the best examples of newspapers that provide value are those that have carved out specialized niches, such as the *Hill Times* and *iPolitics* have for politics, the *Western Producer* has for agriculture, or the *Daily Oil Bulletin* has for energy professionals. These publications are directed at professional constituencies that need access to deeper reservoirs of information and analysis in order to conduct business. Moreover, some of these publications offer auxiliary information services with their subscriptions: intelligence reports, websites that contain highly detailed weather reports or up-to-the minute sales figures, or blogs that provide very specific nuggets of information. Most critically, advertisers are given access to customized audiences that are likely to pay attention to their ads.

One would think that local newspapers enjoy a similar advantage because of their near monopoly over local news. This is certainly the case with small-town newspapers that report on what's taking place at city hall, cover local sports teams, and publish photos taken at bake sales or the local church. Small-town papers can also cash in on old-style classified ads, because their readers don't necessarily need to go to Craigslist or Kijiji or Facebook if their goal is to sell something to people who might live down the street or a few blocks over. The problem for many city papers, however, is that they have already become so weakened and so battered by cuts and debt that they can no longer provide the value that readers are looking for. As one big city newspaper publisher in the US admitted when told of new plans to invigorate his newspaper through intensive local coverage, "This is great, but I don't have anything left in this paper that I think anybody would buy anymore."[44] Moreover, even when it comes to local news, would-be competitors are lurking online. One interesting experiment is *AllNovaScotia.com*, a website devoted to business and political news in that province. Its revenue comes mostly from subscriptions, and it employs close to a dozen journalists.

The unfortunate reality, according to C. Edwin Baker, is that the market never rewards newspapers for the critical benefits that they provide for society. Non-readers receive these benefits even if they don't read or pay for papers. As Baker explains,

> many nonreaders of a newspaper benefit by a paper's high-quality investigative journalism that exposes corruption, hopefully leading to correction and better government. This benefit to nonreaders, however, does not generate revenue for the paper that would give it the incentive to provide this journalism. Even less does the paper known for its deep, hard-hitting investigative journalism receive

revenue for possibly the greatest benefit that its watchdog operation provides: deterrence of government or corporate corruption due to fear of exposure.[45]

To turn the question on its head, one has to ask how society would function if inspection reports on breaches of food safety never made headlines, if dangerously long waiting times for operations or in emergency rooms were never revealed, if dubious and ruinous financial practices of banks and corporations were never exposed, or if hockey concussions had never become a news story. The answer is that we would all have been poorer in tangible ways. The situation is magnified in Canada, where papers are pipelines for national news in a country where the connecting links cannot be taken for granted. The great irony is that there may be no market solution for an institution that is vital to the survival of the market itself.

The issue of who pays for news has become a central question for the future of democracy. This question has provoked both intense debate and a series of experiments. In the US, the Annenberg, Knight, MacArthur, Pew, Rockefeller, and Kaiser Family foundations have supported studies examining various options or subsidized reporting in areas such as health care and religion. A number of institutions have joined forces to fund ProPublica, a news organization that employs roughly three dozen journalists and offers its "deep dive" investigative stories to the mainstream media for free. The key to the kingdom for ProPublica is that its work is non-partisan and it employs experienced journalists. Despite the fact that ProPublica won Pulitzer Prizes for investigative journalism in 2010 and for national reporting in 2011, one of the great success stories in journalism has received little attention within its own arena. Strangely, ProPublica's reports are mostly ignored by the mainstream media. Presumably many of their stories are too hot to handle, media organizations may not want to give credit to an outside organization, and digging deeply into public-policy issues may be of little interest to news organizations that depend on reporting about crime, sports, and celebrities.

Another development is the so-called pro-am movement, which has amateur journalists working side-by-side with professionals. While this appears on the surface to be an exciting development, off-loading work to unpaid volunteers has its dangers. Volunteers need to be trained, may not be around when newspapers need them, have their own agendas, and may eventually feel exploited. Newspapers can't depend on people who, in Alex Jones's words, "want to perform journalism just for the fun of it."[46] So while employing citizen journalists appears at first glance to be cost-effective, the costs in the end may be deceptively high.

There have also been renewed calls for government intervention in the form of tax breaks or increased advertising. Some have suggested that readers receive a tax credit for subscribing to a newspaper or magazine. Quebec's influential *Le Devoir* operates as a charitable foundation and thus has a special tax status. In France, the government now provides over $1 billion annually in subsidies and tax breaks. While there is no shortage of imaginative solutions, all of them require money at a time when funds are in short supply for governments.

The dilemma, according to Alex Jones, is that newspapers are "like the railroad industry in the face of airplanes, automobiles and interstate highways. Railways were forced out of the city-to-city passenger business, which they had once dominated. But the industry survived by hauling freight and now trains move about two-thirds of the total tonnage in the country. Newspapers have to find a way to haul freight."[47] While it is difficult to imagine great old eminences such as the *Globe and Mail*, *La Presse*, and the *Toronto Star* disappearing entirely, they are unlikely to persist in their present forms. Nonetheless, in some way, news, like freight, will have to be moved.

The Great Canadian Television Crisis

By any conceivable measure, television remains the dominant medium, and its reign is likely to remain unassailable, at least for the foreseeable future. While Canadians now spend more time online than they do watching TV, online activity is scattered among a wide range of functions, such as being on Facebook, playing games, watching videos, writing email, and blogging. But TV is everywhere, all the time and inescapable. As discussed earlier, the average Canadian was glued to the TV set or watched TV shows online for roughly 28.2 hours a week in 2012, the equivalent of watching TV for more than a full day every week.[48] This translates into watching TV for an astonishing 50 days a year, and well over 10 years out of an average lifetime. Nor is there a precipitous drop in viewing among digital natives. Those between 18 and 34 watched close to 23 hours a week in 2012.[49] So even as younger Canadians are abandoning newspapers and reading fewer books or magazines, they remain consummate TV junkies.

And for all of the talk about the onslaught of the Internet and social media, a survey taken by the Pew Research Center's Project for Excellence in Journalism during the 2012 US presidential election found that most people still followed the election on cable and local TV news and considered them to be the most useful sources of information. While social media sites were growing as sources of news, they still lagged far behind TV. Newspapers and radio were supplementary media for most of those surveyed.

One of the reasons for TV's continued domination is that the visual sensation of being in front of a TV screen has never been more compelling. Gigantic, flat-screen, high-definition TVs that produce pictures of stunning sharpness and clarity, sling-boxes that allow viewers to take their home TV signals with them wherever they travel, personal video recorders with huge storage capacities, a seemingly endless array of channels and programming, the advent of 3D technology and high-fidelity sound have made this the golden age of TV viewing. In fact, the viewing experience has become so spectacular and indeed comfortable that people who own high-end home-entertainment centres are now spending less time attending sports or cultural events.[50] Why fight crowds, pay for transportation or parking, sit in uncomfortable seats, be overcharged for beer and nachos (and everything else), and take hours getting home, when the best seats are in front of your TV?

Perhaps the greatest change is in the source of TV viewing. Where TV and the Internet were once different media, they are now merging into one. TV programs are now being "broadcast" and more crucially produced by companies such as Netflix, YouTube, and Amazon that are essentially websites. Thirty-three per cent of Canadians watched web-based TV in 2012, with the typical viewer watching three hours per week. This means that conventional over-the-air TV broadcasters such as CTV, Global, and TVA now exist alongside both cable and satellite channels as well as "over the top" broadcasters (so called because signals reach audiences without the need of a cable box).

Each of these broadcasting systems exercises different levels of control over its audience and has a different financial model. Conventional TV networks offer viewers the fewest programming choices in a largely command-and-control system. Networks act as brokers, bringing the audience and advertisers together. The system is based on ratings, so programs are designed to attract a mass audience. Viewing is relatively passive, as schedules and advertising are dictated by the networks. Cable and pay TV, on the other hand, provide viewers with a smorgasbord of highly customized viewing options, but programs and viewing times are still controlled by the broadcasters. The system is based on subscriptions as well as advertising. Web-based broadcasting has an entirely different trajectory. In fact, viewing shows on Netflix or Hulu is in some ways the last spike in terms of me-media: audiences have the power to watch the shows that they want, when they want them, and for how long. This is the heartland of hyper-serialized viewing, or binge watching as some describe it—a TV watcher's version of blood doping. The fix is paid for through monthly subscriptions and micro-payments for each episode watched. Ads that interrupt the flow of viewing are gone; indeed, media economist Peter Miller argues that Netflix's greatest impact may be that it is conditioning viewers to watch TV without ads.[51] In 2013, over-the-top (OTT) viewing represented a relatively small cut of the TV revenue pie in Canada (2.5 per cent), but Miller estimates that this number could easily surpass 10 per cent by 2020.[52] The online TV phenomenon is also more evident in English-speaking Canada than in Quebec, largely because French-language viewers are still well served by the dramatic offerings of conventional and cable providers and seem less interested in US stories.[53]

When the legendary journalist and pop icon Hunter S. Thompson once famously pronounced that "the TV business is a cruel and shallow money trench, a long plastic hallway where thieves and pimps run free and good men die like dogs," he clearly wasn't referring to Canadian television.[54] Until recently, television was as secure and comfortable a business as you could find. Private broadcasters such as CTV and Global could fill their prime-time schedules with hit American shows that they could buy for far less than the costs of producing Canadian shows, receive generous subsidies for the Canadian programming (albeit indirectly, since the fund subsidizes independent producers rather than networks), represent one-stop shopping for advertisers that had few other places to turn to, and keep their licences regardless of how little they poured into news or quality Canadian programming. With the stars aligned, over-the-air TV networks could count on steady profits. During the period from 1996 to 2004, profits (before interest and taxes) for both English- and French-language conventional TV hovered between 10 and 15 per cent of total revenues.[55] While not spectacular, profits were cushy, easy, and seemed to be automatic.

Toward the end of the decade, however, as the networks were hit by the double whammy of media shock and the great recession, prospects turned grim. Perhaps the greatest body blow was the loss of advertising to the Internet. In fact, Internet advertising would surpass TV advertising in Canada for the first time in 2013.[56] Not only did advertising dollars migrate online, but studies found that brand recall was far higher when the same ads appeared both on TV and in cyberspace, so television and web advertising became mutually reinforcing.[57] This meant that in a strange twist, advertisers now had to divert money from TV to the web in order to make their TV advertising more effective.

A second development was that video archives and nascent delivery systems began to attract mass audiences. As Amanda Lotz has pointed out, "it's a stunning shift" when a single low-budget YouTube video can attract many more people than a hit TV show.[58] Canadian over-the-air broadcasters hadn't seen the competition coming, and they certainly hadn't foreseen the extent of the onslaught. A former head of CBC's English-language television, Richard Stursberg, has described the new situation created by the advent of web-based streaming: "Everywhere, everyone was crossing boundaries and moving into old media's territory. What had been fixed was increasingly fluid. What was a television platform? What was a schedule? Who was a producer? Who was a distributor? Who was just around the corner ready to stand everything on its ear one more time? The scope of the changes taking place was convulsive."[59]

The effects of the economic downturn were just as devastating. Suddenly the industry could barely keep its head above water. Between 2008 and 2012, revenues for private conventional TV stations dropped by 1.2 per cent on the English-language side and by 2.8 per cent on the French-language side. Total revenues for conventional TV stations as a whole shrank from $2.138 billion in 2008 to $2.038 billion in 2012.[60] Profits had all but flat-lined. Media lawyer Peter Miller estimates that if the current squeeze continues, revenues for conventional TV could drop by as much as 20 per cent by 2020.[61]

The weakening of over-the-air network TV has produced or ratified a number of long-term changes in the nature of television viewing and production in Canada. First, while apparent for quite some time, the TV networks, at least in English-speaking Canada, seem unable to attract a mass audience. The days of Canadians coming together in a kind of national living room to watch the same shows and experience the same events has mostly vanished. So while shows such as *Hockey Night in Canada*, *Dragons' Den*, *Battle of the Blades*, *Heartland*, and *Rookie Blue* regularly attract over a million viewers and often many more, the vast majority of shows struggle to find a significant piece of the audience pie.

Second, the nature of programming has changed. Between 2007 and 2011, investments by the private networks on Canadian drama and comedy, and on journalism and news programming dropped considerably. We will look first at what can only be described as the wasteland of Canadian drama. Conventional private broadcasters spent only $58 million on Canadian drama and comedy shows in 2011, compared to over $76 million in 2007.[62] They spent $480 million on foreign (i.e., American) programming in 2011.[63]

The economics are clear and inexorable. The costs of producing an hour-long Canadian drama are usually $2 million or more. But Canadian shows tend to lose money by an average of $200,000 an hour. On the other hand, the rights to broadcast Hollywood shows can be bought off the shelf in Hollywood for far less than the cost of producing Canadian shows. American shows, with their higher budgets, more recognizable stars, and vast promotion machines, produce sizable profits for the networks. This upside-down relationship between the amounts spent on Canadian as opposed to American programming, which has been embarrassing for decades, has now reached absurd proportions, with the networks becoming little more than transmission belts for Hollywood shows. Gone is even the semblance of trying to produce a big Canadian show. The mini-dramas and made-for-TV movies that were once the heartland of Canadian content have all but vanished.

The *Globe and Mail's* John Doyle believes that the industry, at least in English-speaking Canada, is awash in "arrogance and delusion" and has abjectly failed to produce shows that are even remotely innovative or compelling. What we see, according to Doyle, "is almost complete creative failure."[64] So at the same time that American broadcasters such as HBO, Showtime, AMC, and Netflix are producing Big TV with shows such as *Game of Thrones, The Walking Dead, House of Cards,* and *Homeland* and have taken chances with large budgets, unknown actors, dark plots, and violent, over-the-edge anti-heroes, Canadian TV seems unable to get up from the couch, unable to do anything more than go through the motions.

The failure to invest in Canadian dramatic programming in dollar terms, let alone take creative risks, masks an even more disquieting reality. Canadian broadcasters, supported by the federal government through Telefilm and the Canadian Media Fund, have for many years co-produced shows with US and other foreign broadcasting partners. But there has been a not-so-subtle turn in the types of shows that are being produced. Although qualifying as Canadian for the purposes of fulfilling Canadian-content requirements, which are based on industrial and job-creation criteria, and thus qualifying for federal support, a number of shows could be easily mistaken as American because the Canadianness of the locations and Canadian cultural characteristics have been either disguised or erased entirely. While Canadian producers had long understood that "anywhere television" was the best way to enter the US and global marketplace, these partnerships "de-Canadianize" shows to the point where even the semblance of being Canadian is gone.

A case in point is the mini-series *Vikings,* which is filmed in Ireland and is an Irish-Canadian co-production that airs on the History channel. While it is an exciting show filled with intrigue and the requisite amounts of gore and human sacrifices and is a valiant attempt to depict life in medieval Scandinavia, there is nothing Canadian about the production. Other than hitting industrial targets and creating jobs—not a small matter—there is no cultural bonus for Canada, no cultural return on our investment. The CRTC's strategy remains "Canadianization through Americanization," that is, allowing broadcasters to "Hollywood up" their schedules so that they can use the profits from airing American shows to offset the costs of producing Canadian programs. With broadcasters becoming ever more brazen about airing "Canadian" shows that barely look or feel Canadian, the theory has turned into a joke.

It should be noted that Canada is the only developed country in the world whose citizens prefer watching foreign programming to watching domestically produced shows. And this phenomenon takes place almost entirely in English-speaking Canada. While the list of the 20 most-watched shows in any given week in English-speaking Canada is usually entirely American, the most popular shows in Quebec are Canadian, that is, programs produced in French-language Quebec. Richard Stursberg describes the reaction among Quebec TV executives and producers when he spoke to them about the viewing habits of English-speaking Canadians:

> I began by projecting a chart showing the names of the twenty most popular television shows in English Canada. Beside each name I placed a little flag showing its country of origin. There was nothing but American flags.... There were cries of disbelief, shock and bewilderment: Calls of "non" and "impossible." The Quebec producers, directors and executives simply could not believe that English Canadians preferred foreign shows to their own. It must be humiliating. How do the writers and directors hold their heads up? How can people show their faces in public?[65]

What's most incomprehensible, however, is not the shocked reaction of the francophone TV executives, but the lack of shock, more pointedly the complete absence of interest or concern, among the vast majority of English-speaking Canadians.

The consequences of this one-way tilt for the broader culture are profound. Arguably without a star system of its own, English-speaking Canada has fewer celebrities and public figures than in most other countries, and viewers consume less of their culture simply because that culture is not on display to the same extent as it is in other societies.

A third change that has taken place is the weakening of TV news, especially at the local level. While the CRTC does not keep statistics on job losses in broadcasting, according to one estimate private broadcasters axed close to 40 per cent of local TV jobs between 2002 and 2011.[66] At many local stations journalists are young and underpaid and are rarely given the resources needed to cover anything but crime and spot news, and staff turnover is almost as great as on professional sports teams, where careers are notoriously short. In fact, in many cases professional hockey players have longer and less bruising careers. The critical point is that there are fewer TV journalists at the same time that newspapers have shed so many of their reporters.

Fourth, the tilt toward pay and specialty channels has continued unabated. In 2012, half of all viewing among English-speaking Canadians was on pay, specialty, and digital channels, while the viewing share for conventional channels was just over 30 per cent.[67] Similarly, pay and specialty channels brought in close to $4 billion in revenue, compared to a little over $2 billion for private conventional stations.[68] Hence, much if not most Canadian programming now consists of easy-to-assemble sports, music, travel, bridal, children's, and food shows. While this cookie-cutter TV culture is not without its successes, in most cases budgets are low and the impact on the broader Canadian culture and identity is almost negligible. The dominant players are the suites of sports channels operated by TSN and Rogers, which are linked to over-the-air broadcasters as well as sports franchises.[69] They exist in an almost separate TV universe.

While the Canadian broadcasting system has been deeply shaken by the developments of the last decade, the next rounds of technological change are likely to hit even harder. As we enter a post-broadcasting era in which over-the-air broadcasters will have to co-exist with both cable and web-based broadcasters, the business model on which over-the-air television networks are based will come under concerted attack. As mentioned above, the key to the kingdom for the networks was that they were positioned at the intersection between programs, advertisers, and audiences. This allowed them to control both the amount and speed of traffic and to charge a hefty price for doing so. As is the case with newspapers, however, the TV bundle is coming apart. Audiences, advertisers, and TV production are increasingly bypassing the networks, and the once central role that they played is being shredded.

In this new post-broadcasting era, a number of developments are taking place simultaneously. One revolutionary change is the personal video recorders (PVRs), also called digital video recorders (DVRs). PVRs now have huge storage capacities, and storage capacities are likely to grow exponentially, giving users an even greater capacity to build giant inventories and bypass network schedules. Unfortunately for the traditional broadcasters, studies of PVR use indicate that viewers skip over at least 60 per cent of the ads, thus disrupting the business model.[70] As Jack Valenti, who headed the Motion Picture Association in the US, once described the effects of videocassette recorders (VCRs) when they first hit, "The VCR is to the American film producer and the American public as the Boston strangler is to the women home alone."[71] The PVR is more effective by orders of magnitude than the old VCR—and arguably more dangerous to the networks.

The biggest challenge for Canadian over-the-air broadcasters, however, is in the explosion of "over-the-top" sites, including ones operated by media and retail giants. What has made this possible are changes in broadband technologies that have not only enlarged capacity but made images far sharper than they were back in the early years of the century. Although the original strategy of some of these online broadcasters was to target small subsections of the audience with highly customized niche programming, hoping that they would find viewers somewhere along the Internet's long tail, online streaming has been instrumental in creating a new mass audience.

A number of different web-TV models have begun to emerge. The big players are Netflix, YouTube, HBO Go, Crackle (which is owned by Sony), Amazon Prime, and Hulu Plus. Hulu Plus, which is a joint venture among Fox, Disney/ABC, and NBC Universal, is a pay-walled service that streams entire seasons of shows to computers, smart phones, and tablets. Canadian players in the OTT market include Shomi (a joint venture by Rogers and Shaw), Tou.TV (launched by Radio-Canada), and Illicoweb.TV (owned by Quebecor's Videotron). CBC has a licensing deal with Netflix that includes shows such as *Republic of Doyle* and *Dragons' Den*.

On another level, there has been an explosion in the availability of OTT set-boxes that enable viewers to access web-broadcasters on their home TVs. Apple TV, Amazon's Fire, Boxee, Slingbox, and inevitably Google TV now dominate this space.

And if the field weren't crowded enough, there are also online pirates and scavengers such as Pirate Bay, LetMeWatchThis, and Project Free TV that lift programs from across the Internet and make them available in the form of bit torrents. Peer-to-peer streaming is a whole other category and is part of the reason why being on the Internet is now increasingly about watching videos.

A critical point already discussed at considerable length is that web broadcasters are doing more than just recycling old movies and TV programs. They now produce their own original programming. Netflix, for instance, has aired shows such as *Sherlock Holmes*, *Hemlock Grove*, *Lilyhammer*, *Orange Is the New Black*, and *House of Cards* that have been produced for it by Sony and other studios. Hulu's offerings include shows such as *Battleground*, *Up to Speed*, and *Spoilers*, and Amazon has built a massive new studio to produce shows for its online audience. As discussed earlier, YouTube has launched over 100 new channels specializing in work that is edgy, experimental, and unconventional.

While this has meant a new revenue stream for US networks that sell the rights to air their programs to over-the-top broadcasters, these revenues don't make up for the losses that they are experiencing as the old advertising-based model breaks down. All of this means trouble for Canadian broadcasters, whose programming is far less in demand. Budgets for shows produced for online broadcasters will soon tower over anything that Canadian conventional broadcasters can muster. In terms of quality, Canadian broadcasters are likely to be out-gunned in every imaginable way. Furthermore, as York University's Wade Rowland has pointed out, with market capitalization seven times the combined worth of Canada's private broadcasters, Netflix is in a position to outbid these broadcasters for Hollywood shows and can make them available to their Canadian subscribers at relatively low costs.[72]

The CRTC has refused to regulate broadcasting on the Internet because it realized quite correctly that web broadcasting was simply too massive, global, chaotic, and amorphous to be controlled. While it has taken a long time for these chickens to come home to roost, web broadcasting now threatens to challenge and perhaps overturn much of the regulatory structure on which Canadian broadcasting is based. The problem for the Canadian broadcasting system is that web broadcasters do not have to adhere to Canadian-content guidelines or contribute to the Canadian Media Fund, which supports Canadian programming. For instance, while BDUs contributed $394 million to support Canadian programming in 2012, Netflix contributed nothing.[73] Simply put, web broadcasters get a free ride and there's little that regulators can do about it. As Simon Doyle, the editor of *Wire Report*, has observed, "What, really, can the CRTC do if foreign-owned web services do not abide by its conditions or orders? Kick the foreign website out of the country? Obviously, no. Block the website from Canada? Does the CRTC really want to get into the business of blocking websites?"[74] It's not hard to imagine that given a choice between supporting the CRTC or keeping Google and YouTube in Canada, the vast majority of Canadians would banish the CRTC.

What's most at stake are the Canadian-content (CanCon) provisions that lie at the very heart of the broadcasting system. Given their importance, it's worth taking some time to examine these rules. In order for a show to qualify as Canadian, it must score at least six out of ten points based on having various creative elements. The show must also have a Canadian producer, and at least 75 per cent of total production expenses must be spent in Canada or paid to Canadians. Once a program is certified as Canadian, the show can qualify for tax breaks and for funding from Telefilm, the Canadian Media Fund, and provincial agencies. This means that the lion's share of the costs of production for any given show are subsidized by public money.[75] And it must be pointed out that this avalanche of subsidies goes to a show's producers rather than to a network. In addition, while the vast majority of this support comes from governments, BDUs contribute 5 per cent of their revenues from broadcasting operations to the Canadian Television Fund to support Canadian productions. Larger BDUs are allowed to divert 2 per cent of this 5 per cent to support their own local community programming channels.

Let's go back to Canadian-content regulations. In addition to setting out production targets, regulations stipulate that for private stations at least 55 per cent of programming aired each year must be Canadian. Over-the-air broadcasters also have to broadcast a certain number of hours of so-called priority programs, mainly drama and variety shows, in prime time each week. Specialty channels must meet lower—and often much lower—CanCon thresholds. Most private broadcasters relegate Canadian shows to the dead zones of the broadcast schedule—to the off-season summer doldrums, to early mornings or late at night, or to Sunday afternoons when viewers are watching sports or spending time with their families. On most private stations, prime-time viewing resembles a sandwich. Local 6:00 news shows are the first slice of bread. Big ticket Hollywood shows, which fill the next three hours, are the meat in the sandwich and bring in almost all of the revenue. Late-night local news or other Canadian programming is the second slice of bread.

Despite these challenges, Canadian programming still attracts close to 50 per cent of all viewing.[76] It's important to note that while American shows dominate prime time—and this is especially the case for drama, reality TV, and variety shows such as *Dancing with the Stars* or the *X Factor*—Canadian audiences still turn to Canadian TV to watch news and sports. These numbers would be far lower if NHL hockey were taken out of the picture.

Some observers question the logic behind Canadian-content legislation. Since the CanCon scorecard is based on industrial targets rather than on cultural criteria, the actual Canadian content of Canadian content can be strangely off the mark. As described previously, many producers hide or downplay any readily identifiable Canadian features in their shows in order to sell their products in the US and abroad. Critics argue that the "anywhere TV" formula has created many lost opportunities. First, I would argue that strong and unmistakable Canadian themes are precisely what many Canadian viewers want and indeed are starving for. Viewers want to experience Canada through television, and the failure to provide those experiences is what is stifling and corrupting much of Canadian production. But the same can be said for foreign audiences; it's the foreignness of Canadian shows that can attract viewers. People are curious and want to travel to faraway places, even while watching TV at home. Besides, great stories reach beyond borders, as the BBC has long demonstrated.

Despite the challenges brought by web streaming, Canada's conventional broadcasters are unlikely to drown in an online tsunami—at least for a while. There is even some evidence to suggest that viewing programs online may supplement rather than replace conventional and cable viewing. For instance, NBC did extensive research about viewing habits during the 2012 London Olympics and found that live streaming had little effect on prime-time ratings.[77] While broadcasting to mobile devices attracted large audiences, these same viewers came "home" to the network in the evenings. NBC concluded that online streaming might boost rather than threaten their audience numbers.

The TV industry has also learned the lessons of the music industry, which was picked apart by free downloading and pirating. The networks now guard their content with the same intensity that prison guards try to prevent escapes. In addition, content providers such as Comcast, which owns NBC, and Time Warner, which owns HBO, are also major cable operators. They are unlikely to participate in their own destruction by offering up content even at high prices.

As we have seen, Canadian media conglomerates are hardly weak or defenceless. With so much influence over information and culture, as well as control over much of the media spinal cord, these media giants hope to construct battlements that will be difficult for others to scale. A number of strategies are at play, one of the most significant being the vertical integration of their companies so that they control both production and distribution. Customers are thus locked into contracts and targeted with messages at every turn. One hurdle faced by vertically integrated companies, however, is a CRTC ruling that programs designed primarily for TV cannot be offered exclusively to mobile or retail companies. This means that media corporations have to make broadcasts that are intended for the mobile devices of their own customers available to their competitors at reasonable prices. The reason for this is to protect subscribers from having to pay for multiple subscriptions in order to get good programming. It remains to be seen how eager broadcasters will be to extend the hand of generosity to their competitors.

A second strategic move has been to limit cord cutting, that is viewers cutting their cable subscriptions, by controlling sports broadcasting. As discussed previously, the prime example is the control that Rogers and Bell Media now have over much of Canadian sports as a result of their ownership of Maple Leaf Sports Entertainment. Rogers has also sewn up the rights to NHL hockey until 2026 and will be broadcasting and streaming hockey on every imaginable platform. The logic is that airing live sports entertainment prevents cord cutting among heavy sports viewers. Peter Miller reports that an estimated 3.5 per cent of viewers cut their cable cords from 2011 to the end of 2013.[78] They probably weren't sports fans.

In addition, over-the-air broadcasters now stream episodes of shows through their own websites and apps. As network websites become the repository for a larger and larger inventory of programs, the networks, as media scholar Amanda Lotz has noted, will have created "a distribution route with lower costs and unlimited 'shelf' space," thus replicating and undercutting their online competition.[79] The question is whether by offering high-quality online broadcasting, conventional broadcasters are helping to destroy the very model on which their existence is based. Here the comparison with newspapers is chilling—the more digitalized papers become, the less money they bring in. Lotz believes that if the major networks aren't careful, the entire house of cards on which TV networks have been built may come crashing down. She suggests that networks could become little more than advertising venues that showcase programs for a few weeks for free before shows are offered up to subscribers.[80] They would be like highway billboards that advertise the next glossy product. And, like billboards, all that they will receive is a momentary glance.

Assuming that the rules and economics of the Internet remain much as they are today, it is almost inevitable that the face of TV will change dramatically. It is likely that a number of TV models will co-exist, creating greater competition and much greater fragmentation. But as is the case with newspapers, any weakening of the networks could have enormous consequences for the viability of local programming, the quality of TV journalism, the production of Canadian drama and culture, and the quality of our national and community life. There is much at stake.

Music and Radio: Hits and Misses

In many ways it's never been a better time for Canadian musical artists. Arcade Fire, Michael Bublé, Justin Bieber, Carly Rae Jepsen, Feist, Drake, Kardinal Offishal, Nickelback, Céline Dion, The Weeknd, and deadmau5, among others, have achieved global prominence to such a degree that Canadians' achievements in music can be compared to their achievements in hockey: Canadians expect to dominate the stage and the playlists. Most importantly it appears that more Canadians are listening to more music by Canadian artists than ever before. According to statistics published in 2010 by Heritage Canada, 27 per cent of the full albums and 25 per cent of the individual tracks downloaded by Canadians were by Canadian artists.[81] There are playlists built around themes such as "I love Canadian music" on Amazon and "Canada Now" or "Toronto 20" available on iTunes. Listeners accessing playlists on iTunes or on social networking sites from a Canadian IP address will find a host of Canadian sounds.[82] Moreover, the Canadian music service Galaxie, which is available through cable and satellite providers and is part of the strategy to keep customers from cord cutting, has been astonishingly successful, reaching 75 million television viewers in over 50 countries.[83]

However—and this is a big *however*—the same forces that are threatening the survival of newspapers and over-the-air television networks have also ravaged the music industry. In fact, the music industry is easily the most prominent casualty of media shock, with sales and revenues plummeting to roughly half of what they were just 15 years ago. The winner-take-all nature of the Internet has meant that there are relatively few big players and fewer musicians able to make a living from their music. While we are listening to more music, the music that we are listening to is being produced by fewer people.

By contrast, radio in Canada continues to be an earnings juggernaut, with profits hovering either above or close to 20 per cent (before interest and taxes) in the years between 2008 and 2012.[84] Nonetheless, even for the most popular and financially successful radio stations there are digital storms gathering on the horizon that may be difficult to outrun.

The Music Industry

We will begin by examining the music industry. The recording industry was totally unprepared for media shock and resisted dealing with the challenges that it faced for years, even as the waves of destruction grew closer and closer. In fact, it is difficult to think of other industries that have experienced as sudden a drop in elevation as has the music industry. According to Music Canada, revenues for the sound-recording industry fell from $765 million in 2001 to just $414 million in 2011.[85] Between 2006 and 2010 alone, album sales in Canada nosedived from close to 50 million to just over 30 million albums.[86] In the US, sales of recorded music dropped from $14.6 billion in 1999 to $6.3 billion in 2009.[87]

While respected scholars such as John Shiga and Dwayne Winseck believe that the claims of crisis are overblown because analysts have failed to account for the revenue streams being opened up by web radio and by social media sites, it is not clear that the industry can ever be what it once was.[88] The would-be rescuers have found it hard to gain traction. iTunes took years to edge into profitability, and it's not clear that popular music apps such as Pandora, SlackerRadio, and Spotify are financially viable.

Illegal downloading is most often cited as the principal cause of the devastation that has rocked the industry. According to *Billboard* executive editor Robert Levine, "so far no reputable study has found a popular file-sharing network where more than 10 percent of downloads are legitimate, and most show that fewer than 5 percent are."[89] George Barker found that some 21 per cent of Canadians engage in file sharing, at a cost of hundreds of millions of dollars to the music industry annually.[90] The Canadian Intellectual Property Council believes that the problem is even more severe than Barker's numbers suggest. They peg the number of Canadians who download music illegally at roughly 7 million, and the cost to the recording industry at over

$1.25 billion annually.[91] Despite efforts to reverse the illegal downloading epidemic by many of the companies that sell music online legally, including iTunes, BBM, eMusic, Zune Music Pass, and iMesh, the piracy culture continues to thrive. For millions of Canadians, illegal downloading has become as natural as drinking coffee in the morning or going on Facebook—and there is no end in sight.

Another major problem for the industry is that digital listeners insist on unbundling albums and buying music by the track. According to at least one study, one-third of the losses in revenue are because people now buy singles rather than albums—although a great deal of money can still be made by a hit song.

But illegal downloading is just one of a number of smoking guns. Big chain stores such as Walmart and Best Buy now account for a sizable portion of all music sales. Because they work on volume and offer customers low prices, they cap prices at levels that make it difficult for other vendors to compete. They also cut into the sizable profits once earned by music producers.

As mentioned above, the same "winner-take-all" sorting system that is evident throughout web-based media has also affected the music industry. Just 5 per cent of songs account for 80 per cent of all music downloads with most songs selling fewer than a hundred copies.[92] This is because the dice are heavily loaded in favour of the "powers that be." As discussed in Chapter Four, just two conglomerates now control most of the industry and far from being displaced by online activity their power is reinforced by the web.

YouTube is a prime example. In the battle between amateurs and large media conglomerates for control over YouTube, the amateurs are clearly in retreat. Existing stars, shows, and labels attract the largest audiences, with YouTube magnifying their power and popularity even more. Moreover as mentioned above, big chains stores such as Walmart tend to sell music that is already popular, thus perpetuating the star culture. Rarely will they take a chance on an unknown artist that is not backed by a major label.

Compounding the problem is the tendency of radio disc jockeys not to stray too far from the mainstream. Their fear of losing their audience if they play new and untested songs too frequently means that they replay the same hit tunes almost constantly. Moreover, with so many internationally popular Canadian artists, DJs have little incentive to undertake a talent search. Hence the pool of music available on conventional radio stations tends to be rather small, even though the amount of available music has increased exponentially. Since the vast majority of radio stations have similar formats and playlists, the cycle is rarely broken.

Robert Levine argues that the loss of revenue has had a cascading effect throughout the industry. Labels promote fewer artists, employ fewer people, spend less on promotions, sponsor fewer concerts, and take fewer risks. In the US, the number of people employed as professional musicians has fallen by almost 20 per cent since 2001.[93] For the vast majority of artists who try to make it on their own by touring from small venue to small venue, paying their own way, transporting and setting up their own equipment, selling albums and T-shirts during breaks, and trying to get media attention, the rewards are few and the chances of eventually signing with a major label remote. And without the backing of a major label for promotion, distribution, and financing, dreams quickly turn to dust. As one former music executive bluntly put it, "a funny thing happens when you don't promote a project: nothing."[94]

The vibrant Canadian indie scene may be an exception to the rule. Bands such as The Dears, Stars, Chilly Gonzales, and Broken Social Scene have been able to extend their reach across the globe though innovative and creative marketing alliances. But it remains to be seen how many indie bands have the staying power to survive beyond the first blushes of success. And despite the spectacular rise of Justin Bieber and the sudden appeal of child singing sensation Maria Aragon, getting noticed has become even more difficult. The irony seems familiar: the very web-based media that allow would-be stars to display their talents also work against them as they are swept up in the same sea as millions of others who are chasing the same dreams.

The vast increase in the amount of music now available has come from amateurs, so-called garage musicians, some of whom are immensely talented. They live in the hope that their next release will reach across the globe and rocket them to fame. When it's obvious that their albums have sunk into oblivion, most go back to their everyday lives, while only some keep their dreams alive even as the odds against them continue to mount.

Radio Stations

As was the case with TV, the Canadian music and radio industries are both guided by Canadian-content regulations. Thirty five per cent of all popular music played each week on radio stations must be Canadian. In order to prevent Canadian music from being relegated to those times of the day and night when there are fewer listeners, 35 per cent of all music broadcast on weekdays between 6 A.M. and 6 P.M. must be Canadian. There is also a two-for-one policy that gives extra CanCon points to stations that play Canadian artists alongside the most popular songs. Canadian artists presumably benefit from keeping company with the leading stars, at least on playlists. Stations that specialize in specific music genres such as concert and country music have lower CanCon targets. On French-language radio stations, 55 per cent of all popular vocal music and 65 per cent of popular music played between 6 A.M. and 6 P.M. must be in French. It's important to note that the radio industry contributes 5 per cent of its revenue to fund Canadian artists and promote Canadian stars.

A key question, however, has been how to define Canadian music. The MAPL system outlined below, which has been in place for decades, is geared to citizenship, not content. To qualify as CanCon a music production must meet at least two out of the following criteria:

- *Music:* The music must be composed by a Canadian.
- *Artist:* The music or lyrics must be performed principally by a Canadian.
- *Production:* If the music consists of a live performance, it must be recorded or performed wholly in Canada and broadcast live in Canada.
- *Lyrics:* Lyrics must be written entirely by a Canadian.

Some argue that this system is riddled with inconsistencies and has produced little in the way of tangible cultural benefits for the country. The most bizarre aspect of CanCon is that songs can qualify as Canadian without having to be about Canada at all. In fact, an editorial written some time ago in the *Ottawa Citizen* blasted Canadian regulators for rewarding artists who shed their Canadian identities in order to sell records. According to the editorial,

> When Canadian singer Alannah Miles crooned about Mississippi and that "slow Southern style" in "Black Velvet," CanCon gave it the Maple Leaf seal of approval. Ditto for Amanda Marshall's "Birmingham" (that's in Alabama, for anyone who hasn't been south of Windsor). All sorts of country artists singing the fake Nashville drawls score, too, because they have Canuck passports tucked into their cowboys boots. In fact, very few Canadian recording artists actually make clear references to things Canadian because they know the real prize, the American market, won't know what to make of them.[95]

However adept Canadian artists have become at sidestepping references to Canada, those supporting CanCon regulations contend that the policy has protected an industry that might have otherwise disappeared. David Young sees CanCon as "fundamental" to the success of the music industry and an example of a "cultural screen" that should never be brought down. But others, especially top stars, are not as supportive. Gordon Lightfoot's view is that

> the CRTC did absolutely nothing for me. I didn't need it, ab-so-lute-ly *nothing* ... and I don't like it. They can ruin you, man. Canadian content is fine if you're not doin' well. But I'm in the music business and I have a huge American audience. I'm going to do Carnegie Hall ... I really like to record down there, but I like to live up here. I really dig this country, but I'm not going to bring out any flags. I'm an entertainer. *I'm in the music business.*[96]

The truth is that the effectiveness of CanCon regulations is sometimes difficult to gauge. On one hand, CanCon can be seen as increasingly futile because the almost limitless array of choices now available to listeners makes any kind of national control or standards difficult to impose. Apps such as Pandora, eMusic, iMesh, and Spotify operate without borders, reach over the eyes and ears of regulators, and allow listeners to create their own music universes—their own me-music. On the other hand, a sizable percentage of all downloads by Canadians are for Canadian music, and the audience for Canadian artists continues to flourish. One can argue that somehow, the fact that CanCon regulations have made sounds by Canadian artists more available than they might otherwise be has altered our cultural landscape and created a different listening culture.

And, unlike the faltering music industry, radio continues to generate sizable profits. However, there is little reason for radio executives to be complacent; media shock may be coming their way. While licences from the CRTC give radio stations the ability to dominate local markets and ensure sizable audiences and profits, offering what until now has been a high degree of protective cover, competition from new sources is increasing. As a 2008 report by the Pew Research Center's Project for Excellence in Journalism bluntly put it, "The audience for what was once called radio is rising—and fragmenting.... The big question is which, if any, of the new audio platforms—satellite radio, Internet radio, HD radio, podcasts, MP3/iPod listening or mobile phone radio—will come out on top. So far, no clear winners have emerged."[97] Even audiences for drive-time radio, until now the safe preserve of local stations, are being threatened as wireless Internet radio becomes more car friendly and satellite radio continues to grow. This is no small matter, as a sizable amount of listening—perhaps as much as 30 per cent—is done in the car.[98]

Ominously, the Pew Research Center's Project of Excellence in Journalism report for 2012 noted that while large numbers of Americans continued to listen to AM/FM radio, relatively few listeners "loved" radio. They listened because it was convenient and because they didn't have an alternative. Smartphone users who did have an alternative preferred listening to apps such as Spotify, Rdio, and Pandora than to digital AM/FM stations. Most crucially, the number of people who listen to music on mobile devices, already close to 40 per cent in the US, is likely to double within the next few years.[99]

Another problem is that conventional radio listening is skewed according to age. While overall audience numbers dropped from 20.5 to 17.5 hours per week from 1999 to 2012, listening among 12- to 17-year-olds fell from 11.3 hours a week, already a low number, to just 6.9 hours. Just as noteworthy is that listening by 18- to 24-year-olds fell from 14.1 hours per week in 2006 to 12.5 in 2012.[100] Clearly, digital natives are slowly drifting away from local radio stations.

The same demographic trends that can be found for newspapers and TV can be found for radio news and for talk radio. As is the case with newspaper readers and people who watch TV news, the audience for talk radio is older. One can listen to shows for a long time, sometimes for days on end, without hearing a younger caller. Surprisingly, CBC Radio, perhaps because it has an older audience, seems to be holding its own. Its distinct programming, national sensibility, and faithful listeners seem to be giving it a larger rather than a smaller place in the media sun. Its combined AM/FM audience in both English and French accounted for 13.4 per cent of weekly listening in the autumn of 2012.[101] In spite of the odds against it, the old lion of Canadian broadcasting continues to roar. How long that roar will continue will be examined in the next chapter.

Are the Traditional Media Doomed to Extinction?

Much of the crisis that the traditional media now find themselves in is the result of media shock. Undoubtedly there is a great deal of truth to the arguments made by Christopher Waddell and others that the failure to invest in strong journalism and excellent programming in the bountiful years prior to the great recession weakened the traditional media to the point where they no longer had the means to respond effectively when the crisis hit. It's also true that the heavy debts that burdened newspaper and over-the-air TV owners such as Global and Quebecor because of ambitious takeovers limited their capacity to bounce back. When the recession hit, the problems compounded. But there is no sense that the newspaper and music industries in particular had anything close to an effective early warning system in place, had any sense of the dark clouds that were looming over the horizon. But even if one takes these missteps and blind spots into account, adequate defences may not have been possible.

First, media organizations have to varying degrees been unable to cope with both the increase in and nature of web-based competition. Selling ads is far more difficult in web-based media, where media giants such as Google, Facebook, Apple, Disney, News Corporation, and Amazon control much of the market and where there are thousands of competitors on every possible topic, activity, and genre. The consequence has been a downward spiral in ad revenue and a devaluing of their products.

A second reality is that "free" media has become part of the culture. Illegal downloading of sound recordings has become a way of life, aggregators scoop up newspaper and magazine articles in vast pillaging operations, and peer-to-peer video streaming attracts audiences in the tens of millions. As Robert Levine has expressed the harsh reality, "Traditional media companies aren't in trouble because they're not giving consumers what they want; they're in trouble because they can't collect money for it."[102] Digital natives are now used to getting their news for free, and as surveys indicate, they remain adamant in their opposition to paying for news. While more and more of the web is inaccessible without making some kind of payment, and less and less is free, the "ring of fire" or "band of brothers" needed to close off free sources entirely is impossible to achieve. News organizations such as the CBC, the BBC, Reddit, and The Huffington Post are likely to continue to produce free news regardless of the pay-walls and micro-payments that are imposed by other media organizations because their mandates and business models depend on it. Breaking the back of the "freebie culture" will not be easy.

Canadian media organizations have responded to media shock by becoming both larger and smaller at the same time. On one level, giant media companies such as Shaw, Quebecor, and Bell Media have stretched their empires across the full length of media platforms, becoming content producers, Internet service providers, cable operators, broadcasters, and mobile-phone providers and becoming larger and more powerful with every gulp. They have developed these enormous wingspans in the hope of gathering and controlling as many customers as possible. On another level, however, Canadian media organizations are becoming smaller. Newspapers are becoming thinner and their stories shorter. They have fewer reporters and fewer bureaus and do fewer investigative stories. Similarly, Canadian TV networks spend less on news, produce low-rent Canadian drama, and seem unable to meet the challenge of Big TV. Cable is a wonderland of low-budget boutique shows aimed at audience segments rather than a mass public.

The fundamental reality is that, from the very beginning, Canadian media organizations have depended on governments in some way to survive. In the early days, reduced postal rates and government advertising were the keys to survival for newspapers. Today, tax incentives to advertise in Canadian publications, cable and broadcast licences that limit competition, the Canadian Media Fund, simultaneous substitution, limits on foreign ownership, and parliamentary subsidies to the CBC have been key drivers of the Canadian media. Arguably with their financial models largely broken or at least under increasing pressure, many players in the traditional media may not be able to survive without a new burst of public support. Yet the possibility of a new era of government intervention is increasingly unlikely. The country faces debts and deficits and crises in many other sectors of public life, from health care to homelessness, from urban transportation to pension reform.

In addition, media shock has shifted much of the basic media infrastructure away from Canadian control. Canadian regulators are likely to have little success trying to bend Google, Facebook, YouTube, or Reddit to their will. As McGill University's Richard Schultz reminds us, in terms of communications policy, the government has gone from "master to partner to bit player" and is now able to influence policy only at the margins.[103]

Yet without strong media organizations the basic work of society and democracy cannot get done. The task of creating and cementing common understandings and memories and shared national experiences cannot be accomplished by bloggers, Facebook sites, or tweets. It's still the mainstream media that organize and carry the culture and set the agenda for web-based media. Some analysts have argued that the steady decline of the traditional media is about to level off and that they will eventually plateau, albeit at a lower elevation. But how low can media institutions drop before they are unable to produce the accountability news that is so crucial to democracy? As Alex Jones has put it with regard to the future of news, "the seas are boiling and the ship may well be foundering. Should that happen, truth will be in shorter supply and that would be a terrible blow to all of us."[104]

Chapter Seven will discuss the plight of Canada's main public broadcaster— the CBC/Radio-Canada. The CBC has been severely weakened by budget cuts, has had to compete against large private corporations that can leverage their influence across multiple platforms—and, like other media organizations, faces strong competition from online media. Public broadcasting, like much of the Canadian media system as a whole, is at a crossroads. It will either be reimagined and reinvigorated or will die a slow death.

Notes

1 Quoted in Auletta, *Googled*, 305–6.
2 Levine, *Free Ride*, 1, 37; Brooks Barnes, "Web Deals Cheers Hollywood, Despite a Drop in Moviegoers," *New York Times*, February, 25, 2012, http://www.nytimes .com/2012/02/25/business/media/web-deals-cheer-hollywood-despite-a-drop-in -moviegoers.html?pagewanted=all&_r=0.
3 Dornan, "Newspapers and Magazines," Table 3.5, 73.
4 Tamara Baluga, "Canadian Media Guild Data Shows 10,000 Job Losses in Past Five Years," *Canadian Journalism Project*, November 19, 2013, http://j-source.ca/article/ canadian-media-guild-data-shows-10000-job-losses-past-five-years.
5 Anderson, *Imagined Communities.*
6 Quoted in Frank Peers, *The Politics of Canadian Broadcasting, 1920–1951* (Toronto: University of Toronto Press, 1969), 9.
7 Jones, *Losing the News*, 3–4.
8 Quoted in Paul Starr, "Goodbye to the Age of Newspapers (Hello to a New Era of Corruption)," in *Will the Last Reporter Please Turn Out the Lights*, ed. Robert W. McChesney and Victor Pickard (New York: New Press, 2011), 20.
9 Jones, *Losing the News*, xvi.
10 Ibid., xiv.
11 James Carey, "The Press, Public Opinion and Public Discourse: On the Edge of the Postmodern," in *James Carey: A Critical Reader*, ed. Eve Stryker Munson and Catherine A. Warren (Minneapolis: The University of Minnesota Press, 1997), 250–51.
12 "Newspaper Killers and the 'Death of Journalism,'" *Mediamorphis: Network Media Industries and the Forces of Change and Conservation*, May 31, 2012, http://dmmw .wordpress.com/2012/05/.
13 McChesney and Nichols, *The Death and Life of American Journalism*, 35.
14 McChesney, *Digital Disconnect*, 176.
15 Florian Sauvageau, keynote address, Conference on How Canadians Communicate Politically: The Next Generation, Banff, AB, 2009.
16 Communic@tions Management Inc., "Daily Newspaper Circulation Trends 2000–2013."
17 Ibid.
18 In all cases statistics are drawn from *Wikipedia*, November 29, 2012. I chose this source because it is a composite based on a variety of industry sources.
19 Jones, *Losing the News*, 187.
20 McChesney, *Digital Disconnect*, 186.
21 Ric Alterman, "Out of Print," *New Yorker*, March 31, 2008, 49.
22 Sauvageau, "The Uncertain Future of the News," 33.
23 Russell Baker, "Goodbye to Newspapers?," *New York Review of Books* LIV, no. 13 (August 16, 2007).
24 Pew Research Center for the People and the Press, *In Changing News Landscape, Even Television Is Vulnerable: Trends in News Consumption; 1991–2012*, September 27, 2012.
25 Sauvageau, "The Uncertain Future of the News," 33.
26 Canadian Media Research Consortium, "Canadian Consumers Unwilling to Pay for News Online."
27 Levine, *Free Ride.*

28 Interactive Advertising Bureau of Canada, *2011 Actual + 2012 Estimates Canadian Online Advertising Revenue Survey*, http://iabcanada.com/files/Canadian_Online _Advertising_Revenue_Survey_English.pdf, "Percent Share of Ad Revenue by Major Medium in Canada: 2010–11," 11.

29 Sauvageau, "The Uncertain Future of the News," 35.

30 Levine, *Free Ride*, 115.

31 Hindman, *The Myth of Digital Democracy*, 56–57.

32 Josianne Millette, Melanie Millette, and Serge Proulx, *Commitment of Cultural Communities to the Media: The Cases of the Haitians, the Italians and North Africans in Montreal*, Cahier-Medias Numero 19 (Quebec City: Centre d'étude sur les médias, Laval University, April 2010).

33 Hindman, *The Myth of Digital Democracy*, 55.

34 Jones, *Losing the News*, 189–90.

35 Jeff Bercovici, "The Story behind Rupert Murdoch's Rants about Google and SOPA," Forbes.com, Jan. 18, 2012, http://www.forbes.com.

36 Christopher Waddell, "The Future for the Canadian Media," *Policy Options* 30, no. 6 (June/July 2009): 17–18.

37 Christopher Waddell, "Berry'd Alive: The Media, Technology and the Death of Political Coverage," in *How Canadians Communicate IV: Media and Politics*, ed. David Taras and Christopher Waddell (Edmonton: Athabasca University Press, 2012), 20.

38 Tamara Baluja, "7 Interesting Facts from the Newspaper Canada 2012 Circulation Data Report," *The Canadian Journalism Project*, April 19, 2013, http://j-source.ca.

39 Will Straw, "Hawkers and Public Space: Free Commuter Newspapers in Canada," in *How Canadians Communicate III: Contexts of Canadian Popular Culture*, ed. Bart Beaty, Derek Briton, Gloria Filax, and Rebecca Sullivan (Edmonton: Athabasca University Press, 2010), 79–93.

40 Levine, *Free Ride*, 123–24.

41 Belinda Alzner, "The Globe and Mail to Launch Paywall on October 22," *Canadian Journalism Project*, October 16, 2012, http://j-source.ca/article/globe-and-mail -launch-paywall-oct-22.

42 McChesney, *Digital Disconnect*, 186.

43 Ibid., 187.

44 Levine, *Free Ride*, 133.

45 Baker, *Media Concentration and Democracy*, 29.

46 Jones, *Losing the News*, 193.

47 Ibid., 200.

48 CRTC, *Communications Monitoring Report*, 2013 (Ottawa: Government of Canada, September 2013), "Television Sector at a Glance," 75, http://www.crtc.gc.ca/eng/ publications/reports/policymonitoring/2013/cmr2013.pdf.

49 CRTC, *Communications Monitoring Report*, 2012 (Ottawa: Government of Canada, September 2012), 63, Table 4.3.2: "National Average Weekly Viewing Hours, by Age Group," http://www.crtc.gc.ca/eng/publications/reports/policymonitoring/2012/cmr2012.pdf.

50 Amanda D. Lotz, *The Television Will Be Revolutionized* (New York: New York University, 2007), 75.

51 Peter Miller, "Three Ideas as We Head into the Meat of the TV Review," *Cartt.ca*, April 23, 2014, https://cartt.ca/, 28.

52 Ibid., 58.

53 Ibid., 49.

54 Quoted in Danny Schechter, "Media Summits," *Media Studies Journal* (Spring/Summer 1996): 84.

55 CRTC, *Broadcasting Policy Monitoring Report 2007* (Ottawa: Government of Canada, July 2007), 67, chart 3.3., https://www.friends.ca/files/PDF/bpmr2007.pdf.

56 Miller, "Three Ideas," 24.

57 *Calgary Herald*, "TV Works Best with the Web: NBC," September 23, 2008: D1.

58 Lotz, *The Television Will Be Revolutionized*, 134.

59 Peter Stursberg, *The Tower of Babble: Sins, Secrets and Successes Inside the CBC* (Vancouver: Douglas & McIntyre, 2012), 284.

60 CRTC, *Communications Monitoring Report*, 2013, 90, Table 4.3.12: "Advertising and Other Revenues by English- and French-language Market for Private Conventional Television Stations," http://www.crtc.gc.ca/eng/publications/reports/policymonitoring/2013/cmr2013.pdf.

61 Miller, "Three Ideas."

62 CRTC, *Communications Monitoring Report*, 2012, 89, Table 4.3.16: "Canadian Programming Expenditure (CPE)—Private Conventional Television," http://www.crtc.gc.ca/eng/publications/reports/policymonitoring/2012/cmr2012.pdf.

63 Ibid., 90, Table 4.3.17: "Expenditures on Non-Canadian Programming—Private Conventional Television," http://www.crtc.gc.ca/eng/publications/reports/policymonitoring/2012/cmr2012.pdf.

64 John Doyle, "Where Is Canada in the Golden Age of TV?," *Globe and Mail*, October 10, 2013: L6.

65 Stursberg, *Tower of Babble*, 2.

66 Mark Burgess, "Canadian Broadcasters Can Take Lessons from FCC Report on Local News, Critics Say," *Wire Report*, June 17, 2011, 17.

67 CRTC, *Communications Monitoring Report*, 2013, 78, Table 4.3.3: "Viewing Share of Canadian and Non-Canadian Services, by Language and Type of Service—All of Canada, Excluding the Quebec Francophone Market (Part 1 of 2)," http://www.crtc.gc.ca/eng/publications/reports/policymonitoring/2013/cmr2013.pdf.

68 Ibid., 90–91, Table 4.3.12: "Advertising and Other Revenues by English- and French-language Market for Private Conventional Television Stations," and Table 4.3.13: "Revenues by English- and French-language, and Ethnic Markets and by Specialty, Pay, PPV and VOD Services," http://www.crtc.gc.ca/eng/publications/reports/policymonitoring/2013/cmr2013.pdf.

69 *Wire Report*, "TSN Grows Annual Profit by 37%, Earns Highest Specialty Channel Profit of $58.3 M," May 18, 2012, 7.

70 Louise Story, "Viewers Fast-Forwarding Past Ads? Not Always," *New York Times*, February, 16, 2007, http://www.nytimes.com/2007/02/16/business/16commercials.html?pagewanted=all.

71 Levine, *Free Ride*, 18.

72 Wade Rowland, *Saving the CBC: Balancing Profit and Public Service* (Westmount, QC: Linda Leith Publishing, 2013), 88–89.

73 CRTC, "CRTC Issues Annual Report on the State of the Canadian Communication System," September 26, 2013, http://www.crtc.gc.ca/eng/com100/2013/r130926.htm.

74 Simon Doyle, "High Noon at the CRTC," *Literary Review of Canada* (November 2011), http://reviewcanada.ca/magazine/2011/11/high-noon-at-the-crtc/.

75 Rowland, *Saving the CBC*, 96.

76 CRTC, "CRTC Issues Annual Report on the State of the Canadian Communication System," September 26, 2013, http://www.crtc.gc.ca/eng/com100/2013/r130926 .htm.

77 Amy Chozick, "NBC Unpacks Trove of Data from Olympics," *New York Times*, September 25, 2012, http://www.nytimes.com/2012/09/26/business/media/nbc -unpacks-trove-of-viewer-data-from-london-olympics.html?pagewanted=all.

78 Miller, "Three Ideas," 18.

79 Lotz, *The Television Will Be Revolutionized*, 135.

80 Ibid., 254.

81 David Young, "Why Canadian Content Regulations Are Needed to Support Canadian Music," in *Communication in Question*, 2nd ed., ed. Josh Greenberg and Charlene Elliott (Toronto: Nelson, 2012), 213.

82 Ira Wagman, "The B Side: Why Canadian Content Isn't Necessary for the Survival of Canadian Music," in *Communication in Question*, 2nd ed., ed. Josh Greenberg and Charlene Elliott (Toronto: Nelson, 2012), 222.

83 Steve Ladurantaye, "Eric Boyko: Stingray's Entrepreneur à Go-go-go," *Globe and Mail*, November 2, 2012, http://www.theglobeandmail.com/report-on-business/ careers/careers-leadership/eric-boyko-stingrays-entrepreneur-go-go-go/article 4887145/.

84 CRTC, *Communications Monitoring Report*, 2013, 66, Figure 4.2.9: "PBIT and PBIT Margin—Private Commercial Radio Stations," http://www.crtc.gc.ca/eng/ publications/reports/policymonitoring/2013/cmr2013.pdf.

85 Music Canada, *Economic Analysis of the Impact of the Sound Recording Industry in Canada*, April 12, 2012, 13, http://musiccanada.com/wp-content/uploads/2014/06/ Music-Canada-Economic-Impact-Analysis-of-the-Sound-Recording-Industry-in -Canada.pdf.

86 Richard Sutherland, "Sound Recording and Radio: Intersections and Overlaps," in *Cultural Industries.ca: Making Sense of Canadian Media in the Digital Age*, ed. Ira Wagman and Peter Urquhart (Toronto: James Lorimer, 2012), 33–35.

87 Levine, *Free Ride*, 37.

88 John Shiga, "Sharing Sounds: Does File Sharing Harm the Music Industry," in *Communication in Question*, 2nd ed., ed. Josh Greenberg and Charlene Elliott (Toronto: Nelson, 2012), 252–63; Dwayne Winseck, "'The Death of the Music Industry' in Canada and Other Copyright Myths," *Mediamorphis: Network Media Industries and the Forces of Change and Conservation*, May 17, 2011, http://dwmw.wordpress.com/2011/05/17/ the-death-of-the-music-industry-in-canada-and-other-copyright-myths/.

89 Levine, *Free Ride*, 55.

90 George Barker, "The Economics of File Sharing, Its Harm to the Music Industry, and the Case for Stronger Copyright Laws," in *Communication in Question*, 2nd ed., ed. Josh Greenberg and Charlene Elliott (Toronto: Nelson, 2012), 243.

91 Sutherland, "Sound Recording and Radio."

92 Levine, *Free Ride*, 52.

93 Ibid., 64.

94 Ibid., 73.

95 W.T. Stanbury, "Canadian Content Regulations: The Intrusive State at Work," *Fraser Forum* (August 1998): 55.

96 Quoted in Ryan Edwardson, *Canadian Content: Culture and the Quest for Nationhood* (Toronto: University of Toronto Press, 2008), 229; emphasis in original.

97 Pew Research Center's Project for Excellence in Journalism, *The State of the News Media, 2008: Radio*, March 19, 2008, 1.

98 CRTC, *Broadcasting Policy Monitoring Report 2007*, 10, https://www.friends.ca/files/PDF/bpmr2007.pdf.

99 Pew Research Center's Project for Excellence in Journalism, *The State of the News Media, 2012: Audio*, 1.

100 CRTC, *Broadcasting Policy Monitoring Report 2007*, 9, Table 2.3, https://www.friends.ca/files/PDF/bpmr2007.pdf; analysis of "audience measurement," in CRTC, *Communications Monitoring Report*, 2013, 58, Table 4.2.3: "Average Weekly Hours Tuned per Capita by Age Group for All Canada," http://www.crtc.gc.ca/eng/publications/reports/policymonitoring/2013/cmr2013.pdf.

101 CRTC, *Communications Monitoring Report*, 2013, 60, Figure 4.2.2: "Radio Tuning by Station Type in an Average Week in Daily Markets," http://www.crtc.gc.ca/eng/publications/reports/policymonitoring/2013/cmr2013.pdf.

102 Levine, *Free Ride*, 9.

103 Schultz, "From Master to Partner," 27–49.

104 Jones, *Losing the News*, xvi.

Seven
The Ever-shrinking World of Public Broadcasting

In most advanced democracies, public broadcasters are the largest and most influential media organizations. The BBC in the United Kingdom, RAI in Italy, ARD and ADF in Germany, NHK in Japan, and RTE in Ireland are just some examples. PBS in the US, which has only a tiny audience and is funded partly through donations garnered through on-air soliciting, is the major exception to the rule. The reason for the dominance of public-service broadcasting is that it fulfills roles that either can't or won't be undertaken by the private sector. The great impetus for establishing the Canadian Broadcasting Corporation (CBC) in 1936, and its predecessor, the Canadian Radio Broadcasting Commission in 1932, was that it was difficult at the time to broadcast across vast distances. Private broadcasters would broadcast only in places where they could make money, leaving large areas of the country under-served. There was also the question of having to counter the power of American broadcasters who were making inroads into Canada. Graham Spry's famous assertion was that Canada's choice in broadcasting was either "the state or the United States."[1] Either the government stepped in to build transmitters, hire performers, and create programming, or the vacuum would be filled by American radio networks such as NBC that already had large audiences in Canadian cities.

The 1951 Royal Commission on National Development in the Arts, Letters and Sciences, headed by Vincent Massey, saw the CBC as being at the centre of the broadcasting system, with private broadcasters having a secondary role. As the commission stridently argued,

> Broadcasting in Canada, in our view, is a public service directed and controlled in the public interest by a body responsible to Parliament. Private citizens are permitted to engage their capital and energies in this service.... That these citizens should enjoy adequate security or compensation for the actual monetary investment they are permitted to make, is apparent. But that they enjoy any vested right to engage in broadcasting as an industry, or that they have any status except as part of the national broadcasting system, is inadmissible ... they have no civil right to broadcast or any property rights in broadcasting.[2]

Indeed, one can argue that the founding of the CBC was one of the great nation-building exercises in Canadian history, comparable in scale only to John A. Macdonald's National Policy of 1891, the building of the social welfare state after World War II, and the creation of the Canadian Charter of Rights and Freedoms in 1981. It took the natural flow of information and entertainment, which was in a north-south direction, and re-directed some of it at least in an east-west direction.

Although the CBC/Radio-Canada (which I will refer to, for convenience, as simply the CBC) is the most prominent public-service broadcaster in the country, a small coterie of educational broadcasters such as TV Ontario, Tele-Quebec, and the Knowledge Network in British Columbia exist on the edges of the broadcasting system. The CRTC has also licensed a category of specialty channels that must be carried by BDUs, such as the Aboriginal Peoples Television Network (APTN) and the Cable Public Affairs Channel (CPAC), operated by the cable industry, that don't quite fit the mould of public broadcasting but have some of its characteristics.

In the early days, public-service broadcasting had a paternalistic, "father knows best" quality. The expectation was that the public broadcaster would not only unify the country but also educate and bring high culture to the masses. The emphasis was on proper language, respect for authority, and broad civic education. The spirit of public broadcasting is vastly different today. The goal is to build social capital by "bridging," "witnessing," and "connecting" and by addressing viewers and listeners as citizens rather than as consumers. This means putting Canadian stories first, doing the heavy lifting in terms of public-affairs programming, being a showcase for national expression and talent, exploring ideas, and offering distinctive and original programming.

In his book *Saving the CBC*, Wade Rowland argues that the ultimate mission of a public broadcaster is to contribute to the "moral economy of the nation."[3] As Rowland puts it, "It should in some way, large or small, leave viewers better than they were. Better, more informed and involved citizens: better fulfilled human beings. I leave it to the readers to judge whether *Law & Order*, *CSI*, and *Desperate Housewives* are 'exceptionally good' in this sense."[4] He argues that ratings should not be the standard for judging success; instead, success should be measured by how programs broaden the human experience and reach for excellence. As commendable as Rowland's expectations are, one wonders whether he is setting standards that are beyond the capacity of broadcasters to meet—except on a very few occasions. After all, much of TV watching is about escape, fantasy, and schlock—and often for good reasons.

Stripped to its core, the CBC might be judged on the amount of Canadian drama that it airs compared to private broadcasters, the depth of its public-affairs programming, and whether it reflects and promotes a distinct popular and civic culture. Using this scorecard, the CBC does far better than private broadcasters, but perhaps not well enough to ensure its survival.

Much of the argument in favour of public broadcasting rests on the assumption that private broadcasters have simply abandoned their responsibilities with regard to ensuring a well-informed public. Critics argue that they do the very least that they can in terms of Canadian content because their business models are based primarily on being re-broadcasters of American shows. As discussed previously, private broadcasters now serve up a sugary diet of Hollywood drama, heavy doses of reality television and cable shock, and as little news as possible. When it comes to airing original Canadian drama that can compete in the era of Big TV, they are largely missing in action. There are no Canadian versions of hit shows such as *Mad Men*, *Homeland*, *The Walking Dead*, *House of Cards*, or *Breaking Bad*. Instead we find cookie-cutter shows that may have brief moments in the sun but do little to stir the imagination.

As Richard Stursberg claims, "The CBC is … the only big network in English-Canada where prime-time is available for Canadian shows. It is the only network in a position to try and solve Canada's most important cultural challenge. The others could not attempt it, even if they wanted to, without destroying the very foundation of their business."[5] Small wonder, then, that in an analysis of the programs aired in deep prime time, between 8 and 10 in the evening, during a typical week in fall 2012, CBC executive Mark Starowicz found that 94 per cent of CBC programming was Canadian, compared to 7 per cent on CTV's main channel, 14 per cent on Global, and 18 per cent on City TV.[6]

Public-service broadcasters are also responsible for maintaining at least some of the checks and balances that make democracies work. News organizations play a crucial "watchdog" role by asking uncomfortable questions, stirring debate, conducting investigations, and helping set the public agenda. As the largest journalistic organization in the country, the CBC is an important part of this mix.

A system of checks and balances must also exist within the media system itself. Public broadcasters act as a counterweight to the crushing power enjoyed by media conglomerates such as Disney, News Corporation, Bell Media, and Quebecor. Public broadcasters give citizens another place to go, another vantage point on issues. Most critically, they also give journalists another place to work, a chance to cross the street if they have to. In short, they prevent the intellectual and cultural suffocation that occurs when big corporate media dominate too much of the landscape. This is particularly the case in Quebec, where Radio-Canada, together with Gesca, is an island in an information sea largely controlled by a single corporation: Quebecor.

Similarly, in New Brunswick, where the Irving family controls much of the media space, CBC is the only other voice.

Furthermore, in a country as divided and complex as Canada, "cross-walks" between English-speaking Canada and francophone Quebec need to be preserved. While the CBC and its French arm, Radio-Canada, rarely connect, the CBC is the only media organization that regularly has English-speaking reporters located in Quebec and French-speaking journalists stationed in the rest of Canada. Again, left to private broadcasters, even these slim connections might not exist. The CBC also broadcasts in Cree and in Inuit throughout the Canadian North, which is hardly a small feat.

The CBC's mandate requires the broadcaster to promote "a shared national consciousness and identity," which it does by covering events such as the Speech from the Throne, the swearing in of a new cabinet, and Remembrance Day and Canada Day ceremonies more thoroughly than private broadcasters do. On a deeper level the CBC allows Canadians to perform and celebrate their Canadianness. Patricia Cormack and James Cosgrove argue that aggressive CBC slogans such as "Canada Lives Here" reflect the public broadcaster's real mission, which is to create a space for the Canadian community to form. Hence for many Canadians, "the experience of listening to or viewing the CBC is more important than what is actually being broadcast at that particular moment" because it is a ritual of citizenship.[7]

One of the great ironies is that a public broadcasting system that did so much to bring the country together also played a role in fuelling nationalist and sovereigntist sentiments in Quebec. There can be little doubt that in creating its own distinct programming style, in marching to a particular Quebec beat, and in serving the needs of the Quebec audience, Radio-Canada contributed to the emergence of the intense nationalism and fervour of the Quiet Revolution. René Lévesque, the first Parti Québécois premier, was, after all, the host of *Point de Mire*, the most popular public-affairs show in the province and rode to political prominence on the coat-tails of his TV fame. Quoting Susan Mann Trofimenkoff, historian Paul Rutherford describes the effects that the first years of television had on Quebec's identity:

> Radio-Canada offered to the Quebecois a concrete, visible expression
> of their own unique places, past and present, and ways. "Television
> in Quebec," Susan Mann Trofimenkoff has observed, "Magnified
> the tiny world of a Laurentian village, a lower town Quebec, or a

local hockey arena into a provincial possession." Its newscasts and its public affairs shows plus the many, many features and documentaries swiftly created a novel means of focusing attention on the activities and concerns of the province....This drama didn't so much create as perpetuate and update a cluster of symbols that gave definition and meaning to community.[8]

One can also argue, however, that in serving Quebec, Radio-Canada has provided perspectives and connections to the rest of Canada that might not otherwise be there.

Another key argument in favour of public broadcasting is that it is one of the only ways in which a country like Canada can cope with the carnage created by media shock. In fact, in an environment increasingly dominated by web-based media and individualized mass communication, public broadcasting is more, rather than less, important. This is because of the need for a country to be able to see and speak to itself amid the cacophony created by individualized mass media. As philosopher John Ralston Saul once put it, "Everybody who is smart in bureaucracies and governments around the western world now knows that public broadcasting is one of the most important remaining levers that a nation state has to communicate with itself."[9] As we have seen, media such as Twitter, Facebook, Reddit, and The Huffington Post reach large and important audiences, but their goal is not to connect regions to one another or to be nation-building institutions.

There is also the issue of what will happen to ordinary citizens when access to media is increasingly available only to those who can pay for subscriptions and micro-payments. What will happen to those who are locked out of the flow of news and information? While Rowland doesn't deal with the issue of pay-walls and tollbooths directly, he has the following warning:

> Think of a world in which all roads are toll roads; in which city parks
> charge admission; in which all medical care is provided for profit;
> in which there are no public schools and universities, just private
> academies; in which there are no public museums of art and history,
> no public libraries, just private galleries and bookstores; in which
> shopping malls provide our only "public spaces." Now think of a
> world in which all media of information and entertainment are for-
> profit ventures that provide content based solely on their ability to
> attract large audiences of consumers.[10]

In a world where less and less of the web is free, public broadcasters may be one of the last places that citizens can go to be informed—free of charge.

Triple Jeopardy: Budget Cuts, *Hockey Night in Canada,* and Big TV

Despite its lofty mandate, the CBC is on life support. A number of challenges have crippled the public broadcaster, turning it into a shadow of its former self. The first issue is the budget cuts that the CBC has had to endure for almost a generation. While public-service broadcasters in a number of Western countries are financed by a licence fee that comes with owning a TV set, and therefore have reliable and predictable revenue streams, the CBC is dependent on the vagaries of an annual appropriation from Parliament. The appropriation has been cut by at least 35 per cent since 1990—depending on how one calculates the numbers. Of the total budget in 2011, $1.166 million (63 per cent) came from Parliament, while $672 million came from advertising and promotions.[11]

The problem with being dependent on an annual allocation from government as opposed to another form of public funding is that the CBC almost always finds itself in the cross-hairs of governments that are never satisfied with its political coverage. The list of prime ministers who nurtured grievances against the CBC is a long one. John Diefenbaker, Lester Pearson, Pierre Trudeau, Brian Mulroney, Jean Chrétien, and Stephen Harper are among those who variously wanted the corporation abolished, attacked individual shows and personalities, or viewed the corporation as an obstacle of some kind.[12] Despite the widespread support for public broadcasting in public opinion polls, the harsh reality is that the CBC has had few friends at the table when its budgets were being decided. The CBC has reacted to these draconian cuts by scaling back and, some would argue, all but abandoning local TV programming, endlessly repeating the same shows throughout the broadcast day, curtailing ambitious projects, cutting budgets for news and documentaries, and becoming more dependent on advertising and on its *Hockey Night in Canada (HNIC)* franchise—that is, until it effectively lost the cross-Canada rights to broadcast the NHL to Rogers in 2014.

Most critically, budget cutbacks have produced a series of "forced errors." Perhaps the corporation's most astonishing miscalculation was its wholesale retreat from local news in key media markets in the early 1990s. Despite having local news programs that were drawing large audiences and making significant profits in burgeoning cities such as Calgary and Edmonton, the network decided to shutter local newsrooms, experimenting instead with regional newscasts that failed to produce the localness that audiences wanted. Audiences whose loyalty had taken years to capture fled in large numbers. Later, when the CBC tried to resurrect local newscasts, albeit with shoestring budgets, these audiences could not be lured back. The corporation would learn the hard way that strong local programming tends to boost national ratings, rather than vice versa. The bleeding from this self-inflicted wound still continues.

Equally devastating was the fact that the CBC did not have the financial capacity or agility—and most importantly the political clout—needed to claim its share of the spoils when the most valuable territories in the cable universe were being divided up. Wade Rowland counts eight separate applications for specialty cable channels by the CBC that were rejected by the CRTC in the 1990s alone.[13] The lost opportunities are simply staggering. While the corporation gained valuable properties with CBC News Network and its French-Language equivalent, RDI, and runs Bold, a channel at the outer fringes of the cable universe largely devoted to re-runs, as well as a documentary channel that it shares with the National Film Board, it has been cut out of the action in almost every other way. One can only imagine how different the financial picture would appear today if the CBC had been awarded lucrative sports, children's, or music licences. While specialty services must stand on their own feet financially, the CBC would have been able to dominate in key programming areas, create economies of scale, and have access to lucrative advertising. Getting even one of the sports channels could have altered the equation considerably. In countries such as Germany and the United Kingdom, governments and regulators protected the interests of public broadcasters by ensuring that the licensing of specialty channels occurred on the public as well as the private side. In Canada, no such consideration was given.

As is the case with other broadcasters, the CBC has had to face the onslaught brought by media change. In fact, the sheer force of media shock by itself would have weakened the CBC, regardless of any other factors. While the CBC has adapted well to web-based media, with a sophisticated website that has made it as much a publisher as a broadcaster, impressive media archives that allow viewers to browse through an almost endless array of programs, and a full constellation of apps, blogs, YouTube videos, and Twitter feeds, nothing has been able to protect it from the explosion of competition that has come from online sources. So despite great efforts, the CBC's digital footprint is remarkably small: the average Canadian will listen to CBCMusic.ca, its streaming service, for just one hour per year, and visit its news and information site, CBC.ca, for roughly three hours per year.[14] There are now so many grains of sand in the digital universe that it is difficult for even a brand-name music or news service to be noticed at all.

Moreover, the CBC's main competition is in the form of multi-platform conglomerates—Shaw, Rogers, Quebecor, and Bell Media—that can reach viewers, promote their products, and sell advertising packages across media streams. The CBC is simply out-gunned at every outpost along the media frontier.

This dire situation is not the same across all parts of the CBC, and sharp distinctions have to be drawn between English-language TV, Radio-Canada (French-language) TV, and English- and French-language radio. English-language TV seems to be in a slow death spiral. While CBC garnered 6.6 per cent of overall English-language viewership during the 2010–11 season, almost 60 per cent of those viewers were tuned to either sports or foreign programs.[15] A single program, *Hockey Night in Canada*, accounted for roughly 50 per cent of CBC TV's advertising revenues in 2011.[16] The rest of the programming schedule is filled with repetitions of often mediocre, sometimes mindless, and all too predictable shows that mimic much of what can be seen on commercial networks.

The *Globe and Mail*'s respected media columnist, John Doyle, wrote in 2012 that the network needed a "new seriousness." As he lamented, "Oh, the ingredients brought to the CBC schedule by *Republic of Doyle* and *Heartland* and *Arctic Air* are fine. But a blinding sheen of lightweight nonsense covers the schedule. Its executives are addicted to ratings bumps for gimmicky TV such as *Battle of the Blades*. There isn't a single serious-minded cable-quality drama on CBC. There isn't a searing comedy."[17] If this weren't enough of an indictment, he saved his harshest words for CBC's flagship news program *The National*: "*The National* is sometimes a disgrace, a meandering journey through the mind of a flibbertigibbet who spent the day garnering news bits from a hodgepodge of online sources. Bizarrely, it treats Ottawa politics with grave and tedious seriousness, failing to see the theatre that is obvious to everyone else."[18] While one might not agree entirely with Doyle's critique, few would dispute that for CBC television the great moments are increasingly few and far between.

One of the dilemmas facing English TV is that it had become increasingly dependent on NHL hockey for its own branding and for much of its revenue. In the largest deal in Canadian broadcasting history, Rogers agreed to pay the NHL $5.2 billion for the rights to broadcast all cross-Canada NHL games for 12 years beginning in 2014. In a side deal, Rogers allowed the CBC to continue broadcasting *HNIC* for 4 years, provided Rogers's own announcers and commentators are used and the revenue from advertising and promotions go exclusively to Rogers. The CBC was effectively cut out of the action, becoming little more than an adjunct of Rogers Sportsnet. It was given a fig-leaf to save its honour—and little else.

The stakes for the CBC were exceedingly high. Not only did *HNIC* produce close to half of the English-language network's advertising revenue, but it also accounted for a third of overall viewing. Most critically it gave the CBC access to the much prized 18–34 age group, with the extra bonus that the majority of viewers visited the broadcasters' website for further information about games.[19] In short, it had given the public broadcaster a way to reach viewers that it normally could not attract. While it will keep its pipeline to younger viewers, at least in the short run, losing *HNIC* is the hardest body check that the public broadcaster has received in a generation. However, there is a small silver lining in the current arrangement. Losing the *HNIC* slot entirely would have meant that at least 300 hours per year of Canadian content would have had to be filled by other shows. The cost of replacing so many hours of CanCon would have been enormous, and arguably impossible. The CBC doesn't have to worry about this problem—at least for a while.

Ironically, retaining *HNIC* also had its dangers. This is because every spring the CBC cancels or re-broadcasts other shows, including *The National*, to fit the contours of the NHL playoffs. It effectively becomes a hockey network masquerading as a public broadcaster. Or, to put it differently, as hockey got bigger the rest of the network grew smaller. But, to add insult to injury, the public broadcaster has been muscled out of virtually all other sports programming. It has lost the rights to broadcast curling, the CFL, and World Cup soccer in 2018 but was able to reclaim rights to broadcast the Olympics in 2014 and 2016 after having lost out to CTV for Vancouver in 2010 and London in 2012.

By contrast, Radio-Canada TV is not in as precarious a position. It has twice the audience share of its English-language counterpart and a large slice of total TV revenues among conventional broadcasters in Quebec.[20] Most importantly, it produces compelling and often riveting dramatic shows in which there is much more character development and where stories evolve over a much longer period of time than is the case on the English side. At least one marquee show, Sunday night's *Tout le monde en parle*, is so popular that it often helps set the cultural and political agenda in Quebec. Moreover, Radio-Canada maintained its stride after losing the rights to broadcast *La Soirée du Hockey* in 2001. By never pinning its fortunes to hockey, it never allowed itself to fall into a deep hockey crevice from which it couldn't escape.

But still, one has to ask whether Radio-Canada is doing its job in other ways. Former English-language CBC-TV vice president Richard Stursberg has lamented the degree to which there is little contact, let alone coordination, between the English and French TV networks. He blames the English side. In his view, "to the English side of the CBC, the French side is all but invisible."[21] In his experience, English-speaking senior managers were so cut off from the shows being aired on Radio-Canada TV that they "might as well be produced in Mongolia."[22] But the same attitudes prevail on the other side of the linguistic divide. A study of stories aired in 2010 on Radio-Canada's main news show *Le Téléjournal* conducted by researchers at Carleton University found a highly Quebec-centred view of the world, with the rest of Canada being more or less an afterthought: 42 per cent of coverage was about Quebec, another one-third dealt with international news, and 20 per cent dealt with "national news."[23] A similar study conducted in 2009 found that "news about other provinces and territories received little attention, even when they were more 'important' for a wide range of reasons."[24]

By contrast, radio is the CBC's happy zone. English-speaking radio's collage of informative, original, fearless, funny, and intelligent shows, including stalwarts such as *Q, Ideas, As It Happens, Quirks and Quarks,* and *The Current* have made the network into the very model of what public broadcasting should be. Local shows such as *Metro Morning* in Toronto, *Early Edition* in Vancouver, *Information Morning Nova Scotia, Ottawa Morning,* and *The Eye Opener* in Calgary dominate drive-time listening and reach closer to the issues and events of local community life than anything else on radio—and arguably in other media as well. As a result, Radio One has maintained a strong audience share, over 12 per cent in 2012, and accounts for well over 60 per cent of all listening to talk radio in Canada.[25] Radio Two, which is devoted to music, does less well, with a little over 2 per cent of daily listeners in 2011. On the French side, Première Chaîne and Espace Musique remain a dominant and creative force, garnering virtually the same audience share as their English-language counterparts.

Placing ads on CBC Radio remains a great temptation for those who worry about the corporation's long-term financial survival. Ads began appearing on Radio Two in 2013, and some observers believe that the public broadcaster no longer has a choice. According to a study commissioned by the support group Friends of Canadian Broadcasting, selling ads on Radio One and Two, as well as on Première Chaîne and Espace Musique, would likely bring in close to $220 million annually by 2015.[26] But opponents of such a move believe that it would alter the very character, the very fabric, of public broadcasting. Indeed, the CRTC has warned the CBC against taking such a drastic and perhaps irreversible step. In one of its decisions the regulator warned,

> A public broadcaster is expected to take risks; to offer diversity, even controversy, and to venture into new innovative forms of

programming. Responding to these objectives requires programming choices that are made with a clear understanding of the CBC's role and the public interest. Such choices should not be unduly influenced by commercial considerations. These considerations, more often than not, lead the CBC's services to become similar to, rather than distinct from the services of commercial broadcasters.[27]

Private broadcasters fear that CBC Radio would draw advertisers away from private stations and depress the rates that private broadcasters can charge. For CBC TV, the battle to be ad-free was lost decades ago. Radio One remains ad-free, at least for now.

Despite its many challenges, the CBC enjoys widespread support from Canadians. Polls taken in 2011 found that over 70 per cent of those surveyed wanted to either maintain or increase public funding for the CBC.[28] Polls also showed strong opposition to the budget cuts imposed by the Harper government in 2012.[29] Support for the CBC tends to be highest among women, among people with higher incomes, and in Atlantic Canada. What's interesting is the obvious disparity between the high numbers of people who support the CBC and the relatively small size of the CBC's TV audience, with the exception of the audiences for *HNIC*. The fact is that many Canadians view the CBC as kind of a national insurance policy. They want the corporation to be there—whether they watch or listen to its shows or not.

Re-imagining the CBC

Despite these votes of confidence, the corporation is caught in the vortex between what it is today and what it might become if it were allowed to reinvent itself. The broadcaster's very weakness has become an argument for dismantling it, since critics can now point to an endless string of failings. The question is this: how can the CBC remake itself in the age of media shock?

Redesigning the CBC has become a kind of national parlour game, with pundits, policy experts, and members of the public proposing any number of possible solutions. Some believe that the key to the kingdom lies in separating TV from radio and running them as two different companies. Radio would continue to prosper without being weighed down by the TV albatross. Others would reverse the CBC's current strategy of being a national broadcaster with weak local roots; they would reinforce the CBC's local presence while forgoing some of the corporation's national programming. A number of commentators are captivated by the notion that the public broadcaster should be a content provider, in effect, a national production studio, that develops programs that can be sold to others. While the idea sounds good, it's not clear how creating a national media production service would actually work, given that private broadcasters might demand the same kinds of fluffy and vacuous programs that make up so much of their schedules today.

Another suggestion is that the CBC give up sports and advertising entirely, in exchange for which private broadcasters would compensate the CBC. Wade Rowland believes that the money that the CBC spends on sales and promotions could then be shifted to programming. Some private broadcasting executives are fully in support of the CBC, provided it doesn't encroach on any of the spaces that they occupy. The problem is that private broadcasters now occupy virtually all of the fertile ground. The CBC would be left on the periphery with only the tiniest mandate. This is also the reverse of the argument made by John Ralston Saul that it is precisely the failure of private broadcasters to produce memorable, high-quality programming that is the principal argument in favour of strong public broadcasting. Still others would like to roll back the clock and award the public broadcaster the specialty licences in sports and music that it was denied in the past. The specialty channel candy box would be re-opened, allowing the CBC to have its pick of the sugary sweets. The likelihood of this happening is very slim indeed.

The Lincoln Report, the product of a two-year study of Canadian broadcasting undertaken by the House of Commons Standing Committee on Canadian Heritage, contained a number of recommendations designed to strengthen the CBC.[30] The 2003 report envisioned a new management system, with the president elected by the board rather than appointed by the government. This would have the effect of lessening the power of the government and ensuring that the president would be someone with direct experience in broadcasting, rather than being an ex-civil servant, corporate executive, or arts professional with little knowledge of the business. A more chilling problem has been that governments have stacked the CBC board with patronage appointments. In 2013, 9 board members out of 12 had donated money to the Conservative Party.[31] The effect has been to create a sense within the corporation of being "watched" and of being judged on "good behaviour" toward the government. Appointments that are above politics and based on experience and independence would go a long way toward inspiring confidence in the board of directors.

The Lincoln Report also recommended multi-year funding so that the corporation could plan with greater certainty. Among its boldest proposals was for a fund to boost local programming, an initiative that was adopted by the CRTC in the form of the Local Programming Improvement Fund. The fund, which was eliminated in 2014, was meant to benefit all broadcasters, including the CBC.

In the end, any discussion of the CBC's future boils down to how it will be funded. One can only imagine how secure the CBC might be today if the government had implemented the recommendations of a special mandate review committee that reported in 1996. The so-called Juneau Report proposed that the CBC's annual appropriation from Parliament be replaced by a tax on the sale of communication services, which today would include the purchase of cable packages, smart phones, video games, online movies, or apps. The proposal blew up in flames after a concerted attack by private broadcasters. The Friends of Canadian Broadcasting recommended that foreign over-the-top broadcasters such as Netflix be required to contribute 10 per cent of their Canadian revenues to support Canadian broadcasting, 5 per cent of which would go directly to the CBC. A Netflix–CBC revenue transfer would bring at least some revenue that is seeping outside of the country back to Canada.[32]

Those who believe in less funding for the CBC argue that with many Canadians being unable to find a family doctor, long waits in hospitals emergency rooms and for basic medical procedures, decaying infrastructure in many cities, and, the widening gap between rich and poor among other problems, money is best spent elsewhere. It's certainly more difficult to ask for an increase in funding when so many Canadians view government with suspicion and want to see a smaller rather than a larger Ottawa.

Moreover, it's hard to envision a new, revitalized CBC when the forces of media shock seem difficult to overcome. On the television side, the CBC seems to be blocked at every turn. It's not clear that Canadian dramatic shows can compete against Big TV; we don't have the budgets—or arguably the sensibility—needed to produce serialized, counter-culture, "bad-ass" television the way Showtime or HBO can do it. The CBC's ability to hang on to sports programming is questionable, and re-entering the local news arena would require Herculean efforts. Too much ground has been lost, and audience loyalties have gone elsewhere.

In the end, the CBC may have to fight on only a few fronts and cut its losses everywhere else. It could leave radio and Radio-Canada TV as they are; why tamper with winning formulas and signature institutions that are deeply respected and popular? English-language TV, however, is just limping along with fewer and fewer bright spots in its schedule. One solution might be for the network to concentrate its efforts on journalism and public-affairs programming. The idea would be to put money and resources into an area where it can make the greatest difference. As news organizations become weaker and the question of who pays for news becomes more acute and desperate, the CBC could become the Canadian version of the *New York Times* or *Le Monde*. It could move the heavy freight of information across vast spaces, as it was first designed to do.

While the weight of history seems to be tilted against the CBC, few have calculated the costs of not funding the public broadcaster. While private broadcasters are indispensable and, despite their critics, have often done outstanding work, the CBC still has considerable journalistic firepower. Think of all of the news stories about government spending and corruption, the direction of the economy, health care, or the plight of Aboriginal Canadians that would go either unreported or underreported if the CBC were not part of the mix. Think of the talent that would be lost to Hollywood, the programs that would never be made, and the vital role that the CBC has played in integrating new immigrants into society. Also think about how little many of our young people know about the country and what needs to be done to inform them. While some of these losses are difficult to quantify, they amount to a great deal. Losing the CBC would come at a great cost, far more than the cost of reinventing it.

As Joni Mitchell crooned in her song "Big Yellow Taxi," "You don't know what you got till it's gone."

Notes

1 Quoted in Peers, *The Politics of Canadian Broadcasting*, 9.
2 Canada, Royal Commission on National Development in the Arts, Letters and Sciences (Massey Commission), *Report* (Ottawa: King's Printer, 1951), 283–84.
3 Rowland, *Saving the CBC*, 46.
4 Ibid.
5 Stursberg, *Tower of Babble*, 63.
6 Mark Starowicz, "Does Canada Still Need the CBC? YES," *Ottawa Citizen*, October 4, 2012.
7 Cormack and Cosgrove, *Desiring Canada*, 27.
8 Paul Rutherford, *When Television Was Young: Prime Time Canada 1952–1967* (Toronto: University of Toronto Press, 1990), 491–92.
9 Chris Cobb, "Saul Enters CBC Debate," *National Post*, January 30, 2001: A10.
10 Rowland, *Saving the CBC*, 116.
11 Communic@tions Management, "A Statistical Profile of CBC/Radio-Canada," vii, October 5, 2012, http://www.cab-acr.ca/english/research/12/study_oct0512.pdf.
12 Taras, *Power & Betrayal*, 129–39.
13 Rowland, *Saving the CBC*, 92.
14 Barry Kiefl, "On Treacherous Ground," *Literary Review of Canada* 22, no. 5 (June 2014): 20.
15 Communic@tions Management, "A Statistical Profile of CBC/Radio-Canada."
16 Friends of Canadian Broadcasting, "Licence Renewals for the CBC's French- and English-language Services," October 5, 2012, 14, https://www.friends.ca/files/PDF/

fcb.crtc2011-379.pdf. See also Christine Dobby, "CBC Expected to Make Deep Cuts Thursday in Wake of Losing Hockey Night in Canada," *National Post*, April 7, 2014.

17 John Doyle, "Memo to the CBC: Suck It Up," *Globe and Mail*, March 29, 2012: R1.

18 Ibid.

19 Steve Ladurantaye, "CBC Closes in on Pricey Deal with NHL," *Globe and Mail*, November 26, 2013: S6.

20 Communic@tions Management, "A Statistical Profile of CBC/Radio-Canada," 26.

21 Stursberg, *Tower of Babble*, 117.

22 Ibid.

23 Bruce Cheadle, "Radio-Canada's Focus on Quebec Doesn't Meet License Mandate: Study Says," *Globe and Mail*, October 14, 2012, http://www.theglobeandmail.com/news/politics/radio-canadas-focus-on-quebec-doesnt-meet-licence-mandate-study-says/article4611766/.

24 Ibid.

25 Communic@tions Media, "A Statistical Profile of CBC/Radio-Canada," 13, http://www.cab-acr.ca/english/research/12/study_oct0512.pdf.

26 Ian Morrison to Jade Roy, Supervisor, "CRTC: Re: Forecast of Potential CBC/SRC Radio Advertising Revenues" (public hearing, November 27, 2012).

27 Quoted in Friends of Canadian Broadcasting, "Licence Renewals for the CBC's French- and English-language Services," 21.

28 Jennifer Ditchburn, "Majority Backs Public Funding for CBC, Poll Finds," *Canadian Press*, November 11, 2011, http://www.theglobeandmail.com/news/politics/majority-backs-public-funding-for-cbc-poll-finds/article4250955/.

29 Friends of Canadian Broadcasting, "Canadians on the CBC by Nanos Research," March 23, 2012, https://www.friends.ca/poll/10624.

30 Standing Committee on Canadian Heritage, *Our Cultural Sovereignty*.

31 Elections Canada reports. See also Taras, *Power & Betrayal*, 136–37.

32 Friends of Canadian Broadcasting, Friends' submission to CRTC, 23.

Eight
Are Journalists and Politicians Abandoning the Public?

Elly Alboim, a former parliamentary bureau chief for CBC TV News, a prominent political consultant, and a professor at Carleton University, is one of the country's shrewdest observers of both media and politics. A cigar-smoking, no-nonsense, larger-than-life figure, he has written a searing analysis of the state of play among news organizations, politicians, and the public. Alboim claims that each of these essential partners in democracy is in the process of disengaging from and turning its back on the others. As a result of this mutual retreat, citizens are being deprived of information that is vital to their lives.

According to Alboim, media rhetoric about upholding democracy, being a watchdog for the public good, and "telling it like it is" is just that—rhetoric.[1] News organizations can no longer afford to cover public affairs and, worse still, no longer feel obligated to do so. Alboim's blunt assessment is that the media "have no interest" in telling citizens about the process of government and no real "attachment" to our current institutions.[2] While news organizations will report about the fireworks of conflict and on what often seems to be the endless parade of scandals and wrongdoings, as they should, they devote little time to explaining how institutions work, the options that leaders face, their beliefs and governing styles, and the major issues that may be simmering below the surface but do not fall conveniently into the news frame. Simply put, conflict wins out over content virtually every time. Alboim also contends that the aggressive and negative style of much political reporting plays to and reinforces the suspicion and cynicism that audiences already have about the political process.

For their part, governments have learned to "stay away from the mass media whenever they can."[3] Given the hard edges of media power, specifically the power of journalists to frame stories, declare winners and losers, and have the last word on any issue, politicians believe that in dealing with the media there "is seldom a win to be had, that playing for ties is about as good as it gets."[4] According to *New York Times* columnist Maureen Dowd, for governments, "wooing the press is an exercise roughly akin to picnicking with a tiger. You might enjoy the meal, but the tiger always eats last."[5] The goal now for governments is to figure out ways to bypass the media filter entirely, or, as Frank Bruni put it, to "present themselves in packages that we can't simultaneously unwrap."[6] Governments and political parties have imposed strict message control, limited the number of people who are authorized to talk to reporters, and choreographed messages and images so that they produce what is in effect a daily advertisement that will be irresistible to the media. Developing a convincing narrative that can be sold to the public has become one of the essential arts of governance.

The main casualty of the politics of mutual withdrawal is that Canadians are increasingly disconnected from and uninformed about public affairs. As mentioned in Chapter Two, Alboim suggests that no more than 30 per cent of Canadians are actively involved in civic life, the other 70 per cent tending to be interested only at election times or when there are particularly prominent and compelling issues—and even this level of engagement may be falling. As he puts it, "Reaching them is extraordinarily difficult. Informing them directly, let alone educating them, is even more so. Most of these people have chosen to disconnect because they have decided that most public affairs are of no practical relevance to them."[7] But Alboim may be too optimistic. In a review of the results of several federal election studies, McGill political scientist Elisabeth Gildengil concluded that "many Canadians are not simply *un*informed about politics; they are *mis*informed about basic policy-relevant facts like the gap between rich and poor, the crime rate and the condition of Aboriginal peoples and this misinformation skews their policy attitudes in predictable fashion."[8]

Alboim believes that what we call media shock has had a corrosive effect on how the media cover politics. In fact, one can argue that political reporting has been one of the main casualties of media shock. Parliamentary and legislative bureaus have been eliminated or reduced in size, the time and resources needed for investigative work is proving to be scarce, and specialist reporters with experience and connections on particular issues have been largely replaced by general assignment reporters. In this case "less" is in danger of producing "far less."

Media shock has also created a highly fragmented public sphere. Alboim, much like Cass Sunstein, Robert Putnam, and others, is worried about the "prospect of closed-loop networks" in which like-minded people increasingly interact only with each other.[9] As these closed-loop networks proliferate, the hope for at least some shared information and a shared public space diminishes. The danger, according to Alboim, is that "if you don't know what you don't know and are unwilling to delegate others to tell you, you begin to narrow your universe to one driven by your pre-conceived interests. Governments can exacerbate the problem when they determine that it is not in their interests to devote extraordinary efforts to engage the disengaged."[10]

This chapter will explore the questions raised by Alboim and others about whether news organizations and political parties are still full participants in public affairs. We will examine current reporting practices in order to gauge whether, as Alboim suggests, news organizations have staged a wholesale retreat from politics. We will also ask whether journalism's supposed long march away from politics is being aided and abetted by a party and political culture that is increasingly fearful of media and public engagement. The stakes for society are enormous. As Lance Bennett and his colleagues have argued, "Like it or not, the mainstream news media are still the only place where large-scale deliberation can realistically occur. The press' job is to host the discussion, and to broaden it...."[11] The task of parties and political leaders is to participate in that discussion, using facts and honest exchange as their weapons. Simply put, without this contest of ideas, hard choices and difficult issues can be avoided and wrongs can't be made right.

We will start by examining whether journalism is disengaging from the public square.

Blind Spots, Cutbacks, and the Decline of Political Reporting

News organizations impose a series of lenses on the stories that they are covering. Because of limited time and resources, commercial or political pressures, or journalistic conventions, each of these lenses distorts reality in some way. In the end, viewers and readers are seeing a highly contrived version of reality through multiple distorting lenses. While much is captured, there are always stories that are missed and aspects of stories that never become news.

For all of the claims from news organizations about facing cutthroat competition and having a unique perspective on the news, study after study reveals a kind of journalistic "mono-culture" where uniformity and sameness are the rule. For instance, in their study of the US media's coverage of the Iraq War and Hurricane Katrina, Lance Bennett and his colleagues concluded that the outcomes of the news system are "stunningly homogeneous."[12] As they put it,

> The press system ... is so uniformly organized across mainstream news organizations that it qualifies as an institution: the media when it comes to news is singular. Though journalists would point to their vigorous competition to get the news first as evidence to the contrary, they also often freely admit that the competition is generally limited to tidbits such as exclusive interviews with inside sources or a scrap of inside information that nobody else got.[13]

The late Timothy Cook arrived at a similar conclusion in his study of media–government relations: "we all know the abiding paradox of news making: news professes to be fresh, novel and unexpected, but is actually remarkably patterned across news outlets and over time … the content of news is similar from day to day, not only in featuring familiar personages and familiar locales, but also in the kinds of stories set forth and the morals these stories are supposed to tell."[14]

Perhaps the most compelling and exhaustive study of news coverage on TV was conducted by veteran journalist Tom Rosensteil and his colleagues over a five-year period from 1998 to 2002.[15] They studied local news reporting at 154 TV stations in 50 media markets in the US, examined 33,000 stories, and did focus groups or interviews with 2,000 news workers from 40 stations, as well as matching audience ratings with stories so that they could determine which types of stories and formats were most popular with audiences. Rosenstiel and his co-investigators found a remarkable similarity among newscasts in local markets across the US. Almost without exception, newscasts had the same structure, led with the same types of stories, and used the same techniques. Sameness in news selection was so pervasive that the authors asked in wonderment, "How is it that more than 2000 news professionals from more than 40 stations working in 250 small groups independently create newscasts that are nearly identical?"[16]

While one might be tempted to argue that studies about the American news media can't be applied to Canada, the reality is that few Canadian newscasts veer from the formulas and agendas found in the US. Local TV news in both countries is predicated on a "hook and hold" philosophy that produces a steady diet of crime, accident, and disaster stories, known as the CAD formula.

While the news selection on local TV news shows varies from city to city in Canada, much of the same coverage can be seen almost anywhere. Crime scenes, fires, and car chases are interspersed with weather, traffic, and stock market reports. A smattering of health, civic, and celebrity and entertainment reporting is stuffed into the middle of the broadcast. Sports news is at the back end. On some nights local news seems like a phantasmagoria of murder and mayhem, leaving viewers wondering whether they are living in the urban equivalent of a shooting gallery. Remarkably, if there are no local crimes to report, the news shifts to reports on crimes in other cities, the grizzlier the better. One Harvard study found that the number of CAD stories appearing in newspapers and magazines and on TV doubled between the mid-1980s and the mid-2000s. At the same time, the number of stories that held those in power accountable was cut in half.[17]

Walter Dean and Atiba Pertilla, who were part of the Rosensteil study, found that there was a mismatch between the content of local news shows and the stories that viewers wanted to see.[18] The stories that garnered the highest ratings were stories that dealt with substantive issues, were backed by hard facts, and offered a diversity of sources including expert opinions. While the "if it bleeds it leads" formula was primal and inevitable, viewers also wanted to learn about what was happening at city hall, at school boards, and in public life. Stories about civic institutions, for instance, were much more popular with viewers than entertainment news. Another study, conducted by Michael Robinson, used the results of Pew Research Center surveys taken over a 20-year period from 1986 to 2007 to rank the news preferences of Americans based on the stories that they actually consumed.[19] Stories about "pocketbook" issues received significantly more attention than stories about crime and violence. Stories about health and safety were virtually tied with crime stories in terms of interest. And stories about celebrities ranked dead last on a list of 14 topic areas. In other words, the media consultants that had for years told news managers that audiences wanted to watch murder and mayhem and gobs of soft news may have been wrong. While viewers did want to know about police chases, traffic accidents, break-ins, and fires, they also wanted a wider lens placed on city hall and on public-policy issues.

Critics might dismiss worries about a journalistic "mono-culture" in the mainstream media because web-based media supposedly offer a kaleidoscope of diverse information and opinions. However, it's still the case, as pointed out elsewhere in this volume, that in the vast majority of cases, news still flows from the traditional media to online media, rather than vice versa. The force of media gravity is still largely in one direction—with mainstream news organizations setting the news agenda for other media.

Crime Stories near You

A key question is whether the emphasis given to CAD is an example of journalism's disengagement from public affairs. It is difficult, at first glance, to make the link between crime reporting and political disengagement. This is because people have always had a fascination with police and guns, innocent victims, deviant behaviour and its punishment, danger, and cruelty. One can argue that not reporting these items would be a disservice, given that people turn to the news at least in part to learn if they are "safe," and they need to be told if they are not. The difficulty is not so much with reporting crimes, but rather with turning crime into an obsession that devalues and displaces other types of reporting. What's also remarkable is the degree to which crime stories are treated as episodic rather than thematic. In other words, crimes are reported as being random, one-off events rather than as part of a wider civic or social context.[20] Edmonton may have become Canada's murder city, but reports rarely put the social pieces together.

There is little doubt that the daily barrage of news stories about sadistic and senseless crimes and innocent suffering has altered public perceptions. As *Globe* columnist Jeffrey Simpson observed some years ago in a column that could have been written today,

> Last week, Statistics Canada reported yet again that most crime in Canada remains in decline. There have been a few blips against the general trend in recent years, but the general direction of violent crime is down. You would never know it from reading newspapers or watching television. In the newsrooms of the nation, it is an unshakable assumption that crime sells.... To what extent, then, are we in the media misleading the public by devoting so much space and airtime to crime, when the underlying story is the reverse of the individually reported ones?[21]

Philosopher John Ralston Saul echoes Simpson's concern about the media's role:

> It doesn't matter that murder and attempted murder rates have been falling since 1990, violent crimes since 1993, and that total crime is at its lowest since 1997. Public discourse is all about getting tough on crime. Our papers—all of them—leap to this subject of fear and crisis at every excuse. Whatever the politics of newspaper, radio or television, they all want people to pay attention to the ads they carry. And fear, they all believe, is the best way to attract attention to the programming that surrounds the ads.[22]

Given the climate of fear that seems to have been created, it is small wonder that political leaders find themselves in bidding wars over who can be the toughest on crime. And regardless of how tough one becomes, the demands to get tougher never stop.

In his classic study *Is Anyone Responsible?*, Stanford professor Shanto Iyengar has demonstrated that the "frames" that are used to cover issues have a dramatic effect on public perceptions.[23] Simply put, journalists impose a "frame" on the events that they are covering. Reporters often arrive at a story knowing in advance what angles they wish to take, who they wish to interview, and the context in which the story will be presented. They always have a choice about what frames to adopt. According to Iyengar, when reporters use "episodic" frames dealing with individual murders, assaults or arrests, audiences tend to blame the individuals involved—including the victims: the victims were in the wrong part of town, they should have known better, and so on. When coverage is "thematic," the focus changes to larger trends such as crime waves, youth gangs, the lack of safety on public transportation, or violence against women and minorities. In these instances the public tends to blame politicians and governments for not doing enough to prevent crime. The majority of crime reporting is of course episodic rather than thematic. So the decision by news managers to focus overwhelmingly on individual crimes has ideological and policy implications. It also represents, some would argue, a decision to disengage from politics since the causes of crime and wider trends have been stripped out of stories.

The contrary view is that crime reporting is in fact the ultimate form of political reporting. Scholars such as Richard Ericson have argued that much of what we call news is about the upholding of social norms and bringing justice to those who have violated them. As Ericson and his colleagues have noted, the media "offer their readers the same kind of entertainment once supplied by public hangings or the use of stocks and pillories. An enormous amount of modern 'news' is devoted to reports about deviant behaviour and its punishment."[24] Their argument is that the media patrol the moral boundaries of society, punishing those who transgress those boundaries by creating spectacles of exposure and then humiliation. The news media administer justice just as surely as the courts do—although justice takes a different form. By showing and exposing disorder, the news helps maintain order.

The Deep Sleep of Financial Reporters

While news is dominated by crime reporting, much of the debate about media responsibility stems from charges levelled against business reporters for their coverage, or lack thereof, of the global financial meltdown that began with the fall of Lehman Brothers in 2008. The resulting economic carnage cost millions of jobs, shook financial institutions and governments to their cores, and created the greatest and most prolonged financial crisis in 80 years. Some scholars believe that news organizations carried out "journalistic malpractice on a grand scale" by being in bed with the corporations they were responsible for covering.[25] They missed the story, in other words, because they were too close to their sources. Dean Starkman of the *Columbia Journalism Review* believes that "there was a bubble all right, and that the business press was in it."[26] I will argue, however, that the issue is not so much about journalistic disengagement as about a type of "engagement" that went terribly wrong.

In a seminal article, one of the world's leading economists, Nobel Prize–winner Joseph Stiglitz, has argued that in the years before the beginning of the great recession the financial press went off the rails almost as completely as the economy on which it was supposed to be reporting. The reason was that "unfortunately, there are at play strong incentives for the media not to serve as part of society's systems of checks and balances, not to 'lean against the wind.'"[27] According to Stiglitz, there were two major factors in the media's failure to adequately warn the public about the financial disaster that was brewing on Wall Street. The first was the tendency of business reporters to embrace the values of the corporate community that was the focus of their reporting. What led to the "cognitive capture" of business reporters was that they needed access to business leaders in order to do their stories. Favourable stories would keep doors open; critical ones were likely to slam doors shut, perhaps forever. Given these realities, reporters wrote glowing stories about business leaders, in some cases painting them as heroes and cult figures. CEOs were the new natural-born leaders who could do no wrong.

On a subtler level, working the street meant inhaling its values to the point where reporters no longer questioned basic assumptions and actions. They succumbed so completely to the corporate and Wall Street worldview that they sometimes ignored dangerous practices, regardless of how grievous or obvious those dangers had become. Few reporters could bring themselves to question balance sheets, regardless of how absurd the level of borrowing had become (with few reporters even aware that many banks and businesses kept off–balance-sheet accounts) or the credibility of exotic and fabricated financial instruments such as credit default swaps on subprime mortgage bonds—schemes that all too often they themselves couldn't understand or explain.

To be fair, some alarm bells were sounded. A small contingent of reporters questioned the fantasy world that Wall Street had created. Gutsy analysts such as Meredith Whitney downgraded expectations about housing prices and the mortgage industry; economists such as Jeffrey Sachs, Nouriel Roubini, and Paul Krugman wrote newspaper columns that warned of dangers; and a small splash of stories focused on the human consequences of predatory financial practices. The problem is that there weren't nearly enough critical stories or blazing columns to help the public understand what was taking place. The response of critics to journalists who claim that "we did those stories" is that reporting a story once or twice or featuring the occasional opinion piece doesn't move the story forward, doesn't ring the alarm bell loudly enough. It was arguably the failure to provide a steady "drumbeat" of stories that constituted a form of negligence.[28]

If they want to have an impact, in fact, news organizations have to go big. Publishing or airing a piece on a given topic every now and then makes little impact. There has to be a decision to campaign on an issue and pursue a story, regardless of where and how the chips may fall. This was certainly the case when the *Globe and Mail* and the CBC launched a campaign about concussions in hockey. They gave the issue prominence, kept with the story over a prolonged period, and brought the matter to a crescendo. In the absence of such a campaign, the public can be forgiven for not paying attention to stories that appear only every now and then.

To Stiglitz, the relationship that business reporters have with their sources mimics the relationship that political reporters have with politicians. As he explains, "Like the business press, they need access. They do not want to lose access, and to retain access they have to provide favorable (or at least not too unfavorable) coverage. Those in the administration work hard to create an artificial scarcity of information so that they have something to trade in return for favorable coverage."[29] Some reporters gain special access to party leaders, are given briefings on developing stories, and are forewarned about an impending decision or appointment. They are so close to those in power that they virtually become members of the team. As with business reporters, refusing to play the game can be harmful to their journalistic health. Reporters can be deprived of the access that they need to write their stories and left to watch from the sidelines as their competitors make headlines. Former BC journalist and Mount Royal University professor Sean Holman has observed that not all governments employ such tactics, however. With the ability to get their own messages out to the public directly, some operatives believe that they no longer have to play the game.[30]

Some would argue that the business press has more than made up for the softness of their reporting by aggressively pursuing companies such as Goldman Sachs, British Petroleum, Barclays Bank, and News Corporation that have engaged in dubious or criminal practices. But, as Laura Way found in her study of media coverage of the oil sands, the way in which business pages are structured tends to make it difficult for reporters not to echo the interests of the industries that they cover.[31] Stories in the financial sections of newspapers tend to be episodic and framed in business terms so that cognitive capture is difficult to escape.

A second blind spot in the media's failure to adequately report on the impending financial crisis, according to Stiglitz, was the journalistic tendency to impose a pro/con—for and against—format without providing the critical analysis or even the basic information needed by readers or viewers to discern the real facts. As Stiglitz observes,

> It is as if, in covering a story about the colour of the sky, a colour-blind reporter gave equal weight to those who claim it is orange as to those who claim it is blue. Of course, it is more complex: it is perhaps more akin to how a reporter in the Middle Ages might have discovered the story about the "discovery" that the world is round. With a majority of those interviewed still claiming that the world is flat, it would be natural for the critics to dominate.[32]

In the case of the financial crisis, charges made by critics would be juxtaposed against the authority of the banking community and thus easily dismissed.

The journalistic norm of "two sides, no real meat" that permeates almost all issue coverage has become particularly controversial with regard to how climate change has been reported. In a study of reporting by the major US networks between 1995 and 2004, Maxwell Boykoff found that 70 per cent of stories suggested that the science behind climate change was open to dispute, despite the fact that a strong consensus existed among recognized experts as well as world bodies studying the issue.[33] Those with fringe views, some paid by interest groups, were often juxtaposed against prominent experts as if their studies and authority were somehow equal.

Indeed, the "for and against" format has become so deeply embedded in journalistic routines that reporters will often drop stories entirely if they can't find people who can take opposing positions. The question that we need to ask is whether this "he said, she said" positioning is a form of journalistic disengagement, however nicely it is dressed up to appear to be the opposite. The conventional wisdom is that viewers and readers will be able to discern the truth from being exposed to two sides. The role of journalists, therefore, is to capture these conflicting views, even though complex issues may have many shades of grey and can't be easily telescoped into two opposing positions. Critics argue that journalists are often forced into creating "false equivalencies" and, worse still, into knowingly promoting false claims.[34] By not digging out and presenting the real facts, thereby taking a position that they can stand behind, they are being unfaithful to the audiences that they serve. However, the advantage of such "balanced" and "viewless" coverage is that it provides journalists with the camouflage of neutrality. The pro/con format protects news organizations from charges of bias that could be levelled by political parties, media rivals, or major interests.

Some observers have also argued that the "Foxification" of news discussed in Chapter Four has changed the nature of news reporting, and with it the need for news organizations to appear to be neutral. According to Jay Rosen, objectivity was part of a "grand bargain between all the different players ...

when radio and television emerged, America's private broadcasters embraced impartiality in their news reporting to maximize their appeal to audiences and advertisers and avoid trouble with regulators."[35] With audiences increasingly splintered along ideological lines, news organizations may be tempted to abandon the veils of neutrality that they now wear and become proudly one-sided in their news reporting. While the tilting of news in a partisan direction is increasing, for now at least the pro/con format remains the gold standard.

Who Shot Political Reporting?

While crime and business reporting provide ample fodder for the media disengagement argument, political reporting provides the starkest example. Perhaps the most persuasive and insightful argument in favour of the disengagement position has been made by Christopher Waddell, who, like Alboim, was a former parliamentary bureau chief for CBC TV News and is now a professor of journalism at Carleton University. In chronicling what he terms "the death of political coverage," Waddell argues that budget cuts have depleted political reporting of much of the oxygen that it needed.[36] Since the mid-1990s, almost all of the country's local newspapers have shuttered their Ottawa bureaus, national news organizations have made sizable cuts to their staffs in Ottawa, bureaus in provincial capitals have been downsized or eliminated, and budgets for investigative reporting have been slashed. Accountability reporting is in shorter and shorter supply.

During Alboim's tenure as Parliamentary Bureau Chief for CBC TV during the 1980s, there were roughly 15 reporters in the bureau. The number of reporters was reduced to 7 or 8 during the period when Waddell served as bureau chief, from 1993 to 2001. Today there are 4 or 5. By comparison, the number of communications personnel that were working in federal offices, including over 80 in the Prime Minister's Office and the Privy Council Office, was more than 3,325 in 2014.[37] Robert McChesney compares the task confronting journalists covering government to that of an NFL team "trying to stop the Green Bay Packers with only two players lined up on the defensive side of the line of scrimmage."[38] But even this analogy may not go far enough: it's as if two linebackers are playing against three teams at once.

For Waddell, the closing of Ottawa bureaus by local newspapers, the loss of specialized reporters, and the advent of "Blackberry journalism" are the principle culprits, the smoking guns, in the saga of who shot political reporting. Waddell argues that the closing of Ottawa bureaus by virtually all of Canada's local newspapers has meant that there is far less coverage of local

MPs and therefore far less knowledge and interest in what they do. We have now reached the point where most Canadians could not identify their local MP if they saw him or her in the street, let alone know about their MP's beliefs or track record in Ottawa. To most Canadians, MPs are almost invisible. To make his point, Waddell compared voter turnout in three Ontario cities where local newspapers had closed their Ottawa bureaus with turnout in three cities that had never had Ottawa bureaus. He found that the decline in voting was more dramatic in the cities whose newspapers had once had Ottawa bureaus. Waddell explains the link in this way:

> Would as many people go to an Ottawa Senators hockey game, a Toronto Blue Jays baseball game or a Winnipeg Blue Bombers football game if all the local radio, television, and print media in those communities simply stopped covering the sport with their own reporters, instead using occasional stories written by wire services such as Canadian Press? Certainly not, so the same principle should apply at least to some degree in the relationship between coverage of politics and interest in voting.[39]

Another problem created by so many cutbacks is that with fewer journalists to work with, news organizations have reduced the number of specialized reporters who had detailed knowledge of specific areas such as foreign and defence policy, the Supreme Court, Aboriginal policies, health care, or financial issues. Instead, specialized stories are now covered by general assignment reporters who often have little background on the subjects they report on. The consequence, according to Waddell, is that, "When a reporter doesn't have the time, knowledge or background to deal with the complexity of an issue there are still two ways that he or she can tell the story—by focusing on conflict or personality."[40] Having less expertise, reporters are more likely to engage in instant research (i.e., through Google or Wikipedia), are less likely to know who the real experts in the field are, and are less likely to challenge the information or story lines that are spun by political parties and interest groups.

This growing journalistic deficit is compounded by the fact that there is less time and fewer resources for investigative work. With fewer reporters available to peer under the hood of government operations, news organizations have lost at least some of their ability to set the public agenda and act as watchdogs. Moreover, without the capacity to produce their own information, they are much more dependent on the scraps that politicians decide to feed them or on spectacles such as Question Period where little effort is needed to come up with a story.

News managers might argue that skilled and experienced general assignment reporters aren't easily fooled. They are trained to know a good story when they see it and where it belongs in the scorecard of political winners and losers. News executives may also feel that the lack of background and nuance in reporting the news is more than made up for by the panels of experts that they call on to appear on cable shows. But it's not clear that these experts provide much depth. In-studio panels are one way to cut costs, and with the exception of CBC's "At Issue" panel, which has become a national institution, many of the Sunday-morning and cable political panels seem to offer few insights. Cable news shows in particular tend to attract small audiences, and the "experts" that appear are typically other journalists, representatives of political parties who come with their predictable talking points, or people chosen for their ideological views. As discussed in Chapter Four, cable news shows are often more about highlighting conflict and creating pyrotechnics than about exchanging useful information.

Compounding the situation, according to Waddell, is that rather than broadening their journalistic horizons, tweeting and texting have made the world of reporters much smaller. The problem is that smart phones have made the flow of political information so fast and intoxicating that it has pushed journalists to value the wrong things.[41] As discussed in Chapter Five, critics argue that Twitter in particular creates an "alternative reality," an "insiders" game in which journalists and politicians deal mostly with each other. The minutiae of the latest Ottawa foible become more important than gauging the pulse of the country. As one journalist told Peter Hamby, "Twitter made me think smaller, when I should have been thinking bigger."[42]

Second, as Waddell points out, "Frequently they [tweeting and texting] result in stories about party strategy, insider political personalities, conflicts within parties and other trivial issues within an environment in which how quickly or cleverly someone 'reacts,' regardless of what is said, becomes in media eyes a key determinant of competence."[43] The danger is when reporters misconstrue the Twitterverse or other social media with the real world of politics. And it's also a mistake to think that tracking stories is the same as covering them—despite the illusion that tracking creates. Of course, as we have seen in Chapter Five, there is another side to this story. Hamby suggests that Twitter has become the centre of gravity for political reporting and is a valuable vehicle for exchange and indeed agenda-setting. There has yet to be a Canadian study that replicates the work that Hamby has done about campaign journalism in the US.

To Waddell, the most conclusive evidence that journalism is failing is the increasing disconnectedness of the public from politics. His conclusion is that "voters have become outsiders and cannot relate to what is being reported. Too much political coverage means nothing to them and has no impact on their lives. As a result Canadians have tuned it out until something happens....."[44] But British scholar Andrew Chadwick paints a far different picture about the influence of web-based media. According to Chadwick, hybrid media have created new forms and a new logic in journalism. He sees the new news system as more open, permeable, and democratic as a result of citizen-based initiatives. The key question, both for Chadwick and for his colleague Nick Couldry, is this: "what are people doing in relation to media?"[45] This perspective contrasts sharply with scholars such as Starkman, Thomas Patterson, Alex Jones, and Christopher Waddell, who ask what the news media are doing in relation to people—and worrying that they are coming up short in far too many ways, especially in accountability.

The Style of Substance

While fewer reporters and limited resources can be seen as main causes for the crisis that has engulfed political reporting, some scholars believe that the blame lies with the values on which political reporting is based. This is particularly the case with television. Neil Postman was among a generation of scholars who argued that television news stories are so visual, so fixated on personalities, so fast-moving, so fleeting, and so intent on entertaining that they give viewers little that is tangible to hold on to.[46] Ninety-second news reports, famously described as "quick and dirty in a minute thirty," can only scan the surface of an issue or event. They can't provide the details or the nuances that are needed for understanding. They have, to borrow a phrase, "an unbearable lightness" or, in Todd Gitlin's words, "the style of substance but not its content."[47] As Jonathan Schell once described the elusive nature of TV reporting, "Television is powerful because it can dominate the moment. It is weak because it cannot outlast the moment—cannot make an impression that lasts."[48] TV can thus signal an event—but it cannot explain it.

The basic critique of TV news is that stories are chosen because they are inherently dramatic, and even then it is the most dramatic aspects of these stories that are highlighted. Issues or events that lack dramatic qualities rarely make it to air. Fox News CEO Roger Ailes has famously described this need for sensationalism: "If you have two guys on a stage and one guy says, 'I have a solution to the Middle East Problem,' and the other guy falls in the orchestra pit, who do you think is going to be on the evening news?"[49]

While criticism that TV news stories are just "bubble gum for the eyes" may contain elements of truth, it's hard to deny that when television news is at its best it is a superb medium for teaching and understanding. In any given news story there are images that stick, facts that are absorbed, and a slice of reality that is given meaning. Even if studies show that audiences often have little recall of the specific details of stories, with stories supposedly washing over viewers like rainwater, the reality is that TV's power comes precisely from the fact that when we are watching we are relaxed, unaware of how deeply its messages are penetrating. Moreover, while it has become customary to think that reporters are too often chosen for their good looks and on-air presence rather than political savvy—and this is increasingly the case in the US—in Canada there are still many ordinary-looking TV reporters who are on air precisely because of their shrewd political eye and sharp instincts.

This having been said, there is growing concern that news is increasingly appearing in smaller and smaller bites, whether as text messages, short headlines, Reddit feeds, factoids floating across TV screens, or tweets. As Florian Sauvageau has reminded us, the trend is for news to be offered more and more as "snacks" rather than as "meals." And the traditional media have gotten the message. A study of story lengths at four great American newspapers—the *New York Times*, the *Wall Street Journal*, the *LA Times*, and the *Washington Post*—found a sharp drop in the number of stories that were over 2,000 words in length. Stories of over 3,000 words are quickly becoming an endangered species.[50] While no similar study has been done on the length of Canadian newspaper stories, even the most cursory review would reveal that "snippets" of news are becoming more prevalent.

Indexing and Framing

In addition to the problem of news-less news, scholars are concerned about structural flaws and potentially dangerous blind spots that seem deeply ingrained within journalism. In an extraordinary study of American media coverage during the lead-up to the US-led invasion of Iraq in 2003, Lance Bennett, Regina Lawrence, and Steven Livingston found that the events leading to war were widely misrepresented.[51] In fact, the invasion of Iraq provided one of the most shocking cases of "missing information" that has ever taken place. Polls suggest that a solid majority of Americans had a least one major misconception about the war, with many Americans believing that there was clear evidence linking Saddam Hussein to the 9/11 attacks, that weapons of mass destruction had been found in Iraq, and that world opinion supported an invasion—all of which was untrue.[52] Clearly the surge in patriotism that existed after 9/11 made it difficult for reporters to challenge the Bush administration's PR juggernaut once the administration had decided to go to war. It may also have been that the reign of terror perpetuated by the Hussein regime, the secretive and amorphous nature of Al Qaeda, and the lack of contact with or respect for foreign sources, particularly in Europe, had made the story especially difficult both to cover and to understand. But some of the explanation for this missing information may lie, as Bennett and his colleagues suggest, with the basic routines and assumptions of journalism.

In an influential study, Daniel Hallin theorized that media reporting takes place only within a "sphere of legitimate controversy."[53] In the case of the invasion of Iraq, coverage was carefully "indexed" or "calibrated" to reflect the debate taking place among Washington power holders. According to what has become known as the indexing hypothesis, if a consensus on a particular issue emerges among political elites, as there was in the US during the run-up to the invasion of Iraq, then reporting reflects that consensus. If all of the main players are singing the same tune, then it's difficult for the press not to join the chorus. When the consensus among elected officials and recognized experts broke down after no weapons of mass destruction were found, and when the horrors that took place in the Abu Ghraib prison were revealed, then news reports started to mirror those differences. Media reporting then acted as an "echo chamber," amplifying the debate among elites but also limiting the discussion to the boundaries set by the political class. The problem is that the rules of engagement for journalists are set by elites. In a study of media coverage of Canadian involvement in Afghanistan a former CBC reporter, Brooks Decillia, found that indexing dictated much of journalistic coverage. On the great majority of occasions journalists would only go as far as the boundaries of elite debate allowed them to go and no further.[54]

The danger of "indexing" is that the boundaries of official debate may be quite narrow. If official views are all that journalists cover, then they may miss the battles raging in the country and certainly overseas. Nonetheless, Bennett and his colleagues believe that for the most part the media system worked well because coverage was able to eventually reflect the true nature of the problems that the US faced. But as they point out, "there is a catch; the press system tends to work well when the political system is already doing its job of debating and giving public scrutiny to policies that affect the general welfare and security of the electorate."[55] If, however, the political system fails to deliver real debate and scrutiny, then it is incumbent on the press to offer a counter-perspective.

Coverage of Question Period in the House of Commons and in provincial legislatures is the principal example of indexing in Canada. Scrums follow closely behind. The highlights of Question Period are dutifully broadcast on the nightly news, and journalistic agendas are dictated, one can argue, by the "sphere of legitimate controversy" that is played out in Question Period. If an issue becomes live ammunition in Question Period, then it becomes a legitimate story for journalists. Most obviously, Question Period provides journalists with the "he said, she said," "you're a jerk, no you're a jerk" ballistics needed for their stories, and it allows them to judge "performance": is the government on top of issues, or has it been caught off balance? Which party leaders or cabinet ministers have star power and which fail the test? Whose fortunes are rising and whose are fading? It also gives understaffed news bureaus a convenient handle for covering Ottawa. Sometimes there is even reverse engineering: reporters and politicians may form tacit alliances to move stories forward so that news stories trigger questions that in turn give journalists the opportunity to keep the story going. While politics takes place at many intersections, most media roads still lead to and from Question Period.

The defenders of the current system argue that despite its theatrical atmosphere, Question Period still acts as a magnet drawing important issues to the centre of Canadian politics and sharpens the differences among political parties for all to see. Governments are kept on their toes and cannot avoid the heat of public exposure when something goes wrong. Critics of the status quo argue that preparing for Question Period now consumes an inordinate amount of everyone's time—time that could be spent on governing and policy-making rather than on coming up with cute one-liners that are endlessly reworked and practised. Moreover, one can rightly accuse journalists of having become enablers, feeding a spectacle that has become contemptuous of both them and the public. Without the media's continuing coverage, the reform of Question Period would probably have taken place long ago.

The most established hallmark of journalistic engagement is the turning of all of politics into a "horserace," with a focus on who is ahead, who is behind, who is gaining, and the strategies needed to win the race, as well as what is taking place behind the scenes. In an analysis of over 10,720 news items that appeared both on TV and in major national newspapers during the 2000, 2004, 2006, and 2008 federal elections, Thierry Giasson, a political scientist at Laval University, found that horserace reporting in various forms dominated coverage. In fact, horserace coverage took up so much space that discussions about issues as issues, rather than as part of party election strategies, were almost completely ignored.[56] Most critically for journalists, the horserace is always on, so all of politics—even during the long breathing spaces between elections—comes to be viewed as a horserace.

Unfortunately, this obsession with what political scientists call the "game" or "strategy" schema has produced a toxic byproduct.[57] Since reporters presume that everything that politicians do is geared to winning, they see and interpret every action, promise, or statement as being either a winning or losing move on the political chessboard. Joseph Cappella and Kathleen Hall Jamieson have described the negative effects of this assumption: "In such an interpretive frame, all actions are tainted—they are seen not as the by-product of a desire to solve social ills, redirect national goals, or create a better future for our offspring but are instead viewed in terms of winning."[58] According to David Broder, since everything boils down to "narrow self-interest" and manipulation, all politicians and all of politics are suspect. Nothing is real; nothing can be believed; "nothing is on the level."[59] As Thomas Patterson points out, journalists seem unable to break the habit of focusing on how the latest events affect the fortunes of political leaders.[60] If the focus were on how the latest events affected ordinary citizens, journalism would improve—and so arguably would audiences.

Strategic framing also means that political leaders and parties in Canada are rarely given credit for having sincere convictions or for being motivated by strong ideological beliefs. The danger is that fierce champions of the Charter of Rights and Freedoms, those who wish to decentralize power away from Ottawa, politicians who are motivated by strong religious convictions, and Green Party activists who care deeply about the planet are painted as opportunists interested only in out-manoeuvring their opponents. In the end, this kind of coverage provides a false and misleading picture of political life. There are many instances in which ideas, policies, and convictions do matter to politicians—even if news organizations are reluctant to discuss them.

Another by-product of horserace journalism is that it has led news organizations to overdose on polling. In Canadian politics, polls are the elephant in the room. Canadian news organizations released over 80 polls about voting intentions in 2009 alone, and some 174 polls were reported in 2008, which was an election year.[61] Poll results are usually reported several times a month between elections and appear at a rate of roughly one every three days during elections. During elections, clients—including parties, interest groups, and news organizations—have access to nightly tracking polls that provide a daily scorecard on how the parties are doing. The reason for the media's obsession with polling is that polls allow news organizations to appear to be on top of the action, they make news themselves, and they are easy to report on. Most critically they provide news organizations with a badge of neutrality because they free them from having to report on policy alternatives, societal divisions, or the state of the country—in other words, from having to report on issues and the consequences of party positions. It's difficult to escape the conclusion that the instrument that has become the very badge of media engagement is in fact its greatest form of disengagement.

Polls shape reporting, and, in turn, reporting shapes elections. Parties that are ahead in the polls raise more money, attract better candidates and more volunteers, and have the glow that comes with being seen as waging a winning campaign. Polls also spur strategic voting: they influence some voters to turn away from their original choices to where they think their votes will count the most. Part of this logic, however, is that polls may suppress voting among those who feel that, since they already know the score so to speak, there is little reason to go to the game. But polling can have other consequences for the political system. For more than a few politicians, polls drive policies. Alberta political legend Ralph Klein once described his political strategy as finding which way the parade was going and then getting to the front of it. Too many "finger in the wind" politicians are afraid to engage in policy debates or take decisive positions for fear of offending public opinion—even though public opinion on many issues can be weak, and easily turned once a convincing argument is made for a particular course of action. Lamenting the ways in which polling has hollowed out public debate, Todd Gitlin has written that, "In the absence of a vital polis, they take polls."[62]

Small wonder, then, that media organizations have been reluctant to acknowledge the crisis that has engulfed the polling industry. The country's leading pollsters were unable to predict a Conservative majority government in the 2011 federal election, a Conservative majority in the 2012 Alberta election, or a Liberal majority in the 2013 BC election. The reasons for the "crisis" are varied, but it has become much more difficult and expensive for pollsters to produce an accurate sample. Busier lives, longer commute times, a greater ability to block calls from unknown callers, a reluctance by cell-phone users to incur the costs of long interviews, an increase in junk calls selling everything from vacations to furnace cleaning, and a lack of interest in and knowledge of public affairs—these factors, among others, have reduced the number of people willing to be interviewed from roughly 70 per cent 20 years ago to between 10 and 15 per cent today.[63] This means that those willing to be interviewed—people who are older, live alone, or have time on their hands, for example—are less representative of the population as a whole. As a consequence, the costs of producing a representative sample have risen considerably.

It has also become more difficult for pollsters to separate voters from non-voters, since almost everyone claims that they will vote even if they have no intention of voting. Translating poll numbers into seats is also tricky, since regional samples tend to be too small to be truly representative. Internet polling, while cheaper, has yet to produce more accurate results, as those surveyed tend to be better educated, wealthier, and arguably more politicized.

One last point needs to be made about the media's addiction to polls. There is a danger that news organizations have attached themselves to an old and increasingly out-of-date technology. By comparison, algorithms using data mined from Google searches, Facebook sites, Apple smart phones, and visits to websites, for example, can forecast whether a movie or TV series will be a hit weeks before it opens, and pinpoint the inflation rate based on tracking hundreds of millions of purchases on a daily and weekly basis. Just as big data is overturning the ways in which corporations and governments operate, it may also be changing the basic methodology of politics. During the 2012 US election, the Obama campaign noticed a discrepancy between the numbers produced by outside pollsters and the numbers produced by its own analytics. The campaign's algorithms were more accurate than the polls.[64]

Reporting Character Issues

Perhaps the most controversial political reporting is on so-called character issues. The parties know that voters often find policy debates too complex to follow and that "character" issues—that is, whether candidates are seen as having the leadership qualities needed to govern—become the basis for their voting decision. Trust, solidity, experience, judgement, and sheer likeability become the barometers of choice. Indeed, according to Internet search data, visitors to political websites sought information about candidates' personal lives, particularly news about their spouses and families, far more frequently than they did information about candidates' political careers, voting records, or policies.

But first some general comments about how the media covers as elusive a trait as character. Before television, political leaders were distant and unseen figures. The American public, for instance, remained unaware that Franklin Roosevelt, arguably the most successful US president of the twentieth century, had been crippled by polio and was unable to walk. This was because journalists had agreed not to photograph or film him in a wheelchair. He enjoyed, in fact, so much protective cover from the journalists who reported on him that his wife Eleanor could live with her lesbian lover in the White House while he enjoyed a long love affair with another woman. Shrewd policies, masterful political skills, a buoyant personality, and a strong radio voice were the keys to success. In Canada, a strange, grey, and squirrelly figure such as Mackenzie King, our longest serving prime minister, could hold séances where he sought guidance from the dead and believed that his mother had been reincarnated as his dog, without any fear of media exposure. He governed because of an almost infinite capacity for compromise and because Canadians never got to see him up-close.

One part of the equation that has changed as a result of media shock is that political leaders have to endure a much greater level of scrutiny. As discussed in previous chapters, at any hour of the day, political leaders face a small army of critics who are sitting in the bleachers of radio and cable, in the blogosphere, and on Facebook or Twitter exposing and refuting their arguments and floating rumours about what's taking place behind the scenes. We now see leaders in all of their awkwardness, frailty, and humanness. Not only are cameras able to record every stammer, every nervous gesture, and every off-hand remark, but these images can be stored virtually forever and can be shown at any time. Moreover, even small gestures can create large and immutable impressions. A cold look, an angry scowl, or an insensitive tweet can sometimes reveal the real person that exists behind the veil of public relations. Even the tiniest morsels of information and speculation can go viral in minutes, and once they become part of conversations on social media sites or are picked up by aggregators such as National Newswatch Canada, Reddit, The Huffington Post, or the Clipboard app, they cannot be ignored by the mainstream media, circumventing at least to some degree the once famous "gatekeeping" role of the elite press. Joshua Meyrowitz believes that by bringing us closer to people and events, the media have corroded and de-legitimized authority, or at the very least made it more vulnerable.[65]

For a variety of reasons, exposing and stripping the private lives of political figures has not occurred to nearly the same degree in Canada as it has in the US. In Canada much of the private realm remains out of bounds. The general understanding is that private behaviour is off limits to reporters, unless it becomes a matter before the courts or becomes a public issue in some other way. Quebec journalists in particular seem to adhere to a European tradition that places a cone of silence around the private lives of public figures. Some believe, however, that this protective cover is receding quickly.

The spouses and family members of Canadian politicians, for instance, still enjoy a zone of privacy that would be unthinkable in the US. After over 30 years in public life and after a decade as prime minister, most Canadians would have been hard pressed to know the name of Jean Chrétien's wife, Aline, or recognize her if they passed her in the street. Little was known about Chrétien's coterie of friends, his religious views, or how he spent his free time. The same can be said for Stephen Harper, although his fanatical devotion to hockey, love of movies, and try-hard piano-playing skills have received a smattering of media attention. Some critics might see these glimpses into his life as part of an image-building campaign, but Harper's book on hockey, *A Great Game: The Forgotten Leafs and the Rise of Professional Hockey*, is detailed, sophisticated, and obviously written by someone with the iron determination needed to write at a pace of 15 minutes a day for years.[66] But his friendships, religious views, and business dealings have not been widely reported on. The other party leaders—Thomas Mulcair, Justin Trudeau, and Elizabeth May—also live within zones of privacy that would be the envy of American politicians.

Once they have departed from the scene, however, Canadian political leaders become fair game. There is now a vibrant cottage industry of Canadian biographies that have excoriated the personal lives of political leaders. C.P. Stacey's, Joy Esberey's, and Allan Levine's excellent biographies of Mackenzie King, John English's masterful accounts of the lives of Lester Pearson and Pierre Trudeau, Steve Paikin's devastating portrait of Ontario's John Robarts, Pierre Godin's and then Daniel Poliquin's shocking descriptions of René Lévesque's inner demons and mental health issues, and Don Martin's tour of the raucous and turbulent side of Ralph Klein's political career are just a few examples of this genre.[67]

The question, perhaps, is whether the American media's obsession with character has degenerated into a kind of journalistic voyeurism that has displaced the reporting of issues and policies. In other words, to what degree has the search for dirt and sensationalism allowed reporters to disengage from politics? Clearly, few business leaders could withstand the level of scrutiny into their private lives that American politicians have to endure. It's also clear that many potential leaders are dissuaded from going into public life because of their desire to protect their own and their families' dignity. For instance, presidential candidates seem to have to pass what amounts to a religious test in order to qualify for office. In 2008, CNN went as far as to schedule a debate among presidential candidates based solely on religious issues. Candidates tried to outbid each other in describing their closeness to Christ. In Canada, there is no equivalent religious threshold, and questions about religious beliefs are rarely asked, except in cases where political leaders have raised the issue themselves, such as when Canadian Alliance leader Stockwell Day touted his qualifications to be Canada's first Christian prime minister.

The more troubling question is whether private behaviour is an accurate guide to public performance. After all, many political leaders have risen above their personal problems to demonstrate great abilities. Winston Churchill's past failures (of which there were many), drinking bouts that often began at breakfast and what he called his "black dog" depressions, did not prevent him from inspiring and rallying his country during the darkest days of World War II and fighting the war with great strategic acumen. John F. Kennedy was able to make clear-headed decisions during the Cuban Missile Crisis despite the debilitating effects of Addison's disease and a dependence on heavy medications. He made little secret of his flings with movie stars and mafia girlfriends, a fact known to the press at the time. Surveys show that Quebeckers rank René Lévesque as their greatest premier despite his predilection for late nights, female companions, and later in his career severe and incapacitating depressions. One of Ontario's most venerated premiers, John Robarts, led a notoriously double life. By day he played the part of a wise and venerated statesman, the very picture of solidity and charismatic power, while at night he seemed to be a lost soul: lonely, damaged, and finding companionship with the bottle.[68]

Spotting erratic or brutal behaviour, chronic lying, or self-deception should be part of what journalists do—although doing it well is difficult. The dilemma for reporters and news organizations is that there is often a big difference between knowing something is happening and being able to prove it. Although reporters had witnessed Toronto mayor Rob Ford's bouts with alcoholism, his loss of control, his incoherence, and his impulsive and dangerous behaviour for years—getting actual proof was not easy. It took an extensive police investigation to finally connect the dots that then allowed reporters to go full blast with the story. And in their widely read book about the 2008 US presidential race, *Game Change*, John Heilemann and Mark Halperin were able to document Republican candidate John McCain's monumental and sometimes uncontrollable temper, his impulsive and haphazard decision-making style, and his shocking lack of preparation on major issues—but only after the election had taken place and people who had observed his behaviour were willing to talk.[69]

Often the better part of valour is for journalists not to go with these stories at all. Playing with live ammunition of this kind can be dangerous for reporters. Journalists can be blamed for taking sides, for scandal mongering, and for calling out behaviours that are not relevant to whether the leaders in question can do their jobs effectively. They can also be sued if they get the story wrong. Moreover, journalists have to be careful not to allow cases of individual wrong-doing to stand for and tarnish the political system as a whole. All too often, scandal reporting feeds into perceptions that all of government is bad and that nothing ever works.

It wasn't that long ago, though, that political reporting was largely an attack culture. As a result of Watergate and the Vietnam War, the prevailing ethic among a generation of journalists was to treat all politicians with suspicion and to see virtually everything that they said as a type of manipulation that needed to be exposed. Prominent writer and magazine publisher Adam Gopnik used the following culinary image to describe the change in journalistic culture that he saw taking place in the 1970s and 1980s: "the tradition ... in which a journalist's advancement depended on his intimacy with power mutated into one in which his success can also depend on a willingness to stage visible, ritualized displays of aggression [against the powerful].... [Those] who used to gain status by dining with [their] subjects ... [now gain it] by dining on them."[70]

What André Pratt has called "obligatory cynicism" had also become an accepted part of Canadian journalism.[71] One of the great landmarks was

CBC's *This Hour Has Seven Days*, a TV show hosted by Patrick Watson and Laurier Lapierre that ran from 1964 to 1966 before it was cancelled by the CBC after pressure from the Pearson government. Politicians were ambushed at their front doors and chased in parking lots. They faced inquisition-like interviews in which they were subjected to close-up shots that zeroed in on the beads of sweat on their foreheads and on their mouths, the insinuation being that they were lying. They were also mocked in songs, dance numbers, and comedy skits. The prevailing ethic during this period was that "bad news was good news," that writing a destructive piece was far more acceptable and easier to defend among one's colleagues than writing a positive piece. Some journalists made a career out of smart-aleck attacks, exposing flip-flops, and the relentless mockery of those in power. Interviews were expected to be combative, even prosecutorial, with easy interviews seen as evidence of journalistic weakness. While there has always been a place for satire, and great journalism is often a "critique," attack journalism took on a life of its own and often came at the expense of dealing with policies or ideas. For some journalists it was, and sometimes still is, simply an easy way out.

The American journalist Elizabeth Drew worried about a journalistic culture that had become too negative, too adversarial, and too destructive. As Drew wrote,

> I wonder if sometimes the sum total of the coverage doesn't tip over to the point where the process is robbed of any sense of majesty, inspiration, where it does become very heavily an approach that runs down just about everybody who tries to get into it.... Again, this is a tough line to draw, but I wonder if we haven't had some effect on the public's reaction, which is: "to the extent that I care: they're all a bunch of bums and fools."[72]

While the press and politicians are locked into a relationship that is based on both mutual need and mutual hostility, one can argue that for a long period hostility won out.

For a variety of reasons there was a cooling off during the 1990s. It is not clear precisely why this shift took place, but one can argue that the country's fierce constitutional battles, the drama of the Quebec referendum, the rise of regional protest parties (Reform in Western Canada and the Bloc Québécois in Quebec), and the severe economic and financial challenges that Canada faced tended to make attack journalism seem less acceptable. The CBC in particular became far more cautious, and some would argue frightened, about attacking politicians, especially those in power. It was also the case that political leaders learned to avoid contact with journalists except under conditions that they controlled. Seeing, as Alboim observed, that they couldn't win the media wars, the political class decided to play the game differently. As we will see in the next section of this chapter, they began to disengage from both the press and the public.

However, not everyone would agree with the theory of media disengagement proposed by the likes of Alboim and Waddell. In fact, the case can be made that the very opposite is true: that we are living in an era of deepening *engagement*. In making this case, proponents could point to the fact that cable news stations in particular have become far more ideological. As discussed in Chapter Four, news and information specialty channels proliferated in the US in the 1990s largely because media managers thought that appealing to small niche audiences that wanted news that conformed to their ideological beliefs would be profitable. Under these conditions cable news shows could dispense with any pretenses to neutrality or objectivity and engage in unrestrained adoration for allies and fierce attacks against opponents. Howard Kurtz has argued that cable news has moved the balance of power in journalism "from those who ask questions to those who seem to have the answers."[73] In the words of media critic Howard Rosenberg, in terms of ideology, cable news shows "slant like drunks who guzzled a couple of six-packs."[74] It's not clear, however, that the model has turned out to be all that profitable, and this is certainly the case with the Sun News Network in Canada.

Perhaps the best comparison with what has taken place in the cable universe is the party press of the late nineteenth and early twentieth centuries—an era in which newspapers in both Canada and the US were either affiliated with or allied to political parties. The party paper's mission was to glorify its friends and bludgeon its enemies. As historian Paul Rutherford reminds us, "In victory the organ gloated, telling its readers right had triumphed; in defeat the organ counseled courage and perseverance, sure evil would fail in the end."[75] One can argue that this is precisely the kind of message that viewers now receive from Sun News Network. It acts as a cheerleader for the Conservative movement and its values, and demonizes both the Liberals and the NDP. While other Canadian cable news outlets such as CBC News Network, RDI, CPAC (which is a consortium created by the country's cable operators), or CTV Newsnet are far more circumspect, the Sun News Network has brought US-style "take no prisoners" political discourse to Canada.

Coincident with the change of culture brought by the rise of cable news shows in the US, there was a return to a deeper hue of partisan journalism in the Canadian press. The tipping point for the renewal of ideological warfare was undoubtedly the founding of the *National Post* by then-media baron Conrad Black in 1998. The *Post* showered right-wing politicians such as Preston Manning, Stockwell Day, Mike Harris, and Ralph Klein with head-lines and protective cover, while spilling mountains of ink attacking Liberal opponents. Under Black, the paper was at the forefront of a campaign to "unite the right," urging that the Reform and then the Canadian Alliance parties merge with the Progressive Conservatives. The merger, or more accu-rately a takeover of the old Tories, was brilliantly engineered by Stephen Harper in 2003. The *Globe and Mail* reacted to the challenge posed by the *National Post* by maintaining its grey respectability as a business newspaper while hugging more closely to the centre on social and cultural policies than it had before. At the same time, the Sun media chain, then owned by Quebecor, hardened its position. The Sun formula mixes right-wing popu-lism with sports, celebrities, and crime reporting. If there is a counterweight to the increased influence of the right-wing press, it's the *Toronto Star*, the country's most unflinchingly progressive newspaper. During the 2011 federal election it endorsed the NDP and urged readers to vote "for the progressive candidate best placed to win their riding."

In an earlier book, *Power and Betrayal in the Canadian Media*, I argued that a right-wing information infrastructure had been created within the Canadian media.[76] This infrastructure consisted of the *National Post*; the Sun newspaper chain; Quebecor papers and TV stations in Quebec; conservative think tanks such as the Fraser and C.D. Howe Institutes, which are turned to for expertise and spokespeople; virtually the entire universe of talk radio; members of the so-called Calgary School such as Tom Flanagan and Ted Morton; as well as a flotilla of pundits. Some would argue that a left-wing information constellation—made up of the *Toronto Star*, the *Ottawa Citizen*, *Walrus* magazine, Rabble.ca, CBC Radio, *The Tyee*, and *Maclean's*, as well as think tanks such as the Centre for Policy Alternatives and the Pembina Institute—has also taken shape.

Quebec journalists tilted toward sovereigntist leaders such as René Lévesque in the 1970s and Lucien Bouchard in the 1990s, and remarkably to Liberal premier Robert Bourassa in his later years. In each of these cases coverage, while rocky at times, sometimes bordered on the reverential. Not surprisingly, the Quebec press always found reasons to dislike Jean Chrétien and paint him as a kind of cartoon character—a native son who was inept, embarrassing, and all too willing to sell out Quebec. Today, the near strangle-hold enjoyed by Quebecor ensures that media opinion in Quebec is far more conservative than it once was.

The argument that we live in an age of journalistic disengagement is not straightforward. The eliminating and downsizing of bureaus, the reduction in specialized reporters, and cutbacks in investigative reporting have certainly made it more difficult for newsrooms to cover public affairs. It's also the case that some of the formats and conceptual devices that journalists routinely use contain traps and blind spots that narrow their range of vision and cause them in some cases to miss the real events that are taking place. Yet at the same time, each of the journalistic routines and rituals discussed in this section has the potential to be meaningful and revealing. Indexing, strategic framing, and pro/con formats can capture important truths. In any case, they are now so "locked into" how journalism functions that their grip is unlikely to be broken any time soon.

According to John Zaller, whether media organizations make it over the threshold of responsible journalism depends on whether they can maintain a "monitorial" function—that is, whether they are capable of sounding the alarm when dangerous political and economic storms are approaching.[77] What one critic described as "watchdog lite" can sometimes be enough.[78] But are the media failing even by these low standards? Or, to put it differently, does an alarm have to be sounded for the media itself?

Totally Scripted: Avoid, Bypass, and Stick to Your Message

The second part of Alboim's thesis is that governments and political parties, knowing that their messages are likely to be contested and twisted out of shape by media reporting, have developed strategies to bypass the media filter. I will argue that despite the remarkable changes brought by media shock, in some ways little if anything has changed in how the political–media game has been played in Canada over the last 40 years. To a remarkable degree, every day in Canadian politics is groundhog day and it's 1972 all over again. In dealing with the news media, politicians still play according to a well-used and aging playbook. Political strategists try to alter the landscape so that media encounters occur on terrain that they control. This involves producing staged events and tightly scripted messages, where the idea is to control the media agenda by giving the media the stories that they want and can't resist.

Yet at the same time, parties now use web-based media to target grassroots supporters and potential swing voters with highly crafted and increasingly individualized messages and fundraising appeals. The science of identifying supporters and getting them to donate, volunteer, and go to the polls has become a key to electoral success. Parties without sophisticated data are parties that are likely to lose.

Since Canadians often make assumptions about politics based on what they know about American politics, it's important to begin by pointing out that there are stark differences between how elections are fought in the two countries. The basic geometry of election politics couldn't be more different. First, if one includes primary battles, American presidential and Senate campaigns last for well over a year. This is far longer than the 36 days that is the usual length of a federal election campaign in Canada. While Canadian parties are in a pre-election fever for many months before campaigns actually begin, in reality Canadian elections are over in the amount of time that it takes major American campaigns just to gear up for the campaign.

More critically, the amount of money spent during an election cycle in the US, now in the billions of dollars, dwarfs anything even imaginable in Canadian political campaigns. The American system allows for so-called super PACs, third-party interest groups (political action committees), which, while not formally tied to major political parties or candidates, run parallel campaigns. Individuals can give anonymously to super PACs, and in some cases tens of millions of dollars have been injected into election races by single donors. By comparison, there are strict limits governing the amounts that can be spent in Canada. During the 2011 federal election, the three main parties could spend roughly $21 million each on their national campaigns, candidates for Parliament could spend between $69,000 and $134,000 depending on the population and geography of their ridings, and third parties were limited to expenditures of a little over $4,000 per constituency. Corporations and unions are prohibited from making donations, and individuals were limited to donations of $1,100 to each party (raised to $1,500 for the 2015 election), a far cry from the $35,000 that US donors can give annually to presidential campaigns—with supporters often leveraging their influence by "bundling" donations from friends and business associates together to have a greater impact—and the tens of millions that individual donors can pour into super PACs. Elections in Canada are also highly subsidized by tax dollars. Parties receive a 50-per-cent reimbursement for expenditures on national campaigns. Candidates that receive a certain percentage of the vote also qualify for reimbursements. People who donate money to parties receive tax credits.

This means that, unlike in the US, Canadian parties cannot afford to saturate the airwaves with tens of thousands of ads, and candidates for Parliament are reduced to running low-rent campaigns, with the vast majority unable to afford TV and radio ads or mount anything close to a professional marketing campaign. In fact, local campaigns are so threadbare that candidates are unable to brand themselves. They depend on the national campaign and party identification to get them over the finish line. This means that their fates can be determined by even the slightest changes of political fortune at the national level. The fact that party leaders are effectively the sole "breadwinners" in elections has meant that the power of party leaders has been magnified, while the power of everyone else has been diminished. Canadian politics has become "presidentialized," because even the most powerful cabinet ministers are dependent on the popularity of the leaders for their own survival. Donald Savoie, a distinguished political scientist, has made the case that Canada is governed by an "Imperial Prime Minister."[79]

Ironically, the very money that allows political organizations in the US to run sophisticated ad campaigns and develop state-of-the-art voter-contact methodologies is also the single most corrupting element in US politics. In order to win or even compete, candidates for office are dependent on wealthy individuals, banks and corporations, and industry associations such as the gun lobby or the trial lawyers' association that want special consideration in return for their support. Media scholar Robert McChesney argues, for example, that communication conglomerates such as AT&T, Microsoft, Google, and Apple have used the "pay to play" system to ensure that copyright, taxation, privacy, and competition policies remain unchanged.[80]

It's also crucial to note that Canadian politics is not as deeply polarized as American politics, at least for now. Political allegiances aren't as tightly wrapped up with identity, and as many as 30 to 40 per cent of Canadian voters change allegiances during campaigns. In the US, the hard crust of political identity means that few voters are likely to change their minds during campaigns.[81]

Despite these stark differences, some aspects of the two systems are similar. The most obvious example is the advent of the permanent campaign. This term was first coined by Sidney Blumenthal in 1980, and the concept was explored in detail by Norman Ornstein and Thomas Mann in an edited volume in 2000.[82] The notion is that where politics, like baseball or the NHL, once had an off-season when politicians were not expected to be campaigning, today the campaign season never ends. The great change came with the emergence of cable news channels and hence a 24-hour news cycle. In this new environment, political parties have to be always on, always ready to respond to the latest controversies or opposition attacks. Talking points, designated spokespeople, and compelling images have to be prepared on a daily basis. The fear is that if you lose the battle of the day, then you can also lose the battle of the week, and before you know it the tides will have shifted against you. Some would argue that the notion of a 24-hour news cycle is now outdated; we now live in a hyper-accelerated news cycle, with stories sometimes appearing and fading in hours and minutes.

Another factor in the creation of the permanent campaign is that as parties can no longer rely on corporate or union donations, fundraising and direct mail campaigns directed at individual donors have become full-time operations. This means that databases have to be continually added to and massaged. The emergence of new web-based media has added another layer: websites, email campaigns, YouTube channels, tweets, and Facebook walls have to be fed and refreshed multiple times a week—and sometimes several times a day or even hourly.

A major new weapon in the permanent campaign has been the use of pre-writ advertising. Designed to lampoon and demonize prospective opponents long before the elections even take place, pre-writ ads have now become standard issue in Canadian politics. Although begun by the Liberals with their "Stephen Harper said" ad campaign launched before the 2004 federal election, pre-writ attack ads are most identified with the Harper Conservatives. Waves of negative ads were launched against Liberal leader Stéphane Dion between 2006 and 2008, and another tsunami of attack ads was aimed at Michael Ignatieff after he became leader of that party. The goal of these pre-emptive strikes was to define the newly elected Liberal Party leaders before they had a chance to define themselves. Dion was painted as "Not a leader," and Ignatieff was portrayed as "Just visiting," a reference to his almost 30 years away from the country. Arguably both Dion and Ignatieff never recovered from these attacks, mostly because voters believed them to be true. The situation was exacerbated by the fact that their subsequent behaviour seemed to fit the caricatures drawn in the ads. More recently, the flights of negative ads directed at NDP and Opposition leader Thomas Mulcair and Liberal leader Justin Trudeau seem to have had little of the same stickiness. The Liberals and the NDP have long had their own pre-writ advertising campaigns.

Perhaps the largest pre-writ ad campaigns are those that shower the airwaves with ads about government programs and initiatives. Susan Delacourt notes that spending on government advertising ballooned from just over $41 million in 2005–06 to $136 million in 2009–10.[83] These spots are an unmistakable part of the TV landscape, especially during the NHL playoffs when audiences mushroom. There are usually young smiling faces, scenes of people working, and views of Canada's burgeoning cities. The government is always depicted as being on top of problems and making a big difference in people's lives. Not surprisingly, little real information about programs is ever conveyed.[84] While paid for by tax dollars, they are political ads under another name. But it gets even better for the government: because they are aired under the guise of "public service," the ads generally fly under the radar of journalistic or even opposition scrutiny. Yet despite the advent of the permanent campaign, and while the political season never stops in Ottawa, the attention of ordinary citizens is intermittent, often waning, and increasingly detached. As noted in Chapter Two, for many Canadians the political season is getting shorter—or doesn't exist at all.

Before we discuss the media strategies used by political parties, it's important to note that new communication tools are changing the ways in which policies and messages are constructed. While the main political parties are brokerage rather than ideological parties, meaning that ideology is often sacrificed to practical politics, they are still anchored by ideological beliefs. Even so, the ways in which policies are packaged are largely drawn from polls and focus groups testing. Political parties practise marketing in ways not dissimilar to the corporate sector. They use surveys to pinpoint the mood of the electorate, determine the issues that are viewed as most critical, and gauge how different policies, appeals, and keywords will resonate with different subgroups. To some degree, party platforms have become exercises in reverse engineering: where platforms were once the starting points for constructing election campaigns, campaign strategies derived from polls now dictate the principles and policies on which parties will run.[85]

The problem with poll-driven policies is that they limit the importance and the possibility of grassroots debates within political parties. While these debates can be messy, inconvenient, and sometimes divisive, one can argue that they ultimately strengthen parties and infuse them with a democratic spirit. As Alex Marland, a political scientist at Memorial University, has warned, "Although technology provides an excellent mechanism to gauge what the public wants ... in practice, it displaces grassroots engagement for it has become an efficient but lazy way for party personnel to devise and promote political products."[86] We can push the argument even further: as creative power has been handed over to party officials as well as friendly pollsters, consultants, and webmasters, parties have become increasingly empty and lifeless vessels with dwindling and increasingly aging memberships.

On another level, given the tight and even brutal party discipline imposed on MPs by governments and parties, ordinary MPs have become little more than "bobbleheads," or, as one MP described it, "potted plants" moved around for decoration.[87] The rules are glaringly simple: you either follow the dictates of the leader, or you search for another line of work. While change is unrelenting in virtually every aspect of Canadian life, the basic architecture of parliamentary behaviour is roughly the same as it was 40 years ago. It's a system based on iron-clad secrecy and only the smallest slivers of freedom for MPs. While Stephen Harper is accused of having an authoritarian, secretive, and command-and-control style of running the Tory caucus and Parliament, shutting off debate through omnibus bills and prorogations and not allowing his own MPs to speak unless they are repeating talking points written by the PMO, Jean Chrétien was at least as draconian when he was prime minister. According to Jeffrey Simpson, during the Chrétien years, the main job of Liberal MPs was to protect the "King."[88] Similarly, in 1969, Pierre Trudeau referred to MPs as "nobodies," and there was little in his behaviour to indicate that he didn't think it was true.

While all of the parties have data-collection and -sorting operations, the Conservative Information Management System (CIMS) is the most extensive and sophisticated. Party databases are based on electoral lists supplied by Elections Canada, telephone soliciting, direct canvassing, and databases purchased from companies and marketers.[89] The Tories retooled their data-scrubbing and -mining operations prior to the 2015 election, interestingly renaming their database the Conservative Digital Nation.

Arguably, however, Canadian parties have not yet developed the more sophisticated algorithms that are the new drivers of American election campaigns. Since American parties play a role in registering voters and have the money and expertise needed to buy and develop more expensive databases, their data-mining operations are state-of-the-art even when compared to those of large Internet companies. As mentioned previously, the 2012 Obama campaign had 75 tracking devices attached to its website and was able to track and "score" the preferences of every prospective voter in the United States.[90] Drawing largely from political science research, the Obama campaign added a number of new conceptual tools to campaigning in 2012. One new twist was to test which messages would work with different subsets of voters by conducting experiments in the field as the campaign was under way. The Obama team was then able to pinpoint not only which issues would resonate with each subset of voters in each community or even neighbourhood, but also the methods that would be most effective in reaching every prospective supporter—an email message, canvassing, a phone call, a brochure, or social media—as well as who the most effective sender or deliverer was likely to be.[91]

While there is worry about corporations such as Bell Canada, Google, and Facebook mining personal data in order to target individual consumers, the fact that political parties have access to reams of personal information is even more disturbing. Data scooping on this grandiose scale can give unscrupulous politicians the ability to sort out friends from enemies—and treat them accordingly. Another problem that emerges when politics becomes reduced to databases and algorithms is that political parties realize that their paths to victory run through certain neighbourhoods and regions, certain age and income groups, and not others.[92] The temptation is to concentrate on making their own supporters happy and to target clusters of swing voters rather than proposing policies that are good for the country as a whole. Those who don't vote—the poor, the uneducated, younger voters—can be ignored.

The Old Crucibles of Power

Despite this new science of elections, political leaders and parties still need to get their messages through the crucible of the traditional media in order to reach the public. Politicians have to deal with journalists who have the power to challenge their claims and assumptions, select which parts of their messages reach the public, and frame stories in ways that fit the media's agenda. It is surprising, therefore, that despite the shock of media change, the main stages on which political performances take place remain much as they were 40 years ago: Question Period in the House of Commons, scrums, formal interviews, leaders' tours during election campaigns, election ads, and leaders' debates. These are the moments when politicians and the political system as a whole are most on display. What these rituals have in common is that they all incorporate strategies of evasion.

One great change, however, is that wide-ranging news conferences where political leaders field a full menu of questions from reporters are now far rarer than in the past. While particularly brainy and charming politicians such as John F. Kennedy, Bill Clinton, and Pierre Trudeau were able to turn press conferences into rhetorical and political *tours de force*, for most leaders there is little to be gained by wandering into a lion's den of hungry reporters. It's all too easy to be thrown off message, say the wrong thing, be gang-tackled by reporters who won't let an issue drop, forget important facts, or appear angry, weak, or uncertain. The strategy is often to appear alongside others—a cabinet minister or a foreign leader, for example—where there is only a single topic on the agenda and lines can be well rehearsed. On the few occasions when Stephen Harper has held open-ended news conferences, he has appeared behind a podium in the Commons foyer with flags on either side of him. His handlers have put the names of reporters on a list and questions have been asked in that order. Reporters rebelled against the system, fearing that only friendly reporters would get on the list.[93]

Most of the rituals of political communication are now highly choreographed and tightly scripted. Political leaders have a well-sharpened message of the day, and they will repeat the same one-liners, the same phrases, and the same sound bites over and over again until reporters have no choice but to go with the intended message. As mentioned previously, in Question Period, weeks and even months can go by without a direct answer being given to a direct question. A main goal for the government side is not to get sidetracked into discussing issues that could be embarrassing or controversial or for which they are unprepared. Or, to put it differently, the goal of Question Period is to avoid the dangers and pitfalls that would come if questions were actually answered in a straight-forward and meaningful way.

As discussed in Chapter Two, most observers believe that the drama and histrionics of Question Period have long since reached the point of irrelevancy. Recalling her many years covering the Hill, one of the stars of Canadian journalism, Chantal Hébert, has written, "The first time I took a seat in the House gallery as a twenty-something reporter, I was wide-eyed. Today, I mostly wish I could look away."[94] Former Liberal Party leader Bob Rae has described Question Period as "totally organized poison."[95]

Furthermore, media scrums, when politicians are surrounded by a bevy of reporters all scrambling to ask questions, now look increasingly like Question Period. Political leaders come prepared with their message of the day, including a battery of one-liners, attempt to stay on message despite attempts by journalists to get more information, and quickly exit once their messages have been delivered. The point is to make news by providing responses that are provocative and dramatic enough to be irresistible to reporters. As Liberal strategist Warren Kinsella once explained, there is a need to give reporters "the fix" that they want. His advice: "Get tough. Go neg. Hit back, hard. Kick ass. It's the only way to get a reporter's attention."[96] The veteran American politician Newt Gingrich once described his own logic in dealing with reporters: "Part of the reason I use strong language is because you all pick it up.... You convince your colleagues to cover me calm, and I'll be calm. You guys want to cover nine seconds. I'll give you nine seconds, because that is the competitive requirement. I've simply tried to learn my half of your business."[97]

One-on-one interviews, on the other hand, are more dignified and arguably more effective than scrums. They are seen as special occasions, and the very act of interviewing a leader helps certify the importance and credibility of the journalists involved. Interviews are often given to a news organization or a reporter as a reward for friendly coverage and with the expectation that questions will be "soft." Interviews are a convenient way to get a message out on short notice, as well as to tilt the media conversation in a favourable direction. Politicians have learned to avoid head-hunting journalists who try to win the interview by jousting with or embarrassing those they are interviewing. But the objectives for political leaders are the same as in scrums: make your points; stick to your message; don't rise to the bait; never answer questions that you don't want to answer; smile, seem warm, and escape unscathed.

The leaders' tours that take place during elections are possibly the main event in the media–political relationship. Originally designed so that citizens could meet and see their leaders first hand—and, just as important, so that leaders could see and learn more about the country and the challenges facing ordinary people—leaders' tours are now almost entirely scripted for television and other media. Party leaders crisscross the country in what is essentially a travelling film set, with neighbourhood coffee shops, sports events, factories, cityscapes, farms, and local supporters used as props and backdrops. Policy announcements are integrated with colourful visuals so that the visuals carry and symbolize the party's message; for instance, Stephen Harper's announcement of a tax credit for children's sports programs in 2006 was made in a karate dojo, with children serving as a backdrop.[98] He announced cuts to the GST while standing at a checkout counter at Giant Tiger.

In fact, visuals are considered so important that the Tories have developed a marketing system based on "message event proposals," or MEPs. No one in government can contemplate any public event or even an encounter unless the messaging and visuals have been approved beforehand. In Canadian politics, everything seems to be choreographed all the time. For instance, during the first week of the 2011 campaign, Stephen Harper, wearing a Team Canada jersey, played pickup hockey with young people in a parking lot in Ottawa. His wife, Laureen, dropped the puck, and the local Tory candidate played as well. The strategy was to portray Harper as an ordinary family man and a middle-class Canadian whose life and interests were not that much different from other Canadians. On another day, he visited then–ten-year-old singing sensation Maria Aragon in Winnipeg. Surrounded by the Aragon family, the Prime Minister and his wife heard Maria sing "Born This Way" by Lady Gaga, and then joined her in a rendition of "Imagine" by John Lennon. The message presumably was that he was current with popular culture, cared about the aspirations of young people, and had a fun side. In a study of visual images of Harper produced by the PMO, Alex Marland found that the same images have tended to reoccur: Harper in business suit attending meetings or at work in the office, Canadian flags, Harper surrounded by the military or the police, or at hockey or curling rinks.[99]

But it was the late NDP leader Jack Layton who demonstrated the most superb mastery of visual symbols during the campaign. He used the cane that he needed after a hip operation as a campaign symbol, wore a Canadiens hockey sweater while serving beer to playoff fans at a bar in Montreal, and strummed the guitar at a height of 30,000 feet. In his interview with the CBC's Peter Mansbridge, Layton was taped sitting with Mansbridge in the back seat of a car heading toward Charlottetown. They sat side by side like friends, each facing the camera. The effect was to create a sense of intimacy, letting viewers join the conversation as if they were in the car themselves. Canadians could not have imagined at the time that Layton would succumb to cancer just a few months after the election. The leaders' tour was a magnificent yet painful last lap.

A main part of the election game is to manoeuvre reporters into going with the stories and images that the parties wish to convey. Speeches are invariably made in controlled settings and in front of the adoring party faithful so that TV reporters have little choice about the words and images that they can use in their reports. They are also given press releases, famously referred to as "daily gainsburgers," that essentially write their stories for them. During the 2011 election, the Conservatives narrowed the range of choice for reporters even further: Stephen Harper answered only five questions a day from the reporters who covered him—two in English, two in French, and one from a local reporter. Christopher Waddell and his colleagues observed that coverage of the 2011 election on all three English-language networks was stunningly the same. Regardless of news organization, coverage was dominated by polls, the horserace, and the visuals that had been created by the parties. Most critically, however,

> One sequence of sound and images appeared night after night in stories about the Conservative leaders' tour—Stephen Harper being applauded by party supporters appearing to be the ordinary voting public…. Most often all three networks used his daily campaign pitch for "a strong stable majority government" followed by enthusiastic cheers from the bleachers.[100]

For all of the excitement about the influence of bloggers and social media, only journalists from traditional media organizations can afford to be on the campaign trail. This differs somewhat from the situation in the US, where at least some of the stars of the blogging stratosphere can afford to be with the campaigns. Indeed, placing even a single reporter with any of the major leaders has become an expensive proposition: it cost at least $45,000 per reporter for a seat on each leader's tour during the 2011 election, not including hotels and other daily expenses. The TV networks pool video coverage so that the same images are available to all of the major news programs. Knowing that reporters can become too attached to campaigns, too cozy, too embedded, and ultimately too susceptible to "cognitive capture," news organizations frequently switch reporters from one campaign to another. There are also reporters who parachute into campaigns for only a limited time—just long enough to get a feel for the action.

During the 2011 election social media played a critical role in creating at least part of the conversation that took place among journalists, campaign operatives, and members of the public. As discussed in Chapter Five, whereas a generation ago reporters could write their stories in relative isolation (except for contact with their producers or editors), they are now linked through Twitter and text messaging to what amounts to a national bulletin board that is alive with updates, comments, rumours, and criticism of their work. Moreover, operatives from the various campaigns are continually tweeting and texting reporters with new information, trying to sidetrack or torque stories even while they are being written. Covering a campaign now resembles a never-ending game of ping pong, where balls come at you at breakneck speed and responses need to be equally fast and sharp. The stresses of the Twitter game can be considerable, as reporters can never escape the pressure to be always on, always edgy, and always inside the loop.

Peter Hamby has described the stress placed on journalists who had to report all day long on several media platforms while covering the moving target of a US election campaign:

> To cover a campaign in 2012, a reporter had to be always on, tweeting with gusto, filing multiple blog posts per day and preparing for television live shots and "phoners," all while fielding calls or emails from editors desperate for nuggets of news in an environment that was often devoid of content. And if you are embed [travelling with the campaigns], you had to shoot and transmit broadcast-quality video in the process.[101]

Despite, or perhaps because of, this frenzy of demands a large number of critical issues were either never or rarely discussed by journalists during the 2011 federal election campaign. The list included the growing deficit in basic infrastructure in Canadian cities, defence policies including the skyrocketing costs of the F-35 fighter, the viability of pension plans, the increasing costs and poor outcomes of the health care system, the lack of environmental monitoring, gun control and the abandoning of the gun registry, Senate reform, the future of Aboriginal Canadians, and youth employment. This is partly because party leaders treated these difficult issues as if they were a kind of political kryptonite: one touch and their political capital would dissolve.

Just as alarming was the wholesale failure of journalists to report on the politics of the campaign. In our review of the 2011 election, Christopher Waddell and I listed a series of questions that were barely touched on by reporters: whether negative ads were effective, the types of appeals being made to ethnic voters, why voters were surging to the NDP despite policy proposals that were vague and had not been costed out, why the Bloc Québécois vote had collapsed and whether this represented a wholesale retreat from sovereignty by Quebec voters, or the reasons behind the deep-seated disdain for the Liberals that was evident in so many parts of the country.[102] It was apparently far easier for journalists to fall back on the old standbys of polls, the horserace, and personalities than to probe the deeper contours of politics.

Strangely, it was a campaign where the political leaders could avoid issues and journalists could avoid politics. The ultimate question is why news organizations continue to commit reporters to the leaders' tours, when it's obvious that the tours are contrived events with reporters being used as little more than a prop and a microphone for party messages. The argument that reporters can understand campaigns only by being on the tour is no longer valid. If anything, the opposite appears to be true: in 2011, it seemed that the closer they got to the action, the less they saw.

There is a fierce debate in scholarly circles about whether campaign advertising has become yet another form of political disengagement. Negative ads, also referred to as attack ads, can be very effective, especially in helping to create a first impression if the public has yet to form a judgement about the party leaders. Negative ads, which are inherently more lurid and shocking, are also remembered far more than positive ads—they have greater stickiness. The best ads, according to legendary ad maker Tony Schwartz, who made political ads during the *Mad Men*–like heyday of advertising, create a context, bring feelings to the surface, and trigger emotions (anger or despair) that are looking for an outlet or a target.[103] The goal of much negative advertising is to find the wart, and then to make the wart stand for the whole. One of the great masters of the art form, former Republican strategist and now head of Fox News, Roger Ailes, expressed the logic this way: "hit the opponent at his weakest point, at the most opportune time, with the least loss to oneself." He also believes, famously, that "if you don't have anything bad to say about the opponent ... why don't you just let him have the job?"[104]

But negative ads may also be why some people don't vote. In the US, Republican strategists in particular have been known to use attack ads to discourage middle-of-the-road or undecided voters from going to the polls.[105] The logic is that while negativity turns many voters off, more ideologically committed voters—*their* voters—will vote anyway. Hence a lower turnout works to their advantage. But critics worry that attack ads create even a greater danger. By slinging mud at each other, political parties bring both themselves and the entire political system into disrepute. The ugliness and brutality of the ads deface all of politics. Moreover, compromises of any kind become more difficult when winning has been based on ads that have mocked and vilified your opponents. Attack ads have even been compared to using nuclear weapons, because the trust needed to make the political system work is then largely destroyed. While news organizations often run "reality checks" to expose inaccuracies in parties' claims, including those in their ads, these checks have little effect because they appear only once or perhaps twice. By comparison, viewers can see party ads dozens of times, and whereas they once disappeared from screens after they had fulfilled their purpose, today's ads are "always up," whether on YouTube, Twitter, party websites, or somewhere else along the viral frontier.

Nonetheless, Jonathan Rose of Queen's University believes that attack ads may have at least some positive effects.[106] He quotes the work of American political scientist John Geer, one of a number of scholars who claim that negative ads tend to focus more on policies than do positive ads and provide voters with real information. This is especially the case with ads that compare party policies—so-called comparative ads. Although Rose argues that negative ads can be beneficial if they spark a debate about issues, his review of Canadian election ads found that attack ads all too often raised issues that were irrelevant to the campaign or were about invented policy "differences" that didn't really exist. Another perspective is that the use of attack ads resembles a game of chicken. The conventional wisdom is that there are two types of political leaders—the quick and the dead. Once attacked, you can never turn the other cheek. You cannot allow yourself to be defined and caricatured by the other side, because once that happens you lose control of the election. The best approach is either to hit first with a decisive knockout punch or to launch an immediate counterattack. Political guru James Carville once explained why no charge can be left unanswered: "Make sure that you go on the offensive right away. Rush the passer. Blitz. Send in the linebackers, send in the cornerbacks. Send the punter in from the sidelines.... Hit back or lose."[107]

Despite the popular fiction that Canadians have different attitudes to attack ads than Americans because Canadian political culture is somehow more gentle and polite, nothing could be further from the truth. In fact,

Canadian campaigns have become all about negative ads. But using them does have its dangers: ads that are seen as mean-spirited or false can create a boomerang effect; they can backfire and devastate those who used them. Two of the most poignant examples are Kim Campbell's vicious attack ad directed at Jean Chrétien during the 1993 campaign and a mindless 2006 Liberal ad claiming that Stephen Harper would put soldiers on the streets of Canadian cities. The Campbell ad showed a close-up of Chrétien's face, emphasizing his facial paralysis, the result of Bell's palsy. The voiceover asked, "Is this a prime minister?" and later intoned, "I would be very embarrassed if he became prime minister of Canada." The reaction was immediate: within hours, even Tory candidates were distancing themselves from the ad. But it was Chrétien's reaction to the ad that seemed to score the most points with voters: "God gave me a physical defect. I've accepted that since I was a kid. When I was a kid people were laughing at me. But I accepted that because God gave me other qualities and I'm grateful."[108]

The Liberals' "soldiers in the streets" ad prepared during the 2006 election was a sure sign that panic had set it. The ad made the following bizarre claim:

> Stephen Harper actually announced he wants to increase military presence in our cities:
>> Canadian cities
>> Soldiers with guns,
>> In our cities
>> In Canada
>> We did not make this up.
>> Choose your Canada.

The ad was nixed before it was aired, but it made headlines in any case.

Some analysts believe that media shock and the massive video culture that it has spawned have made the public much more aware of falsehoods and bullying than was the case even a short time ago. Political ads can be responded to almost instantly, and counter-ads by ordinary citizens and interest groups can be made at little cost. While it is tempting to think that the era of attack ads is coming to a close, the reality is that it may be just beginning.

Let me briefly reiterate the points made so far. All of the means that political leaders and parties use to communicate with the public include some aspect of avoidance and disengagement. From Question Period to leaders' tours, from scrums to advertising, political communication in Canada is as much about disengagement as it is about engagement.

Nowhere to Hide: The Value and Politics of Debates

One great exception to the notion that politics is becoming increasingly disengaged, however, is the leaders' debates that take place during elections. Debates are the only times when leaders have to step out of their protective bubbles of scripted appearances and cheering supporters to face each other and answer questions from journalists and sometimes from ordinary Canadians. It's the one occasion when narratives can be challenged and disrupted, when leaders have to live by their wits and can easily lose control of the agenda, get flustered, or wilt under pressure. Moreover, outside the debates, most Canadians usually see and hear their political leaders in short bursts lasting only seconds at a time. Sound bites normally last 7 to 10 seconds—not enough time for leaders to complete a full sentence or a full thought. During debates, however, leaders are expected to meet a different standard. They have to be eloquent, able to explain and defend policies in some detail, and think on their feet. It's comparison shopping at its very best.

Most important, the debates provide the spectacle and drama that draw in a large, Stanley Cup–sized audience. As many as 10.65 million people watched at least some part of the English-language debate during the 2011 election. The numbers for the French-language debate exceeded 1.4 million. Suddenly there are political discussions at work, in coffee shops, and at kitchen tables—something that rarely happens at any other time.

The conventional wisdom is that debates rarely move the yardsticks during elections because voters tend to view debates through the view-finders of their pre-existing beliefs. They pay attention to what's being said by the leaders that they like or agree with and tune out the views of those they have decided not to vote for. Kathleen Hall Jamieson has described the findings of a generation of studies with regard to American presidential debates:

> Since exposure to extended forms of communication reinforces
> existing predispositions, those who favored the front-runner are likely
> to judge the person the winner. Those favoring the person behind
> in the polls are likely to feel that their candidate has "won" as well.
> In practice this means that the process is rigged to favour a supposed
> "victory" by the person ahead in the polls before the debate even
> begins.[109]

This is not the case, however, when voters are seeing and judging leaders for the first time or if something happens during a debate that is unexpected or that overturns conceptions that are only thinly formed.

Despite the overuse of boxing analogies by journalists and commentators, in debates leaders have landed the political equivalent of haymakers that have left their opponents bloodied and gasping for air. At the same time, there are sometimes "defining moments" that stand for and symbolize the larger campaign.

Some of these winning or losing moments have become famous: Brian Mulroney's upending of Liberal prime minister John Turner during the 1984 debate, when he lectured Turner for making a series of questionable patronage appointments—"Sir, you had an option. You could have said no"—or Lucien Bouchard's demolition of Conservative prime minister Kim Campbell during the 1993 debate, when he repeatedly questioned her about the size of the government deficit—a figure that she didn't know. During the English-language debate in 2011, Liberal leader Michael Ignatieff went into the debate burdened by the weight of high media expectations. If this weren't enough, he was to suffer a deep knife wound at the hands of Jack Layton. After reminding viewers that Ignatieff had the poorest attendance record in the House, the NDP leader added the following zinger: "most Canadians, if they don't show up to work, they don't get a promotion." Ignatieff was too slow to muster a response—and arguably his campaign never recovered its footing.

Sometimes it's just a calm authority, an innate charm or the ability to reach across the screen and connect with viewers in a heartfelt way that makes the difference. During the English-language debate in 2000, for example, opposition leaders took turns lambasting Liberal prime minister Jean Chrétien for being arrogant, high handed, and dictatorial. But what viewers saw was a folksy and modest prime minister who possessed a rough-edged common sense. The other leaders seemed vengeful and bellicose by comparison.

Given that debates attract large audiences and are one of the few times when Canadians come together to watch and talk about politics, one would think that the political system would try to accommodate this interest, even build on it. But that is not the case. The debates are run, not by Elections Canada, but by a consortium of the major broadcasters—CBC, CTV, Radio-Canada, Global, and TVA—who negotiate with the political parties about the ground rules that will govern the debates, including who will be allowed to participate. Green Party leader Elizabeth May, for instance, was included in the 2008 debates but was excluded in 2011. According to tradition, there is a single English-language debate and a single French-language debate, usually held on consecutive nights. The problem with allowing a broadcasting consortium to decide the debate schedule, however, is that broadcasters lose money if there are multiple debates or if the debates cut too deeply into their prime-time schedules.

Election campaigns would be entirely different if there were a series of debates among the leaders or if the scope could be widened so that top cabinet ministers would debate opposition critics on topics such as jobs, the environment, or foreign policy. If the debate schedule were expanded, a number of goals could be achieved. Attention to politics would increase, at least for a few weeks. Party leaders could not evade discussing critical issues, less attention would be paid to the leaders' tours, and journalists might be forced to up their game, as viewers would presumably want deeper insights and analysis. Yet election rituals, the political system itself, and the journalists who cover them are now so stuck in the cement of arcane traditions that any changes, any new formats, seem unlikely.

In addition to the old methods of political communication, parties are fully armed when it comes to using websites and social media. As discussed in Chapter Five, the rules of communicating online are surprisingly similar to the ways in which parties communicate through the traditional media—control the message, avoid interaction with the public, and go negative. Tamara Small found that while the parties like to maintain a "façade of interactivity," communication is largely top-down, with little or no two-way traffic.[110] The reason is that parties don't want their sites hijacked by opponents or their messages sidetracked or disrupted by uninvited visitors. Or, to put it differently, why would parties open up their sites to debates about hot-potato issues such as climate change, Quebec sovereignty, Aboriginal rights or abortion that would throw them off message or highlight internal divisions?

Interestingly, during the 2011 election roughly 80 per cent of tweets from party leaders were broadcast tweets—a one-way message about an event or a news item—as opposed to social tweets in which there were interactions with the public. The exception was Elizabeth May, whose tweets were more or less evenly divided between broadcast and interactive tweets.[111] The same one-way communication was evident in the US. Only 3 per cent of Barack Obama's tweets in a sample month during the 2012 presidential campaign were responses to citizens or re-tweets of messages from outside the campaign. Mitt Romney posted only a single social tweet.[112] While party leaders sometimes post their own accounts on Facebook or compose their own tweets, these tasks are usually outsourced to a staffer or a committee of staffers. According to one account, no fewer than eight different groups are involved in composing and authorizing a single tweet from a federal government department.[113] What scares political leaders is that while the number of people who follow politics and news events on Twitter remains small—at less than 5 per cent of the public—mistakes can be costly.[114] The wrong tweet, with the wrong facts, said the wrong way, can create the equivalent of a viral forest fire that can be difficult to contain.

More ominous is Tamara Small's account of how the parties use websites for what she terms "e-ttacks."[115] In addition to their official sites, from time to time the parties also maintain off-road sites such as Ignatieff Me! and Cheque Republic, whose primary purpose is to deride, smear, and lampoon their opponents. Unlike official party sites, which are festooned with logos, photos, videos, donation and volunteer forms, and policy statements, e-ttack sites are made to look anonymous, with little indication that they are the handiwork of a political party. Just as official party websites are also giant storage systems that can keep campaign materials, including ads, "alive" well past their usefulness, e-ttack sites can linger as ghost sites for quite some time, keeping attacks going well after the battle is over.

One particularly interesting development is the use of emails and tweets to respond to journalists and members of the public. Emails and tweets allow political operatives to answer only those questions or parts of questions that they wish to answer. They also allow for tight responses that can't be mis-interpreted, exaggerated, or taken out of context. Like so much of online communication by governments and political parties, emails and tweets are meant to end the conversation. The downside for politicos is that where the old rule—often credited to US congressional boss Tip O'Neill—was that politicians should never "write when they could speak, never speak when they could whisper and never whisper when they could nod" so that deni-ability could be preserved, today there are email and Twitter trails that can't be erased.

The Last Disconnect

According to Alboim, the final act in this ongoing drama is the withdrawal of citizens from public life. There can be little doubt about the trend line. News shows continue to lose audiences, as many as one-third of the population are "news-less," and many others gobble down news snacks rather than spending time reading longer or more in-depth articles. Even for those who are regular consumers of news, reporting can be painfully inadequate and lead to misunderstandings about what is at stake. Interestingly, a study conducted by Florian Sauvageau and Simon Thibault about reactions to the 2012 student strike in Quebec found that while viewers were aware of events such as demonstrations or negotiations, they had little knowledge of the underlying issues. Moreover, they blamed the media for not providing the explanations and context that was needed.[116]

As for the public's disengagement from politics, poll after poll shows that many Canadians are troubled by the quality of public life. In just one example, a Samara Democracy Report released in 2012 found that only

55 per cent of Canadians were satisfied with the state of democracy, a drop of 20 points from a previous poll taken in 2004. Only a minority, 27 per cent, thought that Ottawa dealt with issues in a satisfactory way.[117]

In Chapter Two we discussed the politics of disengagement as measured by the number of people who volunteer, join civic organizations, donate to charities and social causes, have a basic knowledge about public affairs, and—most critically—vote in elections. The numbers in each case except volunteering are on a downward slope. The falloff is particularly evident among digital natives and those with less education. There are other more inexact measures of disengagement that speak just as loudly. Go into any bookstore and look for the number of popular books on Canadian politics, history, or public life. Look at the magazine racks or app selections. Try to find a Canadian film or TV show that deals with political themes—outside of Quebec at least. Try to find reflections on the public sphere in Canadian art or music or theatre. While you will certainly find them, they are few and far between. If we turn to fiction writing, the number of books can be counted in handfuls.

Canadians are also discussing politics a lot less than they used to. The 1984 Canadian Election Study found that 15 per cent of those surveyed never discussed politics with others. By the time of the 2011 Canadian Election Survey, the number had doubled. The 2011 survey also found that over 80 per cent of those interviewed almost never discuss news or politics online.[118]

While this chapter has focused on fault lines within journalism and politics, one has to recognize, as discussed in previous chapters in this book, that the sources of disconnection are complex, varied, and interrelated. The mix of factors includes how history is taught (or rather ignored) in schools; the nature of identities in Canada; the degree to which web-based and social media can suppress political involvement by giving people the illusion of participation without the reality; the fall of the traditional media, including public broadcasting; and, as Markus Prior reminds us, the growth of entertainment choices to the point where entertainment and commercialization overshadow almost all other categories of media consumption. Added to this list can be the growing inequalities that are tearing through Canadian society and the frustration and anxieties that many young people feel as they are beleaguered by debts, trapped in unfulfilling jobs, and don't believe that their voice can be heard. Ultimately, much of this becomes a self-fulfilling prophecy: the lack of engagement produced by these various factors has created the conditions that have allowed news organizations and political parties to disengage from public debate.

Some might argue that Alboim's assessment is overly pessimistic. After all, we still remain well above the waterline in terms of a responsible and diligent press, as well as an attentive public. This is especially the case during critical moments when reporters often act as a lifeline for their communities and the country. The pundit class, for all of its foibles, can still provide cutting and fearless analysis. Moreover, while the rituals of political life remain strangely out of sync with contemporary society, the public is still savvy enough to see through the charades, and their sense of disgust with how politics works is in fact well founded. Nonetheless, even if one accepts the argument that the standards that we are using in this analysis are too high and that both journalism and politics are "as good as it gets," it's difficult to dispute the fact that there are antiquated and dysfunctional institutions and routines both in news rooms and on Parliament Hill that need to be rethought and rein-vented. Breaking the crust of old habits may prove difficult, as many of these habits have become a way of life.

Notes

1   Elly Alboim, "On the Verge of Total Dysfunction," 45–53.
2   Ibid., 45–46.
3   Ibid., 50.
4   Ibid., 50–51.
5   Patterson, *Informing the News*, 37.
6   Frank Bruni, "Who Needs Reporters?," *New York Times*, June 2, 2013, http://www.nytimes.com/2013/06/02/opinion/sunday/bruni-who-needs-reporters.html?pagewanted=all.
7   Alboim, "On the Verge of Total Destruction," 49.
8   Elisabeth Gidengil, "The Diversity of the Canadian Political Marketplace," in *Political Marketing in Canada*, ed. Alex Marland, Thierry Giasson, and Jennifer Lees-Marshment (Vancouver: UBC Press, 2012), 43–44.
9   Alboim, "On the Verge of Total Destruction," 51.
10 Ibid., 52.
11 Bennett, Lawrence and Livingston, *When the Press Fails*, 194.
12 Ibid., 177.
13 Ibid.
14 Ibid., 46.
15 Tom Rosensteil, Marion Just, Todd Belt, Atiba Pertilla, Walter Dean, and Dante Chinni, *We Interrupt This Newscast: How to Improve Local News and Win Ratings, Too* (New York: Cambridge University Press, 2007).
16 Ibid., 88.
17 Patterson, *Informing the News*, 20–21.
18 Walter Dean and Atiba Pertilla, "'I-Teams' and 'Eye Candy': The Reality of Local TV News," in Tom Rosensteil et al., *We Interrupt This Newscast: How to Improve Local News and Win Ratings, Too* (New York: Cambridge University Press, 2007), 30–50.
19 Michael Robinson, *Two Decades of American News Preferences, Part 1: Analyzing What News the Public Follows—and Doesn't Follow* (Washington, DC: Pew Research Center for the People and the Press, 2007).

20 Shanto Iyengar, *Is Anyone Responsible? How Television Frames Political Issues* (Chicago: University of Chicago Press, 1991).

21 Jeffrey Simpson, "Stop the Presses! Crime Rates Falling," *Globe and Mail*, July 23, 2008: A11.

22 Saul, *A Fair Country*, 198.

23 Iyengar, *Is Anyone Responsible?*

24 Richard Ericson, Patricia Baranek, and Janet Chan, *Visualizing Deviance: A Study of News Organizations* (Toronto: University of Toronto Press, 1987), 7–8.

25 Quoted in Anya Schiffrin, "The US Press and the Financial Crisis," in *Bad News: How America's Business Press Missed the Story of the Century*, ed. Anya Schiffrin (New York: New Press, 2011), 7.

26 Starkman, *The Watchdog*, 214.

27 Joseph Stiglitz, "The Media and the Crisis: An Information Theoretic Approach," in *Bad News: How America's Business Press Missed the Story of the Century*, ed. Anya Schiffrin (New York: New Press, 2011), 24.

28 Chittum, "Missing the Moment," 92.

29 Stiglitz, "The Media and the Crisis," 32.

30 Sean Holman, correspondence, March 15, 2014.

31 Laura Way, "Canadian Newspaper Coverage of the Alberta Oil Sands: The Intractability of Neoliberalism" (doctoral dissertation, University of Alberta, 2013).

32 Stiglitz, "The Media and the Crisis," 30.

33 Maxwell Boykoff, *Who Speaks for the Climate? Making Sense of Media Reporting on Climate Change* (New York: Cambridge University Press, 2011), 56–57.

34 Patterson, *Informing the News*, 40, 52.

35 "Impartiality: The Foxification of News," *The Economist*, July 7, 2011, http://www.economist.com/node18904112.

36 Waddell, "Berry'd Alive," 109–28.

37 Susan Delacourt, *Shopping for Votes: How Politicians Choose Us and We Choose Them* (Madeira Park, BC: Douglas & McIntyre, 2013), 230. For the statistic, see "We've Got a Failure to Communicate," *Globe and Mail*, July 29, 2014: A10.

38 McChesney, *Digital Disconnect*, 181.

39 Waddell, "Berry'd Alive," 113–14.

40 Ibid., 120.

41 Ibid., 126.

42 Hamby, "Did Twitter Kill the Boys on the Bus?," 67.

43 Waddell, "Berry'd Alive."

44 Ibid.

45 Chadwick, *The Hybrid Media System*; Nick Couldry, *Media, Society, World: Social Theory and Digital Media Practice* (Cambridge: Polity Press, 2012).

46 Neil Postman, *Amusing Ourselves to Death* (New York: Penguin, 1985); see also Ranney, *Channels of Power*; David Altheide, *Creating Reality: How TV Distorts Events* (Beverly Hills, CA: Sage, 1976); Gaye Tuchman, *Making News: A Study in the Construction of Reality* (New York: Free Press, 1978); Herbert Gans, *Deciding What's News: A Study of CBS Evening News, Nightly News, Newsweek and Time* (New York: Vintage, 1980); and Todd Gitlin, *The Whole World is Watching: Mass Media in the Making and Unmaking of the New Left* (Berkeley: University of California Press, 1980).

47 Quoted in McKibben, *The Age of Missing Information*, 155.

48 Quoted in Taras, *Power & Betrayal*, 33.

49 Quoted in Ken Auletta, "On and Off the Bus: Lessons from Campaign '92," in *1-800-President: The Report of the Twentieth Century Fund Task Force on Television and the Campaign of 1992*, by Kathleen Hall Jamieson, Ken Auletta, and Thomas Patterson (New York: Twentieth Century Fund, 1993), 69.

50 Dean Starkman, "Major Papers' Longform Meltdown," *Columbia Journalism Review*, May 29, 2013, http://www.cjr.org/the_audit/major_papers_longform_meltdown.php.

51 Bennett, Lawrence, and Livingston, *When the Press Fails*.

52 Ibid., 120.

53 Daniel Hallin, *The Uncensored War: The Media and Vietnam* (Berkeley: University of California Press, 1986).

54 Brooks Decillia, "The Contested Framing of Canada's Military Mission in Afghanistan: The News Media, the Government, the Military and the Public" (MCs dissertation, London School of Economics, 2010).

55 Bennett, Lawrence, and Livingston, *When the Press Fails*, 39.

56 Thierry Giasson, "As (Not) Seen on TV: News Coverage of Political Marketing in Canadian Federal Elections," in *Political Marketing in Canada*, ed. Alex Marland, Thierry Giasson, and Jennifer Lees-Marshment (Vancouver: UBC Press, 2012), 175–92.

57 Kathleen Hall Jamieson, *Dirty Politics: Deception, Distraction and Democracy* (New York: Oxford University Press, 1992); Thomas Patterson, *Out of Order* (New York: Alfred A. Knopf, 1993).

58 Joseph Cappella and Kathleen Hall Jamieson, *Spiral of Cynicism: The Press and the Public Good* (New York: Oxford University Press, 1997), 34.

59 Quoting David Broder in Patterson, *Out of Order*, 54.

60 Patterson, *Out of Order*, 115.

61 André Turcotte, "Under New Management: Market Intelligence and the Conservative Party's Resurrection," in *Political Marketing in Canada*, ed. Alex Marland, Thierry Giasson, and Jennifer Lees-Marchment (Vancouver: UBC Press, 2012), 76.

62 Todd Gitlin, "Bites and Blips: Chunk News, Savvy Talk and the Bifurcation of American Politics," in *Communication and Citizenship: Journalism and the Public Sphere*, ed. Peter Dahlgren and Colin Sparks (London: Routledge, 1991), 120.

63 Pew Research Center for the People and the Press, *Assessing the Representativeness of Public Opinion Surveys*, May 15, 2012, http://www.people-press.org/2012/05/15/assessing-the-representativeness-of-public-opinion-surveys/.

64 Sasha Issenberg, "How President Obama's Campaign Used Big Data to Rally Individual Voters," *MIT Technology Review*, December 19, 2012.

65 Meyrowitz, *No Sense of Place*.

66 Stephen J. Harper, *A Great Game: The Forgotten Leafs and the Rise of Professional Hockey* (Toronto: Simon & Schuster Canada, 2013).

67 C. P. Stacey, *A Very Double Life: The Private World of Mackenzie King* (Toronto: Macmillan, 1976); Joy E. Esberey, *Knight of the Holy Spirit: A Study of William Lyon Mackenzie King* (Toronto: University of Toronto Press, 1980); Allan Levine, *King: A Life Guided by the Hand of Destiny* (Vancouver: Douglas & McIntyre, 2011); John English, *Shadow of Heaven: The Life of Lester Pearson, 1897–1948* (Toronto: Lester, Orpen and Dennys, 1989); John English, *The Worldly Years: The Life of Lester Pearson, 1949–1972* (Toronto: Alfred A. Knopf Canada, 1992); John English, *Citizen of the World: The Life of Pierre Elliott Trudeau, Volume One: 1919–1968* (Toronto: Alfred A. Knopf Canada, 2006); John English, *Just Watch Me: The Life of Pierre Elliott Trudeau, Volume Two: 1968–2000*

(Toronto: Alfred A Knopf Canada, 2009); Steve Paikin, *Public Triumph, Private Tragedy: The Double Life of John P. Robarts* (Toronto: Viking Canada, 2005); Pierre Godin, *René Lévesque: Un homme et son rêve* (Montreal: Les éditions du Boreal, 2009); Daniel Poliquin, *René Lévesque* (Toronto: Penguin Canada, 2009); Don Martin, *King Ralph* (Toronto: Key Porter Books, 2003).

68 Paikin, *Public Triumph.*

69 John Heilemann and Mark Halperin, *Game Change: Obama and the Clintons, McCain and Palin, and the Race of a Lifetime* (New York: Harper Collins, 2010).

70 Quoted in Stephen Clarkson, ed., *My Life as a Dame: The Personal and Political Writing of Christina McCall* (Toronto: House of Anansi, 2009), 68.

71 Quoted in Richard Nadeau and Thierry Giasson, "Canada's Democratic Malaise: Are the Media to Blame?," in *Strengthening Canadian Democracy*, ed. Paul Howe, Richard Johnston, and André Blais (Montreal: Institute for Research on Public Policy, 2005), 233.

72 Paul Taylor, *See How They Run: Electing the President in an Age of Mediaocracy* (New York: Alfred. A. Knopf, 1990), 249.

73 Howard Kurtz, *Hot Air: All Talk All the Time* (New York: Random House, 1996), 19.

74 Howard Rosenberg, *Not So Prime Time* (Chicago: Ivan Dee Publishers, 2004), 41.

75 Paul Rutherford, *A Victorian Authority: The Daily Press in Late Nineteenth-Century Canada* (Toronto: University of Toronto Press, 1982), 220.

76 Taras, *Power & Betrayal.*

77 Zaller, "A New Standard of News Quality," 109–30.

78 Bennett, Lawrence, and Livingston, *When the Press Fails*, 186.

79 Donald Savoie, *Governing from the Centre: The Concentration of Power in Canadian Politics* (Toronto: University of Toronto Press, 1990).

80 McChesney, *Digital Disconnect*, ch. 4.

81 See discussion in Kevin Arceneaux and Martin Johnson, *Changing Minds or Changing Channels: Partisan News in an Age of Choice* (Chicago: University of Chicago Press, 2013), 153–55.

82 Norman J. Ornstein and Thomas E. Mann, ed., *The Permanent Campaign and Its Future* (Washington, DC: American Enterprise Institute and the Brookings Institution, 2000).

83 Delacourt, *Shopping for Votes*, 230.

84 Jeffrey Simpson, "We All Pay for the Government's Hockey Ads," *Globe and Mail*, May 11, 2013: F2.

85 I am grateful to Tom Flanagan for making this point.

86 Alex Marland, "Amateurs versus Professionals: The 1993 and 2006 Canadian Federal Elections," in *Political Marketing in Canada*, ed. Alex Marland, Thierry Giasson, and Jennifer Lees-Marshment (Vancouver: UBC Press, 2012), 74.

87 Quoted by Donald Savoie, *Whatever Happened to the Music Teacher? How Government Decides and Why* (Montreal: McGill-Queen's University Press, 2013), 40.

88 Jeffrey Simpson, *The Friendly Dictator* (Toronto: McClelland & Stewart, 2001), 42.

89 Bennett, "What Political Parties Know about You," 51–53.

90 Ibid.

91 Issenberg, "How President Obama's Campaign Used Big Data."

92 Note the pioneering work done by Philip N. Howard in *New Media Campaigns and the Managed Citizen* (Cambridge: Cambridge University Press, 2006).

93 Delacourt, *Shopping for Votes*, 228–29.

94   Chantal Hébert, "House of Commons No Longer a Source of Wonderment for Journalists," *Toronto Star*, October 19, 2012.

95   CTV News Staff, "Bob Rae's Parting Wisdom to MPs: No More Scripted Remarks in House," *CTVNews.ca*, June 19, 2013, http://www.ctvnews.ca/politics/bob-rae-s -parting-wisdom-for-mps-no-more-scripted-remarks-in-house-1.1332132.

96   Warren Kinsella, *Kicking Ass in Canadian Politics* (Toronto: Random House Canada, 2001), 192.

97   Quoted in Cook, *Governing with the News*, 114.

98   Tom Flanagan, *Winning Power: Canadian Campaigning in the 21st Century* (Montreal: McGill-Queen's University Press, 2014), 87.

99   Delacourt, *Shopping for Votes*, 236.

100 Mary Francoli, Josh Greenberg, and Christopher Waddell, "The Campaign in the Digital Media," in *The Canadian Federal Election of 2011*, ed. Jon Pammett and Christopher Dornan (Toronto: Dundurn, 2011), 224.

101 Hamby, "Did Twitter Kill the Boys on the Bus?," 22.

102 Taras and Waddell, "The 2011 Federal Election," 81–83.

103 Kinsella, *Kicking Ass in Canadian Politics*, 48.

104 Quoted in Taylor, *See How They Run*, 194.

105 Stephen Ansolabehere and Shanto Iyengar, *Going Negative: How Political Advertisements Shrink & Polarize the Electorate* (New York: Free Press, 1997).

106 Jonathan Rose, "Are Negative Ads Positive? Political Advertising and the Permanent Campaign," in *How Canadians Communicate IV: Media and Politics*, ed. David Taras and Christopher Waddell (Edmonton: Athabasca University Press, 2012), 149–68.

107 Quoted in Kinsella, *Kicking Ass in Canadian Politics*, 188.

108 Lawrence Martin, *Iron Man: The Defiant Reign of Jean Chrétien* (Toronto: Viking, 2003), 70.

109 Kathleen Hall Jamieson, *Everything You Think You Know about Politics ... And Why You're Wrong* (New York: Basic Books, 2000), 163–64.

110 Small, "Are We Friends Yet?," 208.

111 Small, "Social Media & Canadian Politicians."

112 Pew Research Center's Project for Excellence in Journalism, *How the Presidential Candidates Use Web and Social Media*, August 15, 2012, http://www.journalism.org/ files/legacy/DIRECT%20ACCESS%20FINAL.pdf.

113 Chris Hannay, "How Many Groups Does It Take to Craft a Tweet in This Government Body? Eight," *Globe and Mail*, February 6, 2013, http://www.theglobeandmail.com/ news/politics/how-many-groups-does-it-take-to-craft-a-tweet-in-this-government -body-eight/article8283424/.

114 Konrad Yakabuski, "What Twitter Is, and Isn't," *Globe and Mail*, May 6, 2013: A11.

115 Tamara A. Small, "E-ttack Politics: Negativity, the Internet and Canadian Political Parties," in *How Canadians Communicate IV: Media and Politics*, ed. David Taras and Christopher Waddell (Edmonton: Athabasca University Press, 2012), 169–89.

116 Florian Sauvageau and Simon Thibault, "See All and Hear All, but Don't Understand!: The Student Conflict and the Failure of the Media," *Recherches sociographiques* 54, no. 3 (Sept.-Dec. 2013): 531–52.

117 Samara, *Samara Democracy Report #4: Who's the Boss? Canadians' Views on Their Democracy*, 2012, http://www.samaracanada.com/research/current-research/who's -the-boss-.

118 Sean Holman, "Why are Canadians Flipping Past Politics?," *The Tyee*, January 29, 2014.

Nine
Finding Citizenship in
the Digital Mosaic

There can be little doubt that media change has brought unprecedented opportunities for learning and connection. The Internet is overloaded with the "cognitive surplus" that has made Clay Shirky and others so optimistic about the future. Think of Ted Talks, the Khan Academy, YouTube videos that made you laugh or cry but also made you think, Facebook walls that kept friendships alive, and the countless apps that have brought us pleasure and made information so much more accessible. But at the same time, media shock has also created a swathe of destruction that has unhinged many of the old moorings on which citizenship was based. We have now entered what Swedish media expert Peter Dahlgren has called "a disturbing era" of democracy in which a confluence of factors has transpired to limit and narrow the very notion of citizenship.[1] These factors have been discussed at length in this volume: the diminished capacity of Canadian news organizations; the increasing costs of being online, such that more and more of the Internet is accessible only through subscriptions and micro-payments and less and less is free; the rise of giant media corporations such as Google, Apple, and Facebook that act as gateways to other media, as well as the increased stranglehold of a small handful of other corporate giants; and the triumph of the entertainment culture such that "entertained majorities" far outnumber "informed elites."[2] All of these factors have created a devil's brew that endangers the capacity of people to think and act as citizens.

A point made throughout the book is that the health and quality of democracy are linked to the future of journalism in general, and accountability journalism in particular. Without great journalistic institutions, publics don't exist. It is journalism that creates and galvanizes publics, raises issues, stirs and hosts debate, and alerts audiences to storms gathering over the horizon. In Canada much of the news about the news is bad. The hemorrhaging of the newspaper industry, the downloading of a great deal of political debate and discussion to the backwaters of cable, the evisceration of the CBC, and the increasing numbers of digital natives that are effectively "newsless" have damaged and weakened journalism and rendered it less able to do its essential task of creating and catalyzing a public. While Facebook, Twitter, and Reddit can form publics at critical moments, creating their own "imagined communities" around certain events, the vast majority of what appears online is still the product of the traditional media. To use the analogy drawn by Harvard's Alex Jones, it's the traditional media, and more specifically newspapers, that are still hauling the freight.[3]

Another concern is that online communities are increasingly ghettoized along ideological lines. People go to sites where they feel most comfortable, to places where their views and prejudices are celebrated and reinforced—and seldom venture beyond these gates. While some scholars would contest this view, arguing that people encounter a variety of perspectives online, evidence suggests that for a great many people at least, information is filtered through a self-reinforcing information loop. Certainly this is the case with Google searches, where the sources that algorithms provide mirror the content of previous searches. Interestingly, Kevin Arceneaux and Martin Johnson found in their study of cable audiences that the food chain created by selective perceptions also creates new two-step flows of communication where elites—who are increasingly the creatures of selective news—influence others; consequently, the effects of hyper-partisanship in the media reach well beyond small circles of viewers and listeners to the public at large.[4]

Perhaps the greatest myth about cyberspace is that the web provides users with an endless cornucopia of choice. While it is true that web-based media provide a vast sea of alternatives, cyberspace is more accurately and relentlessly a "winner-take-all" environment where there are a handful of winners and armies of losers. Sitting at the top of the pecking order are kingpins such as Google, LinkedIn, Facebook, eBay, Groupon, Apple, Twitter, Yahoo, Reddit, YouTube, Netflix, Amazon, Pinterest, Instagram, and Paypal. Millions of competing sites exist in relative darkness, awaiting the liftoff that never quite comes. The survival of the fittest applies most glaringly to news: big news organizations such as the *New York Times*, the BBC, CNN, and Fox News attract an avalanche of users, while the smaller players don't do nearly as well and many face extinction. As Robert McChesney reminds us, there is "no effective 'middle class' of robust, moderate size websites; that segment of the news media system has been wiped out online."[5] While McChesney's argument may be overdrawn there can be little question that the middle class seems to be thinning out.

The crisis of journalism and citizenship is compounded in Canada by the nature of the country. Our sprawling distances, sharp linguistic and regional divides, increasing inequalities, and globalized population has made identity politics difficult, complex, and multi-layered. Whereas "tight-knit" countries such as Italy, South Korea, Japan, Ireland, Argentina, and Denmark are united by a confined geography, the dominance of a single language and religion, long histories, and far less immigration per capita, Canada is "loose" and amorphous and has encouraged multiple loyalties and identities. Added to the Canadian conundrum is the fact that the American media are overwhelming and inescapable and surround us at every turn. Political thinkers such as John Meisel have gone as far as to argue that Canadian culture is in some ways the minority culture in Canada; the majority culture is American.[6] Arguably one of the effects of media shock is to hammer Americanization even deeper into place.

For much of our recent history, the traditional media were the transmission lines of trans-Canadian identity. In fact, they were the great presenters of Canadian politics—projecting political life out to the population and in doing so creating the public square. The traditional media carried out a number of vital functions: they acted as a bulwark against a complete takeover of the culture by the American media and they played a critical watchdog role in Canadian public life. The concern today is that they can no longer carry out these functions. When it comes to acting as a check on power, it is evident that news organizations have been battered to the point where they have less and less to contribute; they employ fewer journalists, pay them less money, do less investigative work, and have shuttered or downsized legislative bureaus, and specialized reporters are becoming an endangered species. In short, the crisis now facing journalism threatens to deprive us of much of the oxygen that citizenship requires.

Another problem is that some of the main media institutions that Canadians deal with, such as Netflix, Apple, Google, and Facebook, are beyond the control of the Canadian government and, of course, the CRTC. While Canadian broadcasters have been protected for decades by laws that prevent foreign takeovers, simultaneous substitution, tax laws that "direct" advertisers to Canadian media, and tax incentives and subsidies designed to promote Canadian programming, much of this infrastructure is being overrun. YouTube, Apple, and Facebook now have a lot more influence over the media lives of Canadians than the CRTC. Governments have never seemed so helpless.

One of the great ironies of media shock is that it has created two very different and contradictory impulses. On the one hand, we have now entered a world of me-media, where each of us has the capacity to create our own highly customized micro-environments. The public square has been broken down into a humpty-dumpty of individual pieces, with every person holding a different piece of the media puzzle. Communication has never been more personalized. In fact, as Manuel Castells reminds us, Facebook and other social media are, if anything, "mass-self-communication."[7] But this hyper-fragmentation and privatization has also meant that Canadian programming and content can be avoided almost entirely. Our individual media worlds may have very little to do with Canada. This is very different, however, in francophone Quebec.

At the same time we have now entered a new era of mass media. The arrival of Big TV has changed the rules of the game. Hyper-serialized shows such as *Breaking Bad*, *Homeland*, *House of Cards*, *Mad Men*, and *The Walking Dead*, produced by cable powerhouses such as HBO and AMC or by over-the-top broadcasters such as Netflix and Amazon, have been able to assemble mass audiences to a degree that has not happened since the 1970s and 1980s. The new technologies allow viewers to binge watch as well as bypass regular schedules and advertising. Whether because of low budgets, an aversion to risk, or an inability to master the new cinematic styles of storytelling, Canadian broadcasters are largely missing in action. They have clearly failed to take the next steps—and perhaps never will.

Perhaps the most perilous issue created by media shock is the emergence of the surveillance society and the threats to privacy that it poses. One of the essential characteristics of web-based and social media is that they ransack data on an enormous scale. One researcher found that he was being tracked by 105 different companies, and, as discussed in Chapter One, virtually every major news organization uses between 50 and 100 tracking devices to follow people who visit their sites.[8] Searches, purchases, and "likes" are sorted, tabulated, and sold to advertisers and third parties. While social media sites in particular are constantly adjusting their privacy policies to persuade users that they can be trusted with personal data, the simple and overwhelming truth is that they could not remain in business if they did not use the data that they collect. Data about their users is in fact their principal product.

It's no secret that businesses and social institutions routinely scour social media sites in order to pry into the lives of prospective employees and applicants. One study conducted in 2013 found that a large number of high-performing students were rejected by universities because of tweets that they had posted.[9] The issue for scholars such as Jeffrey Rosen is that past mistakes can be preserved forever.[10] While we once had the capacity to wipe the slate clean and begin again, it's now far more difficult to escape our past. It follows us everywhere. In addition, sites such as Facebook and Google maintain "back doors" that can be entered at any time by government operatives. Every day, in the name of national security, the US government collects huge caches of email traffic, text messages, and phone calls, evidently without warrants, both from its own citizens and from millions of people in other countries. The Canadian government works hand in hand with the NSA, often conducting surveillance operations on its behalf. While data are aggregated, agencies have the ability to "go deep" at any time.

Also of concern is the extraordinary amount of personal data now collected by Canadian political parties about how people vote, their buying habits, and the organizations that they belong to. While Canadian Privacy Commissioners, the courts, scholars, and political commentators have repeatedly raised concerns about the emergence of a surveillance society, these databases seem to be accepted as part of the new art of politics. They have become essential in fundraising and in organizing "get out the vote" operations on election days. We have to remind ourselves, however—and this is a big however—that the temptation to abuse power comes all too easily in politics. While survey after survey shows widespread distrust of political parties, we don't seem to be disturbed by the fact that they collect reams of data about our lives.

The politics of disengagement has run like a thread through the entire volume. Some of the reasons for this increased disconnectedness from community and civic life, particularly among young people, are not directly related to media shock. Economic inequality cuts into the very fabric of community like a sharp knife. This is because income and education are principal drivers of community involvement: those who are wealthier have far more confidence that their voices will be heard and that their efforts will make a difference—as has been the case throughout their lives; those who are poorer have fewer educational opportunities, have less to give, and are more likely to believe that the cards are stacked against them regardless of what they do. One of the effects of this widening economic and social divide is being felt online. Those who are already active are using web-based and social media to become more active, and those who are already informed are using new technologies to become even better informed. The reverse is also true: those who are uninformed and disconnected in the real world tend to be just as uninformed and inactive in the online world.

As noted in Chapter Two, there are many other societal factors at work in explaining disconnectedness. The abandonment of Canadian history in high-school curricula, the general weakening of community bonds and civic organizations, the "liquid" nature of so much of modern life and the feeling that we are living "nowhere in particular," the increased secularization of society, and the loss of trust in political leaders and institutions have all taken a toll. Another argument made frequently in this book is that some of Canada's political institutions are antiquated, profoundly out of step with how society functions, and in need of drastic reform.

While these societal factors weigh heavily in the equation, a key question is whether media shock has played some role in the unraveling of community. As discussed in Chapter Four, some theorists argue that online communication has created the illusion of connectedness without its substance.

Users feel that they know about or are participating in events if they follow someone on Twitter, watch a video, bounce an article to a friend, or post a blog entry, even if they haven't taken action that could actually move the political yardsticks in any real way. Most critically, however, online media have helped create a diversion economy that has overwhelmed and undercut politics.

On another level, psychiatrists such as Elias Aboujaoude have chronicled the emergence of the e-personality: heavy users who become addicted to pornography, gambling, or video games and become more isolated and despondent the longer they remain online.[11] In their comparison of three generations of learners, Howard Gardner and Katie Davis found that digital natives were less likely to take creative risks or challenge conventional wisdom in their online discussions.[12] They feared that stepping too far outside the box would label them or produce a backlash among their friends. For many users, the less said about politics the better.

Nonetheless, there is no disputing the powerful role that Facebook, Twitter, and YouTube played in helping to ignite and organize political uprisings and demonstrations such as occurred during the Arab Spring, Occupy Wall Street, and Idle No More movements. But it's not clear that cyber-activism can be easily translated into political and institutional power. There are those, such as Malcolm Gladwell, who argue that without concrete plans, goals, and leadership, even the most creative and inspired campaigns cannot be sustained for long.[13] Famously, Manuel Castells takes a different view: he believes that once the forces of change are unleashed and a cyber-community is established to perpetuate revolutionary ideas, then a new consciousness can be created and, as a consequence, some change is inevitable.[14] All that can be said at this point is perhaps, maybe, we will see, and time will tell.

In the end, perhaps Christina Holtz-Bacha, Markus Prior, and Robert Putnam are right in their assertion that attention to public affairs has been lost amid tidal waves of entertainment and distraction.[15] While access to at least some news was unavoidable during the heyday of newspapers and over-the-air TV, news can now be avoided entirely. Or, to put it differently, entertainment trumps news almost all the time, except when news itself becomes entertainment. While Neil Postman could write in the 1980s that as a culture "we are amusing ourselves to death," even he would be shocked by the cable wasteland that has emerged in the twenty-first century.[16] Moreover, as Florian Sauvageau has pointed out, even when digital natives consume news they are more likely to devour news snacks—headlines, tweets, and nibbles of information—rather than full meals.[17]

Chapter Eight dealt with three mutually reinforcing "retreats": the withdrawal of the news media from political coverage, the withdrawal of political parties from engagement with the public, and the withdrawal of the public from both media and politics. These trends set in long before the storms created by media shock were fully felt. In fact, the essential nature of media–political relations has changed very little in decades. While it's difficult to gauge the degree of blame that any one factor has had in creating the new politics of disconnectedness, journalists and political leaders bear a major share of the responsibility.

Peter Dahlgren is quoted in the first chapter as arguing that we may be doing a great disservice by analyzing participation in terms of the old criteria of joining, volunteering, donating, being attentive to public affairs, and of course voting.[18] His contention is that if we extend the boundaries of the "political" to include popular culture, then our assumptions about disconnectedness might be wrong. His argument is that people who actively consume popular culture—voting in a sense when they choose TV shows, films, video games, musical artists, or what makes them laugh, and on the values and beliefs that are being championed or represented by these choices—are creating change. As Harvard anthropologist Stephen Pinker points out, the sensibilities derived from popular culture "find their way into barroom and dinner-table debates where they can shift the consensus one mind at a time."[19] His point is that once an idea becomes accepted by the culture, then the dam has been broken and political and legal change will inevitably follow.

While Dahlgren's argument is a powerful one, popular culture in Canada is a complex amalgam of linguistic divides, a top-heavy American presence, and great ethnic diversity. The critical question is whether English-speaking Canada can continue to produce a vibrant popular culture that is not merely a cookie-cutter imitation or branch plant of the American entertainment industry. Again, we go back to Meisel's dictum that Canadian culture is in some ways the minority culture in Canada: while stirring and triumphant on many levels, all too often it stops short of being mass culture. More pointedly, just as is the case with news gathering, popular culture is still inexorably linked to the survival of the traditional media.

It's Time to Do Better

Clearly there is no stopping the momentum created by media shock. There is no escape from the "acceleration of the acceleration" and the relentless and destabilizing power of media change. To some degree we are riding a wave that is taking us farther and farther out to sea—and there is no turning back. The problem for Canadian democracy is that old institutions are being eroded before new ones fully take shape. Whether it be Parliament, newspapers, the CBC, or the CRTC, old institutions don't seem to be adapting quickly enough. While there is great hope that online media will eventually provide the connecting links that we need, the immediate question of who pays for news and culture and indeed for the ingredients that fuel a vibrant democracy remains unanswered. Moreover, there is no magic bullet, no one easy remedy that will make a difference.

Theoretically at least, the political marketplace should respond to what citizens want. If people want more and better local news, more compelling Canadian drama on TV, apps and websites that enhance the "cognitive surplus" in our communities, investigative reporting that has teeth, and political rituals that force Canadian leaders out of their bubbles at election time, then all of these are within relatively easy reach. The problem is when the political marketplace refuses to respond, even when its own existence and credibility are at stake.

Unless some of these issues are resolved, then the future of the online world will also be in jeopardy. Without quality and dependable news, much of what takes place in cyberspace will be empty and devalued. Just as was the case during the last era of media policy, support systems will have to be put in place if we want a trans-Canadian information and cultural highway to survive. Incentives will be needed to save at least some elements of the traditional media, as well as support the emergence of a new generation of sites, apps, and other tools. We will also have to salvage and reinvent public broadcasting. It's hard to see how we can continue to carry out fundamental tasks such as connecting English-speaking and French-speaking Canada, showcasing Canadian talent, and broadcasting the great ceremonies of Canadian public life if we allow one of the main stages on which our cultural life takes place to disappear.

Furthermore, privacy will have to be protected by governments and the courts and strict limits placed on what others can collect and know about the way we live our lives. If we don't take these steps then we will go further down the road toward a surveillance society with few protections for citizens. While users arguably make a conscious decision to give up some aspects of their privacy in exchange for access to Facebook or Google or Amazon, many Canadians are increasingly uneasy about the bargain they have struck.

For journalists and politicians, the fault may not be as much in the stars as in themselves. The rituals and priorities that drive both news gathering and politics have to be rethought if the engagement crisis is to be reversed. For their part, journalists will have to "inform" the news, to use Thomas Patterson's phrase, and provide "news that matters," to quote Shanto Iyengar and Donald Kinder, to maintain their credibility as well as their audiences.[20] This does not mean that crime reporting and car crashes aren't important— or that graphic pictures shouldn't be shown—but the news needs to be much more. The problem for political elites is that they are increasingly becoming technicians of power, peddling their images and brands through ads, websites, and political spectacles, and trying above all to control the message. In this drama journalists are co-conspirators. Even as political leaders turn Question Period into a carnival and the campaign trail into a movie set, journalists are still playing the game as if it was 1972 all over again. Small wonder, then, that so much of the public is no longer watching.

While each of these steps is relatively small and achievable, taken together they can create new ground rules for both the media and citizenship. The only thing more costly than taking these actions is not to take them at all.

Notes

1 Dahlgren, *Media and Political Engagement*, 6.
2 Ibid., 44.
3 Jones, *Losing the News*, 200.
4 Arcenaux and Johnson, *Changing Minds or Changing Channels*, 162–63.
5 McChesney, *Digital Disconnect*, 190–91.
6 Meisel, "Extinction Revisited."
7 Castells, *Networks of Outrage and Hope*, 7.
8 Ibid., 150.
9 Natasha Singer, "They Loved Your G.P.A. Then They Saw Your Tweets," *New York Times*, November 9, 2013, http://www.nytimes.com/2013/11/10/business/they-loved-your-gpa-then-they-saw-your-tweets.html?pagewanted=all.
10 Rosen, "The Web Means the End of Forgetting."
11 Aboujaoude, *Virtually You*.
12 Gardner and Davis, *The App Generation*.
13 Gladwell, "Small Change."
14 Castells, *Networks of Outrage and Hope*.
15 See Holtz-Bracha, "'Videomalaise' Revisited"; Prior, *Post-Broadcast Democracy*; Putnam, *Bowling Alone*.
16 Postman, *Amusing Ourselves to Death*.
17 Sauvageau, "The Uncertain Future of the News."
18 Dahlgren, *Media and Political Engagement*.
19 Stephen Pinker, *The Better Angels of Our Nature: Why Violence Has Declined* (New York: Viking, 2011), 169.
20 Patterson, *Informing the News*; Shanto Iyengar and Donald Kinder, *News That Matters* (Chicago: University of Chicago Press, 1987).

BIBLIOGRAPHY

Abma, Derek, and Peter O'Neil. "Canadians Trail Only Aussies in Quality of Life: Study." *Canada.com*. May 26, 2011. http://www.canada.com/business/Canadians+trail+only +Aussies+quality+life+Study/4830801/story.html.

Aboujaoude, Elias. *Virtually You: The Dangerous Powers of the E-Personality*. New York: Norton, 2011.

Adams, Michael. *Fire and Ice: The United States, Canada, and the Myth of Converging Values*. Toronto: Penguin, 2003.

———. *Unlikely Utopia: The Surprising Triumph of Canadian Pluralism*. Toronto: Viking Canada, 2007.

Agrell, Siri. "Nenshi Spreads a Gospel of Revenue Sharing." *Globe and Mail*, September 22, 2011: A6.

Akkad, Omar El. "Silver Surfers Boost Canada's Web Usage." *Globe and Mail*, March 9, 2011: A3.

Alboim, Elly. "On the Verge of Total Dysfunction: Government, Media and Communications." In *How Canadians Communicate IV: Media and Politics*, edited by David Taras and Christopher Waddell, 45–53. Edmonton: Athabasca University Press, 2012.

Almond, Gabriel, and Sidney Verba. *The Civic Culture: Political Attitudes and Democracy in Five Nations*. Princeton, NJ: Princeton University Press, 1963.

Alterman, Eric. "Out of Print." *New Yorker*, March 31, 2008: 49.

Altheide, David. *Creating Reality: How TV Distorts Events*. Beverly Hills, CA: Sage, 1976.

Altheide, David, and Robert Snow. *Media Logic*. Beverly Hills, CA: Sage, 1979.

Alzner, Belinda. "The Globe and Mail to Launch Paywall on October 22." *The Canadian Journalism Project*. October 16, 2012. http://j-source.ca/article/globe-and-mail -launch-paywall-oct-22.

Anderson, Benedict. *Imagined Communities: Reflections on the Origin and Spread of Nationalism*. London: Verso, 1983.

Anderson, C.W. *Rebuilding the News: Metropolitan Journalism in the Digital Age*. Philadelphia: Temple University Press, 2013.

Andrews, Lori. *I Know Who You Are and I Saw What You Did*. New York: Free Press, 2011.

Angus Reid Public Opinion. "Canadians Happy with Daily Lives, While Americans and Britons Ponder Moves." December 28, 2011. http://www.angusreidglobal.com/ wp-content/uploads/2011/12/2011.12.28_Greatest.pdf.

Angwin, Julia, and Tom McGinty. "Sites Feed Personal Details to New Tracking Industry." *The Wall Street Journal*, July 30, 2010. http://online.wsj.com/articles/SB100014240 52748703977004575393173432219064.

Ansolabehere, Stephen, and Shanto Iyengar. *Going Negative: How Political Advertisements Shrink & Polarize the Electorate*. New York: Free Press, 1997.

Arceneaux, Kevin, and Martin Johnson. *Changing Minds or Changing Channels: Partisan News in an Age of Choice*. Chicago: University of Chicago Press, 2013. http://dx.doi. org/10.7208/chicago/9780226047447.001.0001.

Atwood, Margaret. *Survival: A Thematic Guide to Canadian Literature*. Toronto: House of Anansi, 2012.

Auletta, Ken. *Googled: The End of the World as We Know It*. New York: Penguin, 2009.

————. *The Highwaymen: Warriors of the Information Superhighway*. New York: Random House, 1997.

————. "Outside the Box: Netflix and the Future of Television." *New Yorker*, February 3, 2014: 54.

Bagdikian, Ben. *The Media Monopoly*. Boston: Beacon Press, 2000.

————. *The New Media Monopoly*. Boston: Beacon Press, 2004.

Baker, C. Edwin. *Media Concentration and Democracy: Why Ownership Matters*. Cambridge: Cambridge University Press, 2007.

Baker, Russell. "Goodbye to Newspapers?" *New York Review of Books* LIV, no. 13 (August 16, 2007).

Baluga, Tamara. "Canadian Media Guild Data Shows 10,000 Job Losses in Past Five Years." *The Canadian Journalism Project*, November 19, 2013. http://j-source.ca/article/canadian-media-guild-data-shows-10000-job-losses-past-five-years.

Balz, Dan. *Collision 2012: Obama vs. Romney and the Future of Election in America*, edited by James Silberman. New York: Viking, 2013.

Baran, Yaroslav. "Social Media in Campaign 2011: A Noncanonical Take on the Twitter Effect." *Policy Options* 32, no. 6 (June/July 2011): 82–85.

Barber, Benjamin. *Consumed: How Markets Corrupt Children, Infantilize Adults and Swallow Citizens Whole*. New York: Norton, 2007.

Barker, George R. "The Economics of File Sharing, Its Harm to the Music Industry, and the Case for Stronger Copyright Laws." In *Communication in Question*, edited by Josh Greenberg and Charlene Elliott, 243–51. Toronto: Nelson, 2012.

Barnes, Brooks. "Web Deals Cheers Hollywood, Despite a Drop in Moviegoers." *New York Times*, February 25, 2012. http://www.nytimes.com/2012/02/25/business/media/web-deals-cheer-hollywood-despite-a-drop-in-moviegoers.html?pagewanted=all&_r=0.

Barney, Darin. *The Network Society*. Cambridge: Polity Press, 2004.

Barnouw, Erik, Richard M. Cohen, Thomas Frank, Todd Gitlin, David Lieberman, Mark Crispin Miller, Gene Roberts, Thomas Schatz, and Patricia Aufderheide, eds. *Conglomerates and the Media*. New York: New Press, 1997.

Barrett, Paul, and Felix Gillette. "Murdoch's Mess." *Business Week,* July 18, 2011. http://www.businessweek.com/magazine/murdochs-mess-07142011.html.

Bascaramurty, Dakshana. "It's Not Your Leave It to Beaver Scouts Anymore." *Globe and Mail*, August 9, 2010. http://www.theglobeandmail.com/news/national/its-not-your-leave-it-to-beaver-scouts-any-more/article1376409/?page=all.

Bauerlein, Mark, ed. *The Digital Divide*. London: Penguin, 2011.

Baym, Nancy. *Personal Connections in the Digital Age*. Cambridge: Polity Press, 2010.

BBC World Service. "Israel and Iran Share Most Negative Rating in Global Poll." March 6, 2007.

Beaty, Bart, and Rebecca Sulivan. *Canadian Television Today*. Calgary: University of Calgary Press, 2006.

Beaty, Bart, Derek Briton, Gloria Filax, and Rebecca Sullivan, eds. *How Canadians Communicate III: Contexts of Canadian Popular Culture*. Edmonton: Athabasca University Press, 2010.

Benefield, Richard, Sarah Howgate, Lawrence Weschler, and David Hockney. *David Hockney: A Bigger Exhibition*. New York: Prestel Publishing, 2013.

Bennett, Colin. "What Political Parties Know about You." *Policy Options* 34, no. 2 (February 2013): 51–53.

Bennett, W. Lance, Regina G. Lawrence, and Steven Livingston. *When the Press Fails: Political Power and the News Media from Iraq to Katrina*. Chicago: University of Chicago Press, 2007.

Bernstein, Carl. "Murdoch's Watergate?" *The Daily Beast*, July 9, 2011. http://www
.newsweek.com/carl-bernstein-phone-hacking-scandal-murdochs-watergate-68411.

Bibby, Reginald. *Beyond the Gods & Back*. Lethbridge, AB: Project Canada Books, 2011.

Black, Conrad. *A Matter of Principle*. Toronto: McClelland & Stewart, 2011.

Blais, André, and Peter Loewen. "Youth Electoral Engagement in Canada." Working
paper, Elections Canada, January 2011.

Bliss, Michael. "Has Canada Failed?" *Literary Review of Canada*, March 2006: 3–5.

———. "The Identity Trilogy: The Multicultural North American Hotel." *National Post*,
January 15, 2003: A16.

———. "Privatizing the Mind: The Sundering of Canadian History, the Sundering of
Canada." *Journal of Canadian Studies/Revue d'Etudes Canadiennes* 26, no. 4 (Winter
1991–92): 5–17.

Blumer, Jay, and Elihu Katz, ed. *The Uses of Mass Communication: Current Perspectives on
Gratification Research*. Beverly Hills, CA: Sage, 1974.

Boczkowski, Pablo, and Eugenia Mitchelstein. *The News Gap: When the Information
Preferences of the Media and the Public Diverge*. Cambridge, MA: The MIT Press, 2013.
http://dx.doi.org/10.7551/mitpress/9780262019835.001.0001.

Boxer, Sarah. "Blogs." *New York Review of Books* 55, no. 2 (February 14, 2008): 17. http://
www.nybooks.com/articles/archives/2008/feb/14/blogs/

Boykoff, Maxwell. *Who Speaks for the Climate? Making Sense of Media Reporting on Climate
Change*. New York: Cambridge University Press, 2011. http://dx.doi.org/10.1017/
CBO9780511978586.

Braid, Don. "Polls Need Personal Touch." *Calgary Herald*, October 16, 2008: A3.

Brin, Colette, and Walter Soderlund. "News from Two Solitudes: Examining Media Con-
vergence Practices in Quebec and Canada." Paper presented to the 16th Biennial
Conference of the American Council of Quebec Studies / 7th Biennial ACSUS-in-
Canada Colloquium, Quebec City, November 2008.

Bruni, Frank. "Our Hard Drives, Ourselves." *New York Times*, November 18, 2012. http://
www.nytimes.com/2012/11/18/opinion/sunday/Bruni-Our-Hard-Drives-Ourselves
.html.

———. "Who Needs Reporters?" *New York Times*, June 2, 2013. http://www.nytimes
.com/2013/06/02/opinion/sunday/bruni-who-needs-reporters.html?pagewanted=all.

Brynjolfsson, Erik, and Andrew McAfee. *The Second Machine Age: Work, Progress and Prosperity
in a Time of Brilliant Technologies*. New York: Norton, 2014.

Burgess, Jean, and Joshua Green. *YouTube*. Cambridge: Polity Press, 2009.

Burgess, Mark. "Canadian Broadcasters Can Take Lessons from FCC Report on Local
News, Critics Say." *The Wire Report*, June 17, 2011.

Cairns, Alan. "The Quebec Secession Reference: The Constitutional Obligation to
Negotiate." *Constitutional Forum* (Fall 1998): 26.

Calgary Herald. "TV Works Best with the Web: NBC." September 23, 2008: D1.

———. "Voters See Liberals as Stale, Dishonest: Poll." September 29, 2008: 5.

Canadian Media Research Consortium. "Canadian Consumers Unwilling to Pay for
News Online." March 29, 2011.

Cappella, Joseph, and Kathleen Hall Jamieson. *Spiral of Cynicism: The Press and the Public
Good*. New York: Oxford University Press, 1997.

Carey, James. "The Dark Continent of American Journalism." In *James Carey: A Critical
Reader*, edited by Eve Stryker Munson and Catherine A. Warren, 144–90. Minneapolis: The University of Minnesota Press, 1997.

———. "The Press, Public Opinion and Public Discourse: On the Edge of the Postmodern."
In *James Carey: A Critical Reader*, edited by Eve Stryker Munson and Catherine
A. Warren, 228–60. Minneapolis: The University of Minnesota Press, 1997.

Carr, Nicholas. *The Shallows: What the Internet Is Doing to Our Brains*. New York: Norton, 2010.

Castells, Manuel. *Communication Power*. Oxford: Oxford University Press, 2009.

———. *Networks of Outrage and Hope: Social Movements in the Internet Age*. Cambridge: Polity Press, 2012.

———. *The Rise of the Network Society*. Malden, MA: Blackwell, 1996.

Cator, Douglas. *The Fourth Branch of Government*. Boston: Houghton Mifflin, 1959.

Cavoukian, Ann, Ron Diebert, Andrew Clement, and Nathalie Des Rosiers. "Real Privacy Means Oversight." *Globe and Mail*, September 16, 2013: A13.

Chadwick, Andrew. *The Hybrid Media System: Power and Politics*. New York: Oxford University Press, 2014.

Cheadle, Bruce. "Radio-Canada's Focus on Quebec Doesn't Meet License Mandate, Study Says." *Globe and Mail*, October 14, 2012. http://www.theglobeandmail.com/news/politics/radio-canadas-focus-on-quebec-doesnt-meet-licence-mandate-study-says/article4611766/.

Chen, Brian X. *Always On: How the iPhone Unlocked the Anything-Anytime-Anywhere Future—and Locked Us In*. Cambridge, MA: Da Capo Press, 2011.

Chittum, Ryan. "Missing the Moment." In *Bad News: How America's Business Press Missed the Story of the Century*, edited by Anya Schiffrin, 71–93. New York: New Press, 2011.

Chomsky, Noam. *Manufacturing Consent: The Political Economy of the Mass Media*. New York: Pantheon, 1988.

Chong, Michael. "The Increasing Disconnect between Canadians and their Parliament." *Policy Options* 33, no. 8 (September 2012): 24–27.

Chozick, Amy. "NBC Unpacks Trove of Data from Olympics." *New York Times*, September 25, 2012. http://www.nytimes.com/2012/09/26/business/media/nbc-unpacks-trove-of-viewer-data-from-london-olympics.html?pagewanted=all.

Clark, Warren, and Grant Schellenberg. "Who's Religious?" *Canadian Social Trends*, no. 81 (Summer 2006): 2–9.

Clarkson, Stephen, ed. *My Life as a Dame: The Personal and Political Writing of Christina McCall*. Toronto: House of Anansi, 2009.

Cobb, Chris. "Saul Enters CBC Debate." *National Post*, January 30, 2001: A10.

Cohen, Richard. "Just Desserts for 'Citizen Murdoch.'" *Washington Post*, July 18, 2011. http://www.washingtonpost.com/opinions/just-deserts-for-citizen-murdoch/2011/07/18/gIQAYn23LI_story.html.

Colarusso, Laura. "Murdoch's Political Money Trail." *The Daily Beast*, July 15, 2011. http://www.thedailybeast.com/articles/2011/07/15/how-rupert-murdoch-s-money-helps-him-makes-friends.html.

Communic@tions Management Inc. "Daily Newspaper Circulation Trends 2000-2013: Canada, United States, United Kingdom." Discussion paper. October 28, 2013.

———. "Sixty Years of Daily Newspaper Circulation Trends: Canada, United States, United Kingdom." Discussion paper. May 6, 2011.

———. "A Statistical Profile of CBC/Radio-Canada." October 5, 2012. http://www.cab-acr.ca/english/research/12/study_oct0512.pdf.

Conference Board of Canada. *How Canada Performs. Canadian Income Inequality: Is Canada Becoming More Unequal?* Ottawa, 2013. http://www.conferenceboard.ca/hcp/hot-topics/caninequality.aspx.

Conover, Michael D., Jacob Ratkiewicz, Matthew Francisco, B. Goncalves, A. Flammini, and F. Menczer. "Political Polarization on Twitter." *Proceedings of the Fifth International Conference on Weblogs and Social Media*. Association for the Advancement of Artificial Intelligence, July 17–21, 2011. 89–96.

Cook, Timothy. *Governing with the News: The News Media as a Political Institution*. Chicago: University of Chicago Press, 1998.

Cormack, Patricia. "Double-Double: Branding, Tim Hortons, and the Public Sphere." In *Political Marketing in Canada*, edited by Alex Marland, Thierry Giasson, and Jennifer Lees-Marchment, 209–23. Vancouver: UBC Press, 2012.

———, and James Cosgrove. *Desiring Canada: CBC Contests, Hockey Violence and Other Stately Pleasures*. Toronto: University of Toronto Press, 2013.

Couldry, Nick. *Media, Society, World: Social Theory and Digital Media Practice*. Cambridge: Polity Press, 2012.

———, Sonia Livingstone, and Tim Markham. *Media Consumption and Public Disengagement*. London: Palgrave MacMillan, 2010. http://dx.doi.org/10.1057/9780230279339.

Creighton, Donald. *The Commercial Empire of the St. Lawrence*. Toronto: University of Toronto Press, 1937.

Cringely, Robert X. "Hard Numbers, Chilling Facts: What the Government Does with Your Data." Notes from the Field blog. October 16, 2013, http://www.infoworld.com/article/2612703/cringely/hard-numbers--chilling-facts--what-the-government-does-with-your-data.html.

CRTC (Canadian Radio-television and Telecommunications Commission). *Broadcasting Policy Monitoring Report 2007*. Ottawa: Government of Canada, 2007.

———. *Communications Monitoring Report*. Ottawa: Government of Canada, July 2010.

———. *Communications Monitoring Report*. Ottawa: Government of Canada, July 2011.

———. *Communications Monitoring Report*. Ottawa: Government of Canada, September 2012.

———. *Communications Monitoring Report*. Ottawa: Government of Canada, September 2013.

———. "CRTC Issues Annual Report on the State of the Canadian Communication System." September 26, 2013, http://www.crtc.gc.ca/eng/com100/2013/r130926.htm.

CRTC, and Telefilm. *Dramatic Choices: A Report on Canadian English-language Drama*. Prepared by Trina McQueen. Ottawa: Government of Canada, May 2003.

CTV News Staff. "Bob Rae's Parting Wisdom to MPs: No More Scripted Remarks in House." *CTVNews.ca*, June 19, 2013, http://www.ctvnews.ca/politics/bob-rae-s-parting-wisdom-for-mps-no-more-scripted-remarks-in-house-1.1332132.

Curran, James. "Reinterpreting the Internet." In *Misunderstanding the Internet*, edited by James Curran, Natalie Fenton, and Des Freedman, 3–33. New York: Routledge, 2012.

———, Natalie Fenton, and Des Freedman. *Misunderstanding the Internet*. New York: Routledge, 2012.

Curtis, Bryan. "Summa Cum Madden." *New York Times Magazine*, September 13, 2008: 31–32.

Dahlgren, Peter. *Media and Political Engagement: Citizens, Communication and Democracy*. Cambridge: Cambridge University Press, 2009.

———, and Colin Sparks, ed. *Communication and Citizenship: Journalism and the Public Sphere*. London: Routledge, 1991.

Davis, Richard. *Typing Politics*. Oxford: Oxford University Press, 2009.

de Kerchove, Derrick. *The Skin of Culture: Inventing the New Electronic Reality*. Toronto: Somerville House, 1995.

Dean, Walter, and Atiba Pertilla. "'I-Teams' and 'Eye Candy': The Reality of Local TV News." In *We Interrupt This Newscast*, edited by Tom Rosenstiel, Marion Just, Todd Belt, Atiba Pertilla, Walter Dean, and Dante Chinni, 30–50. New York: Cambridge University Press, 2007.

Decillia, Brooks. "The Contested Framing of Canada's Military Mission in Afghanistan: The News Media, the Government, the Military and the Public." MCs dissertation, London School of Economics, 2010.

Delacourt, Susan. *Shopping for Votes: How Politicians Choose Us and We Choose Them.* Madeira Park, BC: Douglas & McIntyre, 2013.

———. "Voters Filled with Dashed Hopes, Angus Reid-Star Poll Suggests." *Toronto Star*, April 25, 2011. http://www.thestar.com/news/canada/2011/04/25/voters_filled _with_dashed_hopes_angus_reidstar_poll_suggests.html.

De Pinto, Jennifer. "The Young Voter Turnout in 2014." *CBS Interactive*, November 13, 2014. www.cbsnews.com/news/the-young-voter-turnout-in-2014.

Ditchburn, Jennifer. "Majority Backs Public Funding for CBC, Poll Finds." *The Canadian Press*, November 11, 2011. http://www.theglobeandmail.com/news/politics/ majority-backs-public-funding-for-cbc-poll-finds/article4250955/.

Dominion Institute. *Canadian Views on Prime Ministers.* February 3, 2006, https://www .historicacanada.ca/sites/default/files/PDF/polls/2006_canadian_pm_en.pdf.

———. *The Dominion Institute's New Canadian Icons Survey Reveals Some Not-So-Familiar Faces.* June 29, 2009, http://www.newswire.ca/en/story/467277/the-dominion -institute-s-canadian-icons-survey-reveals-some-not-so-familiar-faces.

Dornan, Christopher. "Newspapers and Magazines: Of Crows and Finches." In *Cultural Industries.ca: Making Sense of Canadian Media in the Digital Age*, edited by Ira Wagman and Peter Urquhart, 53–76. Toronto: James Lorimer, 2012.

———. "Other People's Money: The Debate over Foreign Ownership in the Media." In *How Canadians Communicate II: Media, Globalization, and Identity*, edited by David Taras, Maria Bakardjiva, and Frits Pannekoek, 47–64. Calgary: University of Calgary Press, 2007.

Doyle, John. "Memo to the CBC: Suck It Up." *Globe and Mail*, March 29, 2012: R1.

———. "One More Time Can We Please Have Canadian Arts on Canadian TV, Please?" *Globe and Mail*, October 6, 2011: R3.

———. "Where is Canada in the Golden Age of TV?" *Globe and Mail*, October 10, 2013: L6.

Doyle, Simon. "High Noon at the CRTC." *Literary Review of Canada*, November 2011. http://reviewcanada.ca/magazine/2011/11/high-noon-at-the-crtc/.

Dunbar, John. "A Television Deal for the Digital Age." *Columbia Journalism Review* XLIX, no. 5 (January/February 2011): 34–38.

Easton, David. *A Systems Analysis of Political Life.* New York: Wiley, 1965.

Eco, Umberto. "Sports Chatter." In *Travels in Hyperreality*, translated by W. Weaver. Orlando: Harcourt Brace Jovanovich, 1986.

The Economist. "Impartiality: The Foxification of News." July 7, 2011. http://www .economist.com/node/18904112.

———. "The Rebirth of News." May 16, 2009, http://www.economist.com/node/13649304.

Edwardson, Ryan. *Canadian Content: Culture and the Quest for Nationhood.* Toronto: University of Toronto Press, 2008.

Elberse, Anita. *Blockbusters: Hit-making, Risk-taking, and the Big Business of Entertainment.* New York: Henry Holt, 2013.

Elections Canada. *Estimate of Voter Turnout by Age Group at the 38th Federal Election.* Gatineau, QC: Elections Canada, June 28, 2004.

Ellison, Sarah. "Murdoch and the Vicious Circle." *Vanity Fair*, October 2011: 172.

English, John. *Citizen of the World: The Life of Pierre Elliott Trudeau, Volume One: 1919– 1968.* Toronto: Alfred A. Knopf Canada, 2006.

———. *Just Watch Me: The Life of Pierre Elliott Trudeau, Volume Two: 1968–2000.* Toronto: Alfred A. Knopf Canada, 2009.

———. *Shadow of Heaven: The Life of Lester Pearson, 1897–1948.* Toronto: Lester, Orpen and Dennys, 1989.

———. *The Worldly Years: The Life of Lester Pearson, 1949–1972.* Toronto: Alfred A. Knopf Canada, 1992.

Epstein, Edward Jay. *The Hollywood Economist.* New York: Melville, 2010.

Ericson, Richard, Patricia Baranek, and Janet Chan. *Negotiating Control: A Study of News Sources.* Toronto: University of Toronto Press, 1989.

———. *Visualizing Deviance: A Study of News Organizations.* Toronto: University of Toronto Press, 1987.

Esberey, Joy E. *Knight of the Holy Spirit: A Study of William Lyon Mackenzie King.* Toronto: University of Toronto Press, 1980.

Ewart, David. "United Church of Canada Trends: How We Got Here." January 16, 2006. http://www.davidewart.ca/UCCan-Trends-How-Did-We-Get-Here.pdf.

Faber, Les. "Canadian Social Media Statistics 2013." *WebFuel,* July 20, 2011. http://www.webfuel.ca/canada-social-media-statistics-2011/.

Fainaru-Wada, Mark, and Steve Fainaru. *League of Denial: The NFL, Concussions and the Battle for Truth.* New York: Penguin, 2013.

Fekete, Jason. "Canadians Just Don't Trust Politicians, Poll Says." *Calgary Herald,* July 3, 2012: A4.

Fischer, Herve. *Digital Shock: Confronting the New Reality.* Montreal: McGill-Queen's University Press, 2006.

Flaherty, David, and William McKercher, ed. *Southern Exposure: Canadian Perspectives on the United States.* Toronto: McGraw-Hill Ryerson, 1986.

Flanagan, Tom. "Social Media Change Our Politics? They Haven't Yet." *Globe and Mail,* May 6, 2013: A11.

———. *Winning Power: Canadian Campaigning in the 21st Century.* Montreal: McGill-Queen's University Press, 2014.

Fortney, Valerie. "Facebook Prank a Lesson in Privacy." *Calgary Herald,* February 6, 2010: B5.

Francoli, Mary, Josh Greenberg, and Christopher Waddell. "The Campaign in the Digital Media." In *The Canadian Federal Election of 2011,* edited by Jon Pammett and Christopher Dornan, 219–46. Toronto: Dundurn, 2011.

Frank, Thomas. "Liberation Marketing and the Cultural Trust." In *Conglomerates and the Media,* edited by Erik Barnouw, Richard M. Cohen, Thomas Frank, Todd Gitlin, David Lieberman, Mark Crispin Miller, Gene Roberts, Thomas Schatz, and Patricia Aufderheide, 173–90. New York: New Press, 1997.

Friedman, Thomas L. "Facebook Meets Brick-and-Mortar Politics." *New York Times,* June 9, 2012. http://www.nytimes.com/2012/06/10/opinion/sunday/friedman-facebook-meets-brick-and-mortar-politics.html?adxnnl=1&adxnnlx=1415199813-pHqKER3I37iM8GPvyIRMQA.

———. "This Is Just the Start." *New York Times,* April 6, 2011. http://www.nytimes.com/2011/03/02/opinion/02friedman.html?_r=0.

———. "The Fat Lady Has Sung." *New York Times,* February 21, 2010: 8.

Friends of Canadian Broadcasting. "Canadians on the CBC by Nanos Research." March 23, 2012. https://www.friends.ca/poll/10624.

———. "Licence Renewals for the CBC's French- and English-Language Services." October 5, 2012. https://www.friends.ca/files/PDF/fcb.crtc2011-379.pdf.

Friesen, Joe. "At the Crossroads: The Idle No More Campaign." *Globe and Mail,* January 25, 2013: A6–7.

———. "The World Would Love to Be Canadian." *Globe and Mail,* June 22, 2010: A14.

Frye, Northrop. *Divisions on a Ground: Essays on Canadian Culture.* Toronto: House of Anansi Press, 1982.

———. "Sharing the Continent." In *Divisions on a Ground: Essays on Canadian Culture*, 57–70. Toronto: House of Anansi Press, 1982.

Fullduplex. *Peace, Order & Googleable Government 2013.* http://fullduplex.ca/wp-content/uploads/2014/02/POGG2013.pdf.

Fuller, Thomas. "Does Human Knowledge Double Every 5 Years?" May 28, 2007. http://newsfan.typepad.co.uk/does_human_knowledge_doub/2007/05/index.html.

Galloway, Gloria. "Canadians Share American Anxiety." *Globe and Mail*, June 28, 2008: A4.

Gans, Herbert. *Deciding What's News: A Study of CBS Evening News, Nightly News, Newsweek and Time.* New York: Vintage, 1980.

Gardner, Howard, and Katie Davis. *The App Generation: How Today's Youth Navigate Identity, Intimacy and Imagination in the Digital World.* New Haven, CT: Yale University Press, 2013.

Gendron, Danika. "In Quebec, Quebecor a 'Planet That Creates Its Own Gravity': Enquête Report." *The Wire Report*, November 17, 2011. http://www.thewirereport.ca/news/2011/11/16/in-quebec-quebecor-a-planet-that-creates-its-own-gravity-enqu%C3%AAte-report/23218.

Gerson, Jen. "Twitter and the Alberta Election." Presentation at the University of Calgary School for Public Policy, May 2012.

Giasson, Thierry. "As (Not) Seen on TV: News Coverage of Political Marketing in Canadian Federal Elections." In *Political Marketing in Canada*, edited by Alex Marland, Thierry Giasson, and Jennifer Lees-Marshment, 175–92. Vancouver: UBC Press, 2012.

Giasson, Thierry, Harold Jansen, and Royce Koop. "'Hypercitizens': Blogging, Partisanship and Political Participation in Canada." Paper presented at the Canadian Political Science Association meetings, Edmonton, AB, June 2012.

Gidengil, Elisabeth. "The Diversity of the Canadian Political Marketplace." In *Political Marketing in Canada*, edited by Alex Marland, Thierry Giasson, and Jennifer Lees-Marshment, 39–56. Vancouver: UBC Press, 2012.

———. "Turned Off or Tuned Out? Youth Participation in Politics." *Electoral Insight* 5, no. 2 (July 2003).

Gidengil, Elisabeth, André Blais, Neil Nevitte, and Richard Nadeau. *Citizens.* Vancouver: UBC Press, 2004.

Giroux, Henry, and Grace Pollack. *The Mouse That Roared: Disney and the End of Innocence.* Lanham, MD: Rowman & Littlefield, 2010.

Gitlin, Todd. "Bites and Blips: Chunk News, Savvy Talk and the Bifurcation of American Politics." In *Communication and Citizenship: Journalism and the Public Sphere*, edited by Peter Dahlgren and Colin Sparks, 117–34. London: Routledge, 1991.

———. *Media Unlimited: How the Torrent of Images and Sounds Overwhelms Our Lives.* New York: Henry Holt & Company, 2001.

———. *The Whole World Is Watching: Mass Media in the Making and Unmaking of the New Left.* Berkeley, CA: University of California Press, 1980.

Gladwell, Malcolm. "Small Change: Why the Revolution Will Not Be Tweeted." *New Yorker*, October 4, 2010. http://www.newyorker.com/reporting/2010/10/04/101004fa_fact_gladwell?currentPage=all.

Globe and Mail. Op-ed. "Canadian Authors Celebrated Abroad, Misspelled at Home." December 31, 2008: A12.

Godin, Pierre. *René Lévesque: Un homme et son rêve.* Montreal: Les éditions du Boréal, 2009.

Goel, Vindu. "Facebook Eases Privacy Rules for Teenagers." *New York Times*, October 17, 2013. http://www.nytimes.com/2013/10/17/technology/facebook-changes-privacy-policy-for-teenagers.html?pagewanted=all.

Goldstein, Kenneth J. "From Assumptions of Scarcity to the Facts of Fragmentation." In *How Canadians Communicate II: Media, Globalization, and Identity*, edited by David Taras, Maria Bakardjieva, and Frits Pannekoek, 3–21. Calgary: University of Calgary Press, 2007.

Gordon, Sean. "Quebec City and the NHL." *Globe and Mail*, November 28, 2013: B11.

Gore, Al. *The Future: Six Drivers of Global Change.* New York: Random House, 2013.

Greenberg, Josh, and Charlene Elliott, ed. *Communication in Question.* 2nd ed. Toronto: Nelson, 2012.

Gruneau, Richard. "Goodbye Gordie Howe: Sport Participation and Class Inequality in the 'Pay for Play' Society." In *How Canadians Communicate V: Sports*, edited by David Taras and Christopher Waddell. Edmonton: Athabasca University Press, forthcoming.

Habermas, Jürgen. *The Structural Transformation of the Public Sphere.* Cambridge, MA: Massachusetts Institute of Technology, 1989.

Hallin, Daniel. *The Uncensored War: The Media and Vietnam.* Berkeley, CA: University of California Press, 1986.

Halpern, Sue. "Mind Control & the Internet." *New York Review of Books* LVIII, no. 11 (June 23, 2011): 33–35. http://www.nybooks.com/issues/2011/jun/23/.

Hamburger, Tom, and Matea Gold. "Google, Once Disdainful of Lobbying, Now a Master of Washington Influence." *The Washington Post*, April 12, 2014. http://www.washingtonpost.com/politics/how-google-is-transforming-power-and-politics google-once-disdainful-of-lobbying-now-a-master-of-washington-influence/2014/04/12/51648b92-b4d3-11e3-8cb6-284052554d74_story.html.

Hamby, Peter. "Did Twitter Kill the Boys on the Bus? Searching for a Better Way to Cover a Campaign." Joan Shorenstein Center on the Press, Politics and Public Policy, John F. Kennedy School of Government. Discussion paper. Cambridge, MA: Harvard University, September 2013.

Hannay, Chris. "How Many Groups Does It Take to Craft a Tweet in This Government Body? Eight." *Globe and Mail*. February 6, 2013. http://www.theglobeandmail.com/news/politics/how-many-groups-does-it-take-to-craft-a-tweet-in-this-government-body-eight/article8283424/.

Harper, Stephen J. *A Great Game: The Forgotten Leafs and the Rise of Professional Hockey.* Toronto: Simon & Schuster Canada, 2013.

Harris, Kathleen. "Canadians Losing Their Trust in Politicians." *Canoe.ca*, December 3, 2007. http://cnews.canoe.ca/CNEWS/Canada/2007/12/03/4704388-sun.html.

Hart, Roderick. "Easy Citizenship: Television's Curious Legacy." *Annals of the American Academy of Political Science* 546, no. 1 (July 1996): 109–19. http://dx.doi.org/10.1177/0002716296546001010.

Hartley, Robert. *The Politics of Pictures: The Creation of the Public in the Age of Popular Media.* London: Routledge, 1992.

Hébert, Chantal. "House of Commons No Longer a Source of Wonderment for Journalists." *Toronto Star*, October 19, 2012.

———. "Quebecers Have Become More Detached than Ever." *Toronto Star*, January 19, 2011. http://www.thestar.com/opinion/columnists/2011/01/19/hbert_quebecers _have_become_more_detached_than_ever.html.

Hebert, Sean. "Jon Stewart, Stephen Colbert and the Evolving Role and Influence of Political Satirists in Twenty-First Century America." Master's thesis, University of Calgary, 2012.

Heffernan, Virginia. "The Game of Twitter." *New York Times*, June 12, 2006. http://www.nytimes.com/.

Heilemann, John, and Mark Halperin. *Game Change: Obama and the Clintons, McCain and Palin, and the Race of a Lifetime.* New York: Harper Collins, 2010.

Hemon, Louis. *Maria Chapdelaine.* Translated by W.H. Blake. Toronto: Macmillan, 1973.

Henig, Robin. "What Is It about 20-somethings?" *New York Times*, August 22, 2010. http://www.nytimes.com/2010/08/22/magazine/22Adulthood-t.html?pagewanted=all.

Hildebrandt, Amber. "The 'Twitter Campaign,' but Who Cares?" *CBC News*, April 1, 2011. http://www.cbc.ca/news.

Hiller, Harry. *Second Promised Land: Migration to Alberta and the Transformation of Canadian Society.* Montreal: McGill-Queen's University Press, 2009.

Hindman, Matthew. *The Myth of Digital Democracy.* Princeton, NJ: Princeton University Press, 2009.

Hirschorn, Michael. "About Facebook." *Atlantic*, October 1, 2007: 152.

Holman, Sean. "Why Are Canadians Flipping Past Politics?" *The Tyee*, January 29, 2014.

Holmes, Helen, and David Taras, ed. *Seeing Ourselves: Media Power and Policy in Canada.* Toronto: Harcourt Brace Jovanovich, 1992.

———, ed. *Seeing Ourselves: Media Power and Policy in Canada.* 2nd ed. Toronto: Harcourt Brace & Company, 1996.

Holtz-Bracha, Christina. "'Videomalaise' Revisited: Media Exposure and Political Alienation in West Germany." *European Journal of Communication* 5, no. 1 (March 1990): 73–85.

Houpt, Simon. "Lament for a National Blogosphere." *Globe and Mail*, May 23, 2012: R1.

———, and Steve Ladurantaye. "Is Bell Too Big?" *Globe and Mail*, September 1, 2012: 9.

Howard, Philip N. *New Media Campaigns and the Managed Citizen.* Cambridge: Cambridge University Press, 2006.

Howe, Paul. *Citizens Adrift: The Democratic Disengagement of Young Canadians.* Vancouver: UBC Press, 2010.

———, Richard Johnston, and André Blais, ed. *Strengthening Canadian Democracy.* Montreal: Institute for Research on Public Policy, 2005.

The Huffington Post. "Nenshi AMA: Reditt Peppers Calgary Mayor with Questions During 'Ask Me Anything.'" October 10, 2013. http://www.huffingtonpost.ca/2013/10/10/nenshi-ama-reddit_n_4080833.html.

Ibbitson, John. "Let Sleeping Dogs Lie." In *Uneasy Partners: Multiculturalism and Rights in Canada*, edited by Janice Stein, David Robertson Cameron, John Ibbitson, Will Kymlicka, John Meisel, Haroon Siddiqui, and Michael Valpy, 49–69. Waterloo: Wilfrid Laurier University Press, 2007.

———. *The Polite Revolution: Perfecting the Canadian Dream.* Toronto: McClelland & Stewart, 2005.

Innis, Harold. *The Fur Trade in Canada.* Toronto: University of Toronto Press, 1956.

Interactive Advertising Bureau of Canada. *2011 Actual + 2012 Estimated Canadian Online Advertising Revenue Survey.* 2011. http://iabcanada.com/files/Canadian_Online_Advertising_Revenue_Survey_English.pdf.

Ipsos Reid. *O Canada: Our Home and Naïve Land.* July 1, 2008. https://www.historicacanada.ca/sites/default/files/PDF/polls/canadaday.survey.dominioninstitute.1july08_en.pdf.

Ipsos Reid/Dominion Institute. *National Citizenship Exam: 10 Year Benchmark Study.* June 29, 2007. https://www.historicacanada.ca/sites/default/files/PDF/polls/dominion_institute_press_release_mock_exam_en.pdf.

Isaacson, Walter. *Steve Jobs.* New York: Simon & Schuster, 2011.

Issenberg, Sasha. "How President Obama's Campaign Used Big Data to Rally Individual Voters." *MIT Technology Review*, December 19, 2012.

Iyengar, Shanto. *Is Anyone Responsible? How Television Frames Political Issues*. Chicago: University of Chicago Press, 1991. http://dx.doi.org/10.7208/chicago/9780226388533.001.0001.

———, and Donald Kinder. *News That Matters*. Chicago: University of Chicago Press, 1987.

Jamieson, Kathleen Hall. *Dirty Politics: Deception, Distraction and Democracy*. New York: Oxford University Press, 1992.

———. *Everything You Think You Know about Politics … and Why You're Wrong*. New York: Basic Books, 2000.

———, Ken Auletta, and Thomas Patterson. *1-800-President: The Report of the Twentieth Century Fund Task Force on Television and the Campaign of 1992*. New York: Twentieth Century Fund, 1993.

———, and Joseph Cappella. *Echo Chamber: Rush Limbaugh and the Conservative Media Establishment*. New York: Oxford University Press, 2008.

Jenkins, Henry. *Convergence Culture: Where Old and New Media Collide*. New York: New York University Press, 2006.

Johnson, Steven. *Everything Bad Is Good for You*. New York: Riverhead Books, 2006.

Jones, Alex. *Losing the News: The Future of the News That Feeds Democracy*. Oxford: Oxford University Press, 2009.

Katz, Elihu. "And Deliver Us from Segmentation." *Annals of the American Academy of Political and Social Science* 546, no. 1 (July 1996): 22–33. http://dx.doi.org/10.1177/0002716296546001003.

———, and Paul Lazarsfeld. *Personal Influence: The Part Played by People in the Flow of Mass Communication*. New York: Free Press, 1955.

———, Jay Blumer, and Michael Gurevitch. "Utilization of Mass Communication by the Individual." In *The Uses of Mass Communication: Current Perspectives on Gratification Research*, edited by Jay Blumer and Elihu Katz. Beverly Hills, CA: Sage, 1974.

Kay, Jonathan. "Warning Signs of Patrick Brazeau's Unravelling on Twitter for Everyone to See." *National Post*, February 7, 2013. http://fullcomment.nationalpost.com/2013/02/07/jonathan-kay-warning-signs-of-patrick-brazeaus-unravelling-on-twitter-for-everyone-to-see/.

Keren, Michael. *The Citizen's Voice: Twentieth Century Politics and Literature*. Calgary: University of Calgary Press, 2003.

King, Ross. *Defiant Spirits: The Modernist Revolution of the Group of Seven*. Vancouver: Douglas & McIntyre; Kleinberg: McMichael Canadian Art Collection, 2010.

Kinsella, Warren. "Blogging and the Rise of the Pyjamahadeen." *Literary Review of Canada* 15, no. 7 (September 2007): 27–28.

———. *Kicking Ass in Canadian Politics*. Toronto: Random House Canada, 2001.

Klein, Naomi. *No Logo: Taking Aim at Brand Bullies*. Toronto: Knopf Canada, 1999.

Knee, Jonathan, Bruce Greenwald, and Ava Seave. *The Curse of the Mogul: What's Wrong with the World's Leading Media Companies*. New York: Penguin, 2009.

Kohut, Andrew. "Self-Censorship: Counting the Ways." *Columbia Journalism Review* 42–43 (May/June 2000).

Kotkin, Joel. "Entrepreneurs Turn Oligarchs." *New Geography*, August 8, 2013. http://www.newgeography.com/content/003875-entrepreneurs-turn-oligarchs.

Kroes, Rob. *Them & Us: Questions of Citizenship in a Globalized World*. Chicago: University of Illinois Press, 2000.

Kurtz, Howard. *Hot Air: All Talk All the Time*. New York: Random House, 1996.

————. "The Death of Print?" *Washington Post*, May 11, 2009. http://www
.washingtonpost.com/wp-dyn/content/article/2009/05/11/AR2009051100782
.html.

Ladurantaye, Steve. "CBC Closes in on Pricey Deal with NHL." *Globe and Mail*, November 26, 2013: S6.

————. "Eric Boyko: Stingray's Entrepreneur à Go-go-go." *Globe and Mail*, November 2, 2012. http://www.theglobeandmail.com/report-on-business/careers/careers
-leadership/eric-boyko-stingrays-entrepreneur-go-go-go/article4887145/.

Lasch, Christopher. *The Revolt of the Elites*. New York: Norton, 1995.

Lawrence, Eric, John Sides, and Henry Farrell. "Self-Segregation or Deliberation? Blog Readership, Participation and Polarization in American Politics." *Perspectives on Politics* 8, no. 1 (March 2010): 141–57. http://dx.doi.org/10.1017/S1537592709992714.

Lazarsfeld, Paul Felix, Bernard Berelson, and Hazel Gaudet. *The People's Choice: How the Voter Makes Up His Mind in a Presidential Election*. New York: Columbia University Press, 1944.

Lazarsfeld, Paul, and Robert Merton. "Mass Communication, Popular Taste and Organized Social Action." In *The Process and Effects of Mass Communication*, edited by Wilbur Schramm and Donald Roberts, 554–78. Chicago: University of Illinois Press, 1971.

Leblanc, Daniel, and Rheal Seguin. "Peladeau the Sovereigntist." *Globe and Mail*, March 11, 2014: A6.

Leibovich, Mark. *This Town*. New York: Penguin, 2013.

Letourneau, Jocelyn. *Le Québec, Les Québécois: Un parle historique.* [*Quebec, Quebecers: A Historical Journey*] Montreal: Éditions Fides / Quebec: Musée de la Civilisation [Museum of Civilization], 2004.

Levine, Allan. *King: A Life Guided by the Hand of Destiny.* Vancouver: Douglas & McIntyre, 2011.

Levine, Robert. *Free Ride: How Digital Parasites Are Destroying the Culture Business, and How the Culture Business Can Fight Back*. New York: Doubleday, 2011.

Levmore, Saul, and Martha Nussbaum, ed. *The Offensive Internet*. Cambridge, MA: Harvard University Press, 2010.

Levy, Bernard-Henri. *American Vertigo: Traveling America in the Footsteps of Tocqueville.* Translated by Charlotte Mandell. New York: Random House, 2006.

Lieberman, Trudy. "You Can't Report What You Don't Pursue." *Columbia Journalism Review* 42–43 (May/June 2000).

Lippmann, Walter. *Public Opinion*. New York: Macmillan, 1922.

Lohr, Steve. "Study Measures the Chatter of the News Cycle." *New York Times*, July 13, 2009. http://www.nytimes.com/2009/07/13/technology/internet/13influence.html.

Lotz, Amanda D. *The Television Will Be Revolutionized*. New York: New York University, 2007.

Malenfant, Eric, André Lebel, and Laurent Martel. *Projections of the Diversity of the Canadian Population 2006 to 2031*. Ottawa: Statistics Canada, March 2010, http://www
.statcan.gc.ca/pub/91-551-x/91-551-x2010001-eng.pdf.

Mandiberg, Michael, ed. *The Social Media Reader*. New York: New York University Press, 2012.

Marland, Alex. "Amateurs versus Professionals: The 1993 and 2006 Canadian Federal Elections." In *Political Marketing in Canada*, edited by Alex Marland, Thierry Giasson, and Jennifer Lees-Marshment, 59–75. Vancouver: UBC Press, 2012.

————, Thierry Giasson, and Jennifer Lees-Marchment, ed. *Political Marketing in Canada*. Vancouver: UBC Press, 2012.

Martin, Don. *King Ralph.* Toronto: Key Porter Books, 2003.

Martin, Lawrence. "Is Stephen Harper Set to Move against the CRTC?" *Globe and Mail,* August 19, 2010: A11.

Mayer, Frederick W. "Stories of Climate Change: The Media and US Public Opinion 2001–2010." Joan Shorenstein Center on the Press, Politics and Public Policy. Discussion paper. Cambridge, MA: Harvard University, February 2012.

Mayer-Schonberger, Viktor. *Delete: The Virtue of Forgetting in the Digital Age.* Princeton, NJ: Princeton University Press, 2009.

———, and Kenneth Cukier. *Big Data: A Revolution That Will Transform How We Live, Work, and Think.* New York: Houghton Mifflin Harcourt, 2013.

Mayrand, Marc. "Declining Voter Turnout: Can We Reverse the Trend?" *The Hill Times Online,* February 6, 2012. https://www.hilltimes.com/opinion-piece/2012/02/06/declining-voter-turnout-can-we-reverse-the-trend/29511.

McCarthy, Andrew. "The Voters Who Stayed Home." *National Review Online,* November 10, 2012. http://m.nationalreview.com/articles/333135/voters-who-stayed-home-andrew-c-mccarthy.

McChesney, Robert W. *Digital Disconnect: How Capitalism Is Turning the Internet Against Democracy.* New York: New Press, 2013.

———. *The Problem of the Media.* New York: Monthly Press Review, 2004.

———., and John Nichols. *The Death and Life of American Journalism: The Media Revolution That Will Begin the World Again.* Philadelphia: Nation Books, 2010.

———., and Victor Pickard, ed. *Will the Last Reporter Please Turn Out the Lights.* New York: New Press, 2011.

McCright, Aaron, and Riley Dunlap. "The Politicization of Climate Change and Polarization in the American Public's Views of Global Warming 2001–2010." *Sociological Quarterly* 52, no. 2 (Summer 2011): 155–94. http://dx.doi.org/10.1111/j.1533-8525.2011.01198.x.

McGregor, Glen. "Critical Posts on PM's Facebook Page Deleted." *Calgary Herald,* November 12, 2011: A6.

McGregor, Roy. "Troubles in the Toy Department." Keynote address. How Canadians Communicate about Sports Conference, Banff, AB, November 9, 2012.

McKenna, Barrie. "Mind the Gap." *Globe and Mail,* November 9, 2013: F6.

McKibben, Bill. *The Age of Missing Information.* New York: Random House, 1992.

McLuhan, Marshall. *Understanding Media: The Extensions of Man.* New York: Mentor Press, 1964.

Meisel, John. "Canada: J'accuse/J'adore: Extracts from a Memoir." In *Uneasy Partners: Multiculturalism and Rights in Canada,* edited by Janice Stein, David Robertson Cameron, John Ibbitson, Will Kymlicka, John Meisel, Haroon Siddiqui, and Michael Valpy, 95–117. Waterloo: Wilfrid Laurier University Press, 2007.

———. "Escaping Extinction: Cultural Defence of an Undefended Border." In *Southern Exposure: Canadian Perspectives on the United States,* edited by David Flaherty and William McKercher, 152–68. Toronto: McGraw-Hill Ryerson, 1986.

———. "Extinction Revisited: Culture and Class in Canada." In *Seeing Ourselves: Media Power and Policy in Canada,* 2nd ed., edited by Helen Holmes and David Taras, 249–56. Toronto: Harcourt Brace & Company, 1996.

Meyrowitz, Joshua. *No Sense of Place: The Impact of Electronic Media on Social Behavior.* New York: Oxford University Press, 1985.

———. "The Shared Arena." In *Seeing Ourselves: Media Power and Policy in Canada,* edited by Helen Holmes and David Taras, 218–31. Toronto: Harcourt Brace Jovanovich, 1992.

Miller, Claire Cain, and Somini Sengupta. "Selling Secrets of Phone Users to Advertisers." *New York Times*, October 6, 2013. http://www.nytimes.com/2013/10/06/technology/selling-secrets-of-phone-users-to-advertisers.html?pagewanted=all

Miller, Mary Jane. *Outside Looking in: Viewing First Nations Peoples in Canadian Dramatic Television Series*. Montreal: McGill-Queen's University Press, 2008.

Miller, Peter. "Three Ideas as We Head into the Meat of the TV Review." *Cartt.ca*, April 23, 2014. https://cartt.ca/subscribe?destination=node/40905.

Miller, Toby. *Cultural Citizenship: Cosmopolitanism, Consumerism and Television in a Neoliberal Age*. Philadelphia: Temple University Press, 2007.

Millette, Josianne, Melanie Millette, and Serge Proulx. *Commitment of Cultural Communities to the Media: The Cases of the Haitians, the Italians and North Africans in Montreal*. Cahier-Médias Numéro 19. Quebec City: Centre d'étude sur les médias, Laval University, April 2010.

Milner, Henry. *The Internet Generation: Engaged Citizens or Political Dropouts*. Boston: Tufts University Press, 2010.

Minow, Newton. "Television and the Public Interest." Address. Washington, DC: National Association of Broadcasters, May 9, 1961.

Mitchell, Amy, and Tom Rosensteil. "What Facebook and Twitter Mean for News." *The State of the News Media 2012*. The Pew Research Center's Project for Excellence in Journalism, 2012.

Moisi, Dominique. *Geopolitics of Emotion*. New York: Doubleday, 2009.

Morozov, Evgeny. *The Net Delusion: The Dark Side of Internet Freedom*. New York: Public Affairs, 2011.

Morrissey, Janet. "Poker Inc. to Uncle Sam: Shut Up and Deal." *New York Times*, October 9, 2011. http://www.nytimes.com/2011/10/09/technology/internet/in-online-poker-a-push-to-legalize-and-regulate-the-game.html?pagewanted=all&_r=0&gwh=8ACE827FEC9B13C73C1133A6C464EDEF&gwt=pay.

Mosco, Vincent. *The Digital Sublime: Myth, Power and Cyberspace*. Boston: Massachusetts Institute of Technology, 2004.

Munson, Eve Stryker, and Catherine A. Warren, ed. *James Carey: A Critical Reader*. Minneapolis: The University of Minnesota Press, 1997.

Murray, Charles. *Coming Apart: The State of White America, 1960–2010*. New York: Crown Forum, 2012.

Murthy, Dhiraj. *Twitter*. Malden, MA: Polity Press, 2013.

Music Canada. *Economic Analysis of the Impact of the Sound Recording Industry in Canada*. April 12, 2012. http://www.musiccanada.com/wp-content/uploads/2014/06/Music-Canada-Economic-Impact-Analysis-of-the-Sound-Recording-Industry-in-Canada.pdf.

Nadeau, Richard, and Thierry Giasson. "Canada's Democratic Malaise: Are the Media to Blame?" In *Strengthening Canadian Democracy*, edited by Paul Howe, Richard Johnston, and Andre Blais, 229–67. Montreal: Institute for Research on Public Policy, 2005.

Nagata, Kai. "Warnings from Quebec." *The Tyee*, September 12, 2011. http://thetyee.ca/Opinion/2011/09/12/Nagata_Quebec_Warning/.

Napoli, Philip. *Audience Evolution: New Technologies and the Transformation of Media Audiences*. New York: Columbia University Press, 2011.

Naughton, John. "Tech Giants Have Power to Be Political Masters as Well as Our Web Ones." *The Guardian*, February 26, 2012. http://www.theguardian.com/technology/2012/feb/26/internet-companies-power-politics-freedom

Noelle-Neumann, Elisabeth. *The Spiral of Silence: Public Opinion—Our Social Skin*. Chicago: University of Chicago Press, 1993.

Norris, Pippa. *Democratic Deficit: Critical Citizens Revisited.* Cambridge: Cambridge University Press, 2011. http://dx.doi.org/10.1017/CBO9780511973383.

————. *A Virtuous Circle: Political Communication in Postindustrial Societies.* New York: Cambridge University Press, 2000. http://dx.doi.org/10.1017/CBO9780511609343.

Nossal, Kim Richard, ed. *An Acceptance of Paradox: Essays on Canadian Diplomacy in Honour of John. W. Holmes.* Toronto: Canadian Institute of International Affairs, 1982.

O'Brian, John. "Wild Art History." In *Beyond Wilderness: The Group of Seven, Canadian Identity, and Contemporary Art,* edited by John O'Brian and Peter White, 21–37. Montreal: McGill-Queen's University Press, 2007.

O'Brian, John, and Peter White, ed. *Beyond Wilderness: The Group of Seven, Canadian Identity, and Contemporary Art.* Montreal: McGill-Queen's University Press, 2007.

O'Carroll, Lisa, and Helene Mulholland. "Mayor's Love-in with Murdoch May Yield Backing for Tory Job." *Globe and Mail,* August 3, 2012: A3.

O'Connor, Rory. "Word of Mouse: Credibility, Journalism and Emerging Social Media." Joan Shorenstein Center on the Press, Politics and Public Policy, John F. Kennedy School of Government. Cambridge, MA: Harvard University, February 2009.

Offman, Craig. "'Room with a View': Hotels Mine Social Media to Win Over Guests." *Globe and Mail,* October 14, 2013: A1, 10.

O'Neill, Brenda. "The Media's Role in Shaping Canadian Civic and Political Engagement." *Canadian Political Science Review* 3, no. 2 (June 2009): 105–27.

Ornstein, Norman J., and Thomas E. Mann, ed. *The Permanent Campaign and Its Future.* Washington, DC: American Enterprise Institute and the Brookings Institution, 2000.

Ortutay, Barbara. "Pew Study Finds Tablet Users Don't Want to Pay for News." *Associated Press,* October 25, 2011.

Paikin, Steve. *Public Triumph, Private Tragedy: The Double Life of John P. Robarts.* Toronto: Viking Canada, 2005.

Palfrey, John, and Urs Gasser. "Activists." In *The Digital Divide,* edited by Mark Bauerlein, 189–204. London: Penguin, 2011.

Pammett, Jon, and Christopher Dornan, ed. *The Canadian Federal Election of 2011.* Toronto: Dundurn, 2011.

Papacharissi, Zizi. "Audiences as Media Producers: Content Analysis of 260 Blogs." In *Blogging, Citizenship and the Future of Media,* edited by Mark Tremayne, 21–38. New York: Routledge, 2007.

————. *A Private Sphere: Democracy in a Digital Age.* Cambridge: Polity Press, 2010.

Paquet, Gilles. *Deep Cultural Diversity: A Governance Challenge.* Ottawa: University of Ottawa Press, 2008.

Pariser, Eli. *The Filter Bubble: What the Internet Is Hiding from You.* New York: Penguin, 2011.

Partridge, John. "Citizen Black." *Globe and Mail,* July 25, 1987: D6.

Patenaude, Troy. "Contemporary Canadian Aboriginal Art: Storyworking in the Public Sphere." In *How Canadians Communicate IV: Media and Politics,* edited by David Taras and Christopher Waddell, 317–48. Edmonton: Athabasca University Press, 2012.

Patterson, Thomas. *Informing the News.* New York: Vintage, 2013.

————. *Out of Order.* New York: Alfred A. Knopf, 1993.

Perlmutter, David D. *Blogwars.* New York: Oxford University Press, 2008.

Perreaux, Les, and Rhéal Séguin. "Opposition Calls on Peladeau to Explain How He'll Guarantee Independence of Quebecor Media's Outlets." *Globe and Mail,* March 11, 2011: A7.

Pew Research Center for the People and the Press. *In Changing News Landscape, Even Television Is Vulnerable: Trends in News Consumption; 1991–2012.* September 27, 2012, http://www.people-press.org/2012/09/27/in-changing-news-landscape-even-television-is-vulnerable/

———. *Journalists Avoiding the News: Self-Censorship: How Often and Why*. April 30, 2000 http://www.people-press.org/files/legacy-pdf/39.pdf.

Pew Research Center's Project for Excellence in Journalism. *New Media, Old Media: How Blogs and Social Media Agendas Relate and Differ from Traditional Press*. May 23, 2010, http://www.journalism.org/2010/05/23/new-media-old-media/.

———. *How the Presidential Candidates Use Web and Social Media*. August 15, 2012, http://www.journalism.org/files/legacy/DIRECT%20ACCESS%20FINAL.pdf.

———. *The State of the News Media, 2008: Radio*. March 19, 2008.

———. *The State of the News Media, 2012: Audio*. March 19, 2012.

———. *YouTube & News: A New Kind of Visual News*. November 2013.

Pinker, Stephen. *The Better Angels of Our Nature: Why Violence Has Declined*. New York: Viking, 2011.

Poliquin, Daniel. *René Lévesque*. Toronto: Penguin Canada, 2009.

Pollara. "Question Period Not Working for Most Canadians." The PPF–Pollara National Dialogue Poll. Ottawa: Canada's Public Policy Forum. September 15, 2010. http://www.ppforum.ca/sites/default/files/PPF-Pollara%20FINAL%20ENG.pdf.

Pool, Ithiel de Sola. *Technology without Boundaries: On Telecommunications in a Global Age*. Cambridge, MA: Harvard University Press, 1990.

Porter, Henry. "Over More than Three Decades, No One Dared Question the Perversion of Politics by and for Rupert Murdoch." *The Guardian*, July 10, 2011. http://www.theguardian.com/commentisfree/2011/jul/10/rupert-murdoch-phone-hacking-cameron.

Postman, Neil. *Amusing Ourselves to Death*. New York: Penguin, 1985.

Prensky, Marc. "Digital Natives, Digital Immigrants Part 1." *On the Horizon* 9, no. 5 (October 2001): 1–6. http://dx.doi.org/10.1108/10748120110424816.

———. "Digital Natives, Digital Immigrants Part 2: Do They Really Think Differently?" *On the Horizon* 9, no. 6 (October 2001): 1–6. http://dx.doi.org/10.1108/10748120110424843.

Press TV. "Voter Turnout in 2012 US Presidential Elections 9% Lower than 2008." November 7, 2012. http://www.presstv.com/detail/2012/11/07/270958/voter-turnout-in-2012-us-presidential-elections-9-lower-than-2008/.

Prior, Markus. *Post-Broadcast Democracy*. Cambridge: Cambridge University Press, 2007.

Putnam, Robert. *Bowling Alone: The Collapse and Revival of American Community*. New York: Simon & Schuster, 2000. http://dx.doi.org/10.1145/358916.361990.

Ranney, Austin. *Channels of Power: The Impact of Television on American Politics*. New York: Basic Books, 1983.

Real Clear Markets. "Google Grows Too Successful for Washington." June 28, 2011, http://www.realclearmarkets.com/articles/2011/06/28/google_grows_too_succesful_for_washington_99101.html.

Remington, Robert. "Endangered Species: Service Clubs Struggle to Attract New Members." *Calgary Herald*, January 18, 2009: A1, A6.

Rich, Frank. "Facebook Politicians Are Not Your Friends." *New York Times*, October 10, 2010. http://www.nytimes.com/2010/10/10/opinion/10rich.html.

Richler, Noah. *This is My Country, What's Yours?: A Literary Atlas of Canada*. Toronto: McClelland & Stewart, 2006.

Richtel, Matt. "Attached to Technology and Paying the Price." *New York Times*, June 7, 2010. http://www.nytimes.com/2010/06/07/technology/07brain.html?pagewanted=all.

Robertson, Grant. "TV Networks Losing Ground to Rival Services." *Globe and Mail*, July 9, 2008: B4.

Robinson, John, and Steven Martin. "What Do Happy People Do?" *Social Indicators Research* 89, no. 3 (December 2008): 565–71. http://dx.doi.org/10.1007/s11205 -008-9296-6.

Robinson, Michael. *Two Decades of American News Preferences, Part 1: Analyzing What News the Public Follows—and Doesn't Follow.* Pew Research Center for the People and the Press, 2007.

Rose, Jonathan. "Are Negative Ads Positive? Political Advertising and the Permanent Campaign." In *How Canadians Communicate IV: Media and Politics*, edited by David Taras and Christopher Waddell, 149–68. Edmonton: Athabasca University Press, 2012.

Rosen, Jay. "Politics, Vision and the Press." In *The New News v. the Old News*, edited by Jay Rosen and Paul Taylor, 3–33. New York: Twentieth Century Fund, 1992.

———, and Paul Taylor. *The New News v. the Old News.* New York: Twentieth Century Fund, 1992.

Rosen, Jeffrey. "The Web Means the End of Forgetting." *New York Times*, July 21, 2010. http://www.nytimes.com/2010/07/25/magazine/25privacy-t2.html?pagewanted=all.

Rosenberg, Howard. *Not So Prime Time.* Chicago: Ivan Dee Publishers, 2004.

Rosenbloom, Stephanie. "Got Twitter? You've Been Scored." *New York Times*, June 25, 2011. http://www.nytimes.com/2011/06/26/sunday-review/26rosenbloom.html.

Rosensteil, Tom, Marion Just, Todd Belt, Atiba Pertilla, Walter Dean, and Dante Chinni. *We Interrupt This Newscast: How to Improve Local News and Win Ratings, Too.* New York: Cambridge University Press, 2007. http://dx.doi.org/10.1017/CBO9780511841064.

Ross, Winston. "The Old Person's Guide to Tumblr." *The Daily Beast*, May 20, 2013. http://www.thedailybeast.com/articles/2013/05/20/the-old-person-s-guide-to -tumblr.html.

Rowland, Wade. *Saving the CBC: Balancing Profit and Public Service.* Westmount, QC: Linda Leith Publishing, 2013.

Rushkoff, Douglas. *Present Shock: When Everything Happens Now.* New York: Penguin, 2013.

Rutherford, Paul. *A Victorian Authority: The Daily Press in Late Nineteenth-Century Canada.* Toronto: University of Toronto Press, 1982.

———. *When Television Was Young: Prime Time Canada 1952–1967.* Toronto: University of Toronto Press, 1990.

Sachs, Jeffrey. *The Price of Civilization.* New York: Random House, 2011.

Samara. *The Neighbourhoods of #cdnpoli.* 2011. http://www.samaracanada.com/research/current-research/the-neighbourhoods-of-cdnpoli.

———. *Samara Democracy Report #4: Who's the Boss? Canadians' Views on Their Democracy.* 2012. http://www.samaracanada.com/research/current-research/who's-the-boss-.

Saul, John Ralston. *A Fair Country: Telling Truths about Canada.* Toronto: Penguin Canada, 2008.

Sauvageau, Florian. Keynote address. Conference on How Canadians Communicate Politically: The Next Generation, Banff, AB, 2009.

———. "The Uncertain Future of the News." In *How Canadians Communicate IV: Media and Politics*, edited by David Taras and Christopher Waddell, 29–43. Edmonton: Athabasca University Press, 2012.

———, David Schneiderman, and David Taras. *The Last Word: Media Coverage of the Supreme Court of Canada.* Vancouver: UBC Press, 2006.

Savoie, Donald. *Governing from the Centre: The Concentration of Power in Canadian Politics.* Toronto: University of Toronto Press, 1990.

————. *Whatever Happened to the Music Teacher?: How Government Decides and Why*. Montreal: McGill-Queen's University Press, 2013.

Schiffrin, Anya. "The US Press and the Financial Crisis." In *Bad News: How America's Business Press Missed the Story of the Century*, edited by Anya Schiffrin, 1–21. New York: New Press, 2011.

————, ed. *Bad News: How America's Business Press Missed the Story of the Century*. New York: New Press, 2011.

Schlozman, Kay Lehman, Sidney Verba, and Henry E. Brady. *The Unheavenly Chorus: Unequal Political Voice and the Broken Promise of American Democracy*. Princeton, NJ: Princeton University Press, 2012.

Schmidt, Eric, and Jared Cohen. *The New Digital Age*. New York: Knopf, 2013.

Schramm, Wilbur, and Donald Roberts, ed. *The Process and Effects of Mass Communication*. Chicago: University of Illinois Press, 1971.

Schultz, Richard. "Canadian Communications and the Spectre of Globalization: Just Another Word…." In *How Canadians Communicate II: Media, Globalization and Identity*, edited by David Taras, Maria Bakardjiva, and Frits Pannekoek, 23–46. Calgary: University of Calgary Press, 2007.

————. "From Master to Partner to Bit Player: The Diminishing Capacity of Government." In *How Canadians Communicate*, edited by David Taras, Frits Pannekoek, and Maria Bakardjieva, 27–49. Calgary: University of Calgary Press, 2003.

Schumpeter, Joseph. *Capitalism, Socialism and Democracy*. New York: Harper, 1975.

Schwartz, Alyssa. "Grownups Get Their Facebook Fix." *Globe and Mail*, March 31, 2007: L9.

SCOUT eh! "Scouts Canada, On the Brink? Is This Century Old Institution on the Verge of Bankruptcy?" n.d. http://scouteh.ca/.

Séguin, Rhéal, and Graham Fraser. "Parizeau Book Stuns Separatists. Bouchard, Duceppe Deny Any Knowledge of Plan to Declare Independence Unilaterally." *Globe and Mail*, May 8, 1997.

Seidman, Andew. "Universal Music, EMI Defend Planned Merger to Keep Industry Competitive." *Globe and Mail*, June 22, 2012: B6.

Senate Standing Committee on Transportation and Communications. *Final Report on the Canadian News Media*. Committee Proceedings. Ottawa: House of Commons, 2006.

Sennett, Richard. *The Corrosion of Character*. New York: Norton, 1998.

Sepinwall, Alan. *The Revolution Was Televised: The Cops, Crooks, Slingers and Slayers Who Changed TV Drama Forever*. New York: Simon & Schuster, 2012.

Shiga, John. "Sharing Sounds: Does File Sharing Harm the Music Industry." In *Communication in Question*, edited by Josh Greenberg and Charlene Elliott, 252–63. Toronto: Nelson, 2012.

Shirky, Clay. *Cognitive Surplus: Creativity and Generosity*. New York: Penguin, 2010.

————. "Gin, Television and Social Surplus." In *The Social Media Reader*, edited by Michael Mandiberg, 236–41. New York: New York University Press, 2012.

————. *Here Comes Everybody: The Power of Organization without Organizations*. New York: Penguin, 2008.

Simpson, Jeffrey. "The Best Health Care System: The Numbers Say Otherwise." *Globe and Mail*, November 23, 2012. http://www.theglobeandmail.com/globe-debate/the-best-health-care-system-the-numbers-say-otherwise/article5577290/.

————. *The Friendly Dictator*. Toronto: McClelland & Stewart, 2001.

————. "Imagine Our Politicians' Words Stirring Us." *Globe and Mail*, September 1, 2008: A11.

———. "Quebeckers Want Power, Not Independence." *Globe and Mail*, October 15, 2011: F9.

———. "Stop the Presses! Crime Rates Falling." *Globe and Mail*, July 23, 2008: A11.

———. "To Quebec, Canada Barely Exists." *Globe and Mail*, August 31, 2012: A11.

———. "A University Degree's Value Is Incontestable." *Globe and Mail*, July 20, 2012: A11.

———. "We All Pay for the Government's Hockey Ads." *Globe and Mail*, May 11, 2013: F2.

Singer, Natasha. "They Loved Your G.P.A. Then They Saw Your Tweets." *New York Times*, November 9, 2013. http://www.nytimes.com/2013/11/10/business/they-loved-your-gpa-then-they-saw-your-tweets.html?pagewanted=all.

Skocpol, Theda. *Diminishing Democracy: From Membership to Management in American Civic Life*. Norman: University of Oklahoma Press, 2003.

Small, Tamara A. "Are We Friends Yet? Online Relationship Marketing by Political Parties." In *Political Marketing in Canada*, edited by Alex Marland, Thierry Giasson, and Jennifer Lees-Marshment, 193–208. Vancouver: UBC Press, 2012.

———. "Blogging the Hill: Garth Turner and the Canadian Parliamentary Blogosphere." *Canadian Political Science Review* 2, no. 3 (2008): 103–24.

———. "E-ttack Politics: Negativity, the Internet and Canadian Political Parties." In *How Canadians Communicate IV: Media and Politics*, edited by David Taras and Christopher Waddell, 169–89. Edmonton: Athabasca University Press, 2012.

———. "Social Media & Canadian Politicians." Paper presented to the School of Public Policy, University of Calgary, Calgary, AB, May 2013.

Small, Tamara A., David Taras, and David Danchuk. "Party Web Sites and Online Campaigning during the 2004 and 2006 Canadian Federal Elections." In *Making a Difference: A Comparative View of the Role of the Internet in Election Politics*, edited by Stephen Ward, Diana Owen, Richard Davis, and David Taras, 113–31. Lanham, MD: Lexington Books, 2008.

Smith, Aaron. "The Internet and Campaign 2010." *Pew Internet & American Life Project*. March 17, 2011. http://www.pewinternet.org/files/old-media//Files/Reports/2011/Internet%20and%20Campaign%202010.pdf.

Smith, Joanna. "NDP MP Pat Martin 'Signs Off' after Calling Tories 'Rat Faced Whores.'" *Toronto Star*, December 20, 2012. http://www.thestar.com/news/canada/2012/12/20/ndp_mp_pat_martin_signs_off_from_twitter_after_calling_tories_rat_faced_whores.html.

Soderlund, Walter, and Kai Hildebrandt, ed. *Canadian Newspaper Ownership in the Era of Convergence*. Edmonton: University of Alberta Press, 2005.

Soderlund, Walter C., Ronald Wagenberg, Kai Hildebrandt, and Walter I. Romanow. "Ownership Rights vs. Social Responsibility." In *Canadian Newspaper Ownership in the Era of Convergence*, edited by Walter Soderlund and Kai Hildebrandt, 137–50. Edmonton: University of Alberta Press, 2005.

Solove, Daniel J. "Speech, Privacy, and Reputation on the Internet." In *The Offensive Internet*, edited by Saul Levmore and Martha Nussbaum, 15–30. Cambridge, MA: Harvard University Press, 2010.

Stacey, C.P. *A Very Double Life: The Private World of Mackenzie King*. Toronto: Macmillan, 1976.

Stairs, Denis. "The Pedagogics of John W. Holmes." In *An Acceptance of Paradox: Essays on Canadian Diplomacy in Honour of John W. Holmes*, edited by Kim Richard Nossal, 3–16. Toronto: Canadian Institute of International Affairs, 1982.

Stanbury, W.T. "Canadian Content Regulations: The Intrusive State at Work." *Fraser Forum*, August 1998.

Standing Committee on Canadian Heritage. *Our Cultural Sovereignty: The Second Century of Canadian Broadcasting.* Committee Proceedings. Ottawa: House of Commons Canada, 2003.

Starkman, Dean. "Major Papers' Longform Meltdown." *Columbia Journalism Review* 29 (May 2013), http://www.cjr.org/the_audit/major_papers_longform_meltdown.php.

———. *The Watchdog That Didn't Bark: The Financial Crisis and the Disappearance of Investigative Journalism.* New York: Columbia University Press, 2014.

Starowicz, Mark. "Does Canada Still Need the CBC? YES." *The Ottawa Citizen*, October 4, 2012.

Starr, Paul. "Goodbye to the Age of Newspapers (Hello to a New Era of Corruption)." In *Will the Last Reporter Please Turn Out the Lights*, edited by Robert W. McChesney and Victor Pickard, 18–37. New York: New Press, 2011.

Stein, Janice, David Robertson Cameron, John Ibbitson, Will Kymlicka, John Meisel, Haroon Siddiqui, and Michael Valpy. *Uneasy Partners: Multiculturalism and Rights in Canada.* Waterloo: Wilfrid Laurier University Press, 2007.

Stelter, Brian. "The Facebooker Who Befriended Obama." *New York Times*, July 7, 2008. http://www.nytimes.com/2008/07/07/technology/07hughes.html?pagewanted=all.

Stiglitz, Joseph. "The Media and the Crisis: An Information Theoretic Approach." In *Bad News: How America's Business Press Missed the Story of the Century*, edited by Anya Schiffrin, 22–36. New York: New Press, 2011.

Story, Louise. "Viewers Fast-Forwarding Past Ads? Not Always." *New York Times*, February 16, 2007. http://www.nytimes.com/2007/02/16/business/16commercials.html?pagewanted=all.

Stout, Hilary. "Antisocial Networking?" *New York Times*, May 2, 2010. http://www.nytimes.com/2010/05/02/fashion/02BEST.html?pagewanted=all.

Strangelove, Michael. *Watching YouTube.* Toronto: University of Toronto Press, 2010.

Straw, Will. "Hawkers and Public Space: Free Commuter Newspapers in Canada." In *How Canadians Communicate III: Contexts of Canadian Popular Culture*, edited by Bart Beaty, Derek Briton, Gloria Filax, and Rebecca Sullivan, 79–93. Edmonton: Athabasca University Press, 2010.

Strickland, Eugene. "You'll Always Have a Friend with Facebook." *Calgary Herald*, June 2, 2007: C8.

Stursberg, Richard. *The Tower of Babble: Sins, Secrets and Successes Inside the CBC.* Vancouver: Douglas & McIntyre, 2012.

Sunstein, Cass. *Republic.com 2.0.* Princeton, NJ: Princeton University Press, 2007.

Sutherland, Richard. "Sound Recording and Radio: Intersections and Overlaps." In *Cultural Industries.ca: Making Sense of Canadian Media in the Digital Age*, edited by Ira Wagman and Peter Urquhart, 33–52. Toronto: James Lorimer, 2012.

Swanson, Bret. "Obama Ran a Capitalist Campaign." *The Wall Street Journal*, November 7, 2008. http://online.wsj.com/articles/SB122602757767707787.

Taras, David. *Power & Betrayal in the Canadian Media.* Toronto: University of Toronto Press, 2001.

———, Frits Pannekoek, and Maria Bakardjieva, ed. *How Canadians Communicate.* Calgary: University of Calgary Press, 2003.

———, Maria Bakardjieva, and Frits Pannekoek, ed. How Canadians Communicate II: Media, Globalization, and Identity. Calgary: University of Calgary Press, 2007.

———, and Christopher Waddell. "The 2011 Federal Election and the Transformation of Canadian Media and Politics." In *How Canadians Communicate IV: Media and Politics*, edited by David Taras and Christopher Waddell, 71–107. Edmonton: Athabasca University Press, 2012.

————, and Christopher Waddell, ed. *How Canadians Communicate IV: Media and Politics.* Edmonton: Athabasca University Press, 2012.

————. *How Canadians Communicate V: Sports.* Edmonton: Athabasca University Press, forthcoming.

Taylor, Charles. *Reconciling the Solitudes: Essays on Canadian Federalism and Nationalism.* Montreal: McGill-Queen's University Press, 1993.

Taylor, Paul. *See How They Run: Electing the President in an Age of Mediaocracy.* New York: Alfred. A. Knopf, 1990.

Thompson, Clive. "I'm So Totally Digitally Close to You." *New York Times Magazine*, September 7, 2008: 45.

Thomson, Michael. "Why Apple Shouldn't Censor the App Store." *Complex Tech*, April 11, 2013. http://www.complexmag.ca/tech/2013/04/app-store-controversial-censorship-and-the-social-conflict-behind-it.

Toffler, Alvin. *Future Shock.* New York: Bantam, 1970.

Tremayne, Mark, ed. *Blogging, Citizenship and the Future of Media.* New York: Routledge, 2007.

————. "Introduction: Examining the Blog-Media Relationship." In *Blogging, Citizenship and the Future of Media*, edited by Mark Tremayne, ix–xix. New York: Routledge, 2007.

Tuchman, Gaye. *Making News: A Study in the Construction of Reality.* New York: Free Press, 1978.

Turcotte, Andre. "Under New Management: Market Intelligence and the Conservative Party's Resurrection." In *Political Marketing in Canada*, edited by Alex Marland, Thierry Giasson, and Jennifer Lees-Marshment, 76–90. Vancouver: UBC Press, 2012.

Turner, Ted. "My Beef with Big Media." *Washington Monthly* (July/August 2004), http://www.washingtonmonthly.com/features/2004/0407.turner.html.

Valpy, Michael. "Anglican Church Facing the Threat of Extinction." *Globe and Mail*, February 9, 2010. http://www.theglobeandmail.com/news/british-columbia/anglican-church-facing-the-threat-of-extinction/article4352186/.

Vezina, Mireille, and Susan Crompton. "Volunteering in Canada." *Canadian Social Trends*, no. 93 (Summer 2012). http://www.statcan.gc.ca/pub/11-008-x/2012001/article/11638-eng.pdf.

Vultaggio, Maria. "Young Voter Turnout High on Facebook's 2012 Election Map." *International Business Times*, November 6, 2012. http://www.ibtimes.com/young-voter-turnout-high-facebooks-2012-election-map-862118.

Waddell, Christopher. "Berry'd Alive: The Media, Technology and the Death of Political Coverage." In *How Canadians Communicate IV: Media and Politics*, edited by David Taras and Christopher Waddell, 20, 109–28. Edmonton: Athabasca University Press, 2012.

————. "The Future for the Canadian Media." *Policy Options* 30, no. 6 (June/July 2009): 16–20.

————. "The Hall of Mirrors." In *How Canadians Communicate V: Sports*, edited by David Taras and Christopher Waddell. Edmonton: Athabasca University Press, forthcoming.

Wagman, Ira. "The B Side: Why Canadian Content Isn't Necessary for the Survival of Canadian Music." In *Communication in Question*, edited by Josh Greenberg and Charlene Elliott, 217–26. Toronto: Nelson, 2012.

————. "Log On, Goof Off, and Look Up: Facebook and the Rhythms of Canadian Internet Use." In *How Canadians Communicate III: Contexts of Canadian Popular*

Culture, edited by Bart Beaty, Derek Briton, Gloria Filax, and Rebecca Sullivan, 55–77. Edmonton: Athabasca University Press, 2010.

———, and Peter Urquhart, ed. *Cultural Industries.ca: Making Sense of Canadian Media in the Digital Age.* Toronto: James Lorimer, 2012.

Waldie, Paul. "Charities See Alarming Trends as Donors Become Older, Fewer." *Globe and Mail*, December 3, 2010: A1, A22.

Walt Disney Company. Fiscal Year 2013 Annual Financial Report and Shareholder Letter. Annual Report, 2013.

Ward, Stephen, Diana Owen, Richard Davis, and David Taras, ed. *Making a Difference: A Comparative View of the Role of the Internet in Election Politics.* Lanham, MD: Lexington Books, 2008.

Watkins, S. Craig. *The Young and the Digital: What the Migration to Social-Network Sites, Games, and Anytime, Anywhere Media Means for Our Future.* Boston: Beacon, 2009.

Watson, Patrick. *This Hour Has Seven Decades.* Toronto: McArthur & Company, 2004.

Way, Laura. "Canadian Newspaper Coverage of the Alberta Oil Sands: The Intractability of Neoliberalism." Doctoral dissertation, University of Alberta, 2013.

Weaver, W., trans. *Travels in Hyperreality.* Orlando: Harcourt Brace Jovanovich, 1986.

Webster, James. *The Marketplace of Attention: How Audiences Take Shape in a Digital Age.* Cambridge, MA: MIT Press, 2014.

Wente, Margaret. "The Collapse of the Liberal Church." *Globe and Mail*, July 28, 2012: F9.

———. "Unskilled, Unmarried, Unwanted...." *Globe and Mail*, August 16, 2011: A13.

Wilkinson, Richard, and Kate Pickett. *The Spirit Level: Why Equality Is Better for Everyone.* London: Penguin, 2010.

Winnipeg Sun. "'F--- you,' Winnipeg MP Tweets." November 16, 2011. http://www.torontosun.com/2011/11/16/f----you-winnipeg-mp-tweets.

Winseck, Dwayne. "'The Death of the Music Industry' in Canada and Other Copyright Myths." *Mediamorphis: Network Media Industries and the Forces of Change and Conservation.* May 17, 2011. http://dwmw.wordpress.com/2011/05/17/the-death-of-the-music-industry-in-canada-and-other-copyright-myths/.

———. "Newspaper Killers and the 'Death of Journalism'." *Mediamorphis: Network Media Industries and the Forces of Change and Conservation*, May 31, 2012. http://dwmw.wordpress.com/2012/05/.

Wiseman, Nelson. *In Search of Canadian Political Culture.* Vancouver: UBC Press, 2007.

Wolff, Michael. "Cable's on a Fast Train to Oblivion." *USA Today*, February 18, 2013: B1–2.

Wu, Shaomei, and Jake M. Hofman. "Who Says What to Whom on Twitter." Cornell University/Yahoo Research. https://iriss.stanford.edu/sites/all/files/dsi/Duncan%20Study%201.pdf.

Wu, Timothy. *The Master Switch: The Rise and Fall of Information Empires.* New York: Alfred A. Knopf, 2010.

Yakabuski, Konrad. "Beautiful Machine." *Report on Business Magazine*, September 2007: 50–58.

———. "Neither Practicing nor Believing, but Catholic Even So." *Globe and Mail*, August 15, 2009: A17.

———. "What Twitter Is, and Isn't." *Globe and Mail*, May 6, 2013: A11.

Young, David. "Why Canadian Content Regulations Are Needed to Support Canadian Music." In *Communication in Question*, edited by Josh Greenberg and Charlene Elliott, 210–16. Toronto: Nelson, 2012.

Zaller, John. "A New Standard of News Quality: Burglar Alarms for the Monitorial Citizen." *Political Communication* 22, no. 2 (2003): 109–30. http://dx.doi.org/10.1080/10584600390211136.

Zuckerman, Ethan. *Rewire: Digital Cosmopolitans in the Age of Connection.* New York: Norton, 2013.

INDEX